MYSTICISM

MYSTICISM

Its History and Challenge

BRUNO BORCHERT

SAMUEL WEISER, INC.

York Beach, Maine

First published in 1994 by
Samuel Weiser, Inc.
P. O. Box 612
York Beach, ME 03910

Translated from Dutch by Transcript, Ltd.

Library of Congress Cataloging-in-Publication Data
Borchert, Bruno.
   [Mystiek. English]
   Mysticism : its history and challenge / by Bruno Borchert.
      p. cm.
   Includes bibliographical references and index.
   1. Mysticism--Comparative studies.   I. Title.
  BL625.B6713 1993   93-17157
   291.4'22--dc20   CIP
  ISBN 0-87728-772-4
  EB

Cover art: "Silence" (c. 1911) by Odilon Redon. Oil on gesso on paper, $21\frac{1}{4} \times 21\frac{1}{2}$". The Museum of Modern Art, New York. Lillie P. Bliss Collection. Photograph © 1993 The Museum of Modern Art, New York.

Illustrations and research: Bruno Borchert and Matthijs Schrofer
Advisors for the Dutch edition: Otger Steggink, Kees Waaijman, Loet Swart

Typeset in 11 point Palatino

Printed in the United States of America

99 98 97 96 95 94

10 9 8 7 6 5 4 3 2 1

The paper used in this publication meets the minimum requirements of the American National Standard for Permanence of Paper for Printed Library Materials Z39.48-1984.

TABLE OF CONTENTS

PART III: THE MYSTICAL WAY

PART I

THE PHENOMENON
OF MYSTICISM

MYSTICAL EXPERIENCE

The word "mysticism" has so many definitions and uses that it means little anymore. And yet there is a certain phenomenon that has to have a name, and the only name we can give it is mysticism. This is a phenomenon that seems to occur in all religions and cultures; it is different in external form, but in essence everywhere it is the same: *it is the experimental knowledge that, in one way or another, everything is interconnected, that all things have a single source.*

Perhaps the phenomenon can best be understood in terms of another that also occurs in all cultures and eras—the state of being in love. Being in love is an experience, too: a new world thrusts itself into your consciousness, you learn to know someone in an unaccustomed way, and you experience and long for union.

There are many symptoms of being in love—blushing, feeling weak at the knees, having a pounding heart, being deliriously happy, being blind to all others, walking on air. More soberly, you can write poetry, let people know how you feel, go courting, or keep quiet and ask yourself seriously whether it would not be better to forget the whole thing. How you experience being in love depends on the immediate environment. In Naples the possibilities are not the same as in New York.

Before the Second World War, when the proprieties had to be observed, feelings were probably more intense than they are today when anything goes. The language of lovers keeps changing, too. In the time of the troubadours it was very rich, because courtly love was at the heart of the culture; now it is meager, because—as proved by the many divorces—love fades so quickly.

Being in love is not very important in itself. The experience is often soon over. But it can radically alter an individual's life. A person can want to keep experiencing the "kick" of being in love, or, when life has settled down, can let "being in love" develop into "love." This development of being in love into love is a path beset by many difficulties, for which solutions have been sought in every age and in every culture. Various traditions have had the monogamous marriage, the marriage to more than one wife, the marriage in which it is acceptable to keep a mistress, the marriage with a possibility of divorce, and living together without marriage. None of these arrangements guarantees that the partners will attain to a deep and lasting experience of love. If they really want to come to a mature love for each other, they will have to search hard for the way. Their particular form of contract can be a help, and may just as easily be a hindrance.

Replace the words "being in love" with "mystical experience," and you have a rough and ready description of mysticism in general. As a matter of fact, mystical experience is often felt and described by mystics, themselves, as being in love, and their lives are a love affair with the all-embracing reality that permeates and surpasses mundane existence. Therefore the word "mysticism" indicates an experience and also what grows out of that experience. A *mystic* is someone whose life is governed by that experience.

We speak of a *mystic way* when thinking of how the mystical experience can have a more permanent influence on daily life. *Mystical theology* is doctrine concerning God made transparent by experience. *Mystical cosmology* is a vision of the structure of the universe in which everything is seen to be interconnected. A *mystical culture* or *counter-culture* has its roots in the mystical experience, but is made and supported by people who, without necessarily having had a mystical experience themselves, recognize in some form of mysticism a pursuit of the highest cultural values.

The word mysticism is also used to define something having a touch of mystery or enigma (e.g., we speak of the mystical aroma of French perfume) or for things that are vague. These are derivative meanings. In comparison with the precise language of science, the language of mystical experience strikes us as clumsy, paradoxical and hazy. Experiences are hard to put into words; and we still find that mystics often make use of religious symbol-systems that are incomprehensible to outsiders. What is more, theologians have set mysticism apart as a very exceptional grace of God; and heavy emphasis has come to be laid on such rare phenomena of mystical ecstasy as trance, levitation, and stigmata, so definitions of the word mystical as enigmatic, mysterious, occult, and obscure are secondary, not primary.

Mysticism is not something or other exceptional. There are exceptional mystical experiences and there are a few great mystics; but minor mystical experiences and mystically oriented lives are many, and individuals who consider themselves to be mystical without having had any noteworthy experience are more numerous still.

At the turn of the century, William James was one of the first to discover this. He wrote down as many accounts as he could find, made a collection of witnesses, and tried to introduce some order into this enormous heap of emotions. The result was the seminal work, *Varieties of Religious Experience*.[1] This paved the way for a neutral approach to mysticism, with no reference to a theological framework, but making a clear distinction between the experience itself and the manner in which it is shaped, between enthusiasm and morbid phenomena on the one hand and authentic experiences on the other. William James says of himself:

> Although I do not possess such a [mystical] God-consciousness in the more direct and strong meaning of the word, yet there is something within me that responds when I hear others talk about it. I recognize a deeper voice. There is something that says to me: there is truth in this . . . I have outgrown Christianity so much that any expression of mysticism that sits pat in it has to be dislodged from it—I am inevitably repelled by their involvement—before I am able to listen. Call this, if you will, my seed of mysticism. It is a seed of very common occurrence.[2]

In the following more detailed study of mysticism, I continue on with the philosophy of William James. I start with the experiences themselves as given in the evidence, and shall try to discover the characteristics of the experiences, their shaping, and their psychosomatic symptoms.

Now as always, anyone who wishes to publicize mystical experiences will feel the same as William James: "The subject has literally bathed us in emotion." So how did James manage to separate the wheat from the chaff? For that matter, can anyone who is awash with emotional experiences keep a clear head? Not a few mystics have had to deal with this problem, and it is obvious that many of them have been unsure about what has really happened to them. Formerly, the question that sprang to mind

---

[1] William James, *Varieties of Religious Experience: A Study in Human Nature* (New York & London: Longmans Green, 1902). A recent edition was published by Viking Penguin (New York, 1982).
[2] William James, *The Letters of William James*, Vol. 2 (Boston, 1920), p. 211.

was: is this of the Devil or does it come from God? Now it is more likely to be: have I gone crazy, is my imagination working overtime, or am I living in the land of illusion? There is no law saying that mystical experiences shall occur only in individuals of a stable, steady type.

Naturally, no guidebook is available to tell us how to sort out our emotions and experiences. Each one of us is different, and so is each experience. Nevertheless, enough thought has been given to the subject, both by mystics and by scientists, to provide us with a very accurate idea of what a mystical experience is and of what it is not.

Mysticism is often identified with emotional experience. The two may coincide, of course, but there is no need for them to do so. Religious revivals, Pentecostalism, and guru cults can be attractive because they provide participants with intense emotional experiences—speaking in tongues, charismatic prayer, surrender to the guru. The mind—or reflective, critical understanding—is switched off, and this produces a feeling of release and happiness.

We also find mystics evaluating their feelings of happiness. This also occurs in love affairs. If falling in love were not so delightful and if courting did not make people feel so happy, few would set out on such an adventure with someone else. And yet the emotions are subsidiary. As the feelings fade, the happiness disappears, and only then does the love adventure really get under way. The same applies to mysticism.

Mystics often try to free themselves from emotional blocks. Reason can sometimes block feelings. Yet, releasing the emotions can, itself, become a block, if the ego—which so desires to indulge the feelings—becomes central, and an ego-cult develops. Using our understanding is part of the mystic path, even if all it does is to discern spirits. In other words, we need to identify our motives to see whether these are merely the enjoyment of our own emotions or if this is a reaching out in love beyond ourselves. In any case, revivals are quite different from mystical experiences. A mystical experience is usually of short duration, and is not worked up; it just happens. It is a sudden realization—the knowledge that a previously unknown reality exists. The understanding is also involved. Therefore this knowledge has always been called enlightenment. It resembles emotional experience in that it gives insights that go beyond logic, and it is effective. It is like the knowledge the lover has of the beloved. Now, someone who simply wants to satisfy his or her sexual needs may know something about the partner's skin and eye-color, but nothing about the partner's unique nature. In the same way, giving free rein to religious emotions results in at least a superficial contact with another reality.

In a mystical experience, on the other hand, a deeper layer of reality rises to consciousness. It is a reality that has always been there, though it has been unperceived; it is a reality that is hidden, so to speak, in the ego and in the surrounding real world. It emerges out of the depths of the ego. It breaks through the barrier of waking consciousness. In this sense, mysticism is rightly called "expansion of consciousness." As in dreaming, the unconscious "I" communicates in pictures with the conscious. What we are dealing with here is a deeper level of our being, which is, in fact, the deeper level of reality in all things.

This breakthrough—of another reality into everyday reality—can be very confusing, and may evoke powerful emotions. You do not know what has happened to you, you are like a fish out of water, you are thrown off balance, and quite possibly you are overwhelmed by a feeling of bliss. On the other hand, the experience can take place in profound tranquillity. Looking back over your life, you may find with a shock that, deep inside you, you have come to look differently at yourself and reality. It is only in retrospect that you appreciate how radical the experience has been.

Mystical experiences have also been identified with visions and contacts with hidden forces, with seeing gods and demons, Jesus and Mary, UFO's and extraterrestrial beings, or the dead and previous incarnations of oneself. These can certainly be poignant experiences, and they do happen to mystics, but they are usually distrusted by them, possibly being seen as a delusion of the Devil. Sometimes such experiences are seen as the result of a more profound experience with a much more significant core. However, this core is inexpressible, and cannot be described except in vague images, such as light, darkness, the ocean, love, father, infinity, nothingness, presence, and so on. It is noticeable that mystics do not entertain the slightest doubt concerning what they are trying to convey by these images—they are experienced as the most real of realities. The core of the mystical state is a clear perception of what underlies all concrete shapes and forms. This underlying reality transcends all forms, and is equally the basis of our own egos and of the egos of other men and women; it is the basis of animals, plants, Earth, the Universe, and of the visions of Jesus, of demons, or of anything else that can enter our minds. Visionary experiences often fail to reach this core. If we may credit Jung,[3] the images that appear to our waking consciousness emerge from our unconscious: from our repressed wishes and fears, and more than likely from a deeper layer, the collective unconscious in which , as it were, the experiences of past generations are stored. In the first case, a vision simply tells us something about the seer's desires and anxieties; in the second case, the vision is a myth that can put one in contact with forgotten primitive religious experiences. According to Carl Gustav Jung, UFO sightings are modern myths of this sort, and he devoted a whole book to the subject.[4]

Indulging ourselves in fantasy can be important in order to gain a clearer insight into what (vague and unformed) is going on inside us. In this sense it is important to the mystic, too; but, in itself, it is not a mystical experience, although it can provide a form for the latter.

Esoteric experiences, too, have their value, if they give an intuitive sense of the forces that are hidden from the scientific eye. More things are possible than science is willing to allow. The study of the paranormal, or ESP, endeavors to develop a methodology for detecting any reality corresponding to this intuitive sense. Even so, unlike mystical experiences, paranormal experiences have no reference to the reality underlying all phenomena.

In ecclesiastical circles, mystical experience is more or less equated with conversion. All at once, insight is gained into a certain passage of the Bible, and its teachings make sense. The individual perceives that Jesus is alive, and surrenders himself or herself to God's will. Someone prays to Mary and experiences contact with her, or meditates on Heaven and feels transported there. A living faith! We say, "Faith comes by hearing and hearing

---

[3] Carl G. Jung et al., *Man and His Symbols* (London: Aldus Books, 1964; and New York: Dell, 1964).
[4] Carl G. Jung, *Flying Saucers: A Modern Myth of Things Seen in the Skies* (New York & London, 1958). Translated by R. F. C. Hull in *The Collected Works of C. G. Jung*, the Bollingen Series XX, Vol. 10, published by Princeton University Press, 1970.

by the word of God"; and so the latter suddenly becomes clear. Faith bows to the authority of God's word, and, in conversion, the individual can assent to this word of authority from personal experience. Mysticism, on the other hand, is knowledge from within.

It is immediate knowledge, in the literal sense of the word: nothing mediates between the disclosed reality and the personal experience—no word, no picture, no doctrine, no thought. It is like an embrace. What takes place is an intimate encounter between the mystic and another world. The two are drawn together, become wrapped up in one another, and endeavor to get to know one another through direct contact. In order to explain this intimacy, mystics employ the imagery of sexual conjugation in marriage. They speak of union (*unio*; or `*ichûd* as the Jews term it), of communion (*communio*), of fusion, of absorption in, of being completely taken up by, and so on; and also of touching, arousing, and clasping. Awareness of a separate "I" disappears. Inner and outer flow away.

It is because of this particular aspect of mysticism that we are entitled to refer to the Mystic East. Buddhism is not a religion, has no revelation, and therefore no conflict between, on the one hand, sacred writings and an ecclesiastical authority that interprets everything by means of them; and, on the other hand, personal experiences that convey an indistinct but ineluctable religious knowledge. Religions founded on revelation (Judaism, Christianity, Islam) possess mystical traditions that have sprung up in spite of disapproval, and in this they differ from the Eastern faiths.

Sometimes faith and mysticism are in conflict; but they are not mutually exclusive. In fact, it is possible for their confrontation to do good. The mystic can see his or her experiences in a clearer light, and the believer can certainly be released from the constraints of dogmas, rules, and rituals, and can go in search again of the experiences that lie behind them.

A mystical experience can be called religious, but not every religious experience is mystical. In organized religion, attention is often focused on the power of God. Thus the Children of Israel stood under the condemnation of Almighty God, who instructed them to offer sacrifices, and to release a scapegoat (on the day of Atonement), in order to be reconciled to Him. Religious experience is then an experience of personal dependence on God. Mystical experience, however, is an experience of love—love like that of a partner who does not want to be placated or entreated, but who wants to be desired.

Throughout history, human beings have been making attempts to circumvent the power of God. The most primitive form of this attempt is magic. We tried to increase our own power at the expense of the superhuman powers by dividing their Power into good and evil forces, so that we might win the favor of the former and use conjurations to keep the latter in check. Serving and ruling both stem from religious dependence, and express themselves in ritual and offerings, in exorcism, and in the burning of witches. Plenty of modern mysticism is a reversion to the sphere of religious forces, or a conviction that these forces are very much alive in areas where science is still ignorant.

Science has been laying into the gods all over the place. People have been taught to regard the structure of divine powers as the law of nature, as a process of evolution, as a psychological reaction. They strain to see the furthest corner of the universe and peer into the tiniest space of the atom, and no longer find God in these things. Faith (in so far as it is dependent on a Higher Power) and science are poles apart. The same is not true of science and mysticism, which are two approaches to reality that can complement one another provided they keep within bounds. They must agree to the following rules: mysticism does not call the visible world an illusion, and science does not claim to be able to know the deepest Ground of reality. Reality is governed by laws, develops through the interplay of forces, and bows to the right of the strongest; but, at the same time, the deepest ground of reality is not Power but Love.

However, there is certainly a strong contrast between mysticism and magic: an experience of ultimate reality as Might excludes the experience that this reality is Love. As a matter of fact, magic can permeate mysticism just as love can be taken over by sadomasochism or violation, and union and bliss can be sought by means of artificial methods and "mind-blowing" drugs. Mysticism—when corrupted—turns the individual into a slave instead of into a lover.

CHARACTERISTICS OF A MYSTICAL EXPERIENCE

It is characteristic of a mystical experience that it is short in duration. It is direct, vague, and all-embracing; it encroaches deep into life (in that sense lasting a long time) and imparts a continuing impulse to give form to what is indistinct. It brings the all-embracing within the confines of concrete reality, and mediates the immediate through words and images.

The experience of breakthrough, itself, is short-lived and is actually named the experience of the *nunc stans*—the stationary now. There is no longer any awareness of time, or of any stream of time with past and future. Rather, there is a sense of eternity.

The experience is immediate, without words or pictures, and in fact without anything between the ego and this other reality. The awareness of a separate personal ego that experiences something "other," and feels that the self is enjoying, seeing, experiencing—that awareness is no more. All this sounds very strange, but it could also apply to any embrace that puts you in seventh heaven and simply loses count of time.

Thus a mystical experience is *all-embracing*. It is not just a matter of the feelings, imagination, understanding, and will—although these come into it—but includes all that is. It is a realization—with one's whole being—that all things are one, a universe, an organic whole into which the self fits. A vision of this sort is abstract, not focused on any detail, and in this sense vague. And yet it is like paradise: everything is one and interconnected, and is not divided into good and evil, into I and not-I, into body and mind. Essentially, everything seems to be good.[5] And so, *love seems to be the basis of everything*, the connection of this whole, the heart of this organism.

Obviously a vision of this sort, however brief, implies deep joy and also a desire to hold that joy fast. Whatever in everyday existence undermines the joy of living is seen to be illusory. Death no longer alarms if the ego rises into the immortal universe and is absorbed in a timeless now. The absurdities of society—wealth and poverty side by side, the defense of life with weapons of mass destruction, the use of force to make existence worthwhile, enslavement to various addictions in the pursuit of freedom—vanish in the fundamental love in which everything is one, good, and meaningful.

---

[5] This (possibly for convenience) may be an oversimplification of the range of mystical experience. Keep in mind just two individuals from the list of mystics at the end of this book: Julian of Norwich recounts visions that were far from vague, abstract, or lacking in detail; and Jacob Boehme was moved to explore and, if possible, to explain, the mystery of good and evil.

THE MYSTICAL PERSON

If a mystical experience were so fleeting as to be forgotten as quickly as it came, we should know very little about mysticism. But, in fact, we have libraries full of testimonies, tracts, poetry, and studies, from all periods, cultures, religions, and regions. A mystical experience has something so unforgettable about it, it would seem, that the person concerned feels compelled to spend time clarifying it. That the joy is not untarnished is clear from the literature of the subject. The mystic has had a vision that all is well; but daily cares, or (as in the case of Dag Hammarskjöld) a political career, form a harsh contrast to it. When violence is a fact, peace is a remote ideal. How can two such experiences be driven in tandem—the experience that everything is splintered and a playground of good and evil forces, and this other experience in which everything is so clearly one and good? Mystical literature is important, because it shows what numbers of people have already been sufficiently troubled by this question to try to answer it. Some of them have been so baffled they decided to opt for the hard reality of everyday life and to abandon mysticism. A well-known example is Ionesco.[6] He has since related that he now has an enormous appetite for life and an ardent desire to satisfy all his senses. Others have ended their lives because they could no longer stand the strain. Failures are hardly ever described in the literature of the subject; apparently failures are not felt to be worth recording for posterity. Mystics are looked on as so holy that their suicidal obsessions do not pass the censor. Only in a few cases do we hear of mystical obsession; for example, in Maria Petyt, a 17th-century Carmelite recluse: "I was sometimes tempted to take my own life . . . . Why will you bring your life into such torment? Choose the short pain."[7] Or, do we think that painters like Vincent van Gogh and Nicolas de Stael were not mystics because they did away with themselves, one in a fit of insanity, the other with premeditation?

A mystical experience is not enough to turn somebody into a mystic. We confine the use of the name to one who enters into the experience, tries to give it form, and wants to live it. According

---

[6] Eugene Ionesco, *Journal en Miettes* (Saint-Armand, 1967), p. 97.
[7] A. Deblaere, *De Mystieke Schrijfster Maria Petyt 1623-1677* (Ghent, 1962), pp. 49-51.

to that person's measure of success, we judge whether or not he or she deserves the title of "great" mystic. Mystical literature belongs to mystics. It has grown up out of a struggle to achieve clarity. Experiences that are mulled over but have little to show for themselves on the outside are excluded from the mystical tradition and have played little part in descriptions of what constitutes a mystical experience. Indeed, is it of any use to bother with such strictly personal events?

In recent years, people have started to change their minds on this point. These experiences can be more important to the people who have them than they themselves may realize. Also these experiences throw new light on the place taken by the mystic in society.

In the main it is psychiatrists who collect accounts of experiences that, without making a radical change in the life, are mystical in the sense defined above. Freud termed them oceanic experiences, characterized by the falling away of all the borders of consciousness and by a pleasurable sense of all-oneness. The individual feels as if sinking into and being absorbed by a boundless ocean. Most people have had such an experience, which occurs chiefly in puberty during the transition from one period of life to another. Maslow had the idea of investigating whether experiences of this sort also happen to people who are mentally sound, without an atmosphere of crisis. This seems to be so. He calls them peak-experiences and regards them as the top of a development ending in human adulthood.[8] Rümke associates such an experience with the religious instinct, and regards it as an intuitive grasp of the primary state in which everything is interlocked.[9] Uleyn describes this religious aspect as follows:

> Perhaps the fundamental meaning of religion is rooted in the enduring human desire for peace and harmony. In the individual's hankering after and quest for reconciliation and union on a cosmic level in which all conflicts and frustrations are removed, for the eternal bliss in which every ambivalence will come to an end.[10]

---

[8] Abraham Maslow, *Religions: Values and Peak-Experiences* (New York: Viking Penguin, 1976).

[9] H. C. Rümke, *Karakter en Aanleg in Verband met het Ongeloof* (Amsterdam, 1963).

[10] Arnold Uleyn, Religiositeit en Fantasie (Baarn, 1978).

Here religion and mysticism meet on the platform of common humanity.

Psychiatrists have become aware of the possibility that tension between two experiences of one and the same reality can lead to madness. Formerly, a person demented in this way was thought to be demon-possessed and was either exorcised or locked up. If a mystic psychic was able to keep dementia at bay in spite of the anguish, people were inclined to interpret his or her neurotic and psychotic symptoms as an extraordinary or even miraculous gift of God. In modern times, people have been more inclined to certify the mystic as a psychopath. Only in the last few years has it been realized that mysticism and mental disturbance are not mutually exclusive.

Only recently has the question been hesitatingly asked, how human is mysticism? Can mystical experiences occur in a psychiatric patient and, conversely, must every experience in someone who is severely disturbed be interpreted as a morbid phenomenon? Psychiatrist Mark Gyselen takes the view that:

> On the one hand, mystical experience, like human love, is not the exclusive privilege of neurosis-free individuals (should any exist) and, on the other hand, it offers the human a chance to be more human.[11]

After a careful analysis, he relates an authentic mystical experience in the complicated clinical picture of a seriously disturbed patient, and concludes:

> Psychiatry must come to recognize this experience as a psychic phenomenon sui generis. Only then will the psychiatrist be in a position to help these people who react in an unhealthy manner, and to show them the way that leads out of the blind alley into a new life.[12]

A mystical experience is therefore no guarantee of a joyful and peaceful life. Even less does it guarantee a long and healthy life. Many mystics have continually complained of poor health. St.

---

[11] Mark Gyselen, "Mijn patient was meer dan ziek" in Mark Gyselen, Paul Mommaers, and J. J. C. Marlet, Hoe Menselijk is Mystiek? (Baarn, 1979), p. 42.
[12] Ibid.

Teresa of Avila was subject to much running water, many little birds, and a great deal of whistling in her head, plus chronic headaches, as was Mechthild of Hackeborn. Fainting fits, attacks of cramps, phobias, depressions—it would be possible to draw up a whole list of symptoms out of the lives of the mystics; and many of them did not live long. Hildegard of Bingen reached the age of 81, Ruysbroeck 88, and Thomas à Kempis 91, but Catherine of Siena was 33 when she died, Hugo of Saint-Victor was 45, St. John of the Cross and Jacob Boehme were 49, while even St. Francis of Assisi, who was so in tune with the life of nature, was only 44 years old when he died, totally exhausted and worn out. Hildegard, on the basis of her own observations, once said that God does not often choose to reside in a robust and healthy body.

◆ ◆ ◆

Apparently it is reasonable to conclude that mysticism is not the exclusive terrain of the mystic. A comparison with art is almost self-obvious at this point: non-mystics can have a feeling for mysticism just as non-artists can have a feeling for art. They know what it is about, can "get into" it, and recognize it when they come across it—not from what they have been taught, but from personal experience. And so, a mystic will penetrate more deeply and knowledgeably into ultimate reality than into some passing fancy.

One modern artist, Joseph Beuys, became famous for the fundamental principle from which he worked: everyone is an artist. That is to say, bringing order out of chaos and giving form to the unformed—the essence of art—is a normal preoccupation of humanity. It is what is done by a politician, an economist, a journalist, a teacher, a religious leader, and an artist. As it happens, we call someone an artist if he or she uses a gift for visual imagery. We might say that what Beuys did was to hold up a mirror in front of his fellow-citizens, asking them to take a look at themselves; he begged them not to live like robots, but as artists of life, to see life as raw material needing to be shaped. The mirror he held up gained recognition in a wide circle; and he pointed out something that had been on its way for a long time—the democratization of art. The artist does not occupy a special place, and is not a special kind of person, but is simply a pathfinder who devotes himself or herself to one aspect of life. Mysticism, also, has been democratized. A mystic is not a superperson but a trail-blazer, one who has applied a certain aspect of life to his or her own life experience.

Trailblazers such as these are necessary for a healthy culture. They ensure the continuing vitality of many aspects of life. If, in a democracy, pathfinding is left to the politicians, the value of life is measured by politics. What is not tied in with politics goes by the board. However, life is more than that. A purely mystical culture would also be a poor and limited culture.

THE MYSTIC AND CREATIVITY

Quite a number of mystics are artists with words and quite a number of practitioners of the visual arts are mystics. Eckhart is acknowledged as one of the founders of the German language; Mechtilde von Magdeburg invented a popular idiom for devotion; Hadewych and Ruysbroeck belong to the greats of Dutch literary tradition; St. Teresa of Avila and St. John of the Cross belong to the literary tradition of Spain. People have had little difficulty in seeing Fra Angelico as a mystic—he was a monk and was beatified—but are invariably surprised by any suggestion that some modern artists might be such. And yet there have been mystics among them, apparently in considerable numbers—Marc Chagall, Mondrian, and Vincent van Gogh, for example. For that matter, composers, playwrights, and filmmakers, too, include those who draw inspiration from a mystical experience of things.

Art and mysticism are not the same, but have a lot to do with one another. One of the points of agreement is the mode of handling the vague and chaotic.

Mysticism is not only an experience but is also a creative process in which this experience is given shape in language, pictures, worldview, and behavior. While it is occurring, a mystical experience is clear and plain; but, when it is over, it seems to be obscure and unformed and leaves behind an uneasy feeling of tension, an awareness of something that does not tally with one's usual activities, with daily experience, or with the world around. One can simply try to sidestep the inner conflict, or resolve it by returning to the beaten road; but artists and mystics are not able to do this, or are not prepared to do it. They are troubled by impending chaos; yet find relief by occupying themselves with it and endowing it with form. They come back to it again and again.

Cézanne revisited the same mountain (Mont Sainte-Victoire) twenty times, Mondrian drew and painted the same tree tens of times over many years, Ruysbroeck poured out a torrent of similar-sounding words in eleven treatises and repeatedly traveled circuitous paths of thought trying to achieve clarity.

Like the creative artist, the mystic has the most disturbing awareness that something is not quite right. The social order, with its world of thought, sentiments, speech, and religion, and its entire cultural network, determines our thoughts and actions to such an extent that it is hard to see or accept any alternative. The vague feeling that not everything fits, that there is something more and something different to take into account, is not automatically accompanied by revised thinking. This has to be developed little by little, against the trend, by learning to cope with the tension between a recurring vision that keeps vanishing below the threshold of consciousness, and affairs of daily life that impress themselves so vividly and coherently on the waking mind.

How is it possible to use everyday language to express something that is well-nigh inexpressible, and in such a way that it will be understood, not misunderstood? Only when a thing has been given form, will its value be demonstrated. And usually the satisfaction and relief are short-lived. The tension seems to be relieved only partially.

It will be obvious that anyone who desires mystical experiences, intense or otherwise, must have talent of some sort. This can be literary talent, organizational talent (the ability to bring order out of chaos), artistic talent, or an instinctive understanding of the art of living. Those without the requisite ability need a guide— a person whose wisdom is not gleaned from books, but one who has actually experienced things mentioned in mystical texts; one who has insight into what is going on in someone else. A guide such as this is a familiar figure in all mystical movements, and has various names—master, teacher, spiritual supervisor, guru. One of the most important qualifications for this guide is that he or she shall not foster dependence but will teach the student self-reliance—not herding, but accompanying the student along the way.

The mystical experience people seek is always the same but each expression of it will be different. This law comes into operation as soon as any mystic tries to explain what has happened. A symbolic and timeless event is being expressed in many words that are strung out in time. What is told is told from memory; and omissions, bias, and changed feelings, all have an effect. What is more, each language is culturally conditioned and is a frail vehicle for conveying highly individual impressions to others. Further factors are the personality, psyche, character, talents, and education of the speaker, and whether enough free time is available for putting the experience into words.

The differences between mystics often develop into disagreements when it comes to deciding what has to be done about a mystical experience. It is a question of how the mystic sees his or her surroundings afterward, and of how he or she interprets the experience in terms of his or her beliefs. It is not as if God necessarily manifests Himself to a mystic, as if the latter is made holy, or as if all that he or she says and does is heavenly and good, admirable and trustworthy. The writings of many mystics show that, when the vision ceased, they saw nothing more and had to pass through a "dark night of the soul."

A number of mystics were beatified or canonized, and some of them (by no means the least interesting) were charged with heresy. Those honored at the altar have been much fewer than those burned at the stake.

MYSTICAL LANGUAGE

Mystical language is an attempt to utter the inexpressible. The crux of the matter is not so much how something is experienced as what that something is. The language of love and the language of mysticism have much in common. For example, St. John of the Cross incorporated popular and contemporary love songs in his mystical poetry. However, it is characteristic of mystical language that it is paradoxical. What is asserted is, at the same time, denied. Obviously, there are no words available that would express precisely what has been experienced. Jean-Joseph Surin said that the mystic's work is to destroy, to wreck, to annihilate, and at the same time to recreate, to establish, to resurrect; the mystic is marvelously terrifying and marvelously mild; the mystic is miserly and open-handed, chivalrous and jealous, asking for all and giving all.

These opposites seem to exclude one another: to destroy—to recreate; miserly—open-handed; terrifying—attractive. Because of the tension between opposites, a narrow opening comes into existence and it is through this channel that the mystic sees something which cannot be set down in *one* word. What it is cannot be expressed, but can only be suggested. To those accustomed to expressing themselves clearly, especially in this computer age in which everything can be operated on the basis of "yes" or "no," such use of language is an annoyance. And the annoyance would be justified if we were dealing with a reality that could be described with precision. Then they would be right to combat the vague, hazy, and confused use of speech, and to protest that it is not legitimate to deny what one has just asserted. A politician or scientist who communicates in this way can be blamed; but the case is different when it concerns something the intellect is unable to grasp, something that presents itself as a totality without words or images. Because, as soon as an attempt is made to express it

Figure 1. In the Jewish Sarajevo Haggadah the mystical experience of Moses is depicted as an ascent in a blazing pillar of fire. He is seen standing between his people and heaven. Afterward his face shone so brightly that no one could look at it. (Facsimile-uitgave Rosenthaliana. University Library, Amsterdam.)

in verbal or pictorial form, the experience shatters. The best that can be done with the splinters is to use them to suggest what the totality is like.

In the writings of many mystics we find lamentations over the difficulty they have in expressing themselves. They tell us they are unable to put their experience into words, and yet they long to talk about it. St. John of the Cross says:

> Who possibly can describe what He reveals to the loving souls in whom He resides? And who can put into words what He gives them to experience? And, finally, who knows what He makes them desire? No one is able to do this, that is sure. It exceeds the capacity even of those involved; since, for that very reason, it is in a flood of images, comparisons, and symbols that they release something of what they have perceived.[13]

As stated in this passage, there are several other ways of expressing mystical experiences, including images, comparisons, and symbols, just as mythological stories and parables are sometimes employed to convey religious truth. But whereas symbolic presentations in religion easily petrify by being taken too literally (becoming converted into dogmas and developed into doctrines), a mystic will look for images so personal that their novelty gives them a suggestive force, or else will come to deny the current images, symbols, and comparisons, will shy away from them or will change them until they recover their suggestiveness. Here, too, paradox often plays a part.

While ecclesiatical theology was full of concern over the correct formulation of the doctrine of the Trinity, Gregory of Nazianze once said:

> You are one,
> You are all,
> You are none,
> You are not one,
> You are not all.

Another common reaction is the *silentium mysticum*, the mystical silence. When St. Thomas Aquinas was almost through writing

---

[13] St. John of the Cross, *The Ascent of Mount Carmel*. Translation mine. Tr. note.

Figure 2. Sitting in solitude at the foot of Mount Hira near Mecca, Mohammed receives from the angel Gabriel the message he recorded in the Koran. The mystical nature of the experience is indicated by the fire enveloping his body. It is literally impossible to look into his face. That would be regarded as sacrilege. (Miniature from the 16th-century Turkish MS, *The Life of the Prophet*. Topkopi-Sarayi Museum, Istanbul.)

the *Summa Theologica*, the most comprehensive theological work of the Middle Ages, he had a mystical experience. He said that he had seen that which made all he had written and thought seem like straw. He then lapsed into silence, and his *Summa* was left unfinished.

St. Thomas Aquinas entered into what, centuries earlier, had been discovered by some of the desert fathers: "Truly, abba Joseph *has* found the way, for he has said, 'I know it not.'" In Christian tradition, the path of silence after much has been spoken, and of not-knowing after much has been sought, is one of the oldest forms of mystical usage, called "negative theology." The classic work on this negative theology dates from ca. A.D. 500 and was written by somebody who wanted to pass for Dionysius the Areopagite, a convert of the Apostle Paul. He describes the vast wealth of heavenly reality insofar as this can be conceived, and symbolizes it by celestial hierarchies of angels (these being mirrored on earth in the ecclesiatical hierarchies). But all these "rays from the divine source" end in the "Darkness." God is Darkness behind the light. One can conjecture something about Him, if one refuses to accept that all one sees and can imagine is the ultimate reality. Of this "unimaginable" he says:

> . . .neither one, nor oneness; nor godhead, nor goodness; nor is He spirit according to our understanding, nor filiation, nor paternity; nor anything else known to us or to any other beings, of the things that are or the things that are not . . . [14]

He continues in the same vein, saying that "It" is neither darkness nor light, and ends with a paradoxical picture saying that he is neither darkness nor light. In non-Christian mysticism, too, the same sort of mystical language is employed. The Tibetan Book of the Dead speaks of the clear light of the Void. And Lao-tzu says:

> He who knows the Tao, tells it not:
> He who tells it, knows it not.[15]

This was applicable to St. Thomas Aquinas, when he wrote a commentary on the work of the pseudo-Dionysius without understanding its essence. It also applies to the anonymous 14th-century author who translated pseudo-Dionysius into English and, at the same time, indited a book with the revealing title *The Cloud of Unknowing*, the most well-known work of English mysticism.[16] But East and West alike have produced mystics who have managed to say a great deal about what they did not know.

As soon as mystic silence and negative theology become too easy an achievement, mystics start telling us how much there is to say about God. And here we encounter the typical paradox of mysticism once more. If something is very precisely formulated by a certain mystic and then degenerates into a cliché in the mouths of his or her followers, another mystic will come along and deny it. Thus Ruysbroeck opposed his great German predecessor

---

[14] Dionysius the Areopagite, *Mystical Theology and the Celestial Hierarchies* (London: Shrine of Wisdom, 1923), p. 19.

[15] *The Simple Way of Lao-tsze* (London: Shrine of Wisdom, 1924), p. 12.

[16] For example see: *The Cloud of Unknowing*, an anonymous work, edited by James Walsh (Classics of Western Spirituality Series) (New York: Paulist Press, 1981).

Eckhart, or, to be more exact, he protested against the use being made of Eckhart's teaching by imitators. When words are divorced from experience, they become deceptive. Mysticism is not a form of doctrinaire thought, it is a testimony.

When mystics say something about God, it will often be as a countermeasure against facile devotion. They might say that we can never give an adequate description of God; He has many names. He is a "worm" and a "bear"—see the Bible.[17] He is a "desert," an "abyss," "the great nothingness." Designations of this kind, stand in paradoxical contrast to "fullness of life" and any other names describing Him as all-inclusive and omnipotent, radiant with beauty, or as an excessively sweet and mild love-partner. The grim and hard aspect of reality, experienced as unfairness and cruelty, is often watered down in piety and theology by superficial declarations. And then mystics feel an urge to turn human misery into names of God, in order to bring it back into sharp focus in consciousness: "He is terrible, desolating . . . ."

Buddha expressly cautions us against too easily thinking that something is unutterable. And yet his silence is profound. He never refers to God; not even in a negative suggestion or a paradoxical description. He is a non-theistic mystic. What is more, he employs the term *atakkavacara* (not within the scope of logical thought) a mere five times; once when referring to his enlightenment under the bo-tree. Mystical language is characterized by endless seeking. Evidently the unattainable continues to be unattainable and the inexpressible to be inexpressible.

Varied Use of Language

Mysticism is an affair of the heart involving two parties. And quite often it has to do with a knowledge of and a deeper realization of

---

[17] As regards the name "Worm," if the words: "But I am a worm, and no man" (Psalm 22:6), are intended (because the opening words of the Psalm were quoted by Jesus on the cross), it would hardly be fair to argue. Christians say Christ is divine and they also apply this Psalm to Him, therefore they must agree that God is calling Himself a worm. Christians say that Christ had a human nature, too, and that it was this that was debased to the subhuman level of a "worm" when He was tortured to death. I cannot find any other Bible passage that might even remotely be thought to call God a worm. As regards the name "Bear," God is said to do something *as* a bear in Lamentations 3:10, and in Hosea 13:8, but is not called a bear. Tr. Note.

ultimate reality. This can also be said of theology and philosophy. Starting with the basics, an approach is made to a more precise description of God. For example, the principle of cause and effect is used to infer a Creator from the existence of things that seem unable to account for themselves, and an Inspirer from the existence of holy scriptures. But, in mysticism, the mystic is personally involved. The mystic's knowledge extends as far as his or her experience extends. God becomes known through a human experience of love that takes a varied course.

That is why different names will be given to this Reality, names indicating the nature of the love-relationship. They say something about God as He is experienced, but nothing about God as He is in Himself. All mystics declare their total ignorance of the being of God. Depending on the way in which the mystical experience occurs, develops, and is assimilated within a cultural and religious context, widely differing names are given to what is encountered. We shall mention a few. The *Ultimate Reality*, the *Absolute, All-is-One/One-is-All*, the *Unity of All Things*, the *Ground of Creation, Brahma,* are names for the deeper reality experienced as a oneness in which everything is interconnected. The *true I*, the *Self*, the *Vital Spark, Atman,* are names for the experience that this deepest reality also dwells in the innermost part of the human being. "Brahma is all and Atman is Brahma." Names such as *Ground*, or *Deeps* are also tied in with this experience. The *Other*, *You*, the *Bridegroom*, the *Beloved*, indicate partnership and the personal character of the mystical experience. The adoption of a name like *Father, Son, Corpus Christi, Jesus, Mary, Krishna*, points to an experience of the All-One in which humanity is central.

So the idea of God comes in here, but is also applied to such things as projections of personal needs and desires, fears and twinges of conscience. It is an idea that is narrowed down in religion, but is employed much more loosely in everyday speech. People have a vague idea of what they mean by it. Mystics caution us to be aware that we are using a word for a Reality of which, in the final analysis (so they tell us), we know little more than that it is there. At the same time, they themselves use very suggestive titles for God; titles that make a strong impression—Desert, for example, or Abyss, because this is how they have seen Him—as fascinatingly harsh and perilous.

Therefore the peculiarity of mystical language, as against ecclesiastical and theological language, is not that it is describing another reality, but that it is describing the same reality in another way.

The varied use of language within mysticism is due to differences in culture, vocabulary, tradition, and ideas, and in the religious and social milieu in which the mystic lives (the latter is particularly significant); also to differences in how the experience evolves—what is done with it, its effect on the way in which the everyday world is perceived, and how it is interpreted. Each word is tied to a culture, each human reaction is colored by psyche and character, each reflection is limited by the degree of talent for achieving clarity. No mystic starts from the very beginning with a *tabula rasa*, but relies on some tradition.

In this sense, we can speak of schools of mysticism, of occidental and oriental mysticism, of Italian, German, Dutch, Indian, German, and Slavonic mysticism, and of classical and modern mysticism. In this sense, too, mysticism can become the province of literature as well as of theology. Much of what one mystic says may be derived from another. The lines of thought can be traced and made the subjects of historical study. And there are other ways of exposing mysticism to scientific research. Its manifestations can be compared, and grouped in phenomenological types. There is ecstatic mysticism, the mysticism of internalization, of "sober drunkenness," of "shewings," also dialogic mysticism, and a mysticism of action. What is more, mystical movements and people can be categorized, with the help of theological concepts, under nature mysticism, theistic and atheistic mysticism, quietist mysticism, Christian and Buddhist mysticism, and so on.

Thus, there are many ways of bringing order into the medley of forms of expression by arranging them on the basis of similarity; and an account can be drawn up of the mode in which they influence one another. In the present book we confine ourselves to a few main lines of Western mysticism. We shall return to these. But now we want to examine mystical language in more detail without introducing the story behind it. Let us take a look at the stimuli that trigger these experiences, and the colors and images that are used, the visions and the language of the body.

WHAT TRIGGERS A MYSTICAL EXPERIENCE?

The surroundings in which a mystical experience takes place are not without influence on the way it is put into language. We refer

Figure 3. The mystical experience of Hildegard of Bingen in 1141: a stream of fiery light washes over her face. She makes notes. Her secretary elaborates them. Her woman friend, Richardis von Stade, looks up with one of her eyes. The glory shines through a window with open shutters. Inside the framework stands the Triune God as the Love that crushes evil. Probably this miniature was made in the scriptorium of Hildegard's cloister. (*Liber divinorum operum* [The Book of Divine Works] Bibl. Governativa, Lucca, cod. lat., 1942.)

to the moment when an experience occurs due to some stimulus that arouses a latent mysticism. And yet the stimulus is not by nature a stimulus: any attempt to recapture the experience by repeating the occasion usually fails. A mystical experience that happens to a nun in a convent will be permeated by an atmosphere very different from the one surrounding a successful merchant out walking in a forest, or an intense student who has just played some classical music, or a scientist sitting among books and trying to see the connection between certain data, or lovers who have just been holding hands.

Little research has been carried out into these stimuli; however, one investigation based on contemporary sources by Marghanita Laski,[17a] produced the following results. The most usual stimuli in non believers are: first, sex; second, nature; and third, art. In Christians the order is, art first, then religion, and then nature. Leaving aside unexpected stimuli, the atmosphere in which mystical experiences occur can be cultivated so that they can be assimilated and have a permanent character. When this is done, and the individual is free to meditate, to pray, and to reflect, the experience will be taken on board very differently from the way in which it is taken on board by someone tied to a demanding job. A medieval mystic, answerable to the church, and not wishing to lay himself or herself open to a charge of heresy, would not choose the same words as a Hindu mystic. Confrontation with the Holy Scriptures does not have the same effect on the development of the experience as does confrontation with social pressures. One who has never heard of Jesus will not see Him; but one who lives in a sphere where His name is on everybody's lips is sure to encounter Him when in a mystical state.

Roughly speaking, the main stimuli are religion, nature, the immediate cultural environment, fellow men and women, and the personal ego. The forms of mysticism produced by these have had different names bestowed on them: nature mysticism, dialogic mysticism (see p. 31), mysticism of the soul (see p. 33), theistic mysticism, modern mysticism. These forms are not sharply divided, but tend to overlap. We shall introduce them briefly now, leaving a more detailed discussion of one or two until later.

[17a] Marghanita Laski, Ecstasy: A Study of Some Secular and Religious Experiences (Westport, CT, 1968); Ecstasy (Bloomington, IN, 1961). Now available as Ecstasy in Secular and Religious Experiences (Los Angeles: J. P. Tarcher, 1990).

It is obvious that a *religious stimulus* is behind many mystical awakenings. Examples are a liturgical celebration, the reading of the Holy Scriptures, a certain article of faith, and a guru or religious figure such as Jesus, Mary, Buddha, or Krishna. Ruysbroeck was especially struck by the doctrine of the Trinity. He had a plastic view of it: God as an ocean expanding and contracting in ebb and flow; the divine unity from which three people proceed, three people who flow back together into unity. He applied this to the human being with three faculties (understanding, will, memory) in one spirit, to the mystical experience as a flowing outward and inward in God, and to the three stages through which that mystical experience passes.

For Hadewych (the Dutch mystic), the decisive stimulus was the insight that God is also human, and one worthy of our love, Jesus. She saw Jesus coming to her during mass. This brought her out of an impasse. Until then she did not know how to love a purely spiritual being as she had been trying to do in that era of courtly love. In Jesus she found an outlet for the force of her love. Her mysticism became characterized by this passion for Jesus.

Such a mysticism comes in many varieties. In the East its counterpart is Krishna mysticism—in bhakti yoga, the personal devotion of friendship with the god-man Krishna. Marian mysticism too, has its counterpart in the East—Chinese Yin-mysticism and Japanese Kwan-Non mysticism.

A moment of enlightenment within a religious setting can be decisive in bringing about a change from a more visual, symbolic mysticism to one that is more abstract. This is illustrated in the life of Krishnamurti. In 1927, in the camp at Ommen, where the adherents of the Order of the Star in the East gathered annually to prepare themselves for the coming of the World Teacher, the Maitreya Buddha, whose mouthpiece Krishnamurti was, he said that he saw Buddha and it was a great joy and honor to be permitted to be one with Him. People asked what he understood by "the Beloved." For him it embraces everything; it is Krishna, it is Master KH, it is the Maitreya Buddha, it is the Buddha, and yet it goes beyond all these forms. What does its name matter? He dissolved the Order of the Star in the East, and since then has sought to be nothing more than a teacher, saying that "nobody can give you liberation, you have to find it within. . . . He who has attained liberation has become the teacher—like myself. It lies within the power of each one of us to enter the flame, to become the flame."[18]

A more common stimulus is *nature*. The solitudes of nature can arouse various feelings in us—a sense of being taken up into a greater whole, and a sense of security, but also a shivery feeling of awe at their mighty vastness. These are religious plus romantic feelings, intensified by nature.

Nature can also be experienced as something that goes its own way, with the birds still singing even when we ourselves are utterly miserable. There need be nothing mystical about any of this; what counts is an awareness stealing over the conscious mind that everything is interrelated, and a sense of oneness with this universe. Thus Meister Eckhart speaks of the experience that "all blades of grass, wood and stone, all things are One." And Jacob Boehme says:

> In this light my spirit suddenly saw through all, and in and by all, the creatures: even in herbs and grass it knew, God . . . .[19]

An experience such as this does not have to be tied in with the individual's feelings. St. Francis of Assisi wrote his famous Canticle of the Sun, in which he calls all things in nature brothers and sisters, when he was most wretched. Nearly blind, he praised the Sun as his brother, even though the sunlight tormented him.[20] Nature mysticism can assume delightful forms. It can involve talking with birds and fish, or with insects as Rosa van Lima did (mosquitoes sang the praise of God with her). St. Francis of Assisi cherished the lice in his fur as "heavenly pearls," and Francis de Sales saw the footprints of wisdom everywhere in the world.

---

[18] Mary Lutyens, *Krishnamurti; The Years of Fulfillment* (New York: Avon, 1983), p. 13.

[19] *The Confessions of Jacob Boehme*, compiled and edited by W. Scott Palmer (New York: HarperCollins, 1954). Cited in William Williams, *Unbounded Light* (York Beach, ME: Nicolas-Hays, 1992), p. 135.

[20] However, the Canticle does include a mention of illness: "Be Thou praised, my Lord, of those who pardon for thy love and endure sickness and tribulations." *The Little Flowers & The Life of St. Francis with the Mirror of Perfection* (New York: E. P. Dutton, 1910). Tr. note.

A favorite legend used to be the one about the hunter—usually St. Hubert—who saw a crucifix in the antlers of a stag, and, through this insight into the connectedness of things, renounced the chase. A similar experience happened to the Sufi mystic, Ibrahim-ben Adman (d. 777). Hildegard of Bingen also saw the bad side of the interrelationship of everything. She heard the elements of the universe complain and cry "with a mighty voice."

Probably, the experience of being one with a nature in which everything hangs together is the oldest form of mysticism. It prompted the efforts made in many ancient cultures to determine nature's connections. The pyramids of Egypt and Mexico, megalithic monuments such as Stonehenge, and the complex costume of the shaman all point in this direction. Arabian astrology and mathematics, Egyptian hermetics, number mysticism, and alchemy, are each attempts to fathom the cosmos on the basis of the experience that everything is interrelated and is ultimately a unity.

The Jewish Kabbalah, too, has the same characteristics; seen for example in the classic Zohar (the Book of Splendor), also influential in Christian circles, which was written by Moses de Leon[21] at the end of the 13th century. There we find described, among other things, the connection between the color, scent, and perianth-segments of the lily, between human fasting and the Messianic end-times, between the meaning of the alphabet and its letter forms.

Much of this is now dismissed as occultism, having been jettisoned by science. Yet it has managed to become very attractive in modern mysticism, especially on account of the vision inspiring this esoteric thinking but lost to our technical culture: the vision that the cosmos is an organism in which everything is dependent on everything else, is involved in everything else, and shares the life of the same Soul.

---

[21] Although Gershom Scholem (*On the Kabbalah and Its Symbolism,* New York: Schocken Books, 1969) refers to "Moses de Leon, whom I regard as the author of the main part of the Zohar," Dr. J. Abelson (*Introduction to the Zohar,* New York: Soncino Press, 1984) comments that "no student of the Zohar . . . can believe that it ever could have emanated from the brain of one man." While the perspective A. E. Waite (*The Holy Kabbalah,* New York: University Books, 1960) says, "the theory of the fabrication of the ZOHAR by Moses de Leon puts an almost impossible burden on the shoulders of that questionable personage," and proceeds to defend his skepticism at some length. Tr. note.

What is more, the notion that each human being is a microcosm (an organism on a small scale, that mirrors, sums up, and forms part of, an organism on a large scale known as the macrocosm), has become the object of renewed interest, and it raises the question of the place occupied by humanity in the great relational whole.

Original, modern nature mysticism is to be found in the writings of Teilhard de Chardin. In 1911, he had his first experience of the powerful presence of the universe; five years later, in the trenches, he had the same experience, but now it was bound up with Christ. It seemed as if the surface that separated Christ from the world around him changed into a quivering film in which all borders were dissolved. In 1933 he said that the great ocean that collects all the spiritual currents of the universe is not a mere something, it is a some*one*. He himself has a face and a heart. All his life, Teilhard de Chardin tested this primary experience by the scientific hypothesis of evolution, by the research in which he actively participated, and by the belief in a cosmic Christ as envisioned by the apostle Paul.

Culture, in the sense of an environment created by humans, is another regular stimulus of mystical experience. A poem, a painting, music, a church, Gregorian chant, incense, a city, a book, or even a war, or a cookie and tea, seem at one time or another to have precipitated a mystical experience. Instances of this sort often occur in reports by contemporary witnesses, and in modern writers. The mysticism that emerges has little point of contact with Western religious mysticism, but is more like the mysticism of Japanese Zen, in which cultural pursuits are actually used to encourage the right atmosphere for mystical experiences: archery, raking a garden tidy, tea-drinking, painting, paradoxical speech, Za-Zen during the daily routine.

Culture plays a big role in Western mysticism, too, but often in a negative sense: the individual withdraws from society because its culture is felt to be too coarse, too rich, too oppressive, or a matter of indifference. When this attitude leads to a counterculture, a mystical culture will often arise within the latter, based on experiences of a reality that is rewarding enough to mitigate life's hardships.

Such a counterculture came into being very early, in the 4th century, when Christianity, having become the state religion, clothed itself in imperial purple and employed civil power to enforce a specific doctrine concerning God. Men and women renounced the world and retired to deserts and inaccessible areas where tax-evaders and outlaws also lived. They did not worry overmuch about doctrine, but left us their maxims and stories. They abandoned society to become hermits, but regarded hospitality as a great virtue. They were anarchistic, but treated love as the highest law in a kingdom that is not of this world. Central to their mysticism were the beatitudes in the Sermon on the Mount: Blessed are the pure in heart for they shall see God. In other words, they wished to separate themselves from society's low values in order to experience another world.

A similar counterculture also lies at the root of the imposing medieval mysticism of the Netherlands. In the 12th century, many women of rank and wealth retired from marriage and society. They did not want riches or security, but went to live in cells attached to a church or hospital. They were far from prudish, but did not wish to confine their love within a marriage. If they were already wed, they used all their powers of persuasion to send their husbands to monasteries. They were thought to be such pests by the established church and by society, that many of them were burned at the stake. They were called Beguines. This was a term of abuse until they came under the protection of Rome. The man who changed the attitude toward them was Jacob of Vitry. In his biography of Maria of Oignies (1117-1213), a Beguine who was his spiritual guide, he said that in the midst of worldlings they remain spiritually modest, in the midst of prostitutes they keep themselves pure, in the midst of the hubbub of society they live the life of a recluse.[22]

Hadewych was one of these women. In our own day, too, a counterculture with strong mystical traits is growing up. And, incidentally, it is as chaotic as its predecessor.

Our fellow men and women can also be a means of awakening mysticism. In Gandhi, the encounter with an outcaste pariah in the waitingroom of a station made a fundamental change in him and his way of life. For St. Francis of Assisi lepers were the challenge; he had a horror of them, but showed love to them whenever they crossed his path.

---

[22] Jacques de Vitry, *Vita Beatae Mariae Orgniacensis*. Analecta Sanctorym, Paris. 1863ff, Junii, pp. 542-581, 547f.

The First World War gave many people a conscious shock: how was it possible that so many human beings could slaughter one another so cruelly? The most important mystical work that appeared at this time was that of Martin Buber: *I and Thou*.[23] This book did much to introduce dialogue into mysticism, so that it is no longer confined to an "I," but extends to direct contact between an individual and that individual's fellowman or woman, whose very otherness is important. Martin Buber was strongly influenced by the Hassidim, a Jewish mystical movement from Eastern Europe, which he hoped to see flourishing again. This is a mysticism in which the story is the language, and the rapturous enjoyment of gatherings is central, with an acceptance of life's hardness, too.

The Second World War delivered another shock, not least through the cold-bloodedly organized mass murder of the Jews, an expression of racism that religions steeped in traditional images of God were powerless to resist. Dietrich Bonhoeffer also advocated a Christianity without images of God, without religion. He was put to death by the Hitler regime, but his ideas spread after the war. One post-Auschwitz slogan was "God is dead!" "The seeing of God is the doing of righteousness," says the Jew Levinas. The Transcendent reveals itself in the face of the Other, the face of those who are shut out, of those who are treated as aliens and herded into ghettos away from our society. Mysticism means being receptive, having a sense of wonder, remaining sensitive to fellow men and women who are foreign to us. Only then is there a guarantee that we shall see more than our own egos.

The liberation theologians of South America have carried through the line of Levinas. For them, the Other signifies the repressed, especially the Indians and the peasants, who have been shoveled to the edges of society by economic forces.

The stimulus for mysticism need not always come from outside, from religion, culture, nature, and another person. It can also come from the desire to penetrate deeper into one's own consciousness, or from the notion that God is accessible to us in the depths of our being. The mysticism that arises in this way is a

---

[23] Kees Waaijman, *De mystiek van ik en jij* [The Mysticism of I and Thou] (Utrecht, 1976). See also Martin Buber, *I and Thou* (New York: Macmillan, 1978).

mysticism of the soul; the inner being comes, as it were, to the surface and breaks through into consciousness.

The stimuli are often systematically applied: meditation, yoga, asceticism—especially the Eastern variety—but also the taking of mind-expanding drugs such as used by American Indians and publicized by Aldous Huxley in particular. In his book *The Doors of Perception*, which appeared in 1954, Huxley interprets his experience with the drug mescalin as mystical by appealing to Hindu and Buddhist mysticism.[24] The extent to which the deepest ground of our being (which can be called ultimate reality because it is also the ground of all there is) can be experienced through such stimuli, remains open to question. Now it is thought that mind-expanding drugs lead to a narrowing of consciousness and not to the realization that the personal ego is fundamentally one with everything and must therefore stand open to everything.

MYSTICISM AND THE FIVE SENSES

Mysticism is the experience of a reality that soars above anything we can understand. As we have already seen, it is hard to find a language for it. On the other hand, it involves the whole person. Spiritual though mysticism undoubtedly is, it is also very corporeal. Individuals can hear, see, smell, taste, and feel God with five spiritual senses corresponding to the five physical senses, or so mystics have repeatedly been telling us. This aspect of mystical experience provides the possibility of a language that artists can use pictorially with ease in a way that most people can understand. Many objects of popular devotion, many of the themes of religious iconography in the East and West, and many liturgical feast-days have originated in the writings of mystics.

In his *Confessions*, St. Augustine shows how the senses *do not* and, at the same time, *do* experience God:

> But what is it that I love when I love You? Not the beauty
> of any bodily thing, nor the order of the seasons, not the
> brightness of light that rejoices the eye, nor the sweet
> melodies of all songs, nor the sweet fragrance of flowers
> and ointments and spices: not manna nor honey, not the

---

[24] Aldous Huxley, *The Doors of Perception* and *Heaven & Hell* (New York: HarperCollins, 1963).

Figure 4. The Trinity—three faces in one—beheld by St. Augustine. The abstract idea, however, entered his heart, as pictured by the three arrows. (Painting by Filippo Lippi, ca. 1440, Uffizi-museum, Florence.)

limbs that carnal love embraces. None of these things do I love in loving my God. Yet in a sense I do love light and melody and fragrance and food and embrace when I love my God—the light and the voice and the fragrance and the food and embrace in the soul, when that light shines upon my soul which no place can contain, that voice sounds which no time can take from me, I breathe that fragrance which no wind scatters, I eat the food which is not lessened by eating, and I lie in the embrace which satiety never comes to sunder. This it is that I love, when I love my God.[25]

---

[25] *The Confessions of St. Augustine*, translated by F. J. Sheed (New York: Sheed & Ward, 1943), pp. 215-216.

Therefore symbols are involved here, but not contrived symbols, such as the design of a national flag. Perceiving God in a sensory way is different from perceiving other human beings in a sensory way; yet it is possible to compare the two ways, because in both cases the body enters the picture.

When St. Teresa of Avila says that interior prayer feels as if a very sweet ointment is being rubbed on the innermost part of the soul, in the manner of an excellent perfume, the perfume she mentions is a symbol, but the experience of smelling perfume does have something to do with the experience of interior prayer. What her experience was may best be appreciated by reliving the memory brought back by smelling a perfume. Listening to music, savoring something, looking at something beautiful, are in this sense symbols of what is pleasurable in mystical experience. Key texts were readily found by Jewish and Christian mystics in the Bible; especially in the Song of Solomon (the Canticles) in which much is said about the fragrance of the bride and bridegroom: "Because of the savour of thy good ointments thy name is as ointment poured forth . . . . Draw me, we will run after thee. . . . " (Song of Songs 1:3,4) and in Psalms such as Psalm 34: 8, "O taste and see that the Lord is good."

The most common symbol where spiritual senses are concerned is that of touch, "the coarsest physical and the most refined spiritual sense" according to some mystics. The mystic has the feeling of being touched by a loved hand that reaches beyond the senses. The mystic also experiences palpably what is (to him or her) a transcendent reality, a point illustrated by St. John of the Cross when he says that it is an extremely subtle touch on the soul by the Lover, that sometimes occurs when least expected. It is as if a spark lands on her and sets her alight. Like someone who suddenly awakes, the will is then immediately on fire to love God, to long for Him, to praise Him, to thank, to honor, to heed, to petition. Mingled in is a love that can be felt. He writes in a poem:

> O sweet burn!
> O delicious wound!
> O tender hand! O gentle touch!
> Savoring of everlasting life
> and paying the whole debt,
> By slaying thou has changed death into life![26]

---

[26] "The Living Flame of Love," in *The Mystical Doctrine of St. John of the Cross,* an abridgement made by C. H., with an introduction by R. H. J. Stewart (London: Sheed & Ward, 1953), p. 116.

THE LANGUAGE OF THE LOVER

Roland Barthes has an interesting explanation of his reasons for writing *Fragments d'un Discours Amoureux* (a compilation made from world literature).

> The language of lovers seems to be characterized by an air of isolation. Someone who is in love is alone in a cruel world; cruel because it seems that so many situations cause separation or alienation from the beloved. The lover creates an alternative world out of his own fantasy, in which the image of the beloved determines everything. The lover is full of hope and full of despair, he waits; and must fill in time with words of expectation concerning a new life, and must fill in time often with tears.[27]

Space is devoted in his book to mystics. They have borrowed heavily from the language of profane love, but have also made contributions of their own. One of those who have done so is St. John of the Cross. His mystico-erotic poetry has become world-famous. "What woman would not be glad to receive verses like these from her lover!" exclaimed psychoanalyst Ignace Lepp. And the poet Arthur Symons remarked that this monk could still teach lovers a thing or two. Evelyn Underhill commented:

> It would be strange if he could not: since their finite passions are but the feeble images of his infinite one, their beloved the imperfect symbol of his First and only Fair.[28]

Whether or not this is universally true, is a question. Place the written expressions of mystical and profane love side by side and it is hard to tell the differences; both are emotional, both are passionate, especially for the periods in which they are written. When Hadewych was alive, troubadours were the creators of the language of courtly love. Hadewych (the Dutch mystic) adopts their language, just as St. John of the Cross adopts the Spanish baroque language of love. Not that all mystics have employed such language; in fact, in our own day and age, it no longer seems appro-

---

[27] Roland Barthes, *Fragments d'un Discours Amoureux*, 1977. An English version was published by Hill & Wang in 1978.
[28] Evelyn Underhill, *Mysticism: A Study in the Nature and Development of Man's Spiritual Consciousness* (New York: E. P. Dutton, 1930), pp. 89-90.

Figure 5. St. Bernard suddenly saw whatever afterward inspired him, which was that God had become man and therefore our fellow. And he felt that he, too, might be allowed to drink from the same source—Mary's breast. He set down in solitude what he had seen; and, as he was writing, the vision became tangible and concrete. (Detail from a triptych, ca. 1290, Palma de Majorca, Museo Arqueológico Luliano.)

guage; in fact, in our own day and age, it no longer seems appropriate because, as Roland Barthes observed, people fight shy of it.

The aversion that erotic mystical texts often seem to provoke nowadays (and the modern insinuation that mystics are sexually frustrated) is due not only to the lack of a contemporary language of love, but also to a view of mysticism that consigns it to the realm of the spirit, to the exclusion of whatever might be thought of as physical or profane.

Nevertheless if anything is clear from mystical writings it is that the whole person is involved in mysticism: the passions, the desires, the capacity for love. There is only *one* love, as St. Teresa of Avila observed. Mystics do strive for purity, but it is of the same sort as that required to achieve tenderness in ordinary human love. Their purity is not prudery—far from it. And yet one would misread the erotic texts if one failed to perceive their symbolic side. Bernard of Clairvaux, the creator of "bride mysticism," explains that he renders his mystical experiences in the language of love because he is impelled by a quite similar desire.

He also points out the difference between the two kinds of love:

> Wait, however, before jumping to the conclusion that I regard the union of the Eternal Word with the faithful soul as something physical or something that can be drawn by the imagination. No, I speak in the same vein as St. Paul when he says, "He that is joined unto the Lord is one spirit." I do my best to put into human words the joining of spiritual with spiritual, the rapture of a pure soul in God and God's merciful condescension to her.[29]

In St. Bernard the symbolism is clear. Also he borrows freely, especially from the Song of Solomon (see his *Sermones in Cantica Canticorum*). In Hadewych, the symbolism is much less clear for she doesn't borrow anything, but describes her own emotions and her extremely physical erotic experiences, without cautioning herself (or the reader) that she is dealing with a reality that, in the final analysis is not physical, but unimaginable and not to be pictured. All this is implicit, however:

---

[29] Translation is mine. Unfortunately we do not know where this quoted material was published. Tr. note.

He swallows you into Himself. Where the depths of His wisdom is, there He will teach you what He is, and how wonderfully the one beloved dwells in the other, and lives through the other in such a way that neither perceives himself or herself. But they possess one another in mutual enjoyment, mouth in mouth, heart in heart, body in body, and soul in soul, while a sweet heavenly nature flows through them both; and the two are one, but at the same time remain themselves - yes, they remain themselves continually.[30]

By and large, the language of love occurs in Western mysticism from the 12th century through the baroque period. We encounter it in the East, too, notably in Krishna mysticism, and most of all in the Sufism of Islam. It is always symbolic.

What is more, most religions are acquainted with a connection between sexuality and the divine. In the leading work of Jewish mysticism, the Zohar, Moses of Leon says: "When a man is intimate with his wife, they are wafted by their desire to the eternal hills."[31]

In Catholic theology, a marriage consummated by the sexual act is a "sacramental sign." The sexual act itself is seldom used as a vehicle of mysticism, the most explicit example occurring in Tantra. This is another mystical path: sexual congress, experienced as total union by two people who have in view the deeper unity with the Ultimate! In that form of modern mysticism known as the sexual revolution, sexuality has come to the fore again. Yet even here, the language of love is lacking. There is practically no question of personal commitment; it is just a matter of friendship. Indeed, the same was true of many mystics in the past who often formed very solid friendships on the human level.

---

[30] Brieven Hadewych, Oørspronklelijke Tekst en nieuw-Nederlandse Overzetting met in leidingen en aanteken ingen, bezorgd door F. van Bladel en B. Spaapen, Tielt, 1954, 9. Brief, p. 113.
[31] *The Zohar*, in 5 volumes, translated by Maurice Simon and Dr. Paul P. Levertoff (New York: Soncino Press, 1934).

The Language of Illumination

Mystical experience not only represents the challenge of another reality, but also gives a brief but clear insight into the ultimate ground of everything that exists. The two facets go together, but one may glint more brightly when the experience is recalled. In the language of love, getting to know the Beloved is always involved. In the language of illumination, we have to do with an enlightenment that floods the being, not with an insight born of cold thought.

A fundamental image that constantly figures in the language of illumination is that of divine inebriation. It originates with a Jew, Philo of Alexandria, a contemporary of Jesus of Nazereth. He was a mystic, and bore testimony to his own mystical experiences. In the light of these experiences, he developed a theory about how the Hebrew prophets prophesied, and suggested that they received divine insight in a state of spiritual drunkenness. According to Philo, this drunkenness has to be distinguished from the divine drunkenness provoked by wine in the Dionysian mysteries. That is to say, what he is referring to is a "sober drunkenness" that is "more sober than sobriety itself." He is talking of an insight into life's questions that goes deeper than the place reached by down-to-earth consideration of the facts and carries on from where the latter leaves off. In other words, the possibilities open to mature reflection are greatly increased by a certain state resembling drunkenness—when the spirit is no longer contained in itself but is transported and enraptured by a heavenly passion.

Five centuries later, we find St. Augustine speaking of the same sober drunkenness. This North African had passed through a deep crisis in which he doubted everything, until the moment when he saw in a flash that everything we see may be doubted except the personal will to live: the fact that in ourselves we have an ineradicable desire for life and love. In this he beheld the will to live that is in all beings and things, namely God; and also saw that the primary human desire is focused on this Love: "Our hearts are restless until they rest in Thee."[32] He also said that we should not turn to the outside world, but retire into ourselves for

---

[32] *The Confessions of St. Augustine*, translated by F. J. Sheed (New York: Sheed & Ward, 1943), p. 3.

only in the innermost part of ourselves does the truth dwell. Only the eye of the soul, not the eye of the body, only the inner eye, the eye of the heart, can perceive the primary love—in a flash of clear seeing. Eventually, St. Augustine came to realize that such seeing is rare. But it had aroused in him a passionate resolve to retain and develop his insight. The sober inebriation of a single moment left behind a calm yet eager longing after, and seeking for, the truth in back of things.

The getting to know, the "seeing" of the Truth in the innermost recess of his own being, was the passion that drove St. Augustine. It is not without reason that later inconography depicted him as "the thinker with heart."

St. Augustine has had a prolonged influence on Western mysticism. The high point of his influence was the school of Saint-Victor, an international group of 12th-century monks who, in the abbey of Saint-Victor in Paris, elaborated the Augustinian insights into a theory of contemplation and into a practical guide. The contemplative form of mysticism has always been rather elitist, fit only for monks who have been granted an opportunity for it. It was not considered suitable for people with lots of things to attend to, as Pope Gregory the Great (ca. 540-604) found out when he said that his afflicted spirit, laboring under its burden of responsibilities, remembered how, in former days, it went with him into the cloister, how it rose above all temporal things, and, although it was always in the body, escaped during contemplation from the body's dungeon.

After the Middle Ages, there were movements led by people who were not monks but who also claimed to be illuminated: the "alumbrados" of Spain in the 16th century; the "illuminés" of France in the 17th century; the Illuminati of Bavaria in the 18th century. These were all branded as heretical because they seemed to be too self-assured and too contemptuous of others who had not been enlightened.

Modern humanistic mysticism is, in a certain sense, a return to this illuminism. But it is more democratic, draws from other sources, and uses a different language. Now we hear of "expansion of consciousness," of the true I and the Self; we hear of meditation as a means of preparing oneself for illumination, and of peak experiences and ultimate reality. Much of this language has been borrowed from psychology and psychiatry, and from oriental mysticism. Nevertheless, in essence, we are still dealing with the mysticism spoken of by St. Augustine: reaching the deepest Ground of all things within our own innermost being, so that we "see," and are conscious of the underlying basis of reality. Cosmic consciousness, a rising up in consciousness of a light in which the universe is perceived as an integrated and united whole; this is how the man who framed humanistic psychology, Abraham Maslow, was talking in 1964. He also said that this experience is not merely verbal or intellectual, but drenches an individual's whole being and is so profound and thrilling that it can change the person's character permanently.[33]

THE LANGUAGE OF ACTION

One of the characteristics of a mystical experience is that it enters deeply into the life. In Western mysticism, this aspect has always been seen, because an experience of Love as the ground of the existence of everything necessarily results in deeds of love to one's fellow humans. Mystical language was dominated by this idea after the 17th century in particular. At that time, anti-mystical feeling started to spread in France: mysticism was for special people, not for the ordinary man or woman! The language of mysticism then adapted itself as follows: it is better not to talk too much about such experiences; one must show by one's deeds what mystical experience is.

One of the first mystics to speak this language convincingly was Vincent de Paul (1581-1660), the son of a French peasant and best known for the Vincentian associations and the new type of nun with the "flying headdress," the Daughters of Love. He tuned in with "antennas of love" (Dom Helder Camara) to every cry of distress from galley-slaves, abandoned babies, beggars, neglected children, the physically or mentally ill, the homeless and the fugitives. He spoke a language that everyone understood, even when he used mystical words. A single example of this mystical language should serve to show what we mean:

---

[33] Abraham Maslow, "The Cor-Religious or Transcendent Experience," in *The Highest State of Consciousness*. Edited by John White, (New York: Doubleday/Anchor, 1972). Tr. note: it will be remembered, of course, that the term "cosmic consciousness" had been used earlier by Bucke in a book of that title.

Figure 6. In 1274, when on a retreat on Mt. Randa, Ramon Lull saw a vision; an insight that, for the rest of his life, he attempted to work out scientifically. In this miniature, commissioned by his friend Thomas le Myesier, three phases are represented: receiving the vision in a cave, talking about the vision to a passing pilgrim, and expounding the doctrine before a large audience. (Karlsruhe, Badische Landesbibliothek, parchment manuscript 92.)

Believe me, my brothers, it is an inexorable stipulation
made by Jesus Christ—as I have so often said to you—
that the heart must first be empty of itself; only then does
God come to fill it. For it is God who dwells in and is
active in it; it is this holy humility that frees us from ourselves! Only then does our striving cease, but God strives
through us. And then everything is as it should be.[34]

The advantage of this mystical language is that it makes mysticism
accessible to all. This is an ideal explicitly pursued by the French
mystic to whom Vincent often referred, St. Francis de Sales (1567-
1622) once said that it was a mistake—no, a heresy—to try to banish the life of piety from the army, the workshop, the palace, and
the homes of the faithful.

For the most part, modern mysticism is a continuation of this
mysticism of action. One of the first people in the Netherlands to
define modern mysticism was the Dutch Carmelite Titus
Brandsma. According to him, what is being done will seem rather
empty, and the mysticism of action will quickly get into a rut, if
people keep quiet about mystical experiences because of an atmosphere of hostility to mysticism. Therefore we have to start talking about mysticism again. Brandsma talked about it like this:

First of all, we have to see God as the deepest ground
of our being, concealed in the innermost recess of our
nature. . . .We must worship Him not only in our own
being but equally in all that exists, firstly in our fellow
men and women, but also in nature, in the universe,
omnipresent and permeating everything with the work
of His hands. . . .This indwelling and in-working of God
should not be a matter of intuition, but should reveal
itself in our lives, should express itself in our words and
deeds, and should radiate from our whole being.[35]

A modern mystic of action was Dag Hammarskjöld, Secretary
General of the United Nations. He never personally mentioned
his mystical experience; only after his death was the diary dis-

---

[34] Translation mine. No source of this quotation was provided by the author.
Trans. note.
[35] From Titus Brandsma's commemoration speech given in 1932.

covered in which he had committed it to writing. It then became obvious how greatly all his activities had been motivated by this wellspring of mysticism, which he allowed to irrigate his public life:

> The "mystical experience." Always *here* and *now*—in that freedom which is one with distance, in that stillness which is born of silence. But—this is a freedom in the midst of action, a stillness in the midst of other human beings. . . . Sanctity—either to be the Light or to be self-effaced in the Light, so that it may be born, self-effaced so that it may be focused or spread wider . . . . In our era, the road to holiness necessarily passes through the world of action.[36]

Hammarskjöld could no longer remember the mystical experience, but he was well aware of its far-reaching character:

> I don't know Who—or what—put the question. I don't know when it was put. I don't even remember answering. But, at some moment I did answer *Yes* to Someone—or Something—and from that hour I was certain that existence is meaningful and that, therefore, my life, in self-surrender had a goal.[37]

Many modern mystics who are rooted in the Jewish-Christian tradition are most strongly attracted by the radical character of mystical experiences in the sense that mysticism has to prove itself in the hard reality of everyday life. In one encyclopedia, various witnesses are cited in support of the following description of the "new mysticism":

> Its special feature seems to be that the individual breaks through to mystical depths by confronting life's inner world; and the place where the mystical experience is undergone is not some isolated spot, but the desert of daily life, in so far as the technique allows.

---

[36] Dag Hammarskjöld, *Markings* (New York: Alfred A. Knopf, 1964), pp. 122, 155.

[37] Dag Hammarskjöld, *Markings*, p. 205.

In one of the best anthologies of modern mystical texts, F. C. Happold provides the following opinion:

> The steep and stony way of contemplation entering the full *vita unitiva* is seldom given us to tread. Though one may turn back later, and descend from the heights to the plain, this life initially demands retirement from the world and intense concentration. It is a way not given to the great majority. Their calling is to go and lead a creative, active life. Even that can be a genuine mystical path; different, but after its own fashion hard and steep, and with its own moments of enlightenment and its own spirituality.[38]

ECSTASY, VISIONS, APPARITIONS, PERCEPTIONS

What has so far been said about mystical language may have given the impression that the writings of the mystics themselves, and books on mysticism, are perfectly easy to understand once their cultural and religious context is known. Such an impression would be false: mystical texts are very intractable; and, apparently, many people find them rather disconcerting. When the pages of the books are filled with such unusual items as visions, voices, apparitions, emotional outbursts, levitation, and stigmata, we are inclined to suspect that some mystics were stark raving mad.

Mysticism involves not only an experience of short duration which always has the same characteristics, but also a person who is trying to assimilate this experience into his or her life. What is more, mystics include both the stolid and the emotional types, both the balanced and the unstable, the physically strong and the frail. Also, a balance between two worlds is involved, especially in Western mysticism: one that is flawless, complete, gladdening, and seen in one lucid moment, and another that has to be coped

---

[38] F. C. Happold, *Mysticism: A Study and an Anthology* (London: Harmondsworth, 1975; and New York: Viking Penguin, 1963).

Figure 7. A mystical experience as a dream. St. Francis receives a strong impression that the five wounds of Jesus can be seen in his body. These stigmata are real. St. Francis is dreaming and is lifted up on a cloud, and Jesus is the angel Seraphin. Under the arms of the cross we have *contemplatio* (contemplation) on the left and *actio* (action) on the right: the ideal of the new monastic orders was to combine the two. (Mathias Paris. *Chronica Majora*, mid 13th century, French. Corpus Christi College, Cambridge, MS 16.)

with daily, full of violence, evil, problems and opposition. Between these two worlds the borders are fairly blurred: the borders between daydream and hard reality, between fantastic imagery and true vision, between spiritual and physical impressions. We must now say something about the latter.

DAYDREAMS VERSUS REALITY

We cannot live in a world of problems and responsibilities without taking a break from time to time. The mind needs rest. It must have the liberty to return to a primitive level of consciousness where things exist without the individual having to answer for them. This liberty occurs in dreams during sleep. If dreams are blocked, for example during brainwashing, the subject becomes mentally ill and can no longer think straight.

The heavier the demands made by life, the stronger the desire to daydream in a problem-free environment: to muse amid quiet surroundings, where birds are absorbed in their own lives and clouds float serenely overhead oblivious of our troubles; to read some light fiction, or the latest gossip column, with no intention of taking it seriously. Such daydreams can also be stimulated and made more ecstatic. They can be induced by fasting and asceticism, by drugs, dancing, music, and rhythmic chants; they can be practiced with the help of TM or yoga. Nearly all cultures recognize this need to daydream and have discovered entries to the dreamworld. Alcohol, and the drug peyote, have both been used to produce unusual phenomena in religious ceremonies, as has dancing to a rhythmic beat. The dreamworld visited has been seen as a heavenly place or paradise—the original state in which everything is whole. The experience has been called an ecstasy or trance, and is known today as a high. Alcohol, hash (cannabis), LSD, and heroin have been used a great deal, but a disco-evening, too, serves the same purpose with its movement, flashing lights, and loud music.

Awareness of one's surroundings, of personal problems, and of things that are hard to control, evaporates. Body-consciousness increases and with it self-confidence. The world seems easy to grasp and manage. As already explained, such daydreams are not mystical states, even though they rather resemble them.[39] And even though these daydreams have been used by some mystics, they have not been used by everyone having a mystical experience. If the experience has been intense, coming back to banal reality is rather hard. Everything becomes unpleasantly cold and tepid as when the heat is removed from a boiling kettle, said St. Bernard. The individual will often long for the other world and want to become immersed anew in the depths of the divine ocean,

---

[39] Much the same thing is said by R. H. Ward in *A Drug-taker's Notes* (London: Victor Gollancz, 1957). A lady friend of Ward's, a psychiatrist, ran six tests of LSD on him, and he recorded and commented on his experiences. Some of these were trivial, but others seem profound, as when he says, "The wall was very old . . . . The dust it was made of spoke to me; dust from all ages of time and all parts of the world; living dust-motes" (pp. 84-85). He also passed through times of terror when he needed all the support the doctor could give him. At the end of the book, he recounts the mystical experience of someone he knew and notes that it differed from his own lysergic acid experiments by expressing "knowledge and love of God" (p. 194). Tr. note.

Figure 8. The vision can be so strong that the body exhibits stigmata. Also the body can radiate until it is raised from the ground. Since St. Teresa of Avila, this phenomenon has been treated as a physical one. Here it is used by Giotto as a symbol of ecstasy. (Mural by Giotto in the Basilica Superiore of St. Francis of Assisi. Photo: Scala Archivo Fotocolor.)

and as Johannes Tauler would say: God is inside me, God is outside me, God is everywhere around me. The ecstatic intoxication that can help to reproduce such a mystical experience is often eagerly sought in both East and West. Women in the 13th century did it by cultivating "love" to delirious heights. Love became like a pail brimful of water ready to run over at the slightest touch. Beatrice of Nazareth described herself as feeling herself abounding in a great fullness of heart. Her spirit was wholly absorbed in love; her body gave way, her heart melted and she felt like a vessel that was full to overflowing—one that would spill when anyone disturbed it.

That this striving for ecstatic experiences is not risk free, was obvious even in earlier times. One of the risks is addiction. Jan Van Ruysbroeck describes such an addiction as something that occurs especially in women. The addiction in question is to the holy mass, especially to receiving the host:

> This goes so far that they are in danger of losing their senses and sinking down if they cannot receive the blessed Sacrament. . . .Nobody can do anything to console them, or to calm them down, as long as they have not received the Sacrament. But then they are completely satisfied, and rest in their Beloved, know spiritual enjoyment and abound in sweetness of soul and body. All is well until the grace requires renewal, and this urge in their nature and in all the powers of their soul rises up again: then they relapse into vehement passion and desire, as if they had never received the Sacrament before.[40]

There is a further risk associated with the cultivation of ecstasy, namely that the border between the dreamworld and reality will disappear. What is dreamed seems real, what is seen is like a dream, and there is no longer any hold on reality. A mystical experience has a fairly overwhelming character, and snatches a person away from normal consciousness. This is called spiritual rapture: a thing that can unsettle an individual considerably. St. John of the Cross likens it to a nightmare and said that at such a

---

[40] Translation mine. Tr.

Figure 9. Something like a century before St. Francis, Milarepa in Tibet described how the spirit can rise up out of the body. The body does not levitate with the spirit, but rests in a dream state. This Chinese wood-cut shows, starting at the top, the four stages of ecstasy. In the final picture the spirit fans out in space.

moment the person is seized by fear and trembling, because of the spiritual vision that is then vouchsafed. The body stiffens in an ecstasy of this sort, so that the flesh contracts as in a corpse.

However, according to him, this is more likely to occur when one first crosses the threshold; later one becomes more serene. It will be realized from the above that, in unstable personalities, crossing this particular threshold leads to psychic disintegration. Well-known examples are J. J. Surin and Francois la Combe. Not that we are laying down a hard and fast rule: there have been mystics with unstable psyches who have been able to handle the problem. A notable example is Catherine of Genoa (1447-1510). She was of an extremely nervous disposition, and her marriage was a martyrdom to her until she had an overwhelming mystical experience. Afterward she constantly entered states of ecstasy bordering on madness.

> . . . . I am so plunged and submerged in the source of his infinite love, as if I were quite under the sea and could not touch, see, feel anything on any side except water. I am so submerged in the sweet fire of love that I cannot grasp anything except the whole of love, which melts all the marrow of my soul and body. And sometimes I feel as if my body were made entirely of some yielding substance. . . .[41]

She interprets this as "being submerged in love," but it is demented love; one cannot help thinking she was suffering from a psychosis when one reads that she went and hid under a bed and stayed with her face pressed against the ground, beside herself, in a state of bliss that no one can express who has never experienced it. She remained in this condition for five or six hours. She no longer knew where she was—in heaven or on earth. It was as if she were infatuated and beside herself. This woman was so alienated from herself and so overwhelmed that she looked like a startled animal.

That in spite of these conditions she did not go crazy but, on the contrary, was efficient in her care of plague patients and the poor, was seen by her contemporaries as something very remarkable. Catherine went to work in the big hospital in Genoa. She was responsible for everything, and did all with the utmost care. Yet she fulfilled her task in such a manner that all the pains she took with it never deprived her of her absorption in God. And although her inner life was intense, nothing was ever wanting in the hospital. Everyone looked on this as a wonder. Very exceptional also is the fact that she was able to distinguish the mystical core of her experiences from the way in which she was overwhelmed by an ecstasy of love, and was able to retain and strengthen this core. Probably this kept her sane.

Leading mystics have taken a hard look at ecstasies and aver that ecstatic intoxication is not the same as being "caught up in the

---

[41] Martin Buber, editor, *Ecstatic Confessions* (San Francisco: HarperCollins, 1985), p. 108.

Figure 10. A modern interpretation. St. Teresa remains standing. St. John of the Cross, but also St. Teresa, herself, thought that succumbing or being overwhelmed must be a result of alienation or might even be a sign of weakness. (Drawing by Marianne van der Heijden, 1953, NCI, Boxmeer.)

Figure 11. A well-known representation of ecstasy. An angel of love pierces the heart of St. Teresa with his dart. She suffers an orgastic paroxysm. A piece of baroque art by Bernini. (Marble sculpture in the church of Maria della Vittoria, Rome, 1645-1652.)

Figure 12. The same symbol was used by the performing artist Ben d'Armagnac. In the chilly city of New York, dressed in black and lying on a white-tiled floor, he allowed a stream of cold water to fall on his heart for forty minutes, in order to induce a transcendental experience. (This is the final performance before he perished at home in Amsterdam in 1978. Photo: Cathrien van Ommen.)

spirit." They do not reject ecstasy if it occurs. It is like falling in love: who would start going out with someone without the joyful attraction of being in love? St. Francis said that emotional delights and tidbits are given to our childish souls by God in order to attract us. St. Teresa of Avila, too, speaks in the same vein. She lived through eight ecstatic years, and valued them as spiritual encouragement, but also played them down as feminine frailties that it would have been wrong to suppress prematurely. She thought, too, that ecstasies justify their existence after periods of depression when the individual feels forsaken by God. They would certainly be a timely comfort!

It is a different matter when ecstasy is cultivated as a way of stronger and more lasting union. Many women have chosen this way and even now it is often entered. But the question is constantly raised, "What are the risks when safe limits are exceeded? How far may one enter this frenzied love? Further than the point where one starts to feel like an intruder? Hadewych informs us:

> I was (and still am) so seized by violent desire and impetuous longing that I had the impression, and in fact realized, that I could no longer endure this great restlessness in which I was (and still am) unless God gave me fresh strength.[42]

It seems to be an audacious confidence. However, Hadewych goes on: "And so He did. Thanks be to Him." Yet this reliance on God can easily be false confidence if our motives are not completely pure. St. Augustine long ago gave as a guide: "Love and do what you will." No limits can be set to love. But then we must realize how thoroughly we have to be purged of self-love before following this advice. Love's emotions are untrustworthy; if we decide to surrender to them, we should always use common sense, watch our motives and what we really love, and be aware that personal feelings, however intense, ecstatic, exalted, and loving they may be, are not the Beloved. Even in human attachments, the cultivation of our own feelings of love can shut us up in our own egos and shut out the loved one.

---

[42] De visioénen van Hadewijch, a. a. o. (Anm. 18), xiv, 1-5. Translation mine. Tr. note.

The great mystics do not forbid the emotional path, even when it is strongly erotic, but they do insist on purity. Thus Ruysbroeck says:

> The more attention they pay to themselves and to their disorganized physical feelings, the more these increase. . . .If they wish to surmount this difficulty and to keep themselves pure in the service of the Lord, then they must forget themselves and must fix their gaze wholly on Him whom they love . . . . And so they become clean people who vanquish whatever might hinder them.[43]

St. Teresa of Avila protested against trying to be "superspiritual" to the exclusion of human emotions, but she cautions her ecstatic sisterhood against confusing dream union and real union, for some think that if they swoon in a dream they call spiritual, they see the one instead of the other and let themselves be carried away. Those who try to induce ecstasies by means of fasts, mortification of the flesh, and vigils, find themselves irrevocably trapped in a vicious circle!

St. John of the Cross refers to St. Teresa on the subject of ecstasies. He recognizes the emotional way as a possible way, but finds it rather complicated because it can so quickly turn into "spiritual epicureanism." He said that for him, the shortest way is pure ecstasy, the passionate search for the reality behind things through absolute detachment from one's own ego.

In non-Western mysticism, too, there are similar appraisals of ecstasy. Thus the Sufi mystic al-Qushayri, in his book *Risala* (1046), regards an ecstatic feeling as often fatal for the soul that is seeking God. He counsels that we should be frugal with these delights and refrain from them.

To avoid being ground down by the daily cares that distract us from universal issues, a mystic will always try to have free space where he or she can make contact with another world and can dwell on the vision of it. But this free space need not be that of ecstasy. It can also be created by meditation, yoga, or Zen: by Za-Zen in the home, or by seeking various activities with values that correspond to the mystical experience of Reality. We can do as

---

[43] Ruysbroeck; translation mine. Tr.

Hammarskjöld did and produce a freedom in the midst of activity that coincides with detachment—a quietness in the crowd—free of self-interest.

FANTASY AND TRUE VISION

In the language of mysticism, the part played by creative fantasy is often bigger than that played by the recording, analyzing, and classifying understanding. Mystical experience evokes images: of an ocean in which one is immersed, of a light in which everything looks different, of fire that consumes impurities and also melts the individual, of love and marriage. All these are representations of an invisible reality so intense that personal consciousness disappears. In addition, there are portrayals of the place where the experience occurs: the deepest ground of the soul, the summit of the spirit, the unseen essence, the inner eye, the spiritual spark, the bridechamber.

That the imagery is symbolic goes without saying. Even when mystical language takes the form of poetry, it is clear that an attempt must be made to feel the suggestive power of the words in order to gather what is really being said. Matters are less clear when the language is narrational. Again visions are even more obscure than narrative. We ask ourselves whether we are dealing with what actually happened or with the symbols of what happened.

When St. Augustine says that he can smell, feel, hear, taste, and see God, he is using imagery. But the experience is much closer to reality than is St. Teresa's "garden watered by God." Spiritual perception does have links with sensory perception, but there is little in common between the soul and a garden even though a comparison of sorts can be made between them.

However, when St. Teresa of Avila describes very precisely how an angel appeared on her left side and how "he was not large, but small of stature, and most beautiful . . . . I saw in his hand a long spear of gold, and at the iron's point there seemed to be a little fire . . ."[44] then we get the impression that what she saw was as real to her as seeing a mugger approaching with a knife

---

[44] *The Life of St. Teresa of Jesus*, translated by David Lewis (London: Thomas Baker, 1924), p. 266.

would be to us. But when St. Teresa's vision is rendered by an artist like Bernini and is later popularized in prints, it becomes a symbol.

Does a visionary do something essentially different from what an artist does? The description given by St. Teresa was so vivid that Bernini had no need to exercise his imagination in order to depict it in marble. On the other hand, marble angels holding spears as the symbol of love could be seen everywhere in the time of St. Teresa. When Margaretha Maria Alacoque saw Christ appear "with five wounds shining like five suns," and with His breast opened to display the source of the radiance (His heart), this was exactly what she had seen in an engraving in her missal. When Bernadette Soubirous described the Virgin Mary as she appeared to her in the grotto at Lourdes, her description matched a lithograph of Murillo's "Immaculate Conception" that had been distributed at Lourdes by the government a few years earlier in a nationwide campaign.[45]

Hildegard of Bingen (1098-1179) was one of the great mystical visionaries. Her visions were so graphic that it was possible to illustrate them in miniatures. She herself says of them:

> The visions I had, I did not discern in sleep, or in dream, or in fits of insanity, or with the eyes of my body, or with physical ears, or in secret places; but when I was awake and attentive, and with the eyes of the spirit and the inner ear. I perceived them with open face and by the will of God. . . .But my outer eyes remained open and my other bodily senses were functioning normally.[46]

In ecstatic women, inner sight is quite separate from what is visible to the eyes, and therefore what is seen by them seems more lucid than everyday reality.

Hadewych is an example of this, in the description she gives of how she became one with Jesus:

---

[45] Harder to fit into the "seen-before" category might be the angel who appeared to the three children of Fatima several times, spoke to them, and celebrated mass for them in what sounds like a highly unorthodox, not to say impossible, form. See: C. C. Martindale and S. J. Burns' *The Message of Fatima* (Kent: Burns, Oates & Washbourne, 1950), pp. 145 ff. Tr. note.

[46] Hildegard of Bingen; translation mine. Tr.

> He now took me completely in His arms and pressed
> me against Him, and all my limbs felt His . . .[47]

Often the consequences are unavoidable. Thus Christine Ebner (1277-1355) was big with baby Jesus and bore Him without pain. Margareta Ebner joyfully gave her breast to the copper Christ child.

Inner hearing can be the hearing of voices, inner seeing can be the seeing of an apparition, inner touching makes the whole body tremble. These have been called accidental phenomena of the mystical experience. That may be so, but they have a significant place in the story of mysticism. They speak a fairly intelligible language, and are easier to make graphic and accessible. Nevertheless, we are still dealing with a language; a language of signs and symbols. In legends, reality and sign flowed into one another. The value attachable to reality as a sign was even primary. Indeed, for St. Teresa of Avila, the first question was always, are these signs from God or from the Devil? Because the answer is to be found only in their consequences, it was of the utmost importance to her to see the effect of visions, voices, and apparitions. But a change came about in the 18th century. The Swede, Emanuel Swedenborg (1688-1772) found the partition between the physical and the spiritual world so transparent that seeing spirits was hardly different from seeing humans. He made contact with spirits as easily as he did with the living, and he used this ability to obtain a great deal of information from the spirit world. The results were published in a bulky treatise, *The Arcana Coelestia*. They were eight volumes full of nonsense, according to Immanuel Kant, who wrote a small book to try and prove the point. Kant argued that contact is possible only with beings similar to us, who are bound by the laws of matter. Things that do not belong to our material world cannot be known. Any further statements concerning them are pure inventions, he said.

Kant was a very influential philosopher. His views helped turn the tide of opinion against mysticism, but, strange to say, did nothing to stop a growing interest in its accidental phenomena. People wanted to find out if this other world was knowable. And so the phenomena were seen in a fresh light: no longer as signs of a deeper unity with the Ground of all things, but as traces of real-

---

[47] Hadewych; translation mine. Tr.

ities that should be recognizable in other ways. Is the law of gravitation so absolute that we cannot float in the air? Is the body such a straitjacket that the spirit cannot leave it or be in two places at once? Are there no beings in the other world capable of appearing to humans? Have human beings no spiritual powers by which they can look into the past and future? Are trance, ecstasy, and hypnosis not ways of contacting other entities? Even today these questions are still topical. They have been given the general name "mysticism" (and also "occult science"), but it is clear that any connection they may once have had with genuine mysticism has been severed.

The line between fantasy and reality in the visionary language of mysticism was not drawn until the 18th century. Even then it was not drawn accurately, but it has helped us make a clearer distinction between the reality experienced by mystics and what is being studied in the occult sciences; also it has helped us understand visionary language in a new way: fantasy and reality go hand in hand. What is seen in visions is a creation of fantasy. The reality is to be sought in the experience itself.

Spirit and Body

Mystical experience is all-embracing, in the sense that the whole person is involved in it, body and spirit. This applies to the sphere in which the experience is initiated or encouraged; it also applies to the impact this experience has on the entire individual.

An ancient means of entering a mystical state is the dance. The dance can be used with a view to persuading God to give rain, for example; but more often, especially in the older religions, it represents joining the eternal whirl of creative cosmic forces around a center of rest. So the dervishes danced in Mevlevi in the 13th century. In the same century, Mechtilde of Magdeburg wrote:

> I cannot dance, Lord, unless you lead me. If you want me to skip, then you yourself must sing. Then I will dance into love, out of love into knowledge, out of knowledge into enjoyment, out of enjoyment beyond all human senses. . .[48]

---

[48] Mechtild von Magdeburg, "God Asks the Soul What She is Bringing," in *Ecstatic Confessions*, collected and introduced by Martin Buber (San Francisco: HarperCollins, 1985), p. 55.

Figure 13. In his ashram at Poona, Bhagwan Shree Rajneesh experimented on his followers with many psychotherapeutic techniques. His object was liberation of the ego and a consequent ingress to a mystical consciousness. Most of his devotees were Western intellectuals who had been sated with prosperity. (Photo: ABC-Press Service, Amsterdam.)

Figure 14. A hippy who "dropped out" in order to find a "meaning in life" that was no longer present in society. His clothing was rudimentary and the great outdoors was his home. This flight from the world repeatedly occurs in history, for example in the 11th century. (Photo: Doug Menuez, ABC-Press Service, Amsterdam.)

In her times, a great deal of dancing went on in nunneries. Ruysbroeck even makes mention of it. More than once we read of the ecstatic dance that has been revived by the Jesus People and the Hare Krishna sect—with shouts of joy, uncontrollable laughter and hand-clapping.

Ecstasy can express itself physically in a disorganized and involuntary fashion. The Islamic term for this is "hal."[49] The body suffers various contortions, the person shouts and screams, dances wildly and foams at the mouth, and is not susceptible to injury.

Beatrice stumbled, fell on the ground, was taken to the infirmary and, "all that day, drunken with an unimaginable sweetness of spirit, exulted and rejoiced, and rested in the Lord in peace and calm of mind."[50]

Such states were valued at that time as signs of a passionate love of God, which was thought to be like the love between human beings. Perspiring, blushing, trembling of the legs, exaltation, feverishness, high or low blood pressure, a floating feeling, were common symptoms. "My heart and my veins and all my limbs shook and quivered with desire," Hadewych relates. And St. Teresa of Avila tells us:

> Sometimes my pulse ceases, as it were, to beat at all—so the sisters say, who sometimes approach me, and who now understand the matter better—my bones are racked, and my hands become so rigid that I cannot always join them.[51]

These are obvious psychosomatic symptoms besides being in keeping with the character of the individual and the spirit of the age. In a period when women often fainted, mystics often fainted, too. Food for thought for psychologists. The case is different when we come to such phenomena as levitation, stigmata, bilocation, the odor of sanctity, and haloes. Since the 18th century these phenomena have had a considerable amount of attention paid to

---

[49] "In the opinion of sufis, hal signifieth a hidden event that from the upper world, sometimes descendeth upon the heart of the holy traveller and goeth and cometh, until the divine attraction draweth him from the lowest to the loftiest stage . . . . Hal (which relateth to the zenith) cometh not in the traveller's sway; in its sway is the traveller." *A Dervish Textbook* (1891); reprinted by Octagon Press, London, 1980. Tr.

[50] Beatrice of Nazareth; translation mine. Tr.

[51] *The Life of St. Teresa of Jesus*, p. 167.

them, because they point to other laws than those ruling the material world: gravity is defied, the boundaries of the body are not absolute, the spirit can be smelled or seen. And, according to the witnesses, we do have to reckon with these things. Rome has shown acceptance of this view by carrying out canonizations: the phenomena can be used as a yardstick of holiness.

In a study of mysticism such phenomena are interesting only to the extent that they are psychosomatic expressions of a mystical attitude and (in particular) can be seen as a creative language, even as visions have given rise to mystically oriented popular devotions. In this respect levitation is important, and stigmata are even more so.

Levitation means that a person rises from the ground and hovers over it. In the days when most people had heavenly aspirations, levitation was a common and understandable symbol. Many paintings have been made of Elijah going up in a chariot of fire, of the Ascension of Jesus, of Mohammed on Al Borak, of Alexander the Great, of saints riding on clouds, and of Icarus—the man who tried to fly but was not pure enough. Witches are supposed to be able to fly, but only through demonic power.

Levitation as an accidental mystical phenomenon enters the West in the time of St. Teresa of Avila. According to her, the phenomenon is solely a feature of ecstasies, and is a bodily experience. During ecstasy, one feels one is going to float in the air. St. Teresa remarks on the strength of this feeling, which she sometimes failed to master:

> . . . my soul was carried away and almost always my head with it—I had no power over it—and now and then the whole body as well, so that it was lifted up from the ground.[52]

In this description it is clear that the phenomenon is psychosomatic—the body follows the soul. The testimonies alleging that St. Teresa hovered above the ground at a measurable height are not very reliable. Where one talks of a few centimeters, another talks of meters. People were only too eager to see something like this: it was a sign of holiness. That is why St. Teresa struggled

---

[52] *The Life of St. Teresa of Jesus*, p. 161.

Figure 15. A mystical experience is radical enough for the mystic to want a changed life. Often there will be a desire to mark the inner transformation externally: for example, by adopting a new way of life, different clothing, or an unusual hair style. In monastic orders, which have commonly arisen from the experiences of a single mystic, such changes became permanent. The novice had to conform to them so as to feel dead and reborn. In recent decades the established monastic orders have relaxed their rule on a change of dress, etc., but the "new religions" have taken it over. (A Western Hare Krishna votary. Photo: C. Barton van Flymen.)

against it so ardently. What we learn from her account is that ecstasy can be seen by the bystanders. The person in ecstasy strains upward, and this makes a big impression.

After St. Teresa come hundreds of eyewitness reports of levitation, the best known being those of Joseph of Copertino, and, in our own century, of Gemma Galgani. In the meantime, people with no pretensions to sainthood have been experimenting with levitation in the name of mysticism. Thus TM, in its Siddhi course, offers to teach mystical levitation. Siddhis are supernormal powers developed by yogis, through which one can make oneself invisible, walk on water, and rise in the air. The fakirs imitated the yogis with their Indian rope trick.

Stigmata are wounds that appear in the body as tokens (stigmata) of the wounds of Jesus. The apostle Paul said that he bore stigmata in his body. The piety of the Middle Ages associated these "signs" with the wounds of Jesus.

In the 13th century, there were those who, when in ecstasy, produced stigmata with their own hands, either consciously or unconsciously. St. Francis of Assisi is the first person in history who actually received the stigmata. They just happened. But, after him, there were numerous cases of self-inflicted stigmata, as in Lukardis of Oberweimar (1276-1309). During her ecstasies, her fingers became so stiff that they pierced her palms. The stigmata of St. Francis were those of the five wounds of Jesus. In others after him there were variations, such as the marks of the crown of thorns and of the scourging. There are more than three hundred documented cases.

It is generally agreed that stigmata are psychogenic, i.e., that they have their origin in the psyche. When Theresia Neumann[53] (1898-1962) caused a sensation by refusing all food and drink and by her repeated stigmatization, experiments were performed in Vienna on a labile subject, Elisabeth Kolbe, who knew little or nothing of Jesus. She was told the story of His sufferings very poignantly, and she, too, developed stigmata. To treat a certain individual's camp-sickness syndrome, he was hypnotized to make him relive his prison camp experiences. All sorts of lesions came back. Thus a vivid impression can make injury marks on the body. What is more, we know that many symptoms can be produced by the psyche—rashes, gastric ulcers, paralyses. Not only the eye, but the whole body, is the mirror of the soul. In this sense, stigmata are really the signs of an intense empathy with the sufferings of others, especially those of Jesus.

What happened to St. Francis had not been heard of before, and it made an enormous impression. It was a powerful symbol of contemporary mystical striving in Europe: there was a desire for a more open communion between God and human beings. Through love, the effect of the wounds was to cause not pain but openness.

---

[53] Re Neumann and Kolbe: Titus Brandsma visited both women and compared their symptoms. See his *Mystiek leven* [Mystical Life], an anthology gathered and introduced by Bruno Borchert, chapter 5: "Mystiek en pseudo-mystiek verschijnselen" [Mystical and Pseudo-mystical Phenomena], published by Nijmegen, 1985.

PART II

THE HISTORY
OF MYSTICISM

ORIGINS

The complete history of mysticism cannot be written; at least, not by me. But I can give an account of several moments in its history that have made an impression on me for I would say they belong to the roots, or look as if they belong to the roots, of what we see springing up around us today. It is widely assumed that shamanism is the oldest form of mysticism. The term "shamanism" refers to a central figure in a tribe who is able to make contact with the "Most High dwelling in the heavens." The shaman was a specialist. He could do something others could not. His specialty was the technique of ecstasy.

Shamanism belongs to a prehistoric environment going back to an era when the continents were still joined. The same conditions can still be found among the indigenous people of Siberia, Indonesia, and Australia, and in the land of the Eskimos and the North American Indians. These people enable us to gain some idea of how our ancestors lived in the primeval ages. In addition to archeological finds, prehistory was bequeathed to us the ancient myths found in all cultures, not to mention the archetypes slumbering in the deepest layers of our psyches, or as Jung would say, in the collective unconscious. It was Mircea Eliade,[1] in particular, who uncovered the connection between archeological discoveries, primitive races, myths, and archetypes. The value of his work is that it not only improves our knowledge of primitive times, but also enables us to enter into them emotionally, and to learn about our own deepest drives.

According to Eliade, mysticism as an experience of unity with the Most High belongs to the deepest layer of human consciousness, both historically and psychologically.

ARCHAIC CONSCIOUSNESS

Many of the manifestations of prehistoric religion seem to be magical conjurations of natural forces in order to prevent them from

---

[1] See Mircea Eliade's *Shamanism* (London, 1964) and "Le chamanisme; experiences mystiques chez les primitifs," [Shamanism: Mystical Experiences in Primitive Peoples], in *Encyclopedia des mystiques* [*Encyclopedia of Mystics*], Vol. 1 (Paris, 1977), pp. 1-92.

Figure 16. Prehistoric cave drawing in Les Trois Frères in Arriege, France.

wreaking destruction or to persuade them to promote fertility. But this is not the whole story. People had an idea that the "Most High dwelling in the heavens" was reachable in some way. They were impressed by an experience of the firmament as an endless height, inaccessible to wingless humans. Height was intuitively associated with all that is holy. The rites and myths pertaining to heavenly ascent and descent are very old. So is the thought that it is possible to rise up to the Most High on spiritual wings. One way this might be done was by making a sacrifice at the mid-point—a tree, or pole—around which one lived and from which one ascended with the smoke of the offering. This midpoint imagery is very ancient and is associated with the experience of creativity; that is to say that life can be made pleasant only by introducing order and turning chaos into cosmos.

The induction of trance played a part within this complex of experiences. From the many cave drawings left to us by the late-paleolithic hunting communities (15,000-10,000 B.C.), it has been inferred that it did so even then. What we now know of ecstasy techniques and of shamanism allows us to form the following picture of what went on. The tribe retired from time to time into a pitch-black cave outside their usual territory. By the sole light of a flickering fire and enclosed by walls painted to represent the animal world with which, as hunters, they felt united, they danced to monotonous sounds and had an ecstatic experience of a dimension of life that was different from their hard daily struggle for survival.

If this interpretation is correct, it seems likely that the induction of ecstasies developed from a more or less spontaneous tribal

Figure 17. Life with the animals and the tribe is also experienced as an ascent of the shaman into heavenly space. Just like the birds so often depicted on the shaman's clothing. (Copy of an Eskimo engraving in stone, The Canadian Eskimo Arts Council.)

happening to a fixed social structure in which a single individual controlled and practiced the technique in the service of the group.

In this connection, Mircea Eliade refers to an ancient paradise myth that plays an essential role in shamanism. This takes us back to a legendary time when humanity had direct contact with the celestial gods:

> When they climbed something high, a mountain, a tree, a liana, and so on, they were able to reach the skies without effort. What is more, the gods regularly descended to the earth in order to mingle with humans. And humans knew that they were the friends and masters of the animals. According to the myth, this paradisical unity was destroyed by a ritual fault. The tree was felled. God retreated into the highest regions of the heavens. But, through a technique of which he alone had the secret, the shaman knew how to restore communications with heaven. His ecstasy is a restoration of a paradisical association with God.[2]

Shamanism in its purest form was being practiced not so long ago in Central Asia and Siberia, although allowance must be made for the influence of Lamaism, Buddhism, and Iranian religions. Even if the above description of the origin of shamanism rests on mere conjecture, the phenomenon itself can be described with a great deal of certainty.

---

[2] Mircea Eliade, "Le chamanisme; experiences mystiques chez les primitifs" [Shamanism: Mystical Experiences in Primitive Peoples], *Encyclopedia des Mystiques* [*Encyclopedia of Mystics*], Vol. 1, Paris, 1977. Translation mine. Tr.

The shaman performs a central function in the tribe; this is usually hereditary, but sometimes he receives an inner call. Before he starts to exercise this function, he must undergo an initiation in which he acquires a new personality. The initiation has the character sometimes of psychic disintegration, sometimes of an attack by demons who torment and kill him, sometimes of a descent into hell. If he survives, he is taught the names of the gods and demons. From this he learns to recognize various diseases and cures, and is able to fight the demons and bring back the spirit of the sick person, whether it is still near the settlement or further away. He accompanies the dead to the underworld and can report on them to the living. His most important task is the journey through the heavens to the Most High—the heavenly voyage, or ecstasy. His ecstasy technique is usually the following. Dressed in and surrounded by all sorts of symbols of birds, spirits, and trees, he beats a drum, invokes spirits, and speaks a secret language, the "language of the birds." He climbs into a tree. His spirit leaves his body and travels through the skies. When he comes back, he tells the members of his tribe what he has seen, in a special poetic mode of speech.

The shaman is not only a medicine man, accompanier of the dead, and prophet of the Most High; he is also the poet and sage who preserves and explains the narratives of the past and composes new ones concerning the present. Sometimes he is a sorcerer who gives demonstrations of a world in which anything is possible.

Eliade makes the point that prehistoric shamanism already contained many elements that play an important part in later mysticism—ecstasy and ecstasy techniques, mysticism as a return to paradise, the descent to hell or the mystical death or night which has to be passed through. It is striking, too, that the mysticism of those days had such strong social ties: preserving traditions, creating a corpus of poetry, keeping the tribe together, and treating the ailments of its members. For his own community, the shaman was an important figure; he warded off death by making the realm of the dead visible, and he defended the world of light, health, fertility, and harmony with nature and the gods by fighting the demons.

As I have already said, shamanism still exists among so-called primitive people. In the further development of mysticism, the shaman disappears and makes way for mystics of other types within the context of a more cosmic and more worldly consciousness.

Figure 18. Man in meditative pose at one with the animals. It is not certain how this Celtic representation should be interpreted. Joseph Campbell (*The Masks of God*, IV, 422-423) points out the similarities to the mythic imagery of the steppe dwellers in the Far East. (Detail of a silver cauldron, Celtic, ca. 100 B.C., found in Gundestrup, Denmark. The National Museum, Copenhagen.)

COSMIC CONSCIOUSNESS

Around 9000 B.C. primitive peoples discovered agriculture. The cultivation of grasses and other plants tied them to one spot: towns and villages came into being. Jericho is the oldest of these as far as we know. It was founded ca. 8000 B.C. Farming communities and municipal centers developed in the fertile valleys of

Figure 19. The shaman as central figure in the tribe. Seen by Nicolas Witsen and engraved for his book *Noord en Oost Tartarije* (North and East Tartary), 1705.

the great rivers—the Nile, the Euphrates, the Tigris, the Indus, and the Ganges. Tools for tilling the land and for communication were invented and the plow, the sail, the wheel, and writing came into being.

With these developments, religious experience became more concrete, more directly linked with the earth, with human fertility, and with the organization of town and country. The sacred was seen and felt in the earth and in life on Earth. The macrocosm was represented by the microcosm of the human body. Human seed and the seeds of plants, a wife and the earth, the rhythm of birth, death, and resurrection were all interconnected. Their interconnection went back to the Creator of this system of things. Yet the role played by the Most High was not emphasized. People did not seek contact with Him except as a last resort when they were in extreme need. He was seen as a *deus otiosus* (an unoccupied God), a God at rest, who created the cosmos one time and thereafter remained the guarantor for an order in the world from which further victories over chaos could be won by human beings and inferior gods and goddesses who were more immediately involved in life. The old rituals and symbols—midpoint, mountain, tree, ladder, fire, water—were still revered, but acquired a new meaning: they made earthly life transparent and no longer served as a way of ascent to the Most High God.

In the period when cosmic consciousness was growing, the belief in the Most High God remained alive among the nomads, who had turned from being hunters to being herdsmen: the Indo-

Figure 20. The path traversed by the shaman. Phase two begins with the climbing of the tree via seven branches. After that the spirit travels through heavenly space to the Most High. (Sketch made by a shaman of the Altai region, Siberia.)

European in the steppes of Central Asia and the Semite in the deserts of Arabia and North Africa. They kept cattle and forged close tribal bonds. They worked with the asses and camels of the deserts and the horses of the steppes. The Indo-European races also discovered that the combination of horse and chariot was a powerful weapon of war.

There came from these nomadic peoples a fresh impetus leading to a further development of mysticism. This happened between 1550 and 1220 B.C., when they were involved with the great cultures of the Nile and the Indus, either as rulers or as ruled and oppressed.

THE PRIEST-SHAMAN

The Iranian tribes of the Indo-European nomads have had a decisive influence on the development of mysticism. They populated southern Central Asia, especially the area east of the Caspian Sea, that is to say Turkmenistan and Afghanistan. They had become herdsmen and regarded the cow as a sacred animal, and their cattle forced them to itinerate slowly. There were two classes only: the herders (who were also the warriors when the tribe and their stock had to be defended) and the priests. The priest still had something of the shaman about him: he inherited the priesthood from his father, he was a central figure who legislated for the tribe, he was an expert in contacting the sacred cosmos, and he was a wise man and a bard.

The priest was not initiated by a psychic disintegration, but by prolonged training in a sort of priestly school. There he learned wisdom, that is to say, he explored the secrets of nature. The ecstasy technique that was part of this wisdom was twofold. The kavi priests (kavyas = maker of prophecies) prophesied in a trance after drinking soma (haoma). The ritual karapan priest meditated on a mantra. Mantras are ideas that are revelations perceived in the heart. They become revelatory when learned and meditated on ritually. Hence the name "instruments of thought." The priests of both sorts were poets, makers of hymns and wisdom poems. These poems were later set down in writing and made up into collections. The Rig Veda, a basic text of Hindu mysticism, and the Gathas of Zoroaster, are examples. Soma, mantras, and poems functioned within public worship. Essentially, the worship was very austere. There were no temples, altars, and images, there

Figure 21. The influential magazine *Time* based a cover story on the bestsellers of Carlos Castaneda. Castaneda describes conversations with the Indian Don Juan on a new sort of mystical seeing that can be induced by shamanistic practices with nature, especially with herbs. From *Time*, March 5, 1975.

Figure 22. Joseph Beuys (d. 1986) was a modern shaman with a very up-dated appearance. Looking citified in hat and waistcoat, he exercised his art with animals in the middle of what might be called a tribe of admirers. (Photo: ABC-Press Service, Amsterdam.)

Figure 23. The symbols of
the I Ching and yin-yang
on the liturgical robe of a
Taoist priest. (Chinese,
18th or 19th century,
Metropolitan Museum of
Art, New York.)

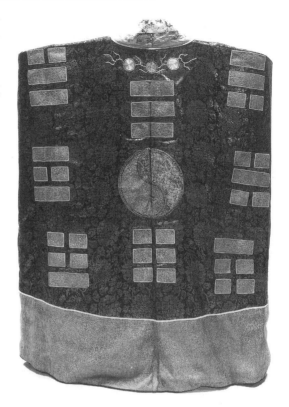

was only fire. Offerings were burned in the fire, and praises and petitions ascended with the sacrificial smoke to the gods who kept the cosmos turning. The object of worship was control of this cosmos. Where tribes were helplessly dependent on the forces of nature, the placation of these forces was a matter of life or death. Peace offerings and performance of the prescribed rituals could achieve this. And the one who had mastered the rituals was a powerful person in the tribe. The functioning of the priest within the tribe was determined not by his mysticism but by his magical powers.

THE ARYANS

Between 1700 and 1500 B.C. at a rough estimate, a revolutionary event must have happened to the Iranian inhabitants of the steppes. Some of their clans invented a wheeled vehicle that could be drawn by their own horses as a rapid means of transport. With a horse and chariot, they were no longer fettered to the tribe and loitering flocks and herds: they could drive off and seek their fortune. A new caste arose, that of the warriors. These had ceased to be herdsmen who defended their livestock and had become heroes who won fame and fortune. The laws were no longer made by the priests, but by the warriors. Their will was supreme. They worshipped new gods of their own, the gods of war. The chief of these was Indra, whom they called "the town-breaker," the mighty warrior who conquered evil. The priests found a new position for themselves next to the warriors; they had exclusive control of the rites and they made these important to the warriors. The worship round the fire was devoted to petitions for riches, success, long life, power, women for the leaders, and descendants. The formula was: praise the gods, let the smoke of the peace offerings ascend on high, and then ask for the benefits conferred by the cosmic powers active in man and nature.

After 1500 B.C. these militant tribes entered the Indus valley and displaced the indigenous culture. They called themselves Aryans (nobles), were pale-skinned and despised all people who were not of their race. In 500 years they had overwhelmed the Ganges valley culture and, in a further 500 years, they reached the southernmost tip of India. They were the creators of the caste system based on racial prejudice and skin color. The higher a person's caste the purer they were deemed to be (*casta* from casto = pure). Eventually the caste system became hereditary, the pariahs being born unclean. Only reincarnation might change this state of affairs.

During this long period, the sacred texts of these peoples grew into two large collections: the Vedas (*veda* = wisdom) and the Upanishads (*upa-ni-shad* = sitting down with the Master). Hindu mysticism rests on these writings.

The non-Aryan Iranian tribes developed less tempestuously. They were held longer by the old tribal ties and were initially taken by surprise and repressed. And then, after 1200 B.C., they trekked slowly southwards. The priest Zoroaster arose among them with a new message. In the sixth century B.C., this message became the state religion of the great kingdom in the region of the Euphrates and Tigris. It is one of the most significant roots of Western mysticism.

The deep divide between Eastern and Western mysticism arose long ago in a far land owing to a new weapon—the horse and chariot.

MYSTICISM IN THE EAST

The Vedas and Upanishads contain a large number of hymns and wisdom texts in Sanskrit, the product of ten centuries of study. It is not possible to distill a consistent vision out of them. Polytheism and monotheism, a personal and an impersonal god, an essentially magico-ritual attitude and a mystical one, are all to be found in them. Yet these writings have led to a pronounced mysticism and can be read as a whole from that point of view. They also reveal how this mysticism grew.

The Vedas comprise four collections. The oldest and most important is the Rig Veda, a thousand hymns used in worship. These display a belief in tens of different gods. They breathe the Aryan hero mentality and are patriarchal, warlike, and hypermasculine; they major on wealth, prosperity, health, an abundance of food and drink, winning power over others as well as over the gods who maintain the cosmic order in which humans feel safe. In the Vedas there is a marked tendency to increase the emphasis laid on ritual sacrifice. Mention is made of a cosmic sacrifice as the origin of the cosmic order. Purusha, the world soul, divided itself, and out of the pieces of its body the universe was made. The rites are magical repetitions of this cosmic sacrifice, and they serve the purpose of creating the world order anew.

The corpus of the Vedic writings was closed around 1000 B.C. with the Brahmanas, a series of texts composed by priests who had been appointed as scholars and teachers. From the Brahmanas it appears that the rituals had become an end in themselves. Placating the gods was no longer an issue. Their control of the cosmic forces had been taken over by the priests. It was not some god who continually recreated the cosmos, but a priest who did so (through ritual) in a mythical way. The mantras are magical formulas encapsulating the cosmos in the same fashion as the seed is in the tree and the tree is in the seed. Understanding a mantra imparts insight into the universe. The old Vedic gods wilted under this development. They were no longer important. There was no longer any necessity to appease them in order to live prosperously.

A parallel development has also been significant. The priests asked questions about the highest god, Indra, in whom the Aryans projected their belief in male superiority. At this time there was neither being nor not-being, there were no worlds and no heavens, neither was there anything beyond. What covered the All? And

Figure 24. Male and female Brahmins meditate and discuss reality. Brahman is symbolized by a golden egg. (Gouache, Rajastan, seventh century, New Delhi, Collection of Aijt Mokerjee. Photo: Jeff Teasdale, Thames & Hudson).

where? And for whose pleasure? Who can know out of what this All has come, from where creation arose, and whether one being gave it birth or not? Only He who surveys everything from on high, only He knows. Perhaps not even He!

Out of these questions grew the concept of an unnameable God. In the beginning there was neither nothing nor something. Again there was neither sky nor atmosphere above. Again there was neither day nor night, neither light nor darkness. . . . The Only-Existing breathed peacefully in isolation, enclosed in Himself.

Upanishad is a collective noun for sets of various speculations dating from between 1000 and 500 B.C. The distinction between the universe and its unnameable maker, already present in embryo in the Vedas, is now a plainly stated basis of every speculation. The creative principle is called *Brahman* (holy power) and is unaffected by any change in space and time. It is said to be an unborn, immortal, impersonal Something, which is the heart of whatever is born in time and space and dies, that assumes a form and eventually leaves it. The universe with all its destructive and vivifying powers has been largely dispossessed of its divinities. The priest with his rites—a sacred center in the Vedic age—makes way for the ego, the deepest center in each human being, the *atman*.

Brahman, atman and "I" are in essence the same—the unmoving midpoint of everything that moves. An excerpt from the Chandogya Upanishad may serve to illustrate this:

Instruction concerning Brahma:

That [plenum], indeed, is below. It is above. It is to the west. It is to the east. It is to the south. It is to the north. It, indeed, is this whole world.

Now next, instruction with regard to the Ego (*ahamkaradesa*). I, indeed, am below. I am above. I am to the west. I am to the east. I am to the south. I am to the north. I, indeed, am this whole world.

Now next, the instruction with regard to the soul (*atmadesa*). The Soul (Atman), indeed, is below. The Soul is above. The Soul is to the west. The Soul is to the east. The Soul is to the south. The Soul is to the north. The Soul, indeed, is this whole world.[3]

This doctrine was blended with a non-Aryan idea borrowed from the indigenous population—the transmigration of the soul. According to this, when the body dies, the soul rises to celestial regions, but eventually returns to Earth. It is born in a better or worse state of existence depending on what it has done. Those who behave well here may expect a happier birth—the birth of a priest, the birth of a warrior, or the birth of a merchant. But those who behave badly may expect an evil birth—the birth of a pig or the birth of a pariah.

The doctrine of reincarnation was used by the Aryans to give an air of sanctity to their caste system: the pariah was a non-person. His only hope of becoming human was a higher rebirth after his death. However, for their own elite, the doctrine of reincarnation was combined with the Brahma-atman teaching and interpreted as offering liberation. It was possible to escape from this cycle of birth and rebirth and from the vicissitudes of earthly existence and to enter the still center of the All, the individual ego, the most real reality. We do not perceive that the one reality exists in our own body, but it is really there. Everything has its existence in that almost imperceptible essence. That is reality. That is spirit. And we all are the spirit.

Thus the way of liberation is a mystical way to what is within. It urges: Be yourself, one with the atman, which is one with Brahman. It is a form of mysticism that is full of itself:

---

[3] "The Chandogya Upanishads," in *The Thirteen Principal Upanishads*, translated from the Sanskrit by Robert Ernest Hume (London: Oxford University Press, 1921), p. 261.

In the beginning this world was Soul (*Atman*) alone in the form of a person. Looking around, he saw nothing else than himself. He said first: 'I am.' Thence arose the name 'I.' Therefore even today, when one is addressed, he says first just 'It is I' and then speaks whatever name he has. Since before (*purva*) all this world he burned up all evils, therefore he is a person (*pur-us-a*). He who knows this, verily, burns up him who desires to be ahead of him.[4]

Or also:

Verily this whole world is Brahma. Tranquil, let one worship It as that from which he came forth, as that into which he will be dissolved, as that in which he breaths. . . . This Soul of mine within the heart is smaller than a grain of rice, or a barley-corn, or a mustard-seed, or a grain of millet, or the kernel of a grain of millet; This Soul of mine within the heart is greater than the earth, greater than the atmosphere, greater than the sky, greater than these worlds. . . . Containing all works, containing all desires, containing all odors, containing all tastes, encompassing this whole world, the unspeaking, the unconcerned—this Soul of mine within the heart, this is Brahma. Into him I shall enter on departing hence.[5]

The personal ego and the divine ego are not the same; yet they are so one with each other as to be indistinguishable: like salt dissolved in water.

THE METHODICAL WAY—YOGA

In this, the main point is not doctrine, but an attitude to life, the object of life being union with Brahma. The achievement of this object is no longer through the ecstasy technique of the shaman or

---

[4] "The Brihad-Aranyaka Upanishad," in *The Thirteen Principal Upanishads*, translated from Sanskrit by Robert Ernest Hume (London: Oxford University Press, 1921), p. 81.

[5] The Brihad-Aranyaka Upanishad, in *The Thirteen Principal Upanishads*, pp. 209-210.

Figure 25. Fragment of a scroll in which different yoga asanas are depicted. (Gouache on paper, Rajastan, 18th century. New Delhi, Collection of Aijt Mokerjee. Photo: Jeff Teasdale, Thames & Hudson).

of the later soma drinker, but through a prolonged practice known as yoga, which is very skilled and involves methodical effort. It calls for control of the breath and of bodily movements in order to bring order into the chaos of everyday life. One can learn to experience timelessness in this cosmos, and can become aware of how nearly the deepest center in the I is one with the deepest center of the universe. This is a sober "ec-stasy" (or stepping out) from the time-bound into the timeless. The goal is absorption in Brahma in the same way all colors coincide in white light.

Yoga contains *asanas* (positions) and techniques intended to regulate respiration and physical movement. It also involves meditation and complete relaxation. The aim of yoga is to stop the incoming impressions on the mind and heart, to isolate oneself in the stream of time, and also to erase past time from the unconscious. By this means the consciousness of guilt is obliterated. Other religions seek for the removal of guilt by rituals such as the scapegoat and the confessional.

In addition to this royal way (*raja yoga*) there are many other varieties of yoga—the way of good deeds (*karma yoga*), of love (*bhakti yoga*), of sex (*tantra yoga*), of knowledge (*gnana yoga*). Any of these forms of yoga can be perverted if its goal is ignored. Yogis are more often exhibitionists than mystics. They gain such control over their bodies that they can even consciously regulate their heartbeats or digestion, and can pull off stunts such as the Indian rope trick, walking on water, and flying. They are ascetics with extreme powers of concentration, people who contemplate their navels. The opposite way, the yoga of venerating the gods, the dancing deity who maintains the rhythm of the universe (Siva) and the female creative energy (Sakti), can descend to mere religious observance or to pleasure.

This is how the essentials of yoga are summed up by Mircea Eliade:

> All forms of Yoga include a preliminary transformation of the profane man—weak, distracted, enslaved by his body and incapable of real mental effort—into a glorious Man with perfect physical health, absolute mastery of his body and of his psycho-mental life, capable of self-concentration, conscious of himself. It is Man thus made perfect that Yoga seeks finally to surpass, not only the profane everyday man.[6]

DELIVERANCE FROM SUFFERING—BUDDHISM AND JAINISM

Aryan mysticism is a piece of elitism meant for the liberated, the Brahmins and the yogis. It is self-assured, optimistic mysticism in which little notice is taken of evil. This mysticism has no language for sympathy or love. The way of union is a stream of consciousness not a stream of love. Against this mysticism, two

---

[6] Mircea Eliade, *Images & Symbols: Studies in Religious Symbolism* (New York: Sheed & Ward, 1961), p. 85.

great mystics opposed themselves in the sixth century B.C.: Siddhartha Gautama, the Buddha, and Mahavira, the founder of Jainism. They played down self-assurance and drew attention first of all to the miseries of life and the need for compassion.

Buddhism starts out from a very pessimistic view of life. Life it says, is full of suffering and nothing is permanent. Even the prosperity that brings happiness is precarious. We keep wanting more—more possessions, more fame, more recognition, more experiences, and a flow of new ideas. Never satisfied, we live in fear of losing what we have or of not being able to get what we want.

How can such beings find rest and stable contentment? Human nature is good, says Buddhism; the cause does not lie there. The cause lies in the web of needs and longings, in a hankering not only after material prosperity but also after loving and being loved, after a solid family life, after a happy life beyond death, after the love of God. An associated cause is the illusion that we are individuals. As if the "I" that we experience as the center of our willing, thinking, and feeling is also a reality, a personality, a soul. But this is an illusion. We are a bundle of feelings, ideas and bodily functions, which develop and eventually dissolve, but in the meantime are always changing. What continually returns in the wheel of rebirth is not an "I" but a flicker as transient as the flame by which one candle is lit from another. According to Buddhism, the thought that the "I" is a permanent entity to be developed in accordance with our needs is a dangerous illusion.

Thus the twofold way of deliverance entails a renunciation of desire and the insight that this "I" that seems so fundamental is merely an illusion. Serenity is achieved by dismissing whatever is painful and mutable in life. Life no longer drifts on a stream of birth and rebirth. Death has been overcome, and *Nirvana* has been realized.

According to Buddha, nirvana cannot be explained, but has to be experienced. He described it in negative terms, such as being not-born, not-made, not-conditioned, or by way of such comparisons as coolness after fever and escape to a refuge, or such paradoxes as a state of contented non-existence. Ego-consciousness with its self-indulgence and greed is no more; a higher form of consciousness, enlightenment, has taken its place.

Gautama Buddha's roots were in Aryan mysticism. He preserved the concept of the mystical moment, which to him meant escaping from the ever-shifting stream of things by becoming one with an unborn, perfectly still center. But he undermined the typical self-assurance of Aryan mysticism. Nirvana is antithetical to atman, it is a not-self. He also rejected the sacred texts and rituals, the priests and divinities of the Vedic religion. He attained to his nirvana without supernatural help and did not explain it in terms of the divine. What is more, he rejected the ascetic way of the yogi. Compassion on the miserable state of humanity is the beginning of his way. He broke with elitism by publishing his insights openly to everyone. His was a level path, not something to learn grade by grade. For the ordinary person, this means that a moral life of good deeds can make of death an entry to nirvana. For those who wish to follow the path to the end and to experience nirvana here and now, it means the monastery.

Jainism is a similar reaction against Aryan mysticism in the very period and area of the world that saw the rise of Buddhism. It, too, lays stress on evil and on having compassion on the miseries of humanity. It also rejected the Vedic religion and the Creator God. Self-assurance was undermined, not as Buddhism undermined it by treating the self as an illusion, but by challenging its uniqueness. Each being, not only man or woman, but plant, stone, water, and even the gods, have souls of the same sort, a little piece of eternity imprisoned in matter. So here the way of deliverance is to deliver oneself from the prison of the body by strict asceticism and by not harming living things. For the ascetics, this sometimes involves starvation and not moving in order to avoid the possibility of killing a single insect. For the ordinary person it means not being a butcher, smith, or farmer, but engaging in trade.

Jainism is still basically an Indian religion. Gandhi was influenced by it. Buddhism, on the other hand, has spread out from India and has become a world faith, having traveled through East Asia via China into Japan. It has two main creeds, the rigid and the popular, and many variants. The best known is Zen in Japan.

LOVING UNION WITH A
HUMAN GOD—THE BHAGAVAD GITA

The writings that come down to us from sixth-century Hindu tradition take the form of an epic poem: the story of the fight between the sons of two kings. The Vedic gods and goddesses again have a role to play. Vishnu is a major god who manifests himself in many forms, especially in that of a person called Krishna. The most famous epic is the Bhagavad Gita (ca. 200 B. C.). On the battlefield Krishna explains his doctrine to the warrior Arjuna: the multiplicity of things and events around us are simply expressions of one and the same ultimate reality, which rises above all ideas and images and is more than its manifestations. The mystical way is manifold, each to his own. One very important method is bhakti yoga, a personal devotion to a personal god-manifestation, Krishna. Emotional surrender to the fervent worship of Krishna can lead to a mystical experience. This is a response to passages like the following in which Krishna says:

> Your mind fixed on me, be devoted to me; Sacrificing to me, pay reverence to me; Having thus a disciplined self and having me as final end, You will come to me.[7]

It is a relationship of love, and always personal.

> He who sees me everywhere, and sees all in me, I am not lost to him, and he is not lost to me.[8]

Here is the basis of the marriage mysticism we find in the ninth century, where the individual has a female attitude to God in the passionate search for union with Him. In the 12th century, the poetess Mahadeviyakka describes her mystical love for Siva in a way that reminds us of Catherine of Siena's devotion to Jesus in the 14th century.

The Bhagavad Gita makes an impact on ordinary people living in a confusing world, a world full of love, grief, emotion, emptiness, joy, and disappointment. The worshipper of Krishna need not withdraw from this uncertainty, but can approach God via a person, in the realization that all things temporal and changeable are manifestations of Brahman.

---

[7] *The Bhagavad Gita* by Antonio de Nicolás (York Beach, ME: Nicolas-Hays, 1990), p. 75 (9:34).
[8] *The Bhagavad Gita* by Antonio de Nicolás, p. 60 (6:30).

Tantra: Sexuality and Mysticism?

The principle of Tantra (which pervades the whole of Indian culture, including medicine and astrology) is that the human body is like the cosmos. Both have the same structure. One is inconceivable without the other. The human spirit is essentially the same as the cosmic spirit. Tantra is not a philosophy but a way, and it seeks to give practical answers to our questions. What must we do to integrate the human being and the cosmos? How must we live in order that human and cosmic sexuality may coincide? There is an interaction, a picture of the cosmos that evolves out the experience of human sexuality, and conversely the manner in which cosmic sexuality is represented is a schooling in human sex.

Figure 26. Creation as a sexual event. Lying on a lotus inside a circle that resembles the world egg, the woman is taking the seed of the man. Streams of blood being drunk by other women are symbolic of the threefold distribution of life-energy in the universe via birth, life, and death. The woman depicts the glory of transient forms. (Gouache, circa 1800, Kangra.)

Figure 27. The heavenly origin of a playful universe. Wood carving on a temple cart. (South India, 18th century. Photo: Jeff Teasdale, Thames & Hudson.)

Figure 28. Cosmic creation based on coitus is also frequently depicted on the outer walls of temples. Many different forms of sexual intercourse are graphically displayed. (Photo: Jeff Teasdale, Thames & Hudson.)

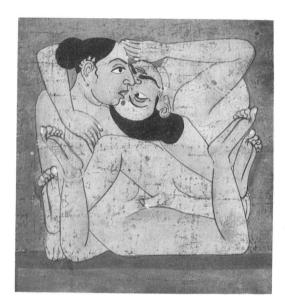

Figure 29. Icon of sexual union as a religious experience. Sex is not seen as passionate sensation but as a feeling aroused through a sexual gaze. Love is a carefully cultivated art, a sustained ecstasy of body and soul. The aim is not orgasm but ecstasy. Stimulation of the sexual organs is directed toward feeling the energy serving their mutual needs. Eroticism is transferred from the outer woman to the inner goddess, of whom all women are paradigms. The man and woman are the keys to each other's welfare, for each is a god in the other. Each loves the other within themselves. (Gouache, 18th century, Nepal. Photo: Jeff Teasdale, Thames & Hudson.)

Figure 30. A more abstract icon of cosmic sexuality. It depicts what stands in the middle of the temple: a *lingam* (phallus) enclosed by the *yoni* (vulva), a stone image honored with such things as flowers. The male partner in the divinity is embedded in the female and can be reached only at their consummation. (Gouache, 18th century, Kangra. Photo: Jeff Teasdale, Thames & Hudson.)

Figure 31. Surrounding the guru in a circle are the five pleasures of life which can lead to enlightenment if experienced in the correct Tantric way. Sex is one of the pleasures. (Painted tapestry, 19th century, Rajastan. Photo: Jeff Teasdale, Thames & Hudson.)

Figure 32. Religious experience as an intense, self-negating sexual activity using exercises and techniques. Instinctive, passionate sexual activity would be quite out of place here. Instead there are traditional rituals, the passing of seed by an enlightened master, genital contact with energy-charged symbols, and also activities shared with a woman who has undergone a secret initiation. (Gouache, 18th century. Rajastan. Photo: Jeff Teasdale, Thames & Hudson.)

Figure 33. The illuminated Tantrist united with the universe while in a state of sexual excitement. The arousal of desire has the aim of releasing energy from the lower parts of the man in order that it may ascend to the mental crown. Desire has to be consecrated and bridled to prevent the mind being lost in fantasies. This is achieved through ritual, yoga, meditation. It is not orgasm that is sought, but the damming up of consciousness until it overflows into an enlightenment in which human energy and the energy of the world seem to be swallowed up in the confined time and space. (Wood carving from a 17th century temple cart, South India. Photo: Jeff Teasdale, Thames & Hudson.)

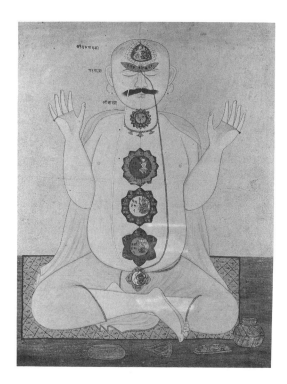

Figure 34. An icon of a yogi releasing and raising his energy. (Gouache, ca. 1820. Kangra. Photo: Jeff Teasdale, Thames & Hudson.)

Figure 35. A yantra employed for a Tantra meditation. The male and female (the triangle as a stylized vulva) are together in the center. This representation divides into more and more triangles, which mesh into one another. The one who follows this movement can become immersed in the creative process expanding outward into the universe. (Painted tapestry, ca. 1700, Nepal. Photo: Jeff Teasdale, Thames & Hudson.)

THE WAY OF SEXUALITY—TANTRA

In the fifth century A.D. an age-old religion penetrated the mysticism of Hinduism, Buddhism, and Jainism. It must have been an indigenous fertility cult, which seems to have many symbols in common with the prehistoric. It was called *Tantra*. This Tantra did not introduce any new mysticism—becoming one with the Brahman, or nirvana, was still part of it—but the method, the yoga, was, so to speak, turned around. In place of saying no to the world, it said a qualified yes. It assented to the dynamics of life, to the creative powers, to fecund sexuality, and did so as a path to mystic union. The ascetic who forsook the world was viewed with suspicion as someone whose sole concern was placid self-fulfillment with not a thought for others.

In dealing with vital forces, it is important to avoid egoism. For this reason the Tantric rituals, images, and formulas have been developed in order to open up the experiences to the creative ground of the cosmos. An isolated experience is worthless. An experience, even an ecstatic one, is fatal if sought for its own sake. The body is perceived as a microcosm; it contains in miniature the creative divinity and the whole universe. The human body and spirit are one with the body and spirit of the cosmos. They are the same organism viewed from different angles. The state of being joined face to face during coitus can signify facing the creative godhead. In Hindu Tantra this is also envisaged as the coupling of divinities and is symbolized by the male and female sex organs.

Tantra is not a religion, but a way in which thinking, reading, and believing are rejected. Tantra is tantra—something done. Body and spirit are transformed in the doing of it; the serpent creeps upward out of the fundament via the head into the cosmos. This Tantra is assisted by mantras, which are continually repeated formulas (often a droning OM), and by visual yantras. The yantra is painted and usually takes the form of a mandala, a circle as a sort of landscape in which one can travel mentally until one reaches the center, a point, the invisible source of existence.

This way of doing, toning, and seeing has to be learned by experience and will lead to mystic union via the enjoyment of sex, wine, meat, ecstasy. The miseries and evils of life could also be experienced in this manner. In Tantra, the dark sides of life are thought to belong to the play of the creative godhead.

DIFFERENCES BETWEEN EAST AND WEST

There are many currents and many mystics in India to describe, and we have mentioned only a few of the more significant. All these currents have been able to coexist, unlike Western religions, which have always taken for granted the purity of their doctrines. Other differences are:

1) Polytheism can accompany striving for unity with the One, and even join forces with atheism. The West knows only one God, who is the exclusive object of worship.

2) Time is a stream of forms known as "maya," or illusion, in which the One manifests. To reach God one stops time; or, at least one lives in time without being confined by it (time being regarded as unreal). In the West, time and events are thought to be moving toward ultimate reality.

3) The East takes the cosmos as its starting point. The individual who seeks union with God must first have some sort of ordered perfection. On the other hand, the West emphasizes sin, and the gulf that has to be bridged between God and humans.

4) Indian spirituality longs to rise above contrasts and tensions, to make reality one, and to recover the primeval Unity. The duality to be conquered here is the discord between visible and invisible reality (*atman, brahman*). The duality can be overcome by the insight that the visible is due to a certain "playing" of the invisible. This insight includes the knowledge that body and spirit are integral parts of the individual, and that the world is an organism of the same kind. All is maya. The West is dualistic on another level, and sees the body as a prison for the spirit or an obstacle on the road to God. Riches and sexuality tend to be frowned upon.

Indian spirituality relies on experience. Everything is taught and learned on the basis of experience. Revelation is not tied to dogma, grace from outside is thought to be unnecessary. Techniques, rituals and exercises are available for achieving enlightenment. Indian spirituality is at first sight more favorable for mysticism than Western spirituality, since it is more directly focused on mystical experience itself. Yet the history of mysticism in the West is also very fascinating.

MYSTICISM IN
IRAN AND ISRAEL

ZOROASTER

Not so long ago Zoroaster was, for Westerners, a legendary figure of the sixth century B.C. whose importance was restricted to the founding of a world faith that has almost died out. However, recent research has shown that he was a contemporary of Moses, not of Buddha. Indeed, he may have flourished before Moses, at some time between 1500 and 2000 B.C. Apparently he was a mystic; in fact the first one whose name is known. He was also a religious genius who has decisively influenced Western mysticism and spirituality. He is the only founder of a world faith who was himself a priest who expressed his experiences in the form of hymns. He is also the first apocalyptic writer.

A compilation of our present knowledge of Zoroaster has been made by Mary Boyce[9] in a very informative history of Zoroastrianism. We rely here on her study to explain the mysticism of the oppressed.

As already discussed, Zoroaster lived at a time when Indo-Iranian warriors in their horse-drawn chariots, and with their hero-mentality, overthrew the old tribalism. Zoroaster speaks of them as "non-shepherds" who glorified the gods of war instead of the eternally righteous Ahura. He refers to their terror and arbitrariness, to the "law of the tyrants"—might instead of right, deceit instead of truth. It seems from the Gathas of Zoroaster that his tribe clung to the old customs and beliefs. Zoroaster himself traveled in a horse-drawn wagon, but his people did not use such vehicles as weapons. The hound was more important than the horse. Their weapons were still made of stone. His tribe had to endure the revolutionary violence and injustice of the invaders.

The sense of despair engendered by these new bloodthirsty heroes was obviously one reason why Zoroaster felt compelled to preach a new message of hope to his people, at the same time laying stress on the strict righteousness enforced by the highest Power—not here and now—but one day at the end of the ages, in

---

[9] Mary Boyce, *A History of Zoroastrianism*, Volume 1: *The Early Period* (Leiden, 1975); and Volume 2: *Under the Achaemenians* (Leiden, 1982).

a kingdom of God on Earth in which every injustice will be remedied; a kingdom to which we can devote ourselves now, and in which we can live one day after rising from the dead. He set a personal choice before everyone: whoever chooses righteousness, truth, and purity in the present will later live with God in his kingdom; but whoever sides with the evil Spirit may expect the awful torments of hell. That his message was not only hopeful, but also made such a sharp distinction between the doers of good and the doers of evil, is perhaps the main reason why he was expelled from his own circle.

Zoroaster was a priest-shaman living in the religious milieu from which the oldest Vedic writings of the Aryans came. In this milieu, shamanism had turned into magic and Zoroaster opposed this. He found the prophecies of the soma-drinking kavi-priests senseless. He himself did not want to be known as a "maker of prophecies." He regarded himself as the communicator of what a personal God had personally revealed to him. Zoroaster set himself against the ritual priests. He called them "mutterers" who repeated formulas mindlessly. He, on the other hand, was one who created mantras out of his own experience and wrote Gathas as a result of personal contact with the All-Highest.

The conflict between Zoroaster and his fellow-priests indicates that he was a mystic who had been taken by surprise by his experiences. In this sense there was still something of the shaman about him; but it was not soma-drinking or ecstasy techniques that had given him a vision of God. A messenger from God stood before him and led him to the All-Highest—a Light in which he viewed the true structure of things. He told others about this Light when his witness was not believed and he was rejected:

> Who comes to help my soul in her loneliness?
> Is there indeed anyone in the universe in whom she can
>   trust?
> There is none but You, O Lord,
> You who are the sole source of all truth,
> From whom there flows a stream of pure thought.

The mysticism of Zoroaster is remarkably fresh and original because personal experience fired his love for the All-Highest and gave him an intense longing for a state of existence beyond our earthly one, "the bridge that still divides us from Thee."

Figure 36. Akhnaten, Egyptian pharaoh, the first of his era to introduce a principle of unity into the divine world. His attempt failed. (Colossus from the temple of Ra-Harakhte. Now in Cairo Museum. Photo: Werner Forman Archive, London.)

Figure 37. Zoroaster was obsessed by purity: pure thought (truth), pure life (environment), pure action (righteousness). His religion dispensed with temples but had places in the open air for the all-purifying fire, and "towers of silence" where corpses were laid to be eaten by vultures, so that even after death the individual should not pollute the earth or the air. (Fire altar of the third century in Naqsh-i-Rustan, Persia [Iran].)

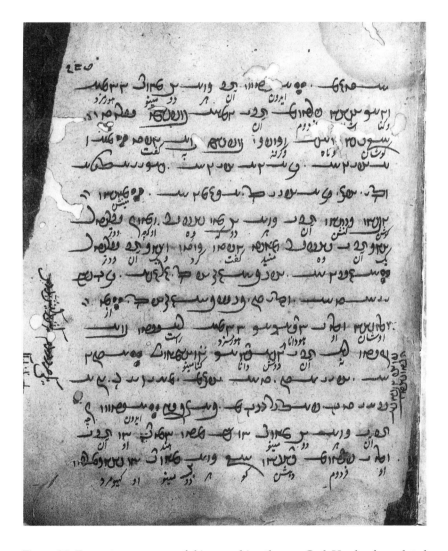

Figure 38. Zoroaster was successful in preaching the one God. He also formulated his message in songs. These Gathas were transmitted orally and are now preserved by the small group of Parsee followers of Zoroaster in India. The oldest extant manuscript was written in 1325. A specimen page is shown here. (The Bodleian Library, Oxford, MS Zend. c.l., f. 190.)

In Zoroaster, mystical illumination led to visions—insights that presented a new view of the whole of reality. He saw an antithesis between the unity of all things and paradisical bliss on the one hand and the wretchedness of everyday life on the other; and he was able to reconcile the two halves of this polarized experience without evaporating either into maya.

Zoroaster's visions take the form of revelations from God to him; but they are elaborated with the help of old Vedic materials. The gods, rituals and theology are not new: it is the context that is different. At a time when the priestly schools were looking for a single creative principle and thought they had found it in a Plant or an Animal (the bull), Zoroaster had the visionary insight that everything, including this Plant and Animal, was created by one Wise Lord (Ahura Mazda, later called Ormazd), himself uncreated, a timeless Light. The gods are servants of this God (they are equivalent to our angels and archangels), or sons and daughters of God (we would call these His divine attributes). They have abstract names: Delight in Immortality, Goodwill, Good Justice, Desirable Lordship, Delight in Devotion, Wholeness, and Health and Life. Zoroaster called them Bountiful Immortals and emphasized their unity within God. In a vision, he saw how they begin creation and remain creatively one in spirit, one in voice, one in deed with the Wise Lord. They who are the creators and form-givers and the makers and guardians and keepers of the creations of Ahura Mazda.

The first product of creation was the spiritual world, including human souls. After this the material world was made, which was better than the spiritual one, because the latter became tangible through it. This world was perfect, stable, and paradisical.

The world we live in now is different. It is no longer stable, but is subject to the process of death and birth, and therefore it is bound to time. According to the theology current in Zoroaster's days, this world of ours, which is bound to time, began with a cosmic sacrifice of the sacred Plant and Animal; but he thought otherwise, and said that Paradise had been disturbed from outside by an attack of the Destroying Spirit (Ahra Manyu, later known as Ahriman). This evil Spirit existed in the timeless beginning near the Wise Lord. In order to challenge him, the Wise Lord made the spiritual creation tangible. The Destroying Spirit penetrated every layer of creation, filling air, earth, and fire, and corrupting human beings with sin, disease, and death. The purpose of this life in the time-bound world is that we may take part with the Wise Lord in the final defeat of the Destroying Spirit. The cosmic offering is meaningful within this purpose: life is sacrificed to bring forth life in the battle with death-dealing Ahriman.

And we also have the apocalyptic messenger. The return to paradise, so typical of many mystics, was not something immediate as far as Zoroaster was concerned: it was not something to be enjoyed at present, but with others at the consummation of history. The mystical way to union with God was that of action. Active cooperation with God down here would be rewarded by a timeless paradisical life in God's very presence. Zoroaster speaks of a divine promise, a hope that creates security and provides a cosmic goal for humanity as a whole and for each human being in particular. In this respect, too, Zoroaster was original. The Vedic religion saw nothing but an unremitting succession of generations like the waves of the sea, without end and without purpose.

When reading the Gathas, one feels Zoroaster's intense longing for the end of time, and his expectation that this was not far away. Equally intense is his struggle against the Destroying Spirit. He sees his might as formidable. Not only does he corrupt human beings, but the good have to suffer from his legions, who falsely and cruelly persecute people of goodwill, trample on their rights, and infect life, land, and air. This evil power can be defeated only if the righteous join the ranks of the Wise Lord's army or the army of one of his servants, especially Mithras the all-seeing sun-god.

Zoroaster is stern, but not ascetic. The world is good. Matter is good. Enjoying it is good. Happiness is a blessing for which it is legitimate to pray. Zoroaster is strict when it comes to personal choices—between truth and untruth, between justice and injustice, between purity and impurity. And he is not talking about truth, justice, and purity in a spiritual sense only: the material world is also involved. Thus corpses may not be buried or burned, the vultures must devour them, otherwise the earth and air would be defiled. Fire is the sole image of worship, and represents the purifying light.

The struggle ends at the Last Judgment, which will be a decisive victory for good and an extermination of evil, and a final settling of accounts. This applies not only to the human race at the end of its history, but to each individual at the end of his or her life. Those who hope to cross the narrow bridge have to be pronounced strictly righteous. No intercession or other influence is

Figure 39. The tomb of Cyrus in Pasargades. The mausoleum is hermetically sealed and forms a seventh step above the Earth. The whole is made of spotless white stone. The lowest step is as tall as a man. (Photo: Roger-Viollet, Paris.)

Figure 40. Zoroaster was the first in history to speak of a Last Judgment of all human beings at the end of time. His imagery is very graphic: there are the scales on which good and evil are to be weighed; the bridge everybody has to cross is "as sharp as a knife." Whoever is impure tumbles off it into the lake of Hell. (Bibliothèque Nationale, Paris, Indian MS 722, f. 24.)

Figure 41. Zoroaster knew only one good God. Evil was a temporary disruption of creation. In a later "heretical" development known as Zurvanism, evil was given more independence as one of the twin zones of Zurvan. This is "Time," the one supreme God; dualism enters into creation, itself. The design reproduced above is interpreted as Zurvan with his good and evil sons (Ahura Mazda and Ahriman). However, the assistant curator of the Cincinnati Art Museum, Ellen B. Avril, has drawn my attention to the fact that the ornament shown here is much older and belongs to an Iranian tradition in which dualistic thought and the myth of the cosmic bull was already central before it invaded Zoroastrianism. (Chased silver ornament. Iran, Luristan, 10–17 B. C. Cincinnati Art Museum, Cincinnati, Ohio, U.S.A.)

Figure 42. Where dualism and the idea of the Judgment has led: the soul of a child has to make an early choice between heaven and hell. (Plates from a book intended to prepare children for their first Holy Communion, ca. 1930.)

possible. The person's deeds are counted and weighed in the balances, the good against the bad. Whoever is found wanting falls from the bridge into hell, where there awaits a long period of misery, darkness, horrible food, and cries of woe.

At the end of time, fire will melt the metal in the mountains and everyone will have to pass through this fiery sea. The good will wade through it as if it were "warm milk," the others will sink in it. Then the earth will be finally purified, time will be no more, and human beings will live for ever with the All-Wise Lord in peace and happiness.

The message of Zoroaster spread westward very gradually along the trade routes. In the eighth century B.C., Raga, just south of Teheran, seems to have been a center of Zoroastrian priests. Cyrus turned Zoroastrianism into a world faith in 550 B.C. after a successful revolt during which he welded the Medes and Persians into the greatest world empire of those days. This empire was later overthrown by Alexander the Great, who laid waste Persepolis, the center of the Zoroastrian priesthood, causing a break to occur in the transmission of the priestly texts.

Zoroastrianism itself, especially in its heretical form of Zurvanism, remained the state religion of the great kingdoms of the Parthians and the Sassanids. Islam nearly extirpated Zoroastrianism, but it survives in a small community of Parsees in India.

Zoroastrianism, in its pure form, was very tolerant of other religions. It was not for or against certain gods, but sided with all

Figure 43. There are numerous caves in which inscriptions have been left behind by people of many kinds—nomads, traders, soldiers, pilgrims—from 6000 B. C. until today. The Italian archeologist Emmanuel Anati published studies of a series of these graffiti. (*Felskunst im Negev und auf Sinai*, Lübke Verlag, 1981). War-chariots were in use around the time of the Exodus.

virtuous gods and men against evil. Cyrus recognized Ahura Mazda as the sole lord of all mankind, and especially as the god of his chosen people, the Iranians. However, he acknowledged and showed respect for national divinities and their worship; the Jews were among those who benefited from this policy. He was the first king of the first great world power in history to understand how enemies should be treated after war: that they ought to be encouraged to be themselves and to employ their skills for the benefit of all. This is opposed to the form of rulership mystique that strives to impose unity by its own power and ability.

MOSES

That new weapon, the horse and chariot, which started a revolutionary process in the steppes of Asia, also produced a revolution in the southern cultural region spanning the Euphrates, Tigris and Nile. Suppression of large sections of the ordinary population was carried out by the new military elite, and those suffering exploitation later revolted in the hope of regaining their liberty. This brings us to the history of Israel. The oldest poem in the Bible, made by Miriam, the sister of Moses, refers to this weapon as a symbol of tyranny when describing her nation's new sense of God:

> Sing ye to the Yahweh,
> For he hath triumphed gloriously:
> The horse and charioteer
> Hath He thrown into the sea (Exodus 15:21).[10]

Moses and Zoroaster have much in common: experiences of oppression, of the Almighty who invites people to work with him for freedom, of hope for a better future. Even so, they differ as fundamentally as the steppes differ from the desert. The nomads of the desert enjoyed few natural resources. For survival they were dependent on wells and oases linked by trade routes, and on one another—on the members of their own tribe and on a code of

---

[10] All biblical quotes come from the King James Bible. The translator has changed wording for "Yahweh" and "charioteer," as the author had done.— Ed.

Figure 44. Moses receives the Torah on the mountain and transmits it to the people below. (Miniature in the "Birds' Head Haggadah," ca. 1300, so called because the Jews themselves did not represent faces and therefore used birds' heads. Jerusalem: The Israel Museum.) [This could not have been a strictly observed rule, however, as can be seen in illustrations from the Golden Haggadah (1320-1330) and similar Jewish books of the same period in which human faces are represented (see *Hebrew Manuscript Painting*, Joseph Gutmann, Chatto & Windus, London, 1979). Tr.]

hospitality. Indeed solidarity, tribalism, and hospitality were typical of desert nomads. Desert spirituality is an intensification of such values as tribal solidarity, rather than the fertility of the soil or the forces of nature.

The tribes were not large. They were nothing like the big city communities in which each quarter, trade, and aspect of life had its own god. All these gods together formed a pantheon with a supreme deity enthroned high above everyday life, a *deus otiosus*. The nomads had a simple tribal structure. Each was equally responsible for the life of the tribe. Only the patriarch had a special place. He was a central figure—leader, priest, bearer of the religious experiences of his clan, guardian of its traditions, and invested with the power to bless and curse as a means of preserving acceptable social behavior. Whoever complied with the patriarch knew that he was free. He was answerable to none except the members of his own tribe.

A simple understanding of God accompanied the simple tribal structure. The Almighty had unqualified power jointly and severally over the lives of the tribe and each member of the tribe, including the patriarch.

The religious experiences recorded for us in the Bible do not tell, as shamanism does, of an All-Highest dwelling in a heaven to which journeys are made, but of One who has a relationship to the tribe and in some ways could be called its highest Patriarch: the "God of my fathers"—of Abraham, Isaac and Jacob. What is involved is the religious experience of a whole tribe, described in narratives in which the patriarch always has the central role. God says, "Fear not, Abraham: I am thy shield" (Genesis 15:1) when promising to protect the tribe; also, "I will bless thee . . . and I will bless them that bless thee, and curse him that curseth thee: and in thee shall all families of the earth be blessed" (Genesis 12:2,3). God was also known as "the Fear of Isaac" and even as the one who wrestled with Jacob. Jacob was so affected by God that his body was permanently marked by the encounter. He became lame. This is a paradoxical experience that is typical in mysticism—the One who wounds is the One who binds the mystic to Himself. Again, what Isaac underwent is typical of a great many mystical experiences—they are terrifying, upsetting, and unexpected.

The desert nomads lived on the edge of a cultural area which was alien and yet fascinating. Some tribes infiltrated it. For others it remained a land of promise—prosperity beckoned but they stayed put in their old territories.

The relationship between these desert nomads and the established cultures was peaceful until the horse-drawn chariot and other new weapons of war were developed and led to the creation of a new class of leaders, the military. Around this military upper class there grew a bureaucracy whose task it was to handle finance. Taxes were levied to pay for the horses and chariots. Towns were enclosed by walls and became the nuclei of city states. The land of Canaan was full of such city states, but these had lost their independence and were controlled by the Egyptian empire. They, in turn, set out to subjugate the farmers and shepherds of the hinterland.

Around 1250 B.C., these farmers and shepherds of the Canaanite hinterland staged a revolt. At the same time, an enslaved people escaped from Egypt. They were nomads who had gradually settled there after 1500 B.C., but had been forced by Ramses II (1263-1234 B.C.) to work as slaves and to build the cities of Pithom and Rameses (Exodus 1:11). When Ramses II died, they seized their opportunity, along with associated border groups known as "Abiri" or "inferior foreigners" (apparently the appellation *Hebrew* is derived from Abiri), and other elements picked up later during their flight through the wilderness. Around 1200 B.C. this mixed multitude of refugees reached Canaan and joined forces with the insurgents. Out of this hodgepodge of nomads, semi-nomads, peasants, collaborators, unwanted strangers, vagabonds, and camp-followers, the nation of Israel grew within a period of two hundred years.

The undisputed leader in this history of liberation was Moses, the "greatest prophet" of Israel. What is said of him in the Bible indicates a mystical process of character formation: from a man thoroughly versed in Egyptian culture he became a desert dweller, from a desert dweller he became a mystic, and from a mystic a political leader. His experience of God began when he was arrested by the sight of a burning bush that did not burn up. At the time, he was in the "backside of the desert" in the "mountain of God." Here he heard the voice of God. With his shoes removed from his feet because the ground was holy, and with his face covered in the presence of the mighty Light, he received an illumination that gave him a deep insight into God's being and into the relationship of things. God is the All-Highest who comes down:

And the Lord said, "I have surely seen the affliction of my people which art in Egypt, and have heard their cry by reason of their taskmasters; for I know their sorrows. And I am come down to deliver them out of the hand of the Egyptians. . . . Now, therefore, behold, the cry of the children of Israel is come unto me" (Exodus 3:7-9).

His name is Yahweh: I am: I am He.[11] His help cannot be extorted by magic or liturgy. He is a dynamic power within the process of deliverance. Moses had a personal experience which he was impelled to express not in words but in a process of liberation. Through him the Exodus from Egypt became a highly charged symbol, powerful enough to weld a horde into a nation and profound enough to grow into a religion.

Moses gained a new insight into the relationship of a people with their God. This insight is described in another narrative in which Moses, on the selfsame mountain of Horeb (Sinai), received the Ten Commandments (the "Ten Words") when he was "face to face" with God. The fire, on which he then gazed, shone from his own face so brightly that he had to cover it with a veil to hide it from view. The first three commandments contain a prohibition against making graven images, and against taking God's name in vain. The nomadic tradition is still perceptible here. God is a "jealous God" who does not allow the deification of the forces of nature or other aspects of life. Neither does he allow petrification. According to the experiences of Moses, He is a God who stirs things up, who has a feeling for the human condition, and moves with the times. Therefore He cannot be locked up in images and names.

From the experience that Yahweh rescued an insignificant people out of a mighty land there grew the realization that new forms of solidarity had to be achieved in a new society, in which there was a caring attitude toward the nobodies and the

---

[11] Out of fear of being irreverent, the Jews have always avoided uttering the name of God, so we do not know its true pronunciation. "Yahweh" not "Jehovah" is now a widely accepted form. Kitto's *Cyclopaedia of Biblical Literature* (3rd ed., Adam & Charles Black, 1876) casts doubt on "Yahweh" and gives grammatical reasons in favor of "Yih'veh" or "Yeheveh." Tr. note.

oppressed, and an aversion to rulers becoming too powerful. This ethic, too, was enshrined in the Ten Commandments. The deepest connection between the latter came to be expressed in the double command:

> And thou shalt love the LORD thy God with all thine heart, and with all thy soul, and with all thy might (Deuteronomy 6:5) and love thy neighbor as thyself (Galations 5:14).

This calls for basic respect of others. Knowing Yahweh involves a recognition of their rights, too.

The experience of Yahweh was kept alive in psalms, prayers, and narrations, and, above all, in a just society; these were reinforced by simple religious rites. Some of the psalms have to do with a historical event—liberation. The nation had had firsthand knowledge of the weakness of armed might. Egypt had sunk under its own weight. Horses and chariots foundered while trying to cross the Red Sea. Evil does not reside high in a spiritual world, but comes out of human beings.

A NEW AWARENESS
OF HUMAN HISTORY

At a time when Aryan mysticism had passed its peak, Buddha having rejected its elitism, the teaching of Zoroaster became the state religion of a world empire; and Judah, recovering from a deep crisis, was left with a broader view of mankind and its history. The sixth century B.C. is important in the history of mysticism because a "universal" consciousness broke through—the realization that one's own tribe belonged to humanity, that there are such things as world history and one common origin of the human race, and that the All-Highest is also the creator of all and everything. This expanded awareness meant that the message of Zoroaster could be translated into politics and that the Exodus of Moses and his people could be experienced as the deepest meaning of the history of mankind.

Two hundred years after the Exodus, the mixed multitude had made good, and people whose ancestors once lived on the edge of cultured society were now one nation. Israel was a kingdom with a king, soldiers, officials, legislation, judges, an elaborate ritual, and a temple. In a land "flowing with milk and honey," Israel had to contend with the Canaanitish Baal worship, a fertility cult involving both country folk and city dwellers. The Mosaic inspiration looked as if it would not be able to compete. The quest for social justice and for a living dialogue between God and humans was bogged down in the power structure, the fossilized worship, the soulless judiciary, and the deification of fertility.

After Solomon, the kingdom split into two. The northern kingdom, with Samaria as its new capital, was overthrown in 722 B.C. The cream of the population was deported. Samaria never recovered. The southern kingdom, Judah, with Jerusalem as its capital, suffered a similar fate in 597 B.C. when the top layer of society was carried away to Babylon. Ten years later, Jerusalem was destroyed, the temple burned down and the middle class deported. These "Jews" (the name is derived from Judah) were forced to dwell in an "unclean" land where another god was treated as greater than theirs. They were left with no social or religious structure, and nothing but each other and the memories of their former slavery and deliverance. They looked for a new liberator and saw him in Cyrus, who became king in Anshan (or Anzan) in 558 B.C. Without striking a blow, Cyrus took possession of Babylon in 538 B.C. and a year later gave permission to the Jews to return to their land and to rebuild the temple. In 485 B.C., Ezra, who was "a ready scribe in the law of Moses" attached to the Persian court, went up to Jerusalem, and was followed in 445 B.C. by the court official Nehemiah acting in the capacity of governor. Ezra was known as the second Moses. He completed the work of Moses by making the five books of Moses the basic law of the Jews. This book, the Torah, became the religious foundation of a religion that no longer stood or fell with central structures. Instead of a central place of worship there were local houses of instruction (synagogues) where those skilled in Mosaic law helped to apply it to everyday life. Worship was also celebrated in the home. One day in every week, the Sabbath, was set aside for divine worship. Coming from a court that observed the Zoroastrian laws of purification, Ezra also laid great stress on the Mosaic laws of cleanliness. This may be the reason why, in spite of its universality, Judaism (like Zoroastrianism) has never really spread as a world faith. The underlying idea was (an idea shared by Cyrus) that all groups would be saved in the coming kingdom of God, but that this salvation would be brought only through the chosen people. Therefore this people must keep itself free from all foreign contamination.

The Prophets

During this period certain prophets played an important role by keeping faith with Moses, criticizing the court and the temple, and pointing out new ways when all seemed lost.

There were nabi-prophets (spokesmen) in Canaan as long ago as 1700 B.C. These lived in groups, strove after ecstasy in the context of fertility rites, were linked with sacred places and with the court, foretold the future, and gave advice and warnings to the leaders. They stammered out their ecstatic experiences. In the wilderness, the Israelites knew prophets of another type: the seers. These still had the characteristics of the patriarch and of the shaman—the journey to heaven, miracles, healings, charismatic leadership. Often they were poets and used language that could be clearly understood. Elijah and Elisha (in the ninth century B.C.) were such seers. They were "fathers" of a large group of prophets. After them a line was drawn between, on the one hand, professional prophets attached to the royal court and the temple (and therefore no longer well-placed to deliver stinging rebukes to the establishment) and, on the other hand, those who had received a "call" and, after a profound experience, had given up their professions in order to travel through the land on their own, testifying in words and symbolic actions concerning the gulf between the ideal and the actual. They gave their hearers a choice—either to carry on as usual, which would mean disaster, or to restore a just society which would bring recovery. They also unmasked a hypocrisy in religious life that was hindering genuine conversion.

As opposed to the "false prophets" who invoked Yahweh without having had any experience of Him and toadied to the rich and powerful, they spoke from personal experience and as the mouthpieces of Yahweh. They repeated the time-honored message that He pitied the oppressed and desired justice for everyone. These prophets were mystics who, out of a staggering experience, spoke of Yahweh as a flaming fire that either destroyed or purified. Theirs were often ecstatic experiences, but the prophets were convinced that these should be shared with everybody; what is more, they explained them in remarkably clear language.

Figure 45. Elijah's ascent to heaven in the chariot of fire is in keeping with a long tradition that is shamanistic in origin. Ascensions have been ascribed to a number of great figures—Alexander the Great, Jesus, Mohammed. Dante's *Divine Comedy* comes in at the close of this tradition. (Painted woodcut from the Koberg Bible, 1483.)

Figure 46. Elijah was a prophet. As a mystic he inspired a group of Christian hermits who lived around Elijah's Well on Mount Carmel in the 13th century. This group had to flee to Europe where they formed a mendicant order. For these Carmelites, Elijah played a big role as an active fighter for the true God and as a seer. On Mount Horeb in Sinai he retired into a cave, but God called him outside. "And behold, the Lord passed by." After stormy winds, and earthquakes, and lightning, there came a "still small voice" and, when Elijah heard it, "he wrapped his face in his mantle." (Woodcut by Marianne van der Heijden, made for a Carmelite publication in 1961.)

While there were plenty of professional prophets, there were few mystics. The best known are Amos, Hosea and Isaiah in the eighth century B.C., Ezekiel and Jeremiah in the seventh century, Deutero-Isaiah[12] in the sixth century and then, five centuries later, John the Baptist and Jesus of Nazareth. The latter included Himself among the prophets who were not honored in their own country, and was seen by others as "Elias" (i.e., Elijah).

DEUTERO-ISAIAH

Deutero-Isaiah is a made-up name, given to an [alleged] Jewish exile living in Babylon before Cyrus conquered the city. He prophesied that Yahweh was now going to liberate His people once more, using Cyrus as His servant. This is what actually took place, although not with all the bloodshed anticipated. From the writings of Deutero-Isaiah it is clear that there was close contact between him and the Zoroastrian priests. The message of Zoroaster strongly influenced the Jews in their new conditions.

The soil was well prepared to receive its influence. The word of hope announced by this Jewish prophet could not be a strict repetition of what had been said before: it was no longer a question of the God of Israel vanquishing the foes of His people. The old message could be true only if Yahweh was the God of all human beings. This was in line with what Zoroaster had taught: there is only one God, who in the course of history will conquer injustice with the cooperation of all people of goodwill. What had entered Jewish consciousness sporadically now became self-evident: Yahweh is not only a national God, but the Creator of the universe and the Lord of human history. In announcing this doctrine, Deutero-Isaiah adopts the scheme of one of Zoroaster's yasnas: individual parts of the universe are mentioned and the

---

[12] A scholarly rejection of the theory that there was a second or "deuterr" Isaiah can be found in *The Unity of Isaiah* by Dr. O. T. Allis (The Presbyterian and Reformed Publishing, 1950). Dr. Allis argues that the whole of Isaiah was written by the eighth-century prophet. There is no record of a sixth-century Deutero-Isaiah (who, if he had existed, would have been as important a figure as Ezra or Nehemiah); e. g., the Jewish historian Josephus had never heard of him. According to Dr. Allis, Deutero-Isaiah was invented because of disbelief in the possibility of accurate long-range prediction by Isaiah himself. However, his existence is assumed below. Tr. note.

question is asked, "Who has created these things?" He clearly distances himself from the idea that Yahweh has an evil Antagonist, the origin of all that is bad. He reports Yahweh as saying: "I am the Lord, and there is none else. I form the light and create darkness: I make peace, and create evil."

Also when Deutero-Isaiah gazed into the future and the end of history, he did not see Hell and the purification of the world by fire. He expected the final kingdom to come very shortly, as did the other prophets; but with this difference—that the choice (repentance for salvation or refusal to repent with resulting calamity) is given a place in history. That is to say, the present is seen as a time of calamity, and the future as a time of salvation. Repression and injustice afflict the whole human race. Only the Creator can bring deliverance by a mighty creative act.

This eschatological expectation (eschaton = end) was not realized after the return of the Jews to their own land, but it survived and grew in intensity among the lower strata of society, who were suffering renewed oppression. The world was experienced as an utter mess and people felt the urge to get away from this impurity, intolerance, and hardness, and to await the servant of Yahweh who will destroy this unclean world, will free Israel and transform it into a holy community, and will convert the rest of the nations. They looked for a new Israel, embracing the world with Jerusalem as its capital.

In practice this new eschatological expectation created enormous tensions. In the dark, miserable present, it did no more than give a glimpse of a brighter future; and who could say when this would come? Passionate longings and extreme devotion to the ideal always seemed to end in disappointment and in feelings of guilt. People felt they were saddled with the responsibility for the whole development of world history; a responsibility they were unable to discharge. Everyone and everything was involved in the eschatalogical drama, but Israel had the central role to play in it. Out of these tensions there have continually arisen eschatological, messianic, and apocalyptic movements, right down to this very day. Sometimes such movements are the products of a deeply felt mystical homesickness.

There also came out of these tensions an extensive apocalyptic literature from the second century B.C. through the second century A.D. This was not included in the Jewish Bible, but in the Christian Bible we find the Apocalypse.

THE BIBLE—A MYSTICAL BOOK

The compilation of documents we now know as the Bible is the result of a centuries-long development. The first collection of texts, the book of Deuteronomy dates from the seventh century B.C. Ezra began with the Pentateuch, the five books of Moses. After this the Bible grew through the admission of a great number of old and new texts from very varied sources, which supplemented the ideas presented about God and the world. The Bible contains legal codes, and historical, prophetical, and poetical books, wisdom literature and love poetry. It gives us a distillate of what Israel underwent, thought, wrote, and found important in other cultures. Many texts were borrowed.

The story of Cain and Abel occurred in the tribal records of the Kenites, that of Sodom and Gomorrah refers to an event in 1250 B.C. Wisdom literature was familiar in the old cultural areas. The Song of Solomon (Canticles) is a collection of amorous songs, which may have come from fifth-century B.C. Egypt. It is a colorful anthology reminiscent of the writings of Hindu mystics. However the Jewish Bible is not a patchwork; it is unified by a fundamental vision. If we grasp this fundamental vision as we read it, it informs us of a mystical process: how men and women gain freedom and achieve unity in a just society, and also come to realize that God is not a being who can be grasped within the confines of an image. The Exodus from Egypt is a key narrative. It is placed in a cosmic setting as an event toward which the creation of the universe and of mankind had moved, and from which the history of mankind can be perceived as evolution toward an earthly paradise. What other races had already experienced and

Figure 47. The throne of God as seen by Ezekiel. This vision helped to give rise to the later Jewish Merkabah mysticism. (Woodcut from Luther's translation of the Bible, 1545; reprinted Munich, 1972.)

expressed in myths was given another significance in these sagas. For example, consider the story of the garden of Eden. Jews understand it differently from Christians. Hyam Maccoby offers this interpretation:

> When Adam was expelled from the earthly paradise, he realized that he would be obliged to work in the sweat of his face, and that he had to learn to distinguish between good and evil. The acquisition of this knowledge was not simply something involving guilt, but something involving the possibility of realization. "Man," said God to the angels, "is become as one of us." But we should guard against reading this passage in the light of later Christian theology. By sinning, Adam lost his protected position; but, at the same time, he became a being with responsibility, in a state to receive the Torah.[13]

The Bible is unlike the mythology of other races. Scant respect is paid to nature and the cosmos. The heavenly bodies are lower creations, and mankind stands apart from them. Humans are created "in the image of God" and are the center of the cosmos and of history. There is no higher world and no hereafter. Human beings have to realize paradise here on earth. There are no escapist possibilities. Our task is not to travel out of this world to a spiritual world where God dwells. We have to transform this world into one ruled by the higher values of unity and love, freedom and justice. The Exodus from Egypt is a very fundamental myth that lays bare the deepest meaning of world history: growth to adulthood in a loving relationship with God, through trials, failures and sins, in spite of longings to be dependent on Him and to be secure in Him; growth out of every form of slavery and subservience. Evil, too, belongs to this process. Secular love lyrics can be assimilated by this mythology, because the love relationship with God is not a spiritual matter. The law is very concrete. A law of love has no meaning if it is not made concrete again and again. The mystical process also signifies a new communal ideal in which all men and women are equal before God. It has social implications that need to be continually realized.

---

[13] Hyam Maccoby, in *De joodse wereld* [The Jewish World], Elie Kedourie (Antwerp, 1980), p. 56.

Figure 48. Carmelites looking out of a cave on Mount Carmel. For the Jews this mountain was a symbol of the land flowing with milk and honey. St. John of the Cross turned the ascent of Mount Carmel into a mystical symbol. (Detail of an altar-piece dedicated to Anna and Joachim in the Carmelite church in Bruges. It was painted by a Flemish master in the 16th century. Now in Saint-Salvador church, Bruges. Photo: NCI, Boxmeer.)

The Bible is not a mystical book in any formal sense. It does not speak of absorption in the One, but of a mystical attitude that is visibly blessed by the love that seeks unison: by an increasingly mature and therefore purer love, which proves itself in everyday life. God is not brought before us as the ground of things, but as the challenge in mundane reality. Union with God is not absorption, but a growing out of every form of dependence, even religious dependence.

A SCIENTIFIC WORLDVIEW

Following the period of growing consciousness just described, came a period of research. People wanted to understand the place occupied by humans and human history in the totality of the universe. An attempt was made to learn this by careful scrutiny and reflection. The first discovery was the importance of numbers. Babylonian astronomers made mathematical models of the paths of the heavenly bodies. Zoroastrian priests applied these calculations to their master's eschatological doctrine of salvation. Greek ecstatics searched the universe and found it to be full of harmony. They discovered the same harmony in music, and saw number as the basis of cosmic harmony.

ASTROLOGERS IN BABYLON

Around 500 B.C., after many years of observation and painstaking analysis of the motions of the heavenly bodies, the stargazers of Babylon discovered that these motions occur in fixed paths, are interconnected, and are tied to time. They found that their results could be calculated and expressed numerically.

The ancients thought of the heavenly bodies as gods who had a direct influence on humanity. Even to the learned astronomers, this was a self-evident fact. They drew the conclusion from it that their calculations of the heavenly motions could be applied to the motions occurring on earth, and to the history of people in the mass and as individuals. A result that became significant in later mysticism is that all heavenly motions are completed in a period of a thousand years. The astronomers named this millennium "the great year." Each great year is an exact repetition of the previous one. For human history this meant that history is an endless recurrence of millennia. A deluge, or "the great fire," forms the end of one great year and the beginning of the next. Human beings have no influence on this.[14]

---

[14] My edition of *Brewer's Dictionary of Phrase and Fable* (Odhams Press Limited, n. d.; an edition edited by Ivor Evans is published by HarperCollins, New York, 1989) says the Platonic, Great, or Perfect year was estimated at about 26,000 years by early Greek and Hindu astronomers, at the end of which all the heavenly bodies were imagined to return to the same places as they occupied at the "Creation." As the planets do not orbit the sun in periods that repeat every thousand years, it is hard to credit that experienced watchers of the skies ever thought that great years lasted no more than a thousand ordinary years. Even the Egyptian Sothic Cycle (of the heliacal rising of Sirius) "wandered over all the days of the calendar, and found its right place again at the end of 1460 years" according to George St. Clair in his *Creation Records Discovered in Egypt* (David Nutt, 1898). Tr. note.

This discovery did not fail to make a deep impression on the Zoroastrian priests among others. They fitted the findings of the astrologers into Zoroaster's vision of history: a prolonged struggle between good and evil ending in destruction by fire and the resurrection of the good. They measured this struggle in terms of episodes: twelve millennia divided into four periods of 3000 years. They said that Zoroaster would appear in each period, returning three times, born of a virgin. What is more, for them the central problem was not evil, it was time. They interpreted the teaching of Zoroaster thus: the two principles of good and evil, Ahura Mazda and Ahriman, are twin zones of the one All-Highest known as Zurvan, i.e., Time. This deviant form of Zoroastrian doctrine was therefore called Zurvanism.

This Zurvanism took firm hold in Western Iran under Artaxerxes II (404-358 B.C.). It undermined the mystical vein of Zoroaster. The conviction that Ahriman would reign for 9000 years, that the end of the ages would not come until after this, that humans had no influence over this course of events, and that both good and evil are concealed in the bosom of the highest God Himself, took away all incentive to join the good God in fighting the power of evil. Yet the "millennial kingdom" has figured in apocalyptic literature and in eschatological mysticism from that day to this.

Insofar as it encourages fatalism, astrology is rejected by the purer form of Zoroastrianism, by Judaism, and by Christianity. An individual's lot is determined by God and by his or her fellow humans! But astrology has always played a part in underground "occult" movements. The idea that we are related to the stars and composed of the same materials, and that the movements of humans and stars are connected, has never wholly disappeared from Western mysticism.

GREEK SHAMANS

Partly due to the influence of the Scythians, who were Indo-European nomads from the Asiatic steppes, Greek shamans put in an appearance in the sixth century B.C. They had all the characteristics of Central Asian shamans, but belonged to a completely different culture; their social function was different, too.

It is preferable to call them by the name their contemporaries gave them. Ion Petru Culianu,[15] who described the phenomenon of Greek shamans in a recent study and revealed their significance, uses the name *iatromantis*, which means "physician and soothsayer." This name indicates what they were essentially. Other names they were given refer to various facets of their activities such as: "traveler in the air," "purifier," "speaker of oracles," and "thaumaturgist." They were key figures—not in a tribe, but in a cult. Their ecstasy culture was linked with the worship of Apollo and contrasted with that of the Dionysians.

The worshipers of Dionysius practiced group ecstasy; they intoxicated themselves (usually with wine) in order to immerse themselves in nature. Notorious among the Dionysian orders were the Bacchantes, groups of women who, crowned with wreaths of ivy and clothed in skins, danced in the mountains, drank the blood of living animals, and ate raw flesh, to try and feel an ecstatic oneness with Life. . . .This was an earthly impression of religious unity. There was no longer any perception of a high and heavenly holiness; the sacred was sought in life down here—in the earth, in woman, in plant seed, in human seed, and in the seasonal death and rebirth of the year. The sacred was sought in the fruitfulness of the earth in which humans shared.

The Dionysian orders were hostile to the iatromants—sometimes to the extent of manslaughter and murder. The two groups differed fundamentally. The iatromants felt called to practice ecstasy as individuals. Instead of seeking unity with nature, they distanced themselves from it. Their food was very meager and they abstained from strong drink and sex. In order to control their hunger they ate *alimos* (= "not hungry"), a plant that is in some ways comparable with the coca leaf used by the Indians of Peru. The body had no share in their ecstasy. While the spirit traveled to the land-of-Apollo-in-the-air, the body remained behind—often in what looked like a state of death. A Greek physician described it as a "possession by Apollo, who keeps the body alive but without pulse or respiration."

---

[15] Ion Petru Culianu, *Psychanodia I. A survey of the evidence concerning the ascension of the soul and its relevance* (Leiden, 1983).

Figure 49. How Pythagoras discovered that number can express the structure of sound and also of the world. An Italian woodcut of 1492 links him with Jubal, the Biblical "father of all such as handle the harp and organ."

We know several of these iatromants by name: Aristeas, Abaris, Bacis, Empedocles, Epimenides of Crete, Hermotimus of Clazomenae, Pythagoras. The latter is the most renowned. He founded a commune and a school. The Pythagoreans believed in the transmigration of souls and in the need to live a pure life. Purity was required out of respect for all living things, because in all a soul can dwell, and it was a necessary condition for obtaining clearer insights. They discovered that music could be expressed numerically—an octave, for example. They saw that human society and the universe are changeable relationships of unchangeable numbers.

The iatromants combined mysticism with the acquisition of knowledge. For them, the hereafter was not an object of faith but of sight. On their ecstatic journeys they saw the heavens and the underworld. Heaven was above, hell was below, and the earth was situated in the middle. All this was experienced as a harmonious whole. The harmony of the spheres is related to musical harmony. All things have their measure and all measures are mutually coherent. Number is the structural basis of the universe and it is the task of mankind to solve the riddle of number.

The ecstatic experience in which the spirit leaves the body—and the body seems as if it were left behind for dead—can easily be interpreted as the body is the dungeon of the spirit. The spirit itself does not die, but migrates through the universe from one body to another, from earth to the kingdom of Apollo—a kingdom in the north or in the air, a paradise where matter is lighter and more aerial.

This world picture was adopted by Plato (429-347 B.C.). However, he based his research not only on ratio and proportion, but primarily on the human individual. He taught that the human being can become acquainted with the universe through self-analysis, discovering in himself or herself that the burden of the

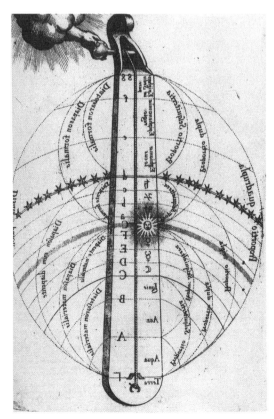

Figure 50. The Divine Monochord, designed by R. Fludd and engraved in 1617, is an interpretation of the leading thought of Pythagoras on the music of the universe.

body and the mutability of earthly life may be triumphed over by the spirit. The individual can form "ideas." For example, there are many humans, and they come and go, but "the human," the idea that applies to all human beings, is unchanging.

On examining the microcosm or small cosmos (ourselves), we recognize the structure of the macrocosm or big cosmos: an immutable reality of Ideas originating beyond this material world and yet animating it. Thus the entire cosmos is structured vertically, with pure spirit at the top and pure matter at the bottom. This doctrine offers an explanation of the harshness of everyday existence. What is lower is less real than what is higher; also it is less good, less valuable, coarser and heavier.

Plato was also influenced by the teaching of Zoroaster. His friend, Eudoxus of Cnidos, had come to know this in the form of Zurvanism when he was in Babylon. It is probable that Plato owes to him the notion that the source of everything is the "One Good" and that evil is hidden by Him, that evil is a peripheral phenomenon, just as darkness borders light wherever light does not penetrate. The more completely the Ideas realize themselves during the creation of the cosmos, and descend (so to speak) into concrete matter, the more fully they are reflected. In this sense, good and evil are connected with higher and lower. In line with Plato, the underworld was transferred from "beneath the earth" to "beneath the moon": beneath the moon evil begins, above the moon good begins. Later, and little by little, even the celestial spheres above the moon were seen as bad. But, by that time, the search for knowledge had been overtaken by the religious longing for redemption.

THE HELLENISTIC WORLD

The incentive for a new culture in which mysticism could hold an important position was given by Alexander the Great when he crossed the Hellespont in 334 B.C. and conquered the Persian empire, Egypt, and the Indus region. This immense realm broke up after his death in 323 B.C., but a permanent result was that the Orient had been opened up to the Greeks: to Grecian scientists, officials, and young people; also to the demobilized soldiers, poverty-stricken peasants, and merchants who settled there. Greek became the official language of trade and learning. Whoever wished to succeed in life had to learn Greek. Other nationalities spread in the same way. New kingdoms with new centers arose: the Greco-Macedonian kingdom with Athens, the Seleucid Syro-Persian kingdom with Antioch, and the kingdom of Egypt with Alexandria, as their capitals. Together they created a very stable balance of power—the Hellenistic world.

Alexandria was the undisputed center of this Hellenistic world. It was a city founded by Alexander the Great himself (332 B. C.). His satrap, Ptolemy, turned it into a metropolis. It contained huge temples, immense sports palaces, a great synagogue, a famous library with approximately 700,000 manuscripts, and a museum for the arts. The learned came to it. They studied philosophy and also more practical subjects, such as medicine, astronomy, and languages. The distances between about 350 places were measured and recorded on maps by the librarian, Claudius Ptolemaeus. He also devised a model of the universe: a spherical earth as the midpoint, with the heavenly bodies circling round it. Ptolemy's map and his Ptolemaic system eventually reached Western Europe, where they made a deep impression. It was also in Alexandria that the Hebrew Bible was first translated—into Greek.

After 200 B.C., Rome slowly extended its power and influence; and, with the defeat of Cleopatra in 31 B.C., the Romans held sway in Egypt. However, even after this, Hellenistic culture determined all facets of life both in Egypt and elsewhere. And then, in 330 A.D. the emperor Constantine founded a new city, Constantinople, which later became the capital of the Byzantine Empire. Christianity was made the state religion and it took over the leadership of cultural life.

The Hellenistic civilization was characterized by an amalgamation of the Greek culture with that of the ancient East. It mingled a Greek culture in which everything knowable was recorded and classified, in which people were not frightened of the stars, calmly bowed to fate, and had a passion for building a "polis" or harmonious and orderly civic community, with an oriental culture in which religion was central and people expected improvements in society to come from the divine world. The Greek emigrants to the East felt they were surrounded by "barbarians."

Other people also spread out over the great empire, especially the Jews. For the latter it meant a life of exile, and also the search for a new identity because they felt rootless in their immediate surroundings. Where so many who were foreign to one another were crowded into new cities, it was only natural that the administrators should look for new ways of doing things when setting up a city, and also for new moral ties. Already, Ptolemy had not only designed a city on the drawing-board, so to speak, he had also presented himself as a "Soter," or preserver, clothed with divine power. He created an artificial religion, the Serapic mysteries, in order to bind Egyptians and Greeks together through their religious sensibilities.

In the Eastern countries themselves, the lower classes and the peasantry tended to cling to their own cultures. The Hellenistic city culture was felt as a threat, and this feeling was later intensified by the Roman occupation. The Roman aim was not only cultural cohesion but political cohesion, too, with a network of roads, and well-defended borders containing a hundred million inhabitants of the empire that also kept out the barbarians. But, as we have said, there were those who resisted this threat to their own identity; none more so than the Jews of Palestine.

Within the whole tangle of rival cultures and religions, and out of the alienation and tensions that changes always create, a new climate came into being. It was a pessimistic climate. The world was experienced as a place where the individual was not at home. Reflection on human existence impressed on people the rhythm of death that hid under the semblance of life. They were persuaded that the world was a place of slavery, where men and women are earthbound and are compelled to toil away all their lives or else suffer boredom. They thought of a gloomy world with only a few sporadic gleams of light.

In this climate that seems to have pervaded the first century of our present era, men and women discovered that they had souls. They became self-aware, aware that there was something inside them that did not correspond to the environment. They analyzed their experiences, were interested in finding personal identity and the meaning of individual life, and they wanted to know their place in an expanse in which they were lost. They wanted to be saved—from the hollowness of existence, from dark everyday banality, and from the fear of death.

A Religious Worldview

In this climate there grew a new world picture of human beings and the cosmos, in addition to the Greek scientific world picture expressed in the Ptolemaic system. The new picture was made up of the same elements as the scientific one, but it was elaborated differently, and its main emphasis was on where the fatherland of mankind really lay. The main elements of this religious world picture are as follows:

◆ *Men and women are composed of parts of the universe.* They are the cosmos in miniature. If we subject this microcosm that is ourselves to analysis, we discover how the great cosmos is structured.

◆ *The soul can ascend out of the body.* This soul is pure spirit. It is not unconditionally bound to the body. Human beings are composed of a body and a spirit united by the psyche, a soul that links body and spirit and gains information through the senses. The cosmos is therefore a world of pure spirit and an earth of pure matter. Between these two are spiritual beings who are tied to matter—humans, and various angelic beings, including the angels of the stars.

◆ *The stars determine the nature and earthly lot of humans.* This fundamental idea is interpreted as follows: the spirit of each human being was once in the spirit world; however, it descended to earth through all the heavenly spheres. In this descent, it was "clothed" by the stars with the virtues and vices peculiar to the stellar beings.

◆ *Human thought processes can teach us how the process of creation was carried out.* Even before we express something, there is the mind. To show what is in our mind we use some concept or other, we verbalize it, and present the Word in symbols and dogmas. More and more of the original is lost at each step. Mystical experience makes this still clearer. The experience itself is timeless and ineffable. Thinking about it and putting it into words spoils the perception of unity. The same was assumed to be true of creation. When the Creator expresses Himself in a Word, then there is less of the spirit. This effect becomes stronger the more tangible and material the creation becomes. Creation is dogged by imperfection.

This world picture can be seen as positive or negative according to whether the person takes a positive or negative view of his or her living conditions. Creation was seen by some as the radiation of God's spiritual power, though very incompletely; by others it was seen as a degeneration and therefore intrinsically bad.

Owing to negative religious experiences, the world picture was drawn harshly in varying ways.

◆ *The distance between the Creator and mankind was felt to be too vast.* This distance was filled up with creative beings of all kinds, and these were the subjects of endless speculation: the "unknown God" and His Creative Word (Logos) or His Wisdom (Sofia) or His Architect (Demiurge). Then there were "heavenly rulers," beings we would call angels. These were seen as militia (Archons).

◆ *The question of evil was often shifted to these heavens.* Did evil originate with Sofia being seduced, with the Demiurge building badly, with the fallen angel Satan, with a Fall of Adam on the moon?

◆ *The underworld was removed to the heavens.* For the earth is a prison of the spirit, but the bondage of the latter to material things cannot be maintained if it travels through the skies toward its true fatherland. Therefore, the heavens are often thought to be full of demons, the stars being ruled by demonic Archons. Many of the occupants of the Hellenistic culture area lived in a world from which they longed to be rescued. They looked into the sky and tried to discover the way to their true fatherland. Some thought they would need passwords in order to get through the heavenly cordons. A deliverer, coming down from heaven was said to be able to reveal these passwords.

Another way was this: initiation into the mysteries so that, while still on earth, one could learn how to detach oneself from matter. Still another way was that of "insight" by which one penetrated into one's deepest self—a direct path to the divine plenitude where this self was thought to reside.

Again, there is the Stoic response, made by those who did not think that the heavens were populated by adversaries, or that earthly existence was something from which they had to be delivered. They conformed to the cosmic order and rejoiced in it.

Releasing the Alienated Soul

The stoic attitude to life is doing what my own nature assigns me. Everything is in motion, but there is a fixed point amid variability. All things stand side by side and are often antagonistic, but are kept in balance by a mighty Mind. This is how Heraclitus

(544-484 B.C.) saw the universe. He named the principle of unity the Logos. Logos means Word, Reason, and Proportion. In the first of these senses it was later used by Gnostics and by Jewish and Christian mystics. In the other senses it was incorporated in the philosophy of Zeno (335-263 B.C.) and his school. The place where Zeno taught, the Stoa in Athens, gave the name Stoicism to this vision of life. His doctrine spread over the Hellenistic world. Famous representatives of the Roman Stoics were the magistrate and philosopher Seneca (ca. 4 B.C.-A.D. 65), the freed slave Epictetus (ca. A.D. 55-135) and the emperor Marcus Aurelius (A.D. 121-180).

Their fundamental concept was invariably the same. They said that the whole universe is based on divine reasonableness—on a Logos that creates everything and produces harmony in everything. According to them, there was a spark of the Logos in men and women themselves. As people learned to live by this spark, they would share in the cosmic harmony, and would achieve the goal of life—contentment here and now, rather than in the hereafter. Entry into the inner depths of one's being was determined by one's virtues and vices. The Stoics drew up long lists of these, rather like those drawn up by the apostle Paul and others. But the essential feature of their way was tranquility—an unruffled acceptance of fate. Thus Epictetus described himself as "a lame old man" whose one aim was to make his life "a hymn of praise to God." Stoicism lent itself outstandingly to mysticism with its view that God always dwelt in the individual. "You are a principal work, a fragment of God himself, you have in yourself a part of Him," said Epictetus.[16] And Seneca said that God is near, with us, in us, and pure spirit has its seat within us. It is the observer of our good and evil, and our guardian angel.

In his impressive *Meditations: or discourses with himself*, the emperor-general Marcus Aurelius teaches that "thou shalt cease to be a stranger in your country,"[17] namely by living in the present, and by doing what your own nature assigns you. He said that we should love what is given to us for the "All" has given it to us. Although differently expressed, the Stoic philosophy of life comes very close to the Chinese mysticism known as the Tao, the "Way"

---

[16] Whitall Perry, *A Treasury of Traditional Wisdom* (Cambridge, England: Quinta Essentia, 1971), p. 43.

[17] Marcus Aurelius, *Meditations*, tr. M. Staniforth (New York: Viking Penguin, 1964); New York: The Limited Editions Club, 1956), p. 217.

Figure 51. Bust of Marcus Aurelius. (The Vatican
City Museum.)

taken by the cosmos, the nameless beginning of all things, to
which mankind must conform by "non-action." Stoicism was confined to the upper class of society.

THE MYSTERIES—
WITHIN THE CIRCLE OF THE INITIATES

The word "mysticism" was coined in the Hellenistic world in connection with the celebration of the mysteries. It meant, "to do
with the mysteries" (*mysteria*) and is also cognate with the Greek
verbs *muo* (to shut the eyes) and *mueo* (to initiate). Mystery cults
were associations of initiates possessing secrets to which non-ini-
tiates were not allowed access. The same attitude was held toward
Christian themes by people like Clement of Alexandria, who
regarded mysticism as an "insight into the hidden divine things"
to which an initiate comes via the Christ-mystery.

In these mystery cults there was a new form of religiosity. In
place of the public sacrifices intended to make the gods propi-
tious, there now came acts of worship that were focused primarily on the needs of the individual. The latter wanted to feel part of
a close-knit fraternity and to have good prospects of salvation.

Figure 52. The new form of religiosity—the mystery cult. Imposing remains in which the ritual of a typical mystery celebration can be traced and the atmosphere of the room in which it took place can still be felt, are to be seen in Pompeii, especially in the House of the Mysteries. Here is a fragment in which the initiate is being scourged in order to feel purified.

The mysteries grew out of what were sometimes very old local cults. Those cults, in particular, that also paraded in public at official festivals without however losing their secret character, became of more than local significance. From these arose the Orphic, Dionysian, and Eleusinian mysteries in Greece, the Isis cult and the artificial Serapis cult in Egypt, the Mithras cult originating in Persia, and the Christ cult from the Jewish diaspora. The last two eventually became the most important. Mithraic temples have been excavated in the furthest corners of the old Roman empire. However, the cult was reserved for men, especially military personnel. This was in contrast to the Christian church which was open to men and women, to the wealthy and to slaves. Although the Christ-cult remained a city phenomenon for a long time (*paganus*, meaning rustic, acquired the sense of pagan or heathen), it soon became a world faith, and actually absorbed very many aspects of surrounding cultures and of other religions, including the Mithraic. The mysteries offered the possibility of experiencing life as something that survived death; of experiencing it with the help of rituals with many symbols, tokens and myths. There were narratives of resurrection: of Isis seeking her dismembered brother

Figure 53. In the Mithraic mysteries, the sacrifice of the cosmic bull holds a central place. In this representation Mithras is rising out of the cosmic egg. In his left hand he holds a torch as an emblem of the light that is coming into the world, and in his right hand is the knife with which he will slay the cosmic bull. He is encircled by the Zodiac. (Museum of Antiquities, The University of Newcastle-upon-Tyne.)

Figure 54. Gnosticism held a great attraction for people. And it was characterized by a bizarre mythology. This neolithic celt has been taken and engraved with one of the Gnostic mythological "intermediate beings." (The British Museum, London.)

and spouse and bringing him back to life, of Orpheus who was beheaded and yet kept on singing, of the life that sprang from the blood of the world bull slain by Mithras, of Christ who was crucified and rose again from the dead.[18]

The Greek and Egyptian mysteries are close to nature. The phallus and the seed play a big role in them. The cults of Mithras and Christ are more tied to the cosmos, to the struggle between Light and Darkness. In the mysteries of Isis and Osiris we hear of "enthusiasm," which means that the god entered the initiate and gave a sense of intoxication. In the Christian and Mithraic ceremonies there was a more sober process of death and rebirth. It began with a baptism, in water (in the first case) or in blood (in the second). In the Mithraic cult, the candidate was ritually raised from death after several days of abstinence from sex and food. Tied up, and lying on the ground as one dead, he was lifted into a standing position by the leader and was dipped in blood, standing in a pit above which an animal was slaughtered. Afterward, he shared a meal of bread and wine with those already initiated. This was the beginning of a way to the higher Light, and it was followed by an ascent of seven steps. He had to purify himself like this, and to enter into training for the journey he must eventually take through the seven planetary heavens. His courage and powers of endurance were being put to the test.

The extent to which mystical experiences took place on his life long journey it is hard to say. In any case, we are concerned with a mystical process here. Not only was there a conflict shared with the divine warrior, Mithras, who formed an alliance with the "invincible sun" in the service of the Good God, but there was also a process of enlightenment and purification from everything preventing union with the Light. "And you have also saved us by shedding blood that makes us immortal," runs an inscription in the Mithraic temple on the Aventine in Rome. By immortality

---

[18] It has often been pointed out by Christians, not always approvingly, that a number of things have been imported into Christianity from outside sources. But even though Clement of Alexandria spoke quite early on Christian "initiation," there was always an openness in Christianity that was very unlike the secrecy of the mystery cults. And today we see that the "sacred mystery" of the Catholics, for example, is not literally hidden like the secrets of Freemasonry, which has a much greater affinity with the old mysteries. Tr. Note.

was meant sharing personally in the Light that stands above time, and therefore above darkness and death.

GNOSTICISM

One of the most important religious movements in the Hellenistic world was Gnosticism. The name comes from *Gnosis* (knowledge) and was given to this movement because it made knowledge central as the means of salvation. In answer to the question as to what gnosis is, Clement of Alexandria repeated a gnostic formula:

> Gnosis is the knowledge of who we were and of what we have become; of where we were and where we have been tossed; of the place to which we are hastening and the place from which we have been delivered; of what is birth and what is rebirth.

Thus Gnosticism is concerned with questions about the place of human beings in time and space, about their destiny, and about the meaning and purpose of their lives. It is also concerned with liberation by a second birth, from a world into which we have been born but within which we feel like foreigners, liberation into a world in which we feel at home.

The answer to these questions is found through self-knowledge. To the Gnostics, self-knowledge is the insight that the individual, in the core of his or her soul, is essentially oriented toward God, and that this "spark of the soul" is just a sample of a spiritual world high above all matter and darkness. Having become preoccupied with the material world, the individual has forgotten the inner spark, and although feeling like a foreigner in the world, does not know why. However, everything changes when awakening from this state of sleep. The individual becomes keenly aware of what he or she is—a spirit imprisoned in a body but belonging to a divine world. Then the problem is to return to the true fatherland.

Gnosticism was rather loosely associated with the spirit of the age. It was "in the air" and gradually became more clearly structured through the formation of its own congregations, mythologies, and methods of deliverance. Its history is still under active investigation, and has been the subject of considerable revision, especially after the discovery some forty years ago, in the

Egyptian Nag Hammadi, of a second century B.C. Gnostic library. Prior to this, Gnosticism had been known chiefly through the writings of its opponents.

The distinctive mythologies that developed after the first century seem to be very rich and far from uniform. Those who elaborated them built on Jewish mythology, reinterpreted Paul and John, and invented new gospels and often quite whimsical cosmologies. To the outsider, their writings look like a heap of fantasies; but we have to remember that every religion has something in it that outsiders find fantastic. Be that as it may, under the obscurity of expression we can find allusions to enlightenment, to mystical experience, and to being at one in one's own spirit with the divine "fullness" of Spirit.

Here are a few specimens of this pluriform mythology.

◆ *The creation*. The Gnostics did not believe the Biblical account of a Creator who saw that "all was good." They made up their minds that the world is essentially evil and that there is no better one to expect. They said that the unknown God whom we know through Christ, the Father, is good. All that is good flows from Him, from the spirits down to and including the human spirit. Taken altogether this is the "fullness" of God. God is all in all to it. And it is a self-development in which He makes Himself knowable. This is the eighth heaven, exalted above the seventh heaven and the earth. The seventh heaven and the earth did not flow from the good Father, they said, but were made by an inferior creator. For the human being this mythology meant that his or her inner self was born of God, while the body and the world around was the work of some inferior creator. The spirit was good, the body was bad.

◆ *The Fall*. For Gnostics, the cause of evil lay in the creation of a time-bound material world. Who, they asked themselves, had thought up this unfortunate project? Was it the Logos (the Word) trying to comprehend the incomprehensible Father? Or Sofia (Wisdom), who wished to act apart from mankind and fell into chaos? Or the Demiurge? Or was it the Creator described in the Hebrew Bible not wishing to satisfy human thirst for the knowledge He had reserved for Himself? In all these mythologies the creation is treated as something sinful because it is intended to make the incomprehensible God comprehensible.

◆ *Simon Magus and Helena.* The relationship between the male and the female in humanity, and the mystical longing for unity of soul, come to the fore in various mythologies. In the more abstract mythologies, the divine Wisdom abandons her partner and so falls into chaos until the Logos restores her insight and marries her. In the more concrete mythologies, historical figures such as Jesus and Mary Magdalene, and more especially Simon Magus and Helena were used. Let us take a look at the latter pair.

In the Acts of the Apostles (New Testament), Simon is described as a man of renown in Samaria. People said of him, "This man is the great power of God," which is something the iatromants used to be called. He became a Christian. During a meeting with Peter, the cloven hoof came out: he wanted to obtain the gift of being able to impart God's Spirit and offered money for it. Peter distanced himself from him. Further details are supplied by Clement of Rome: Simon studied in Alexandria and returned to Samaria in order to take charge of a sect that had been founded by a woman called Dosithea.[19] Here he met Helena. They set themselves up as an ideal pair in which God manifested the Power of God in Simon, and the Wisdom of God in Helena. Clement also gives the content of the discussions between Simon and the apostle Peter, and says these hinged on a Gnostic interpretation of the Jewish Bible. In the second century there was already a strongly cultivated myth, with hymns describing how Wisdom brought forth angels, and how these angels created worlds in which, out of envy, they kept Wisdom confined; how Wisdom then took another body, sinking deeper and deeper into prostitution, and how finally Simon was sent to rescue her. Helena is here the symbol of all women who cause chaos; like Helen of Troy, who was the *casus belli* of the Trojan war.

In Gnostic movements, women often played a prominent role—as leader, inspiration, and symbol. Helena was symbolic of

---

[19] According to an article on Simon Magus in *A Dictionary of the Bible,* Vol. IV, ed. James Hastings (London: T & T Clark, 1902), Clement informs us in his Homilies that Simon was "The chief of the disciples of John the Hemobaptist. . . . The death of John occurred during the absence of Simon in Alexandria, and Dositheus succeeded to his place." Simon then contended with Dositheus and took over the leadership of John the Hermobaptist's group from him. Here it is John, not Dosithea, who founds the sect, and the person Simon supplanted was not Dosithea, a woman, but Dositheus a man. It may be that the author is quoting from an alternative source. Anyway there is a discrepancy somewhere along the line. Tr. note.

the feminine side of the soul, as Simon was of the masculine. Separated from one another, feminine and masculine create tensions. When they come together, the individual finds his or her soul. Through the strength of sexual love, the divine "Power" will free the individual from chaotic emotions and acquisitiveness. It can be a fire that consumes everything until only the purified soul is left, says Simon in one of his Gnostic writings.

Quite unconnected with the above, was the idea that human beings were originally both male and female, as suggested by Philo of Alexandria and by certain monks. But then the conclusion was drawn that a complete person does not marry.

All Gnostics took as their starting point contempt for the world and desire for the spirit. They experienced the world as darkness, ruled by the rhythm of death. They saw it as a place where the spirit is dulled and the soul is absorbed in the satisfaction of needs, where life becomes banal, and people with ambitions quickly reach their limits and sigh over what fate has written for them in the stars. The thing to do, therefore, was to live in the spiritual sufficiency at the center of one's own being, which was the same as living in the eighth heaven.

It was claimed that whoever had reached the Self, did the right thing automatically. Moral instruction was unnecessary. The thing to do was to detach oneself from the material world. However, this detachment meant different things to different people. For some Gnostic groups the correct path was amoral: going against established morality, against social norms and against natural laws. They were anarchistic, and believed in sexual promiscuity. For other groups the way was strict asceticism, and abstention from sexual and other enjoyments.

Gnosticism was a broad movement which penetrated milieus and religions of all kinds, but its appeal was limited to persons of a certain type. It was no cure for the carnal nature, as the Gnostics themselves discovered. We shall come to Christian Gnosticism later.

Egyptian Hermetics

One of the most important documents of "heathen" Gnosticism is a collection of works, a sort of bible, that circulated in Egypt under the name of Hermes Trismegistus. Its various sections date from the third century B.C. through the third century A.D. This sheaf of documents has been particularly significant because the scholars of the Italian Renaissance discovered it, highly regarded it as a very old revelation, and placed a great deal of reliance on it. The European esoteric tradition is very much indebted to these writings. Because of the reference to Hermes, later held to be a prophet, this form of Gnosticism is known as hermetic. The writings in question include old texts of popular origin as well as later Gnostic speculations. The popular texts have to do with research into the occult forces that rule the universe, and into the underlying sympathies that bind things together. This research is often conducted in the interests of magic, with the object of learning how to control the said forces. To know, for example, when the force in a certain plant is strongest due to planetary placements, so that the plant can be picked with the maximum amount of fruit. In the speculative texts this knowledge is given a Gnostic complexion, and is presented not as a result of painstaking research but as due to immediate mystical enlightenment.

In the treatise known as *Poemandres*, there is the description of a mystical experience of this sort, in which everything becomes clear in a moment, although the knowledge acquired has to be unfolded. The writer relates how he was meditating when suddenly a being of "indefinite size" was plainly present. This being revealed himself as Poemandres, the Mind of the Supreme Power and asked him what he wanted.

> I say, "I wish to learn the Entities, and to understand the nature of them, and to know God. . . ." He says to me again, "Have in thy mind whatsoever things thou wouldest learn, and I will teach thee."[20]

After this comes a Gnostic view of the formation of the cosmos and human beings. In the *"Secret Discourse"* (Chapter 13 of *Poemandres*), Hermes tells his son how to acquire this gnosis:

> Draw to thyself and it will come; wish and it becomes. Lay to rest the senses of the body, and it will be the generation of The Deity; purify thyself from the irrational avengers of the Matter.[21]

---

[20] *The Divine Pymander and Other Writings of Hermes Trismegistus,* tr. John David Chambers (London: T. & T. Clark, 1882). Reprinted by Samuel Weiser, New York, 1972, p. 1.
[21] "Poemandres," in *The Divine Pymander,* p. 89.

We are also told how Hermes's son follows this way, experiences ecstasy and then exclaims:

> I am in heaven, in earth, in water, in air. I am among animals, among plants, in the womb, before the womb, after the womb, everywhere.[22]

The ecstasy described has the character of a journey through the cosmos and beyond death. What is learned in this ecstasy must be retained as one reviews everything that has been seen and then enters into it. "Climb higher than all heights, descend deeper than all depths." The human spirit resembles the divine. It can encompass everything and be everywhere, and thus can come to know everything. To this end, the individual must be still, and free from the emotions that rouse the senses; and, after a mystical experience, must examine its implications: "Then shall contemplation take possession of them and draw them to it."

This sense of being at one with the cosmos also involved that preoccupation with matter which was later called alchemy, or the Hermetic art because it was described in Hermes Trismegistus.[23] The idea that there are just a few primary elements, and that new elements arise from the changing combinations of these, was current at about the same period in China, India, Greece, and Egypt. Alexandria was one of the main centers of alchemical research. The very famous alchemist, Zosimos (350-420), worked here. He referred to the Hermes scripts. Alchemy was concerned with a refining process carried out by various manipulations of matter, similar to chemical experiments but essentially religious in nature, the aim being to distill the pure divine principle out of impure substance. Gold was regarded as the noblest metal, and as the symbol of divine illumination and purification. This interaction with matter was experienced mystically as a process of transmu-

---

[22] "Poemandres," in *The Divine Pymander*, p. 91.

[23] I do not find a clear reference to alchemy in the *Poemandres* or in the Hermetic extracts of Stobaeus, although alchemists may well have seen some justification for their own doctrines there. C. G. Jung, in his *Alchemical Studies*, RKP, 1967, does mention the krater (or great baptismal cup) in *Poemandres* and calls it "the *vas Hermetis* of later alchemy" (p. 73). But the connection seems rather tenuous. My own impression is that the later Hermetic writings, and writings such as *The Book of Crates* in which Hermes was a prominent figure (see J. C Brown, *A History of Chemistry*, J. & A. Churchill, 1920), had diverged from the original philosophy. Tr. note.

tation in which the alchemist was very much involved. Matter was "killed" in order to eliminate all its properties, and was then restored to life so that new matter could be built out of it. Dissolve and coagulate was the watchword. The hardness of matter was put to the test. It was established that the forms of matter are no more fixed and permanent than a human being is. Alchemists were not gold-seekers, but people who, by operating on nature, tried to purify themselves to become worthy of God, the ground of nature. In the treatise *The Virgin of the World*, accredited to Hermes Trismegistus, God Himself is described as an alchemist who, in order to break through the inertia of the spiritual world, makes souls of all sorts out of the various elements of his breath.

ANSWERS FROM THE JEWISH WORLD

The Jews hold a special place among the nations that were over-run by the Hellenistic culture. They had become conscious of their historic significance and were now forced to find a place in a culture that was not their own. Consequently they developed defense mechanisms and also attempted to adapt—in many forms. There were groups who withdrew and cultivated their own identity. They were people like the Essenes, who lived in monastic communities and established themselves in caves bordering the Dead Sea. Some were expecting a new society that would be set up after a traumatic end to the existing one, and were wondering how this would happen. Their speculations led to the growth in the second century B.C. (and after) of an extensive apocalyptic literature. Others, however, were not looking for any end of the age, but intended to found their ideal state by force of arms. This led, in A.D. 70, to the destruction of Jerusalem and to the Dispersion of the Jewish people as a whole. Among the Diaspora, the Bible began to fulfill another role: it was no longer simply a book one heard being recited in the liturgy, but was also a book one could see—characters written on paper. There arose a mysticism that sought to explore the secret world behind the letters. And out of this came the "Merkabah" mysticism, in which the journey to the "Throne of God" (merkabah) is a central concept in creation mysticism and, some centuries later, in the Kabbalah. Dominant figures in the later development who, although Jews, reached out to the non-Jewish world, were Philo of Alexandria, Jesus of Nazareth, and Paul of Tarsus. They were contemporaries of one another.

ASCENT TO THE THRONE OF GOD

The idea of an ascent to God's Throne owed much to the prophets, especially to Ezekiel, but was also influenced by new trends from the Hellenistic world. It entailed a journey through the heavenly spheres, which lay in wait like so many ambushes. The adept had to use magic formulas and mystical signs in order to overcome them; and, on successfully negotiating these difficulties and dangers, appeared before God's throne, filled with awe at the divine glory majestically supreme over all. Singing played an essential role in this ascent, and the name of God was central in it. The shining King is "clothed in tissues woven by song." This ascent to the Merkabah is actually a jumping-off point for a mystical process. That is to say, it is also a descent into the inner being of the individual. Therefore the ones who practiced it were also called "those who descend into the Merkabah." They made a perilous journey. How risky it was thought to be is apparent in a story of four rabbis who traveled to God's throne. One died there, one became a heretic, one went mad, but the fourth "stepped into peace and ended in peace." This form of mysticism was therefore unsuitable for the masses. Yet it was not a fringe activity, peculiar to sectarian groups of initiates; even rabbis practiced it.

Culianu points out that Merkabah mysticism was prominent in apocalyptic literature and that this literature had a direct influence on the eighth-century account of a journey to heaven and back (*miraj*) and nocturnal journey (*isra*) made by Mohammed.

This, in turn, penetrated the Christian part of Spain and, in 1141, was taken to Cluny by the abbot Peter Venerabilis. After that, the Jewish and Arabic heavenly journeys encouraged the production of an extensive Christian literature of travels to the world beyond, culminating in the work of Dante. Whether authentic experiences underlay the latter is something that is open to doubt.[24]

---

[24] A very accurate translation of Dante's *Divine Comedy*, with useful notes, was made by the poet Longfellow. Tr. note.

Simultaneously with Throne mysticism there developed another form of mysticism aimed at penetrating the secrets of the Torah—the so-called "Creation mysticism." The main document for this is the *Book of Creation* (*Sepher Yetzirah*), dating from some time between the third and the sixth century.[25] Its inspiration is the idea that cosmic events must be seen as a gradual realization of God's name, the four letters YHWH. This form of mysticism would later come into prominence, especially in the Kabbalah.

PHILO OF ALEXANDRIA

There was a large Hellenized Jewish community in Alexandria. Philo belonged to its wealthiest section. His family was on friendly terms with the Roman Caesars. In 40 B.C., he led a delegation to the emperor Caligula to plead for Jews who were in revolt against the obligation to pay the emperor divine honors. Philo's whole life is characterized by a thoroughgoing attempt to reconcile and enrich Jewish tradition with Hellenism. He made this attempt from a mystical standpoint.

Philo knew mysticism from personal experience. He said he was not ashamed to share his experiences, and described these as a sudden ecstasy so overwhelming "that I have become greatly excited and have known neither the place in which I was, nor those who were present, nor myself, nor what I was saying, nor what I was writing. . . ."[26]

"A penetrating vision," "an insight that gives great joy," "light," "sober drunkenness," are some of the expressions he used. This vision is transitory and beyond all understanding. It is a glimpse of God even though His features cannot be distinguished. One stands with one's back to Him, but realizes that one is standing near Him. Whoever has had this experience has been initiated into the mysteries. In this connection, Philo referred to the initiates of the Dionysian mysteries. Their transports were not unlike his. His, however, was a purer inebriation. He read the

---

[25] Modern scholars may be interested in Aryeh Kaplan's work because it thoroughly researches *Sepher Yetzirah* (York Beach, ME: Samuel Weiser, 1990).
[26] Evelyn Underhill, *Mysticism: A Study in the Nature and Development of Man's Spiritual Consciousness* (New York: E. P. Dutton, 1930), p. 64.

Bible in the light of this insight. He looked for meaning that went deeper than the literal meaning. Thus, whenever something is said about a well, he sees it as describing what is within each one of us, the almost unattainable hidden in our depths. This mode of interpretation, known as allegorical (the discovery of the spirit in the letter), eventually became a school of interpretation.

Because of his mystical orientation, he recognized mystical overtones in Biblical figures such as Abraham, Moses, and the prophets. And in the narrative of the wandering of the children of Israel in the wilderness, he saw the way that has to be taken by the mystic. Those who set out and turn to God will find that God turns to them. Therefore Philo greatly respected a group of Jews, the Therapeutae, who went to live well outside the city in small houses they had built, subsisted on bread and salt, dressed in white garments, and devoted themselves wholly to contemplation. They did not suffer from distractions and were able to recover the unity in their own souls in order to be more dedicated to the "One." Philo himself looked back nostalgically to the period of solitude he once enjoyed before he had saddled himself with political tasks.

Prompted by his mystical insight, he also assimilated the concepts of Plato and of Stoicism, and reworked them to fit the currently accepted picture of the world and mankind.

He postulated that God is unapproachable and beyond all understanding, although He has announced Himself in history, in scripture, and in creation. This revealed God is the Logos, or Word. And the Logos is the Image in which God radiates His being. The whole of the Platonic "Ideas" were called "Logos" by Philo. The shining forth of the inaccessible God takes place strongly and immediately in the Logos, and in everything that is born of this Word in spirit. It takes place more weakly and indirectly in the material creation. Thus human beings are a duality. Their spirits are direct emanations from the Logos, and are flashes of the image of God. On the other hand, their bodies are only a faint ray of His creative power.

Philo was not like a fish out of water. It is obvious that he felt at home in the Hellenistic world, even as a Jew. For him, the way to God was to concentrate on the good and the beautiful. Yet he saw the physical and material as something from which one should turn away. The way to the "Unity" is the way within, with the "eye of the soul" averted from material things. What the contemplative has to guard against is putting a representation of God on a level with God, Himself. For when the soul that loves God looks into the nature of existence, it begins an invisible exploration. The most significant discovery will be that God is beyond our comprehension, and the most significant insight that He is unseeable.

JESUS OF NAZARETH

The greatest figure in turbulent Palestine before the destruction of Jerusalem was Jesus of Nazareth, who had been born into the family of a carpenter. He was amazingly open to everyone around him and to every living thing. At the same time, he always took a very personal view of them. He, himself, came from the circle of the Pharisees, who were lay-scribes belonging to the middle class and, in a certain sense, formed a bridge between the Hellenizing upper class and ordinary people. Jesus set himself against Pharisaism by taking, not the letter, but the spirit of the letter, as his starting point in interpreting the Scriptures. He had himself baptized by John the Baptist but, in contrast to the ascetic Essenes he "came eating and drinking." He prophesied the end of the age, but went against the Zealots by preaching non-violence, and against an attitude of expectation that was too passive by emphasizing the kingdom of God *now*, and what has to be done *now* in order to bring it nearer. And yet he raised expectations that the end would be ushered in by him. This persuaded the Romans to condemn him to death.

His ministry of three years started with a mystical experience, in which he saw "the Spirit of God" descend on him and heard the voice of God saying, "You are my beloved Son; in you I am well pleased." As mystics have often done, he withdrew into the desert to clarify the experience.[27] Not that he said anything about it, but his ministry itself reveals what the experience contained. He spoke as, and presented himself as, a perpetual "well of living water." His teaching was not based on external authority, but on his own authority: "I say unto you." He called the Reality he experienced and from whom he lived, not the Almighty, but Father. What had to be brought into being was his Father's king-

---

[27] . . . the spirit drives him into the wilderness (Mark 1:12).

dom; not in an arbitrary way, but because nothing else would do. The kingdom of the Father is outside us and inside us at one and the same time. Prayer is prayer only when we seek contact with the Father. Jesus used to retire to a quiet place for this purpose.

But the power of prayer was to be seen in action. "Who has seen me has seen the Father," he said. And it was clear that Jesus was not imitating anybody. His was a unique voice in debates with bystanders and enemies. He contacted people who made no claim to be very religious, and had a special care for those on the fringes of society, receiving them and healing them: people such as tax-farmers and sinners, women and children, and the sick, the frail, and the possessed; people who were shunned, like the lepers and the mentally ill, and those who were handicapped in their social contacts because they could not hear, see, talk, or walk. Jesus got in touch with them, restored their self-respect by publicly showing his regard for them, and healed them, in response to their cry, "Have mercy on us."

What is striking about Jesus is how ordinary, straightforward, and human he was. He praised the effortless growth of the lilies and the spontaneity of children. "Seek ye first the kingdom of God, and his righteousness; and all these things [i.e., the necessities of life] shall be added unto you," he said. There is no "must," no straining after piety, no parade of keeping the commandments. Whoever is in living contact with the Father knows inwardly what to do or not to do. He explained this attitude to life most clearly in the sermon on the mount, in which he calls for unqualified goodness without discrimination against anybody or shutting anybody out:

> That ye may be the children of your Father which is heaven: for he maketh his sun to rise on the evil and on the good, and sendeth rain on the just and on the unjust (Matthew 5:45).

What is more, he warns against doing good deeds "before men, to be seen of them." They should be done before your Father who sees in secret. He preaches a way of the spirit in place of the letter, of conversion in place of asceticism, of a pure heart in place of a craving for possessions or a hunger for power.

Nevertheless, Jesus lived wholly within the Jewish tradition. He himself realized that he was fulfilling it. According to him, the commandments in the Law of Moses are definitions of love. This love is grafted upon trust in the Father who created all things and will therefore be compassionate to all and everything. The endeavor to bring about a caring society has to come from within. God is not only within history but also within the life of each one of us in our common round and daily task. In renewing the tradition, Jesus answered the questions that, in his days, were on everyone's lips: From where do I come? Who can I trust? What is the meaning of my life?

Jesus' experience of the Father was not untested. He underwent trials, conflicts with his family, with his disciples, and with the religious leaders. He knew the death agony and the feeling of being abandoned by God. On the cross, his trust in God was challenged. In this situation, his union with the Father seems to defy all the conventions, as does his confidence in the primary basis of existence, which is like a father. Even when he felt forsaken by the Father, he committed his spirit into his Father's hands.

It was only after his death that the meaning became clear of Jesus' trust in life without any other security than his submission to the Father. First of all to the women who had believed in him. They found that Jesus had risen from the dead and that his spirit had survived. This was something quite new at that time. Deliverers who died and rose again were known; Osiris, for example. So were people who had become divine deliverers. Journeys to heaven were also popular concepts. But a savior of the world in whom God appears, whose life ends in rejection, failure, capital punishment, the death agony and being forsaken by God, but whose trust in God is not discredited by these things—such a deliverer was unique.

The first Jesus-communities reflected his brief but amazing appearances after his resurrection, and were convinced that the Spirit would teach them all things. The fruits of this initial awareness are the Gospels. They are not history books, but books about the historical Jesus as people had come to see him later.[28]

---

[28] Luke would probably deny this. He refers to the reports of eyewitnesses, and asserts that he himself had had "perfect understanding of all things from the very first." (See the start of Luke's Gospel). Tr. note.

PAUL OF TARSUS

Paul was a Jew born outside Palestine in cultured Tarsus. He was influenced by the Stoic climate of his native city, but educated in orthodox rabbinism in Jerusalem. He was open to Hellenistic culture, and thought that one should appropriate what was helpful while using discretion. "Prove all things; hold fast that which is good," he advised.

Paul was an ecstatic mystic, and describes how he was "caught up to the third heaven . . . into paradise" where he "heard words that cannot, and indeed must not, be translated into human speech."[29] This mystical experience remained engraved on his memory even though it had taken place more than "fourteen years ago." And he referred more than once to another ecstatic experience which had revolutionized his life. He was traveling to Damascus when "suddenly there shined round about him a light from heaven" (Acts 9:33). This literally blinded him and struck him to the ground like lightening. It was several days before he recovered. He heard Jesus speaking to him. Later on, while he was praying in the temple at Jerusalem, he was in a trance, and saw and heard Jesus again, although not so intensely. He realized who Jesus was, and that he, Paul, had to devote his life to him.

Paul sounds a note of warning on ecstatic experiences in which unintelligible sounds are uttered. To the Christians in Corinth who coveted spiritual gifts, he said that he speaks with tongues more than they do (I Corinthians 14). So he is not against the practice, but insists that it must be useful within the group and not get out of hand: members had to take their turn, and had to have an interpreter. Should none be present, they had to remain silent. Otherwise the "unlearned"[30] would think they were mad. He says of himself that it would not be profitable "except I shall speak to you either by revelation, or by knowledge [gnosis], or by prophesying, or by doctrine" (I Corinthians 14:6), in other words, unless he spoke plainly.

---

[29] J. B. Phillips, *The New Testament of Modern English* (Geoffrey Bles, 1960).

[30] The author translates Paul's word *idiotes* as "uninitiated," but it really means a private person or an uninstructed lay person (as here). If he had wanted to imply that Christians were initiates of a mystery cult, and that outsiders were uninitiates, he would have been more likely to use *atelestos* or *amuetos* for the latter. Tr. note.

Figure 55. This miniature is a composite of what in the original sixth-century Cosmography of Cosmas Indicopleustes was depicted in separate scenes: Saul of Tarsus is on the road to Damascus, is arrested by the vision, and so becomes the apostle Paul. The Cosmography is a very important book in the Byzantine picture of the world. It shows how Christendom was working out its own description of history and the universe. (Vatican City, MS. Bibl. Apost. Vaticana, Vat. Gr. 699, f. 83.)

In fact, he did speak plainly. Paul had a clear view of the human race, of history, of the cosmos, and of the place occupied in it by Jesus and those who have become "new creatures" in him. Jesus is the first of a new human race—"the firstborn among many brethren." As such, he is the "Lord's Anointed" (the Christ or Messiah) and the Church is his body. He is the Lord (*kurios*) of history, throned on high at the right hand of his Father "far above all principality, and power. . . ." In Paul's vision, not only humanity but also the cosmos was ruined by Adam's sin. The corruption was so total that nothing in humanity or the cosmos could salvage anything from the wreck. But salvation has now been achieved by the Christ, who came down from and has returned to heaven, who was born of a virgin and has suffered the deepest humiliation of death on a cross, saving us from sin by "being made a curse for us." In principle, the whole world has been redeemed by him. Redemption will be complete at his second coming, due to happen shortly. In preparation for it, believers must put off "the old man" and put on "a new man." In other words they must become people of a new type, living in Christ.

This vision fired Paul with a mission. He wanted to convert the known world quickly. In A.D. 49 he broke away from Judaism in its nationalistic aspect, visited the towns and cities of the vast empire, organized churches in them, and tried to reach everyone.

All were one in Christ Jesus—male and female, slave and master, Greek and Jew. The only difference was between those who were prepared to believe in Christ and those who were not. Why there were unbelievers was, for Paul, a mystery hidden in God. He was often attacked by Jews who clung to the Law, was threatened with death, and eventually was taken prisoner in Jerusalem. From there he was sent under armed guard to Rome; where, according to tradition, he was beheaded in A.D. 64.

The life in Christ as Paul preaches it in his epistles (letters) has a mystical character. It involves a process of transformation from a fleshly life to a spiritual life. Not in the Gnostic sense, as if the body were an evil thing from which the individual needs to become free, but in the sense of relinquishing a selfish mode of existence for one that is unselfish.

They that are Christ's have crucified the flesh with the affections and lusts [. . .] Walk in the Spirit and ye shall not fulfill the lust of the flesh. For the flesh doth desire contrary to the Spirit, and the Spirit contrary to the flesh.[31]

He refers to Christ as present in the Spirit, and speaks of being "in the Spirit" in the sense of: "I live; yet not I, but Christ liveth in me" (Galatians 2:20). He talks of the love of God which "is shed abroad in our hearts by the Holy Ghost which is given unto us" (Romans 5:5), and of being conformed to the image of his [God's] son [Jesus Christ]. Others of his expressions are: ". . . until Christ be formed in you" (Galatians 4:19), and: "the new man, which is renewed in knowledge after the image of him that created him: where. . .Christ is all, and in all" (Colossians 3:10,11). Paul also uses terms borrowed from the mysteries: "initiated," "secret," "insight." A Christian was given insight thus:

But we all, with unveiled face reflecting as a mirror the glory of the Lord, are transformed into the same image from glory to glory, even as from the Lord the Spirit.[32]

However, Paul's understanding of insight was not the Gnostic one of something that individuals discover inside themselves; it was of something bestowed in response to faith in the sense of trust. Trust in oneself was given in exchange for trust in God. Also insight did not determine the outlook on life. The core of morality was love: "all the law is fulfilled in one word, even in this; Thou shalt love thy neighbor as thyself" (Galatians 5:14).

This aspect is also central in the Gospel and epistles of Jesus' friend, the apostle John. He, too, at times, employs language that sounds mystical.

GOD IS LOVE; and whoever continues in love, dwells in God, and God in him . . . because love is from God; and everyone who loves is born from God, and knows God. He who does not love, does not know God; for GOD IS LOVE.[33]

---

[31] Galations 5. King James version for verses 24 & 16; Young's Literal Translation for verse 17. Tr. note.

[32] 2 Corinthians 3:18, Revised Version.

[33] 1 John 4:16 & 17. Ferrar Fenton's version, New York, 1919.

In the Gospel according to John, we read of Jesus saying:

> If a man love me, he will keep my words: and my Father
> will love him, and we will come unto him, and make
> our abode with him. [. . .] He that has seen me has seen
> the Father [. . .] the Father that dwells in me, he does the
> works. Believe that I am in the Father, and the Father in
> me; or else believe me for the very works' sake.[34]

Texts such as these, especially those that speak of being indwelt by
God and being born of God, lend themselves to the description of
mystical experiences, and they were used for this purpose in later
Christian mysticism.

Paul and John follow Jesus with a mysticism that is oriented
toward love in action and the mutual unity of human beings.
They differ from him, however, by displaying a fairly strong
Hellenistic influence in their thinking. Their outlook on life is pessimistic; they see a tragic transient existence on earth, in a world
and cosmos that is thoroughly corrupt. Their world-picture is vertical. Jesus descended into the lower parts of the earth, and then
ascended on high, far above all heavenly beings at the right hand
of God. The highest world is Light, the earth is Darkness. "That
was the true Light [the Word made flesh] which lighteth every
man that cometh into the world. He was in the world, and the
world was made by him, and the world knew him not (John
1:9,10). This was a realm of thought that Gnosticism was able to
invade. Paul, and John in particular, were well aware of this. They
rejected the Gnosis that claimed to be superior to love, and warned
against those who (on the grounds that the flesh is evil) were
denying that Jesus Christ had come in the flesh. Nevertheless it
was a long time before Christianity and Gnosticism were disen-
gaged. The Gnostic answer to life's problems held a fascination for
Christians and, although it was vigorously attacked, it kept on
raising its head because of the mystical vein running through
Christendom. But the ecclesiastical authorities were obviously
worried that the survival of the Church was threatened by loosely
worded formulations of a Gnostic sort.

---

[34] John 14:23, 9 & 10-11. King James version slightly modernized.

HELLENISTIC MYSTICISM

"Here the worshippers of Serapis are also Christians, and those who call themselves bishops worship Serapis too. Here there is no Jewish synagogue leader, no Samaritan, no Christian priest, who is not an astrologer, haruspex, and anointer." This is taken from a letter written by the emperor Hadrian to the consul Servianus. It refers to Alexandria.

At the beginning of the second century, Alexandria was a melting pot into which everything had been thrown—old Egyptian religions, the deliberately invented Serapis mystery cult, new Greek and ancient Persian religions, Judaism, Christianity, and Gnosticism. In addition to religion there were philosophy, science, and sport. The unification then attempted is known as "syncretism." The different religions did not oppose one another but tried to grow nearer to one another. In ancient Egypt the rationale behind this syncretism was a deep-rooted political determination to unify the country. Pharaoh Akhenaton (ca. 1358 B.C.) tried to unify it by imposing unity of belief in one God, but everything he achieved was ferociously destroyed after his death.

In Alexandria a mystical attitude gave added impetus to the political motive for syncretism. The mystics said that, as the One is unknowable, all images of God are mere hints at his nature, although they may serve to supplement one another. One of the questions arising out of a mystical experience is: how solid is sensory reality? When a reality has been experienced that is "more real" than everyday reality, there is a tendency to interpret the spiritual reality as the source of the material world. Material reality becomes, as it were, transparent, an image of the spiritual, and capable of being changed by the spirit. Unity has to be reached "in the spirit." All forms are then relative. Mysticism is prone to take on board a great deal—even things that are apparently antithetic. All the older mystical writings are sheaves of very discrepant texts, which are connected at some more or less undivulged deeper level.

At Alexandria this mystical attitude was perceptible in everything. Philo stated that mystical experience gave a deeper insight into reality than that given by knowledge. Alexandria was a noted center for the exact sciences, but mystical "insight" was regarded more highly there. However, it was not seen as being in conflict with knowledge. This was the prevailing attitude in religious matters, too. The holy scriptures were "spiritualized" by the Jews and Christians who read them. The concrete forms of religion were compared, and interpreted in terms of the mystical insight. Christians with leanings toward Gnosticism queried the ecclesiastical institutions, and declared that a choice had to be made between building up the church by the spirit and building it up by ritual, a settled organization, and hard doctrine.

Alexandria and Rome were antipodes. Both were crucibles of change, but in Rome a genius for organization and in Alexandria a mystical genius was at work. This is something of an exaggeration, because the battle lines were not quite so clear, and it was a long time before the two came into open conflict and Rome won. We shall now give a few examples showing how some Christians used Gnosticism to reach the most radical conclusions opposed to the specifically monotheistic structure of the church; and how the same mystical attitude in others matured in a way that had a decisive influence, even on the Church of Rome.

GNOSTICISM AND CHRISTENDOM

One of the most important documents of Christian Gnosticism has been preserved because Hippolytus of Rome quotes it in order to refute it. His citations were recently analyzed and reconstructed by Josef Frickel.[35] The document now seems to be a basic pagan text that was adapted by a Christian who interpreted all religions in terms of Christ. It is called *Concerning Man* and its object is to answer the question of man's doubts about man. We find all religious movements represented in it. The fundamental idea of this work is that God is the "Unknown" who arouses a great longing. He is sought by all people, whatever their religion. Christ revealed him as the Father and is the way to him. This document was later reworked in Gnostic terms by a disciple of Valentinus.

Other Gnostic writings take the form of apostolic epistles or profess to be words spoken by Jesus during the forty days between his resurrection and his ascension. Also there were teachers and scholars in Alexandria who tried to frame an exhaustive scheme of reality from a Gnostic viewpoint. The first exegesis of

---

[35] Josef Frickel, *Hellenistische Erlosung in christlicher Deutung, Die gnostische Naasenerschrift* [A Christian view of Hellenistic Salvation, the Gnostic Naasene Writings]. (Leiden, 1984).

Figure 56. The catholic Church sees Gnosticism as a temptation and a danger. Simon Magus became increasingly singled out as "the father of Gnosticism" and a symbol of menace. The way in which his fall is depicted on a 12th-century capital in the cathedral of Autun speaks for itself. (Photo: Bildarchiv Foto Marburg.)

the Bible was that of Basilides who had a school in Alexandria. What Philo had already done with the Jewish Bible was continued here: the Gospels and Paul's epistles were read as mystical texts and strong emphasis was laid on the mysticism of Jesus, Paul, and John.

One of the most authoritative Gnostic teachers in Alexandria was Valentinus. He founded a school and later went to Rome. We have no reason to believe that he was treated as a heretic there. He was even a candidate for the papacy, although he never became pope. He was a gifted man—a mystic and a poet. After receiving a classical education in Alexandria, he converted to Christianity. It is possible that the reason for this change was an experience similar to that of St. Paul: a vision in which Christ appeared. Valentinus saw him as a newborn child who revealed himself as the "Logos," and he spent the rest of his life elaborating his vision poetically. He regarded this newborn child as a symbol of the birth of the Logos in God as follows: the "Deep" rested in "Silence" (Sige),[36] in which He planted the "Thought" (Ennoia) of creation like a seed. "Silence " bore "Mind," who in her turn was fertilized by "Self-reflection" and so bore "Logos." This process was envisaged as continuing up to and including the birth of Jesus. Such speculations weary us now, but they fitted in well with the philosophical notions of their times. More radical was the scale of values that Valentinus applied in judging genuine reality.[37] The spiritual individual stood at the top of the ladder, the fleshly [hylic] individual at the bottom. Between them stood the psychical individual. When applied to Christianity, this meant three sorts of church: the spiritual church made up of perfected and elect ones, the soulish church of those who have been called, and the fleshly church of the great majority who are past saving.

The strength of the Christian Gnostics lay in the fascinating way they talked about a mystical core of the Bible. Their weakness was an inability to equate this mysticism with what others saw as "the hard facts." So they turned the church into a place for the elite, and then started deleting any texts from the Gospels that did not suit them. Finally they rejected the Old Testament [the Hebrew Scriptures] too, as a mendacious account in which the evil demiurge was represented as the good God.

The two greatest teachers in Alexandria, both of whom steered clear of these rocks without jettisoning mysticism, were Clement and his pupil Origen. They taught at the earliest known school for Christian catechumens. In both, the perfected individual is a Gnostic, someone with mystical insight and a likeness to God. They said that spirit and body are two different realities, the body being a covering of the spirit, and that there are two sorts of church member, spiritual and fleshly. They treated mysticism as a higher form of the human condition. Whereas the mystic "is

---

[36] The author equates *Ennoia* with "Silence," but the Greek for "Silence" is *Sige*; *Ennoia* is "Thought" (see Vol. II, Chap. IX of *Forerunners and Rivals of Christianity*, by F. Legge, Columbia University Press, 1915; reprinted by Peter Smith, New York, 1950. Legge gives a slightly different list of emanations). Tr. note.

[37] It seems, however, to have been variant of what the Gnostic Ophites had taught, namely that "the soul of man consisted of three parts corresponding to the three worlds, that is to say, the pneumatic, psychic, and earthly. . . [to] attain to the light. . . [the] soul must first pass from choice to psychic, and thence to pneumatic" (Legge, op.cit., Vol. II, chap. VIII). Tr. note.

always praying internally," others simply say their prayers at certain times. But this does not mean that the masses will not be saved; on the contrary, Origen sees in a great vision that God is doing His utmost to bring all things back to Himself, and that His purpose will be achieved when the cycle comes to an end. Then everyone, even the evil spirits, will be saved.

A mystical experience centered on Christ was not too difficult at this time. Had not Paul talked of the Spirit of Christ and John of His pre-existence as the Logos? The human spirit does not belong to this world of Spirit and Logos, but is born outside it. In Clement's exposition, the man Jesus who became Christ remains rather shadowy. He is a teacher: the logos who from God became human in order that this human should teach you how you can become God.

After the martyrdom of his father, Origen was brought up with a Gnostic by a wealthy lady. He, himself, died of tortures inflicted because he was a Christian. He was a versatile man with a persuasive turn of speech and he had a passion for combining things such as Gnostic belief and Christian belief, the church of the perfected ones and the church of the people, Christ as the Logos and the historical Jesus, mysticism and knowledge, gnosis and love, love and responsibility for others. He holds an important place in the history of mysticism because he was the first to treat the Jewish "Song of Solomon" as a description of the mystical union of the soul and the Logos, and the mystical path an intense love affair in which everything "fleshly" has to be burned away. He speaks from personal experience:

> God is my witness that I have been often aware of the coming of the Bridegroom and that He has been as close as possible to me. Then He has withdrawn suddenly and I have been unable to find what I sought. I long for His coming and sometimes He returns. Then, after He has come, and it is as if I could take hold of Him with my hands, He departs; and, when He has disappeared, I go in search of Him once more. He does this frequently, until I really grasp Him and ascend, leaning on my Beloved.[38]

---

[38] Translation mine. Tr.

The Gnostic movement, as such, was gradually outflanked and overcome by Christianity. Christendom developed a more powerful organization with a central hierarchy, and kept honing the formulation of doctrine so that deviations could more easily be identified and rejected. The canonical New Testament books were distinguished from all the others, which were apocryphal. Of course, Gnostic elements were fitted into this framework by such people as Clement and Origen. On the other hand, Gnosticism sailed more and more under the Church's colors, but ran aground on dogmatism and libertine morals that no longer had any relevance to experience itself. Nevertheless, it has certainly been a lasting influence on Christian mysticism.

The mystical impulse was preserved not only by Christians, such as Clement and Origen, but especially by two non-Christians—Plotinus and Mani. Both cleared the ground of rubbish and built something new on it. One came from Alexandria, the other from Babylon. It is said that they met beside the Euphrates in 243, when the emperor Gordianus III gave battle to the Persian monarch Sapor. Plotinus was a friend of Gordianus and wanted to go to the East. Mani was a protégé of Sapor and wanted to go to the West.

PLOTINUS

The Egyptian, Plotinus, studied in Alexandria for most of his life. He had a predilection for Plato and the Stoa, and also for Gnosticism, but felt that something essential was lacking in everything he examined: he could not find a convincing answer to a question that had arisen from an intense mystical experience and had haunted him all his life. He worded it like this:

> Often when I awake from the body to myself and step from otherness into myself, I behold a most wondrous beauty. It is then that I believe most strongly in my belonging to a higher destiny. . . . I don't know how it can be that the soul once got into my body, considering what the soul is in itself, as it has now revealed itself to me even though I am in the body.[39]

---

[39] Plotinus, as stated in *The Enneads IV: 8:I* in Martin Buber's, *Ecstatic Confessions*, edited by Paul Mendes-Flohr (San Francisco: HarperCollins, 1985), p. 32.

Figure 57. Plotinus was a shy man, somewhat asthmatic. He had a hoarse voice and a weak stomach; his discourses are rambling. He was worried by the religious-emotional chaos in the Roman Empire and conferred with the Roman administrators about it (even the emperor heard him with respect). He cured Porphyry of a deep depression that had bordered on the suicidal. This is the best likeness of him. He lived very soberly, "as if he were ashamed to be found in a body." (Bust carved in 255 by the sculptor Carterius, in accordance with a description given by Plotinus' pupil Amelius. The American Academy, Rome.)

We think of it as the connection between mystical self-awareness and the self-consciousness of everyday life, between the "true I" and the ego, but Plotinus did not have this terminology at his disposal. He had an idea that he would find the answer in the East, which is why he wished to accompany the army of Gordianus III.

The expedition was a failure and he did not return to Alexandria, but settled in Rome, purchased a large villa, and invited all sorts of people to come and discuss this central problem with him: do we live in an alien world into which we have "strayed," or have we a meaningful task to perform here? Are what we do and refrain from doing determined from outside, or do we live from within as responsible individuals? Is the path to human completeness something for the elect, or can anybody travel on it? In his rather chaotic discussions—he goes into all the interruptions—he obviously clarified his thinking. After his death, his student Porphyry wrote an account of what had been said, and has also left us a description of his teacher's person and life. He issued the collected writings of Plotinus in the form of books. From these it can be seen that Plotinus came very close to Eastern mysticism as expressed in the Upanishads. Indeed, some people think he must have read the latter, but there is no proof of this. It is true that the Hellenistic world was full of itinerant yogis known as "gymnosophists" (naked philosophers), but nothing indicates that Plotinus knew any of the Eastern texts. It would seem that his formulation of mysticism, although similar to the one found in the latter, was made independently.

Plotinus sees the mystic way as an ascent to a higher world through spiritualization; but at the same time, and more often, as an entry into oneself in search of the center of one's being—which coincides with the center of all things. He said that we should retire into ourselves and remove anything superfluous, so that the divine light can make its appearance, and we become one with ourself in purity. He regarded the center of the soul as coinciding with the center of the All—the Atman and Brahman of Hindu mysticism.

The strength of Plotinus lay in the fact that he tested Platonic knowledge and Stoic sobriety in the laboratory of mystical experience, and also tested Gnostic mysticism by pure critical reasoning. In this way, he arrived at a systematic doctrine in which mysticism and rational thought agree, and the chief virtues of Hellenism come into their own. This parting shot of Hellenistic culture exerted a powerful influence (in the form of neoplatonism) on the thought and mysticism of Western Europe, mainly because St. Augustine and pseudo-Dionysius took their stand on it.

Plotinus had much in common with the Gnostics, but distanced himself from them when he encountered them in Rome. He even wrote a treatise *Against the Gnostics* with the revealing subtitle: *Against those who Assert that the Creator of the World Order is Malicious and that this World is Evil.*

Plotinus possessed artistic talent and appreciated beauty. So he was appalled when Gnostics spurned beauty, even though he agreed with them that the earth is imperfect, unsatisfying, and temporal. He regarded their teachings as willful blindness to the harmony of creation. Like them, he thought that everything issues from a single source and that this source is unknowable; being called the One, the Good, and God, simply for reference purposes. Yet he sets himself against their fantastic mythologies purporting to show how everything came forth from the One. Going back to Plato, he pared this mythology down to a simple reference to the flowing of the Spirit out of the One and of the World-Soul out of the Spirit. Plotinus made a point of comparing the mysticism of the Gnostics with their deeds. He showed how they cheated. What stung him more than anything else was their arrogance. They looked on themselves as elect mystics, and said that mysticism was suitable only for their group; outsiders were beyond the pale. What is more, they were outrageous know-it-alls. In the end he threw them out of his villa, saying, "It is hopeless trying to persuade them to change their minds. [. . .] They suppose that everything is as they think." Abjuring their brand of self-importance, Plotinus explained in detail his view that the mystic way is open to all who wish to tread it; and he thought it right to indicate this way.

Plotinus was fond of using the illustration of the midpoint. Consider a universe with the Sun at its center, and eliminate the Sun while keeping the light-source. Each being, including each man and woman, is a universe of this sort. The midpoint in each thing is the same creative Spirit. Everything flows from this Spirit and everything has a tendency to become one with the One again. This tendency is a cosmic stream, an impulse, a cosmic eros, which Plotinus also calls insight. Thus, for him, mystical insight is not something that has to be bestowed, it is a discovery of what everything is. It is not an intellectual pursuit, but obedience to the deepest law of nature: an ardent desire to be at one with existence and so to become complete. Whoever goes this way and becomes complete will burn with love for all things just because they *are*.

MANI

When he was 12 years old, Mani had an experience that made a deep impression on him. He understood that he must test this insight within the sect his father had joined. This was a Christian sect, with its own rules concerning diet and ritual washing, which were said to go back through the Gnostic Elchasius to Jesus himself. He became a member of the sect but reached the conclusion that its pretentions were false. His argument was that the purity to which Jesus referred was really purity by Gnosis. He also gave a wider meaning to the belief in a constantly returning deliverer, and declared that he himself, Mani, was such a deliverer: the latest "apostle of the Light" in a long line of prophets. But the sect did not consider that he was another Jesus, or Zoroaster, or Buddha. After another visionary experience, Mani left the sect and retired to a cave for a year. He emerged with a book in which he had drawn, rather than written, what had been revealed to him. He became a fanatical missionary, taking the apostle Paul as his inspiration. Like Paul, Mani traveled through the known world, from the Indus valley to the far-flung borders of the Roman Empire. He won many disciples of high rank, but faced fierce opposition from fanatical Zoroastrian priests. In 276, he was charged with heresy, imprisoned, and after twenty-six days, put to death.

Mani had the notion of founding a new universal religion that would include all that went before it and would incorporate features found in the teachings of Zoroaster, Buddha, and Jesus; all in the line of Gnostic mysticism. He set out from the pessimistic dualism peculiar to Gnosticism, and was essentially interested in Gnosis. Mystical insight sheds light in darkness, rescues spirit from matter and opens the road to paradise. From Zoroastrianism, Mani adopted Ahriman, the Darkness fought by the Light, and also the idea of a historical process in which the struggle between Light and Darkness takes place. He envisaged three phases in this process, so his doctrine was called "the doctrine of the two principles and three periods." From Buddha, he borrowed karma, the

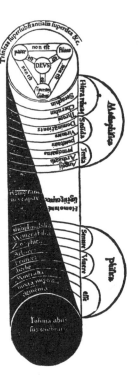

Figure 58. A drawing that illustrates the cosmology of pseudo-Dionysius as seen by Nicholas of Cusa. The radiant Triune God creates by letting His light flow out downwards. As creation descends further, the light decreases, and darkness—the reverse of the light—increases. This dualistic picture of the universe formed the basis of Christian Gnosticism, Manicheism, and Catharism. (Woodcut from the edition of the *Mystical Theology* of pseudo-Dionysius by Jean Eck in 1519. He himself borrowed it from an edition of *De coniecturis* by Nicholas of Cusa.)

cycle of rebirths evaded only by turning into the self. All this he elaborated in fantastic visionary mythologies, his basic idea being that the now fragmented Light is imprisoned everywhere in matter. The Evil Spirit wants to swallow these sparks in the Darkness. The Redeemers of the Light make every effort to gather it out of matter and take it to the Realm of Light. Because the desire for redemption is continually obscured by the binding of Light to matter, people will always need exhorting to seek enlightenment. For this purpose, deliverers are constantly being sent out to preach "Gnosis." Men and women being what they are, the individual is unlikely to be "perfected" during a single reincarnation unless he or she finds the way inwards[40] and is spiritualized to become

---

[40] It is interesting to find this concept mistakenly regarded as an innovation by the Rev. Benjamin Holloway back in 1751, when it became the subject of his ire: "Trees have been their Oracles, and Schools of Science, in the Main, till our Times; wherein some have chang'd the old Object and old Method of seeking to acquire Knowledge by a Tree or Stock, for one if possible, yet more Brutish and wicked; I mean, by setting up to find it within Themselves." *Originals Physical and Theological, Sacred and Profane*, Vol. I (Oxford, 1751, p. 27.) Tr. note.

Figure 59. These two paintings on a temple banner belonging to Manichaeans in Turkestan reveal how Mani's message was spread: it was reproduced in the local artistic language. Because it was adaptable, Manichaeism penetrated far into the East. In 742-840, it was the state religion of Turkestan. Women held an honored place in it. Here we see a man and a woman on equal terms as "chosen ones." Each is holding a book as a sign of wisdom. (Sections of a temple banner from Knocho, Turkestan, 19th century. Public Museums of the Prussian Cultural Heritage, Berlin: The Museum of Indian Art.)

pure light, and able to collect light from any sparks struck from matter. At the end of the ages, all the sparks of light will have been released from matter. Matter, itself, will then sink back into the Darkness. Mani differed from Zoroaster in supposing that the separation of good and evil is also the separation of the material and spiritual worlds.

Mani's strength lay not in his convoluted mythology, but in the simplicity of his options: matter is evil, spirit is good; therefore choose spirit. He placed human beings in three classes: the Just, who lived ascetic spiritual lives and were liberated from matter; the Hearers, who were prepared to live in the spirit yet still resided in the world either willingly or of necessity; and the Sinners, who were not amenable to the spirit and were therefore predestinated to eternal Darkness.

Mani was very artistic[41] and he attached great importance to imagery. At the same time, he knew how to relativize forms. He founded monasteries where books were made and art was practiced. He illustrated his visions himself and also composed hymns. This artistic activity was meant to extract sparks of light from refractory matter. He created his own script in order to have a neutral basis for his preachers, and he told them to clothe his message in the forms and languages of the countries to which they went. The murals—discovered in the oasis of Turfan in Central Asia—are not different from the Buddhist murals as far as their form goes. On the other hand, Mani himself made a list of his authentic writings, to avoid forgeries being fathered on him as the Gnostics had tried to father forgeries on Jesus.

Manichaeism was stoutly resisted by Christianity. Its dualism was seen as too pessimistic, and as an oversimplification into the bargain. Its most intelligent adversary was St. Augustine, who, in his young days, had been a "Hearer" in a Manichaean community. But he retained some of the pessimism and predestination, and these have come down in a diluted form to modern times. Contempt for the body resulted in a piety that is rather leaden.

---

[41] Hans-Joachim Klimkeit, *Manichaean Art and Calligraphy, Iconography of Religions,* XX (Leiden, 1982), p. 5.

THE MYSTICAL RETREAT

When the Byzantine Empire took over from Hellenism, mysticism no longer occupied a central position in cultural life. The attempt made by the Gnostics (in particular) to give mysticism this centrality had run out of steam. The emphasis was now placed on devotion to Christ's Majesty and, on a lower level, to the imperial might around which the culture crystallized. Court theologians—like Eusebius—provided a doctrinaire basis for it, and artists created a new iconography. Those who were mystically inclined abandoned society and moved to the fringe of the cultural area to live as recluses. Inspired by the "desert fathers," they set up "cloisters" outside the towns—self-contained units in which a community could flourish without interference from church and state, and where mysticism could be encouraged in accordance with the principles laid down by Jesus in The Sermon on the Mount. These refugees continued to look on mysticism as the highpoint of human life. Even the townsfolk saw them as specially gifted and sought them out.

Simon Stylites, who sat on top of a pillar near Antioch, was consulted by hundreds of town-dwellers, even on medical matters. "God's fool" Andreas came along and wandered round the city of Constantinople, being taken seriously as a fool. The liturgical calendar of the Roman Church still honors thirty-six similar simple souls. Because of this appreciation, the monastic system was able to reject established society in an acceptable way. It functioned as a critical spur, and thus performed an extremely useful role. At least, it did so in the good days when mystical inspiration was alive and well.

The withdrawal of the mystics from society began in Egypt, when St. Anthony (251-356), at age 20, went to live on the outskirts of his town, Koma, and then retired further and further into the desert. He was inspired by the words of Jesus to the rich young ruler: "If thou will be perfect, go and sell that thou hast, and give to the poor, and thou shalt have treasure in heaven: and come and follow me" (Matthew 19:21); also by the fact that the early Christians actually did this.

From *The Life of St. Anthony the Great* by St. Athanasius, it appears that St. Anthony was as strongly motivated by disgust at the softness of society. He wished to embrace martyrdom in a

Figure 60. Hermitages sprang up in the Egyptian desert and spread as far as Turkey. The hermits hollowed out many cave dwellings in the mountains of Goreme in Cappadocia. These may still be seen. (Photo: ABC-Press Service, Amsterdam.)

Figure 61. The first hermits were not Westerners, but Buddha and his followers. Hermits' cave dwellings on both sides of a huge Buddha, in the mountains near Bamiyan in Afghanistan. (Photo: Robert Harding Picture, London)

Figure 62. Simeon Stylites, the first saint to live on top of a pillar, is shown sitting on a column that is in the coils of a serpent, the symbol of sin and temptation. (Gold plate from a fifth century Syrian shrine. The Louvre, Paris.)

new way. He fought with demons and discovered that these also had their good side, and that the battle was really with himself. St. Anthony had many followers, both men and women. They aimed to live a perfect life through strict asceticism in solitary hermitages; sometimes with a few disciples, sometimes immured, and sometimes in colonies sheltering in caves and grottos. They spent their time learning Biblical texts, in prayer, and weaving baskets for sale in the city. In summer they would often leave their cells to work as hired hands in the harvest.

Theirs was an alternative lifestyle in religion, too. They shunned the endless theological disputes of the Gnostics and later of the Christians, and would not speculate even on mysticism. Instead of teaching some special way of becoming one with God, they exerted themselves and concentrated on doing. They aimed at a mode of life in which the sole authority was that of the charisma: experience, love, and wisdom; in which all were equal without some who were successful imposing on others who were not. They received many town-dwellers hospitably, and kept in touch in order to learn from one another. But they have left no written records, and no teachings—only stories.

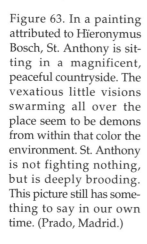

Figure 63. In a painting attributed to Hïeronymus Bosch, St. Anthony is sitting in a magnificent, peaceful countryside. The vexatious little visions swarming all over the place seem to be demons from within that color the environment. St. Anthony is not fighting nothing, but is deeply brooding. This picture still has something to say in our own time. (Prado, Madrid.)

The first cloister was founded in 320 in Tabennisi on the Nile by Pachomius (286-346). By the time he died there were, around Tabennisi, some nine thousand monks in eight monasteries, besides the nuns in two convents. An enormous concourse, which confirmed what Pachomius had guessed, namely that a solitary life was not suited to everybody and that there must also be an opportunity for people to live communally like the apostles—but well away from the influence of the city. Afterward, Basil of Caesarea (330-379) built monasteries in Cappadocia, closer to the city and more involved in the community. Within the cloister walls, social work, such as caring for children, orphans, and the sick, was carried out. He was led to adopt this policy after seeing monastic life in Palestine ruined by ego trips, ascetic exhibitionism, and a lack of love for others.

The first hermit to write books was Evagrius of Pontus (346-399). From his writings, we can infer how repose was cultivated.

Those who practiced it sought holiness and completeness as human beings through a "state of stillness" (hesychia) in which it was possible to experience God. This condition of rest is said to occur when an individual becomes inwardly free from all passions (the "apatheia" sought by the Stoics). In this stillness, one can be continually occupied with God in the deepest ground of the soul, which was created in the image of God and was therefore designed to see God.

The thought resurfaces in the "Cappadocian fathers," especially in Gregory of Nyssa; his doctrine being an extension of the Hellenistic view that God is unknowable. Nothing can be said about Him; and yet He can be experienced in the ground of the soul, where the spirit is free from all passions. Unlike his predecessors, Gregory emphasized the transcending of one's own being. The mystic is taken up into God more and more, but never permanently, for the true vision of God embraces the knowledge that whoever looks for Him never ceases to desire Him. Gregory did not come to this conclusion with the help of Christian dogma, but by analyzing the mystical experience, itself, insofar as this ultimately passes all understanding. He said that the more you catch sight of God, the more clearly will you see that, in Himself, He is invisible. Only when you have an experience, do you recognize that you have seen God. In other words, only when you have the experience do you know that the essentially divine transcends all experience and understanding.

In contrast to Gnostic mysticism, monastic mysticism was characterized by optimism and joy, although tears flowed freely, too. Even Gregory liked to see the world and the cosmos as a ray from the Christ-Logos.

This monastic mysticism, which was simultaneously Stoic, Neoplatonic, and Christian, with a strong emphasis on the ineffability of God, the inaccessibility of His being, and the constant lack of fulfillment of our longing for unity, this mysticism took shape in the book of pseudo-Dionysius that had such a great influence on the West as I discussed in our first chapter.

The Hesychast method is still practiced in Eastern monasticism, especially on Mt. Athos in Greece. It has a certain similarity to yoga. The body is kept still, the gaze is directed inward, and the thoughts are made to descend from the brain to the heart. A short, powerful sentence, such as the Jesus prayer ("Lord Jesus, Son of

God, have mercy on me"), is repeated over and over again to the rhythm of the breath.[42]

Monasticism was introduced to the West by John Cassianus (360-430). He stayed with monks in Palestine and Egypt, described their mode of life and collected many conversations with desert fathers. He died in Marseille. Benedict of Norcia (480-547) then did a great deal to promote Western monasticism. His instructions are still observed. He said we must preserve harmony in the life of a simple community, seen as a family, separate from society, self-supporting, and with no interests outside its walls. The monastery is a school for "seekers after God" under the headship of a father (abbas, or abbot).

St. Augustine (354-430), too, created resorts for mysticism. He is a figure who summed up the past and, at the same time, laid a basis for the future. He was strongly influenced both by Mani and Plotinus. He was a mystic and a pastor; he held an important position in the Church, but remained a monk at heart. He wrote a rule for clerics who wished to realize an ideal communal life in accordance with the Sermon on the Mount, a life that is not normally possible in the present state of society, but a new form of living together, outside society and against the flow. According to his rule, alternative relationships have to be created in which authority does not depend on might, but is a benevolent service in which one is more loved than feared. This is what is expected of those who desire to become monks. St. Augustine describes the latter as those who are called "monks" who, through their united gathering, become, as it were, *monos* (or a single entity), possessing only one heart and one soul in God.

What had come into existence on the margins of society became in Western Europe a center of culture when the Roman Empire was overrun by the barbarians. In an uncivilized environment culture was preserved in the cloisters. Only the cloisters housed libraries of ancient manuscripts, and supplied education, scholarship, and medical care. They offered military protection to travelers, reclaimed land, and were the only places with a stable economy. The monasteries were populated with the sons of

---

[42] For further details, see *The Power of the Name, the Jesus Prayer in Orthodox Spirituality*, by Bishop Kallistos of Diokleia, SLG Press, Oxford, 1977. According to this booklet, these techniques are used today. Tr. note.

nobles and of barbarians, with rich and poor, and with the clever and the stupid. The communal life of so many disparate individuals was possible only through "righteousness," that is to say, not through everyone receiving equal shares, but through everyone receiving his due: "according to the measure of each one's need," "without respect of persons," and "supporting the weak." The yardstick was the individual, and a middle way was taken between, for example, the extremes of work and prayer, both of which are valuable in the eyes of God. The word "pax" (peace) stood over the gateway. Monasteries were sheltered plots and it was felt that behind their walls lay an earthly paradise.

Within their precincts, the recluse could savor something of the glory of God in the heavenly Jerusalem.[43] This was also cultivated as a desire. "They eat hungrily without ceasing and while eating never cease to hunger," said Petrus Damianus (1007-1072). The desire is as if the person is "touched by pangs of love," expressing themselves in "sighs" and in the "gift of tears."

WESTERN EUROPE

When the centuries of misery that Western Europe had endured from foreign marauders and invaders finally came to an end, a new culture arose there very abruptly. It sprang out of the ground, so to speak, around the year 1000. Almost everyone (90 percent of the population) made a living from the land in one way or another. Those who owned land were also able to get people to work on it or to defend it. The latter—the serfs—were entitled to sustenance and protection in exchange for their servitude. Nearly 70 percent of the people were serfs. Even those who became monks promised "stabilitas loci" (to stay put). Each person was tethered to the place where he or she lived.

All at once, around A.D. 1000, this static, fragmented, barbarian Europe became a turbulent, rapidly developing cultural area, full of initiative. A breakthrough occurred due to something that

---

[43] See the 12th century *De Contemptu Mundi* by Bernard of Cluny, on which J. Mason Neale based the famous hymn "Jerusalem the Golden," which he included in his *The Rhythm of Bernard de Marlai on the Celestial Country*, 7th ed., London, 1865. Tr. note.

had been in the air for quite a long time: a new mentality characterized by a strong awareness of personal responsibility, and owing much to Irish missionaries who, in the eighth century, had managed to convince the peasants that trees and other plants are not inhabited by spirits and that, therefore, they would not be offending any spirits by encroaching on nature. The sense of responsibility was further strengthened by the auricular confession introduced by these monks: absolution after the confession of one's sins privately to a fellow man. This was something unheard-of and unlawful at that time. The Church knew only public confession once in the life.

The success of the Irish monks meant that the peasantry set out to make nature productive with technical implements without feeling guilty. Difficulties were seen as problems that human beings had to solve while taking full responsibility for what they did and did not do.

Out of this attitude arose the culture that surfaced in the 11th century. One of the first inventions was a new kind of plow. Longer strips of land were necessary if full advantage was to be taken of this invention. And so woods and wastelands were reclaimed and swamps were drained. The harvests were strikingly improved and there were fewer famines. Surplus produce was sold elsewhere. Annual fairs required an extensive network of roads. As the peasants increased in numbers, many of them migrated to the cities to avoid being tied to the land, and built up new industries there. These industries were powered by natural energy sources, which turned windmills and waterwheels. Trade developed at the same time. All this is described in detail by L. White in his studies of the relationship between religion and technology in the Middle Ages.[44] It seems from his research that a technical approach by the North European peasantry in particular formed the basis of the new culture that arose in the eleventh century and lasted through the sixteenth century. Our modern "technical culture" has not dropped from the skies.

Also of great importance for European culture was the initiative of the monks at Cluny who established themselves as

---

[44] Lynn White, Jr. *Medieval Religion and Technology* (Berkley: University of California, 1978). For a critical review of this standpoint, see A. Verhulst's, "De zogenaamde agrarische revolutie van de middeleeuwen" [The So-called Agrarian Revolution of the Middle Ages], in *Spiegel Historiael*, 1988, nr. 5, pp. 239-243.

Figure 64. The abbey of Cluny. (Woodcut of 1481 from Werner Rolewinck, *Fasciculum Temporum*.)

exempt, that is to say, not subordinate to bishops or temporal rulers. They placed themselves under the direct authority of the pope and recognized no borders. That was in 909. A century later, there were more than eleven hundred exempt cloisters scattered throughout Europe and linked together by a single authority, and, in a physical sense, by roads. It is no accident that all the great pilgrim ways passing abbeys ran from Cluny. These abbeys afforded protection and shelter to the increasing numbers of laymen who went through the whole of Europe on pilgrimage.

The contribution made by Cluny was that a stagnant Europe became full of movement and also that a single central authority emerged which knew no frontiers within the European area. Naturally, political control was seized in Western Europe by this central authority; so it is hardly surprising that religion, too, underlay the new culture. There was an intense desire to establish a single commonwealth of the Christian faithful, and to build Jerusalem on earth.

BUILDING THE CITY OF GOD

In the 11th century, the memory of Charlemagne, the man who had unified Western Europe for a brief period, was still fresh. He resided in Aachen and lived from 742 through 814. He wanted to forge one Christian nation out of the many "heathen" tribes that came under his sway, and saw himself as a "king and priest" crowned by God. In this he was inspired by a book called *The City of God*, written by St. Augustine in A.D. 410 in response to the fall of Rome.

The people of the 11th century hoped, like Charlemagne, to establish the city of God, but in the opposite way: not through

Figure 65. When, at the beginning of the 15th century, the city of God finally disintegrated, Christine de Pizan had the original idea of women building a city of their own. She wrote a book about this city and populated it with women. We reproduce from one of the richly illustrated manuscripts three miniatures illustrating the construction and occupation of this city. Her intention was to lodge a protest against the repression of women that began in her times, but it was to no avail. (MS "La cité des dames." Bibliothèque Nationale, Paris, ms. fr., f.l.; f. 31 v; f. 67 v.)

Figure 66. The city of God did not come up to expectations, but degenerated into an establishment. In this miniature it is being defended against a mob of heretics (blindfolded) and deadly sins (women). (French miniature, 15th century, Berlin, Archiv für Kunst u. Geschichte.)

political might wielded by a ruler who is also a priest, but through religious might wielded by a high priest who is also a ruler.

Augustine had drawn a picture of two cities. The evil city, Babylon, was founded on Cain, and the good city, Jerusalem, was founded on Abel. Augustine had suggested that human history occurred as an increasingly distinct growing apart of these cities—in seven stages, analogous to the seven days of creation. According to Augustine, we are now in the evening of the sixth period and on the threshold of the seventh, in which everything will be completed and come to rest. God will then be all in all. All will then rest in the one God. The date of the transition to this final period is unknown, although we do know, in the opinion of St. Augustine, what we should be doing now, and what the meaning is of our existence here on Earth: that we should be turning society into a state ruled by God who is to be all in all. Thus, according to St. Augustine, the deepest impetus in human history is a mystical one, which may be expressed best perhaps when he said that his heart is restless until it finds rest in God.

The fashioning of medieval society was mystically inspired from the start. Mysticism was still very evident in the Church leaders of the 11th century. Not only did they strive for a holy city of God, but they looked for ways of combining mysticism with leadership. Right from the beginning (ca. 1050), people wanted to know if mysticism could legitimately be active; that is to say, is a vision of God compatible with active leadership, and how would that work? Lives of the saints were written from this point of view.

The attempt to model communal life after the city of God, was initially made in the abbey of Cluny and led, in 1046, to a reformation of the Curia in Rome. The popes decreed that they, the monasteries, and the churches were not subject to the temporal powers. At the same time, they built up a central authority within the church itself; the right to hold office in it being conferred by the laying on of hands in a chain of succession said to go back to the apostles. It was decided that this office should be confined to priests who had no family or financial responsibilities—in other words, to celibates. In the 13th century, the city of God was realized. Pope Innocent III (pope 1198-1216) turned Central Italy around Rome into a papal state. He appointed emperors and was more than a match for the politicians.

Figure 67. The City of God founded in Münster by the Anabaptists under the leadership of the [Dutch] Haarlem baker Jan Matthijs and the tailor Jan van Leiden, shown here as a king. After a year of terror inside the city and of siege outside it, this idealistic venture ended in a bloodbath (1535). (Woodcut from a pamphlet issued at the time of the siege.)

Every pope after him monopolized the Gospel, and decided who would preach what. And God's grace was allegedly conveyed through his ecclesiastical channels, and through them alone. After purgatory had been invented and proclaimed a dogma, his power was thought to reach into the hereafter. Sufferings in purgatory could be cancelled by the purchase of papal indulgences. Every European, no matter where, fell under his direct authority, and was tied to a parish by the obligatory Easter confession. Innocent also found ways of bringing potential troublemakers into his ecclesiastical set-up or else liquidating them.

The city of God became a colossal, absolute emblem of salvation, ruling over body and soul, affording comfort and security, but not doing much for the mystical impulse. Yet this impulse remained alive. The desire for personal responsibility was present from the beginning. People were prepared to put their faith in revelation, but they also wanted to understand it, as St. Anselm of Canterbury (1033-1109) observed. Anselm was the author of a revolutionary treatise with the challenging title: *Why Did God Become Man?* People wanted to feel the truth of what had been revealed, not only to be able to grasp more of the reality of it, but also to enter into it more. It was not for nothing that St. Bernard called the Biblical Song of Solomon the "book of experience."

However, mysticism was fostered in the main by protest movements which began as experiments and ended either as full-blown heresies or as monastic orders.

HERMITS AND PILGRIMS

In the 11th century, the old frames of reference, which had had such a stabilizing influence, no longer met the desire to know more and to experience more. People turned away from the cloisters to immerse themselves in nature or to wander through towns and villages. They studied the gospel without bothering about monastic rules, because they wanted to find themselves or discover an effective answer to the question: How can I lead a true Christian life?

These hermits and pilgrims compelled respect; they were much sought for their advice or made disciples. Typical of this questing spirit in the 11th century is Bruno "the Carthusian," born in Cologne in 1032. He was a canon there, became a chancellor in Reims and then an archbishop, said farewell to this office and went to the abbey of Molesmes. A year later, he withdrew to the mountains, where he and six others founded a monastery that is still there—La Grande Chartreuse. After six years, he was summoned to Rome. On one of his travels with the pope, he stayed behind in an isolated part of Calabria and founded a second monastery. Only after his death there in 1101 did something permanent grow out of both monasteries—the Carthusian order. This, and other monastic orders which arose at the same time, emphasized the individual, even though their members lived under a single obligation. That was an innovation—a feeling for the value of the person, of the concrete individual, even in the setting up of a religious community.

The groups that formed around those who aspired to be saintly included people from every stratum of society. Women, too, joined the search for a Christian lifestyle. People were often ascetic, and abstained from meat, sex, and marriage. Many advocated a reformation of the Church, to make it holy, stainless and devoid of luxury. Robert of Molesmes was one of them. He and his followers were vegetarians, worked on the land, and formed a community without a central authority and without privileges. He also built a convent for women. The Cistercian order owes its existence to the monastery he founded in Citeaux in 1098.

Figure 68. The 11th century was a time of experimentation. Many people retired—even from the abbeys—in order to achieve clarity on their own. Some of them discovered that, even among the distractions of natural beauty, such isolation is very conducive to mystical experiences. Their experiments occasionally acquired fixed form in an order of recluses. One of the most important of these hermits was St. Bruno the Carthusian, whose order is still in existence. (*St. Bruno*, painted on glass by Marianne van der Heijden, 1956. Photo: Lambert van Gelder.)

Robert and Bruno survived as saints and founders of orders; but most seekers in this century died in obscurity or are remembered as fanatics, like Leutard, the peasant from the Champagne area, who was taken out of his depth by a dream in which a swarm of bees flew in and out of his body. He took this dream as the starting point of his preaching and managed to gain adherents; but he was condemned, lost his followers, and committed suicide.

AGGRESSIVE RELIGIOSITY

The unorthodox lifestyle for these religious seekers, who wanted to purify themselves in order to make themselves receptive to the Holy Ghost, aroused opposition. They were called "new-lighters," "slippery snakes," or "messengers of antichrist who had come out of their hiding places." Often they were branded as heretics with such well-known names as "Arians," and "Manichees." However, in the 11th century, they certainly had nothing to do

Figure 69. The dark side of the endeavor to create an ideal community, the city of God, was the exclusion and excision of all who were not wanted in it, especially heretics and Jews. In this miniature from a "moralizing Bible," a passage from the Old Testament is brought up to date: Cathars and Jews, stereotyped as a false lover and a money-grabber, are being driven to hell. In a previous miniature the pope is expelling them both from the city of God. (Bodleian Library, Oxford, MS 270 b, f. 78 r.)

with heresies like these. They belonged to original, local movements, with one leader, but with no clear doctrine, and having no other ties to similar groups apart from a general religious desire to live a Christian life. And yet sometimes they were even put to death—on the grounds of heresy—not by the Church leaders, but by a maddened populace who did not relish being confronted by their high moral standards. It was by order of Robert the Pious that, in 1022, a number of learned canons were burned at the stake. And it was the burghers of Monteforte who, in 1028, against the wishes of the bishop, burned a group of nobles and the local countess as heretics. And it was townspeople who lynched some illiterate peasants at Chalons in 1048.

Illustrative of the confused situation in this century was the burning of a priest in Kamerijk, in 1077. He qualified as a heretic because he thought that simoniacal and unchaste priests should not be allowed to say mass. And yet, at the same time, Pope Gregory VII was carrying out a reformation aimed at cleansing the Church of unworthy priests such as these. No wonder he called this heretic-burning a crime. Unfortunately, he was powerless to prevent it.

L. White attributes 11th century aggressiveness to the feelings aroused by fear of chaos and of the new. The cultures of both town and country had been thrown into disorder. A new situation created unexpected problems which, for a long time, seemed to be intractable. People took their fears out on some scapegoat—on the innovator, the stranger, or the separate group.

Things were different in the 12th century. Humble preachers of another ilk suddenly put in an appearance in Cologne in 1145. These Cathars wanted to have a public debate. They were willing to be convinced that they were wrong, but only by genuine arguments. The clergy accepted the challenge, but before matters could be taken any further, the civil authorities stepped in and sent the preachers to the stake. Twenty years later, Cathars were again being burned, but now after being heard and condemned by the clergy themselves. Forty years after that, Innocent III made short shrift of this group by organizing a very ferocious crusade against their stronghold in the South of France (1208-1229) and by setting up an ecclesiastical tribunal, the Inquisition, to catch and burn anyone who might attempt to revive their ideas at some future date.

Evidently the mood of aggression was not passing. Certainly, from the 12th century onward, the Church sought to turn it into other channels, but this does not mean that it had lost any of its force. In contrast to the static and exalted inwardness of the Eastern Church, Christendom in the West was assertive, worldly, and passionate. People wanted to have an intense, almost human, relationship with God, and they looked for a Church that could make this immediately possible. They were filled with a sense of mission to turn the whole world into a single Christian city of God if possible. They tried what human mysticism, full of fervent emotion, would do. They went to extremes. Whatever did not fit in was thrown on the fire. This religious passion led to increasing bloodshed; the search for new mystical ways was literally a matter of life and death. And Western mysticism is bedevilled by morbidity. One of the less attractive sides of some of the beatified female mystics is that "blood" figures so largely in their writings. In Catherine of Siena, the word occurs on average once in every five sentences.

THE STRUGGLE FOR
A SPIRITUAL CITY

Mystically oriented movements in the 11th century were all inspired by the Bible; by such texts as: "Blessed are the poor in spirit: for theirs is the kingdom of heaven. . . . Blessed are the pure in heart: for they shall see God" (Matthew 5:3, 8), and by the promise Jesus made to send the Holy Spirit to His disciples to teach them all things after He had gone away. People wanted to experience these things for themselves and claimed the right to preach about them.

In the 11th century attention was focused on the poverty and chastity of individual priests, monks, and nuns, not on the religious institutions themselves. This changed in the 12th century, immense wealth having flowed into the cathedrals and abbeys. The most magnificent edifice in Europe was no longer an imperial palace but the Abbey of Cluny.

Various areas had become affluent, with a new rich class and a new poor class. The Church took no interest in the poor people. Those who desired to embrace poverty in the 11th century had become monks and nuns, shut up away from the cities in cloisters; and, traditionally, this was felt to be the best place for them. Now, however, especially in the rich regions of Southern France and Northern Italy, new groups arose that positively refused to live behind convent walls. They wanted to be poor with the poor, as Jesus had been before them. Robert of Arbissel called this, "Following the naked Jesus nakedly." They wished to recover the apostolic lifestyle. The members of these groups were drawn from the nobility and from the nouveaux riches, the merchants. They did not want to have plots of land, cattle, or fixed abodes. Their exemplar was Jesus who had "not where to lay His head." They went preaching from place to place, barefoot and with longish hair, in imitation of Jesus and His apostles.

It did not deter them to encounter opposition, to be hooted after, and even to be persecuted and sometimes sent to the stake by the Church; for Jesus had given His followers advance warning of this, and had called them blessed on account of it. The Gospel was their sole standard, and in it they learned that Jesus had identified Himself with the poor, that they must go into all the world and preach the glad tidings, that it was incumbent on all

Figure 70. An important inspiration for mysticism was the life of Jesus of Nazareth. People tried to gain release from desire by following Him. Therefore, like Him, they abandoned their personal possessions; and they preached that others should do the same. This poverty-ideal was in stark contrast to the practice of the church, which relied on riches and power, so it was often an unmistakable protest. On these two pages from a Bohemian MS, Jesus is standing with Peter opposite the papal throne and raising his finger. Texts from the Bible are being quoted in Czech by Jesus: "Provide neither gold, nor silver, nor brass in your purses" (Matthew 10:9), and by Peter: "Behold, we have forsaken all, and followed thee" (Matthew 19:27). (Göttingen, Niedersächsische Staats-und Universitätsbibl., cod. theol. 182, pp. 140-141.)

Figure 71. One of the many poverty movements was that of the "humiliaten." They wanted to live genuinely humble communal lives, supplying their needs by manual work. This miniature illustrates how the women wove and spun in their community. (*Historia ordinis humiliatorum*, ca. 1421. Pinacoteca Ambrosiana, Milan, ms. G 301, f. 3 r. [= S. P. 66].)

Figure 72. The poverty ideal was a favorable context for mysticism, partly because Jesus had said that whoever gave bread and water to the needy was giving to Him. The face of the God-man appears in the poor. This vision is taken literally in a painting of Elisabeth of Hungary bestowing clothing on the destitute. (Cologne master, 14th century, Museum Wallraf-Richartz, Cologne.)

Figure 73. The most important representative of the poverty movement was St. Francis of Assisi. He combined this ideal with humility, and with the desire for comradeship between human beings (who would renounce the use of force), and for friendship between humans and animals. Since all creatures come from the hand of the same Maker, none may be regarded as inferior. According to legend, St. Francis could talk to animals and he preached a sermon to the birds about the Creator. (Drawing by Mattheus Paris, 1236-1250. Corpus Christi College, Cambridge, MS 16, f.66 v.)

Figure 74. The poverty ideal also made it clear that action had to go hand in hand with mysticism, "doing" with "contemplation." In this miniature from a Psalter of 1217, we are shown how both are to be combined. Over it is written "Contemplativa vita" and "Activa vita" with an explanation of what these two things imply. (*Elisabeth-psalterium*, Museo Archeologico Nazionale, Cividale. f. 173.)

Christ's disciples to do so, and that they must obey God rather than society. Groups of all kinds—with different names and purposes—were motivated by this basic vision. For most of them, poverty was a spiritual ideal. They had to become poor like the poor; they did not think it was important to relieve poverty. In the main, they wished to build up the Church as one Christian people. The mighty symbols of salvation that had sprung up, the great cathedrals and abbeys, were regarded as displays of wealth and prosperity, and, thus, as symbols of degeneration. They wanted a different sort of Church, a Church composed of people who took Jesus' life and teaching seriously, that is to say, literally. They themselves practiced what they preached; but, in those days, a social revolution or political stance by Christian people against a rich Church with absolute power was still unimaginable and, in any case, doomed to failure.

One of the few who took the ideal of poverty into the political arena was Arnold of Brescia, an Augustinian choirmaster. He was fascinated by the papal "Gregorian reformation" and also by a popular movement in his own religion (called *pataria*, for the rag market in Milan) which aimed to get this reformation off the ground. Its ideal was a Church free from every taint of power and money. Arnold criticized the hoarding of wealth by prelates and the Church. A powerful preacher of the duty to forsake the world, he also supported the struggle to liberate the towns from the clutches of the princes of the Church. He was exiled and hounded through Europe, but was brought back to Rome by a papal legate and rehabilitated. There he repeated his sermons against the wealthy clergy, and was once more embroiled in the struggle of the city-dwellers, the burghers of Rome who, in 1142, were resisting the papal ambitions. Eight years later, he stood at the head of this democratic movement, and was pushing for the creation of an ideal city of God in the midst of the Church. However, he was not blessed with sufficient political acumen to perceive the game being played by the pope and the emperor, and he ended up being extradited by his patron Frederick Barbarossa to the pope, who had him hanged in 1155.

Large-scale movements combining a humble existence with a life of prayer spread through Lombardy (the *humiliaten*, the lowly ones) and the South of France (the "Poor Men of Lyons," followers of Pierre Valdès, otherwise known as Peter Waldo, a rich merchant of Lyons who had distributed his wealth to the needy in

1170). These movements were excommunicated in 1184 because they demanded the right for their members, both men and women, to go out and preach. Pierre Valdès refused to give up this right. When the issue was made a matter of doctrine rather than one of right, he conceded everything that Rome required. He did this in a reply to a condemnation in 1179, but it did no good.

THE PURE CHURCH

The mystical impulse aimed at reforming the Church also expressed itself, in the 12th century, in movements that sought genuine spirituality. One of the earliest and most powerful of these movements was that of the Cathars. They showed all the signs of an alternative Church, and were well-organized. They were named, not for a leader, but for an attitude to life: *katharos* means "pure." Men and women lived in groups, separately and chastely, but giving one another mutual support, and they went round preaching in the same way. It was indeed an alternative Church; set up, not on the principle of a legally defined "apostolic" office, but on the principle of "perfection." The purest among them filled the highest place.

The Cathars originated in Bulgaria. There they were described in A.D. 980 by the priest Cosmas as "the newly arisen heresy of the Bogomili." Bogomil was a Bulgarian priest who gave the teachings of Mani a Christian form. In the writings of Cosmas we are given the following picture of these sectarians. They are as gentle and humble as lambs, modest and pale with fasting. No unseemly word, no laughing lips. They are seen as good Christians and consulted as perfect saints.

According to Cosmas they used a ploy: "They sigh and make answer very modestly as if they really know what will be done in heaven." In Constantinople in the 12th century the Cathars were described as somber and dreary in their appearance, in their gait, and in their dress. Hypocrites, too; wolves in sheeps' clothing; they kept all the Christian precepts and meanwhile proclaimed another doctrine, that of Mani. A similar description and condemnation was issued in Germany at about the same time, in a sermon by Hildegard of Bingen. She portrayed them as pale people in cheap clothes, with strange-colored hats, quiet and gentle, living without money, and celibate. She, too, sees them as wolves in sheeps' clothing who would help to destroy the Church unless they were stopped. The Cathars are upright in everything, but the core of their teaching is false. Moreover they say of themselves that they are holier than others, and they act like saints in public and sin in secret.

This last aspect was heavily emphasized by their adversaries. By the end of the 12th century, the popular idea of the Cathars was this: they indulged in pornography and promiscuity, and performed child sacrifices in order to get rid of their illegitimate offspring. Not all "pure ones" had the same doctrines or the same lifestyles. The Cathars were somewhat different from the Bogomili, who were somewhat different from the Manichees. Nevertheless they did have much in common. God, for them, was light, spirit, love, and goodness. Satan was darkness, materiality, and wickedness. They said that the world was created by Satan, and that mankind was originally born of God as a spirit, but became a fallen angel and thus bound to a body. Glimmers of light are hidden in all material things. These sparks must be harvested. The purpose of life is for us to choose goodness, light, and the spirit, and to reject evil, darkness, and the flesh. The final redemption of the world will be a universal conflagration that absorbs everything into the light. Real life begins with death, a life of spirit with the Spirit. And those who want to experience this superior life before the time comes for them to die, must make "perfection" their object.

The Cathars understood by this: renunciation of profane love, abstinence from flesh foods, forsaking the love of possessions, being members of a non-authoritarian church, and avoidance of worldly affairs. Whoever could not reach so high, but who shared these ideals, was counted as faithful to the Church. They saw their lives as weaving, and often called themselves weavers.[45] Even though held to the earth by black desire, as believing ones they could weave the sparks of light in all things into a heavenly garment—an artistic occupation that frees the soul from the heavy, oppressive, dark earth. Not for nothing did the Cathars meet with a wide response in Provence, the land of the troubadours, where so much was achieved in the field of creativity.

---

[45] "These persons were scattered all over Europe: in France they were called 'Tisserands,' or weavers." *The Book and Its Story*, by L. N. R. (London: Samuel Bagster & Sons, 1854). Tr. note.

The Cathars were also anarchists of a sort: they did not respect traditional institutions, and they had their own manifesto. They were against the bond of marriage, despised wealth and luxury, were opposed to the abuse of power and to social injustice, and did not believe in working for a master. They wanted to improve the living conditions of their fellow men and women. For example, many of them were physicians, and many of them shared their goods with others. A further feature of the Cathar culture was the cultivation of desire. Thus death could be understood as a desire for a higher life. Even suicide was sometimes an expression of this. Usually it involved a specific situation in connection with *endura*, a sort of baptism by the laying on of hands. Through this baptism a person was perfected, was no longer allowed to sin and any sin was irrevocable. For example, anyone who received this *endura* when sick had to die if he or she did not feel strong enough to live a sinless life from that time forward. Such an individual would fast to death if not killed by the disease. Desire was also cultivated in connection with love, which had to remain unfulfilled, for fear the person would become bound to the body. The spiritual spark contained within the longing for love was supposed to become a fire by which passion was consumed.

The Cathar Church was extirpated early in the 13th century, along with all the other movements that had been undermining the outwardly powerful Church of Rome. Among those suppressed at that time were the followers of Joachim of Fiore (Gioacchimo da Fiore) and Amalric of Bena (Amalric de Bène).

The Flowering
of the Spiritual Church

What St. Augustine saw in his picture of the city of God was seen in an original manner in a surprising vision by a mystic of South Calabria, Joachim of Fiore (ca. 1130-1202). This Cistercian abbot left his abbey, founded a monastery in Fiore, and spent the rest of this life elaborating his vision in relation to the Bible, in relation to the theology of the Holy Trinity, in relation to the changing seasons, and in relation to the plants and the stars. Like St. Augustine, he regarded human history as a gradual growth toward the seventh day—the moment when the faithful will know the drunkenness that the Holy Spirit pours out on the souls He visits.

He felt that this kingdom of the spirit is growing in secret and will speedily break through after an apocalyptic day in which the era of the Son ends. In contrast to St. Augustine, he distinguishes three periods: that of God the Father, in which the flesh and law hold sway; that of God the Son, in which the Church exercises priestly rule; and finally that of the Holy Spirit, in which each individual will discern the spirit of the Sermon on the Mount and in which the letter of the Gospel will no longer be needed any more than sacraments and priests. There will be no more hatred, and everybody, even the Jews, will belong to the Church in freedom under the leadership of a spiritual pope without pomp and power. Joachim's fame and importance were great. He showed how a church could be represented that was different from the contemporary clerical Church. What is more, he helped people to feel what this different Church would be like. Hidden under the foliage of the clerical Church, the mystical Church had already budded, and was on the point of blossoming out. He thought the time had come when the clerical Church could safely join forces with the covert mystical Church in anticipation of the apocalypse.

Joachim said that the moment of the apocalypse was unknown, but he did give cryptic indications, which were later thought to point to the year 1260. In any case, the apprehensiveness of people living in the Middle Ages concerning the end of time led them to fix on this year, which they awaited with mixed feelings. But there were others who wanted to make the hidden Church more powerful without waiting for a particular year, and they hoped to achieve this by adopting a mystical attitude to life. Groups of Franciscans saw themselves as the new order that Joachim had foretold would herald the new Church. They called themselves spirituals. There were also the *Amalricians*, who combined the teaching of Amalric of Bena with that of Joachim of Fiore.

Amalric of Bena, a professor at the University of Paris, had been resting quietly in his grave for several years when, in 1210, the hierarchy of the Church discovered the harmfulness of his doctrine, dug him up, and tossed his bones away. The harmfulness lay in this, that in his teachings he seemed to have given the blueprint for a new human being with a new morality; a human being who has no knowledge of sin, and therefore no knowledge of remorse and repentance, or of vengeful justice. Amalric harked

Figure 75. Joachim of Fiore saw history as an ascent to an increasingly spiritual society. According to him, the age of the Spirit was immanent, when the external church and the letter of the Bible would probably be made redundant. In this illustration, his theory is shown as the growth of two trees rooted in the ground and circularly intertwined. Each circle is a period of time—the periods of the Father, Son, and Holy Spirit (*Pater et Filius et Spiritus sanctus*), 13th century miniature, Bibl. Apostolica, Vatican.)

The Russian painter Wassily Kandinsky read the mystics and was particularly impressed by the writings of Joachim of Fiore. He recognized in them what he had vaguely wanted to do: to make visible the spiritual reality hidden behind everyday reality. He began with an icon on the subject of "All Saints' Day," the new spiritual kingdom of God that will be seen hereafter. In a series of paintings and woodcuts, with titles referring to the day of judgment, the subject itself seems resurrected into a new world of shapes and colors. The familiar motifs disappear to make way for novel abstract forms. His works were epoch-making.

back to Plato, Scotus Erigena, and, in some degree, to St. Augustine, all of whom saw evil as non-being, or as darkness in the sense of lack of light. He also quoted St. Paul's words: "God is all in all"[46] and argued that as evil is not included in that "all" then it does not exist. What we call evil and sin is not the reality of things with which God is identical, it is unreality. Everything we call sin must somehow go back to God, he thought; and the sinful disappears when we banish the darkness from our consciousness by the mystical knowledge that God works all in all.

This teaching was elevated into a philosophy of life by his rapidly growing band of followers, to whom Paradise was mystical consciousness, a knowledge that God is in everything, here and now. There is no hereafter, and we do not rise from the dead. We rise out of the darkness by the second birth, prompted by the Spirit through a mystical enlightenment. The kingdom of the Spirit

---

[46] This seems to be a misquotation. Paul does not say that God is all in all now, but that He will be in the future (I Cor. 15:28). Tr. note.

Figure 76. W. Kandinsky, "All Saints' Day." (Painting on glass, 1911, Städtische Galerie im Lehnbachhaus, Munich.)

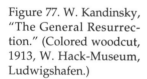

Figure 77. W. Kandinsky, "The General Resurrection." (Colored woodcut, 1913, W. Hack-Museum, Ludwigshafen.)

Figure 78. W. Kandinsky, "The Last Judgment." Only the angel's trumpet is still recognizable, at top right. (Oil on canvas, 1913, Städtische Galerie im Lehnbachhaus, Munich.)

has already arrived. The group professing this saw itself as the vanguard of the approaching kingdom of the Spirit that had been prophesied by Joachim of Fiore. For them, no further faith and hope were needed, because the kingdom of God is already present in mystical consciousness. Only love is necessary. The power of love conquers all. The forces of gentleness lead the way. It was an optimistic philosophy of life.

Such an attitude of life was appealing, because it freed people from the frustration of having to live in a Church that said it was holy but seemed unable to cleanse itself from corruption. And it was appealing because it gave a foretaste of the paradisiacal happiness of the "free children of God." Unlike the flagellants who walked through the streets with blue and swollen limbs and blood-stained clothing announcing the end of the age of the Son, the Amalricians were inspired, not by fear, but by a cheerful expectation of a mystical era: "Within five years everyone will be able to say, I am holy spirit," they said. But within five years, between 1210 and 1215, they had all perished at the stake in Paris and Rouen. Yet something had been evoked by them that continued to emerge in different forms: the idea that the paradisiacal Church is always a reality if we find her within our inmost souls.

The spiritual currents running in the direction of a mystical brotherhood and sisterhood devoted to poverty ran deep. Suppressing them seems to have been a short-term solution, because they kept taking new forms and threatened to continue as sects outside the Church, so undermining the ideal of one city of God. At the beginning of the 13th century, there was an impasse. The mainstream of European Christianity had turned away from mysticism, and spiritual movements had an increasing tendency to become peripheral. Nobody wanted this to happen—mysticism was highly valued—but the Church knew no other answer than repression.

In Europe, people wished to bring the spiritual and divine to earth. They no longer thought in terms of black and white, but envisioned a Purgatory between Heaven and Hell, because most people were neither saintly nor utterly evil; and they set "merciful Mother Mary" against the stern justice of God. Instead of concentrating on Christ in Majesty, the Divine Logos, glorified after His "blessed" sufferings, they concentrated on the earthly nativity of Jesus and on His resurrection after bitter sufferings. The notion of God as our Fellow had broken through into consciousness—a startling discovery.

It was not thanks to Rome but to a few reprieved mystics (especially Dominic, Francis of Assisi, and Jacob of Vitry) that the new spiritual currents managed to flow into the mainstream to produce monastic orders rather than sects. Jacob of Vitry succeeded in finding a place for the new feminine religiosity, of which more later.

DOMINIC GUZMÁN
AND FRANCIS OF ASSISI

In 1203, the Spaniard Domingo de Guzmán (1170-1221) was traveling through Cathar lands in France when it struck him that there was much of value in the faith of the Cathars, and in the conduct of their lives, and that this ought to be preserved. He drew a distinction between what had turned people into Cathars—dissatisfaction with the affluent society and with the corrupt Church—and what they had become as Cathars. His practical response was to found an order in which the first aim was to seek the truth and the second was to live a life of poverty like the Cathars.

He made sure that women had the same facilities as men, and the first cloister he founded, in 1208, was allocated to women. Monastic orders of a new type arose at this time—the mendicant

Figure 79. The oldest portraits of St. Francis of Assisi. 1) Fresco in the Benedictine monastery at Subiaco. Without halo and stigmata. Apparently ca. 1224, commissioned by Cardinal Hugolinus; 2) Painting on the cover of St. Francis' tomb in the Maria degl' Angli, Assisi, attributed to Cimabue, ca. 1230; 3) Fresco in the lower church of San Francesco in Assisi, ca. 1280.

orders. These were the Dominican and the Franciscan, and two older ones that changed into mendicant orders—the Augustinian and the Carmelite orders. They settled in towns, won the right to go about preaching everywhere, and sought no possessions other than those received for services rendered or as the proceeds of begging. They saw activity as a result of, not as a hindrance to, mystical vision, and esteemed this mixed life more highly than a purely contemplative life. Their form of government was strictly democratic, with brothers and a prior who was the first among equals. And those who became their leaders had to be reselected every four years. The mendicant orders have produced great mystics: after St. Francis have come the Dominican Meister Eckhart, the Augustinian Martin Luther, the Carmelite St. John of the Cross, and St. Teresa of Avila.

The man in whom the mystical impulse of the poverty movement is most clearly seen is St. Francis of Assisi, born in 1182, the son of a rich merchant, Pietro Bernardone. He chose to be poor with the poor after shaking the hand of a leper.

> Then as he departed, in very truth that which had aforetime been bitter unto him, to wit, the sight and touch of lepers, now changed into sweetness.[47]

Later, when asked what was his highest happiness, he simply replied: "To be treated as 'repulsive' and 'riff-raff' and then to bear this evil and injustice joyfully." The poor people whose poverty he wanted to share belonged to what we call the "lumpenproletariat" (dirty, smelly, and scruffy). He, himself, performed the most sensational deeds, while on the outside he looked like a disreputable person—shabbily dressed in peasant's clothing, exhausted, and nearly blind. And yet he was able to persuade many young people from well-to-do circles to live as "friars minor." He stripped himself naked in public and gave back all the clothes he wore to his father. Together with St. Clare, he married "Lady Poverty." He repaired an insignificant little church as a sign of the restoration of the Church of Christ, and built a stable in order to make visible the birth of God in all its poverty. His

---

[47] Thomas of Celano, Legenda Prima, cap. vii; 3 Soc. Cap. iv; in Underhill's *Mysticism* (New York: E. P. Dutton, n. d.), p. 224.

devotion was such that he received in his body the marks of Christ's crucifixion. He carefully chose a place to die and lay naked on the ground sprinkled with ashes. All this with impressive naturalness and lack of ceremony. His joy was expressed in singing and dancing, but he said very little about his mystical experiences. He retired into a cave and came out a different man, so something very significant must have happened to him at that time.

St. Francis had a special talent for doing what had to be done while managing to stay in the Church. He was a layman and gave other laymen access to the Bible by preaching in the open air, using narrative without dwelling on dogma. He responded to the love of St. Clare, and provided many places of residence for women and showed how lay people could follow the Gospel at home and at work. He did not try to justify this, but stuck to deeds; hence there were no propositions or principles for inquisitors to seize on as heretical. What is more, he rescued the poverty movement from its straitjacket of Church reformation. He did not

Figure 80. St. Francis was "married to Lady Poverty" but he loved St. Clare. Their affection was mutual. (Fresco by Simone Martini. Assisi, lower church of San Francesco.)

want a conflict with the Church, and the decadence of the Church interested him hardly at all. He looked beyond the manifest corruption and did not assume that others had to live as he did.

He was unwilling to find fault that once the earlier poverty movements had been assimilated by the Church, their followers had been shut up in old-style abbeys; but he made his own arrangements for his own followers, both men and women, for the married, and for those who were in work. He made for them "rules," which he took to "my lord the pope." What he wanted was a brotherhood, not an imposing order. Actually, he was not a good organizer. It was someone else, as in the case of Jesus, who gave his ideas a solid shape that would endure down the centuries. Brother Elias created three orders: the first for men, the second for women, and the third for lay people in the world. St. Francis wished to assemble a people of God from all countries and all stations in life to live out of a pure heart and to be poor in spirit, just as Jesus had preached and practiced in His own life. He did not imagine that this people of God was going to coincide with the Church; even Moslems were welcome.

He sent friars to Syria and Morocco, and joined the Crusade of 1217 as a non-combatant in order to be able to speak to the sultan Melek-El-Kamel. This he managed to do during the siege of Damascus, and learned from the experience that theological wrangles are offensive to those whose beliefs differ from our own, and later on he prohibited them. He distanced himself from any martyrdom that arose out of a dispute, and also from his own longing to be a martyr. His friars were not allowed to do anything insulting. From the Crusades themselves, he learned that resorting to force is hard to avoid when religious motives come into play. He managed to get the pope to agree that the indulgences granted to the Crusaders should also be granted to pilgrims to his little church in Portiuncula, and that they should be gratis and full. Instead of the holy places that had to be captured from the Moslems, he, himself, built such a place—a stable of Bethlehem in Greccio.

One of the fruits of his mystical experiences, and the one that would probably appeal most to people today, was that he wanted to live in unity with all things, with his fellow humans and also with animals, plants, and the sun, and with natural phenomena such as fire, night and day, and death. It is remarkable that not only did he see all these things in relation to God, as "God's footprints," or "vestigia Dei" as the saying was at that time, but he relished their individuality. And he saw the harshness and cruelty in nature connected with the softness and gentleness; aspects that are also seen in the lives of each one of us. He talked to animals "as if they had understanding" says the legend. He called all created things his brothers or sisters—a great family of the one Father.

The democratic form of government that had been introduced as an ideal into the poverty movement and had been made a rule in the mendicant orders—all are equal and the master is the servant of all—was extended by St. Francis to the whole of creation. In this, he was most original, even for his own day and age. He made common cause with the poverty movement, but interpreted it in a way that was diametrically opposed to the way in which the Cathars interpreted it. In his view, creation as a whole is good, even where it is harsh and cruel. Also, the most sinful creature can be converted. Thus the story is told of how he reproved a wolf that was devouring sheep, and of how the wolf became as meek as a lamb. Everything is worthy of love, and we ought not to be sparing with our love, provided it is poor in spirit: love must be kept entirely separate from possessiveness or covetousness. His democratic attitude is also seen in his concept of poverty, which is based, not on a belief that material things are fundamentally bad, but on the insight that everyone has received all things from the Creator and that, in this, all are equal. "We commit theft against the great Almsgiver if we do not give away to those who are more needy than ourselves." That is why he called himself a minor, or lesser, brother. He wanted to have less than others, for to have more is stealing. And what he tried to do for the poor was not to enrich them, but to restore their self-respect. He was a rich man's son who gave his hand to lepers—to people others avoided like the plague.

Near the end of his life he was often wretched—owing to deep depressions, and also on account of St. Clare. But at the same time, he wrote his famous *Song of Brother Sun* in which he even praises the negative forces of nature. All give glory to God in their own way. In this vision, too, St. Francis shows his originality. Before him, created things were seen as symbols, simply existing for the sake of humanity—the center of the cosmos—to help us to love and extol God for our spiritual benefit. To St. Francis, everything also existed for its own sake, all created things are brothers and sisters, placed in the world for a reason that we do not know. God's ways are past finding out, and we cannot say that any one of his creatures is more important than another. The importance of each is derived from the one God, of whom we know that, in three persons, He is the emblem of love, even though we cannot be acquainted with Him in His unity. God is the inexpressible.

L. White points out that this new vision of nature presented by St. Francis provided a suitable emotional basis for the objective study of nature we know as natural science.[48] And he adds that it is hardly surprising that later on at Oxford it was the Franciscans who devised a new kind of science. In St. Francis' vision, nature is always interesting and important for its own sake. St. Francis created one great, democratic family, not only of his own followers, not only of men, not only of Christians, but also of non-Christians, of animals, plants, the sun, the heavenly bodies, the forces of nature, and also of what happens to us, including death. All of them are sisters or brothers. And the human being is no longer seen as central, and ought not to pretend to be the owner or controller of everything else. Authority does not belong to anyone unless they are chosen.

St. Francis built a city of God without might, under the authority of the elect, with mysticism as its deepest incentive; a polity that is "Catholic" in the broadest sense, in which all can be treated fairly, whether they be cleric or lay, man or woman, married or unmarried. Everything is welcome within the walls of this city—nature, the passions and events, even evil forces and negative experiences, such as Sister Death. This City is the city of the "poor in spirit," because life is lived in the realization that everything is given by the one Father, and that nobody is or possesses anything in his or her own right. All are poor in the same sense. In the realization of the nobility of each being, the socially disadvantaged, the outcast, and the ostracized can recover their self-respect.

GOD—LOVER AND BELOVED

In the poverty movement there was very little reflection on the experiences themselves—on love is of God, or God is love—until the 12th century in the monastic milieus that had come into being

---

[48] Lynn White, Jr., *Medieval Religion and Technology* (Berkeley: University of California, 1978).

in the previous century, especially in Central and Northern France—the Cistercians, the Carthusians, and the School of Saint-Victor. Here, too, arose a completely new mysticism in which "love" was the central theme. This mysticism grew out of the spirit of "longing" cultivated in the cloisters before the 11th century.

The most extensive description of this mysticism of longing was given by Jean de Fécamp, an Italian who died as abbot in Fécamp near Rouen in 1078. His book was later widely read, usually as a "meditation" of St. Augustine. Here is a typical text:

> One eats according to the hunger that has to be satisfied, one rests according to the extent that one is tired; so also one seeks Christ, unites with him, and loves him in so far as one longs for him.[49]

Love was being taught about quite early on—for example, in a treatise written ca. 1005 *On the Fruit of the Flesh and the Spirit*. It was said that the capacity for love is a source from which two rivers flow: one in the direction of earth, and the other in the direction of God. But only during the 12th century did it register that God had become man and that He is Love: that is to say that He is both our Fellow and our Lover. Much was made of two texts in John's Gospel at this time: "God is love," and "Love is of God" (I John 4: 7,8). They were interpreted thus: seen from our human standpoint, God is the same as "love." God longs for our love in response to His. This response is love that is from God, human love that is directed toward the innermost part of the soul, the ground of existence from which love flows. The Lover lives in the deepest innermost part, awakens love there, and waits there for the person who, inflamed by love, desires to be united with Him. There, too, one learns to know God. This love is the eye of the soul.

Through the School of Saint-Victor, this tendency became a subject of study in the 12th century. Many pictures were discovered in the Bible to reinforce the new form of mysticism: Adam created in God's image, the new birth from God, the child of God. Ideas were also borrowed from St. Augustine and pseudo-Dionysius; for example, the idea that an individual ascends to

---

[49] Jean de Fécamp. Translation mine. Tr.

God by turning inward into his or her own soul, and that the way heavenward rises above all knowledge. According to Hugh of Saint-Victor (d. 1141), meditation is a form of thought that has to be practiced if one wishes to pray fruitfully, but vision is characterized by the cessation of all thought, when love and knowledge coincide. Hugh describes his own experience as an embrace: "I know not where I am, because my Love has embraced me."[50] In agreement with Plotinus, Hugh thought that any one of us can become a mystic, given the will to do so. Love is the basis of the existence of all things. It is the deepest motive of all that lives within us. Each individual can plug into the foundation of love. This love is God. The mystical process itself was studied in Saint-Victor. Richard of Saint-Victor (d. 1175) summarized it thus:

> In the first degree God enters the soul and it turns inwards into itself. In the second degree, it ascends above itself and is elevated to God. In the third degree, the soul that is raised on high to God is merged wholly and completely in Him. In the fourth degree, the soul passes utterly *into* God and is glorified in Him.[51]

The essence of the process is therefore not that individuals remain lost in God, but that an experience of losing themselves in God leads them to live a changed life.

Another important mystic was William of Saint-Thierry (1085-1148), a native of Liège. He joined the Benedictines in Reims, made friends with St. Bernard of Clairvaux (1090-1153), became a Cistercian after a long period of indecision, visited the Carthusian monastery of Mont-Dieu in the diocese of Reims around 1144, and wrote the "Letter to the Brothers of Mont-Dieu." This work became the guide of later medieval mysticism. It was attributed to Saint Bernard.

William of Saint-Thierry (Guillaume de Saint-Thierry) takes for granted that the residents of Mont-Dieu are specialists in mysticism and he says:

---

[50] From Hugh of St. Victor's mystical tract, "De Arrha Animae," quoted in Evelyn Underhill's *Mysticism: A Study in the Nature and Development of Man's Spiritual Consciousness* (New York: E. P. Dutton, n. d.), p. 245.
[51] From Richard of Saint-Victor, "De Quatuor Gradibus Violentae Charitatis" (Migne, *Patrologia Latina*, Vol. 1. cxcvi, col. 1207). Translation is mine. Tr.

> That is your vocation: to seek Jacob's God; not in the usual, human manner, but to seek the face of God seen by Jacob, who said: "I have seen God face to face, and my life is preserved."

With him, too, the beginning of the mystic way is "Know thyself."

> The soul is the image of God and, because it is His image, it comes to understand that it can be and must be united with Him whose image it is.

Even without God's grace, individuals are able to experience a measure of mystical union; but, for the higher union of love, the grace of God is essential.

> The will is a natural propensity of the soul. In some it inclines towards God and the inner life, in others it inclines towards the body and material things. When the will arises, it is like a fire that blazes up and seeks its origin. This occurs when it is united with the truth and reaches toward the highest. Then there is affection. But when it receives, retains, and enjoys God's grace, then there is a union of spirit. Then there is God: for God is this supreme union of love.

He formulates the Christian aspect of love mysticism thus:

> So this love grows until it starts to resemble the love that constrained God to make human beings in His likeness. When the love has grown like this . . . it benefits the person by helping them to humble themselves with the supreme power, to be poor with the Son of God, to conform to the divine wisdom, and to feel inwardly what is in Christ our Lord.[52]

In this formulation, the mystical element of the poverty movement resurfaces.

---

[52] The previous quotes by William of Saint-Thierry. Translation mine. Tr.

Figure 81. Embrace with eye contact in a "Commentary on the Song of Solomon," manuscript that Saint Bernard must have seen, emanating from the abbey of Clairvaux. The bride here is obviously the Church. (Bibliothèque de Troyes ms 1869, f. 176 v.)

Figure 82. The oldest medieval representations of physical affection are found, surprisingly, in religious books. Here, in Bede's commentary on the Song of Solomon, it is shown in an embellishment of the "O" of "osculetur me" ["Let him kiss me"]. Originally, at the end of the 11th century, the bride was clearly the Church: a church-building was held in her arm, or stood in the background. But before long, the reference to the love between Christ and His Church disappeared. This miniature, for instance, symbolizes the love between Christ and the soul. (King's College, Cambridge. MS 19, f. 21 v.)

What William of Saint-Thierry had formulated, we find again in his friend St. Bernard of Clairvaux, but the tone is much more emotional. The latter was no thinker. Theology, or the formal study of God, left him cold. He was more interested in knowledge gained from experience. In his mysticism, purely spiritual experience is associated with the incarnation of God, or what he called the "abbreviation" of the Word: "Even from everlasting to everlasting Thou art God, and behold, He has become a day-old child."

He devoted thirty-one sermons to this child, Jesus, and his mother. He experienced his insight as an appeal that God decided to become like us because it means that He invites us to become like Him. It also means that mystical love can be expressed in human terms. In order to express it in this way St. Bernard used the Song of Solomon (Song of Songs) in the Jewish Bible.[53] He was not the first to do so, but his style was original in being intensely emotional, copious, and based on personal experience.

St. Bernard felt like a woman in love who enjoys the love of a man. This approach develops into a love affair with highs in which the two are absorbed in one another, and lows when the man is absent and does not satisfy the longings of the woman. In this manner, the language of ordinary human love was turned into a mystical language.

Typical of bride mysticism is that, on the one hand, mystical experience is interpreted as love and not primarily as enlightenment, and, on the other hand, strong emphasis is laid on the difference between God and the human being. They are, and remain, partners with their own individualities.

Yes, St. Bernard was an emotional man, but he did not get carried away by his emotions. Although, in his highest ecstasies, he was not aware of any difference between his own love and the creative Love, he observes that this was so only in the feelings, not in reality. In reality, the creature retains its difference. He illustrates what he means by the example of a piece of iron glowing in the fire. When white hot, it seems to vanish there. Even more clearly, he pictures what happens to a drop of water falling in wine. In the same way, the person continues to exist during

---

[53] Sermones in Cantica Cantorum. Left incomplete. Included in S. Bernardi's, *Abbatis Primi Clarae-Vallensis, Opera Omnia*. Editio Nova, Paris, 1854. Tr. note.

Figure 83. Love toward God as love between humans was mainly the discovery of St. Bernard. He described it in his commentary on Canticles, and he experienced it in visions as a love for the crucified Jesus, whom he embraced and covered in kisses. (Painting by the Westphalian master, Körbecke, ca. 1475. Alte Pinakothek, Munich.)

absorption in the immeasurable reality that encompasses him or her during ecstasy.

St. Bernard did not regard blissful ecstasies as the only, or the most important, part of mysticism. He said that rapture is, as it were, sleeping in the arms of God, but the soul returns, filled with a fire of extremely vehement love for God, with a spiritual zeal for righteousness, and a burning desire to do whatever needs to be done.

Especially in the last years of his life, St. Bernard managed to combine his mystical experience with incredible activity in the outside world. He became a prominent figure wielding a decisive influence on the course of affairs in the Church. His influence on the devotional life of the laity was considerable, too, and must not be underestimated. He, himself, was represented as drinking from the breast of the Virgin Mother or as someone who embraced the crucified Jesus. He describes the latter activity as a sort of vision. St. Bernard tried to immerse himself in what he saw and heard. When he read of the salutation of Mary by the angel, he imagined what he, himself, would have replied. So, too, with incidents in the life of Jesus.

A FEMININE WORLDVIEW

A noteworthy fact is the rise of women since the 11th century. The initial impulse came from the convents. The nuns followed the rule of St. Benedict, but were independent, with their own abbesses, who carried the crozier like bishops. Usually, they were good "all-rounders" and sometimes very original, like Herrade of Landsberg, who compiled a *Hortus deliciarum* ("Garden of Delights") containing at least a hundred miniatures.

HILDEGARD OF BINGEN

The leading light in this galaxy of ladies was the abbess of Bingen, Hildegard. She penned more than three hundred letters to the pope, the emperor, and other great personages, and preached in the cathedrals of Cologne and Mainz. She wrote poems, books, and some eighty musical compositions. She devised a secret writing with her own alphabet for internal use, made architectural drawings for her cloister, led a center producing manuscripts, and was personally involved in the miniatures that were made there. Her curiosity was boundless and she recorded her findings about herbs, natural processes, what happens to people during the sex act and during menstruation, what should be done to preserve health, what human types there are, and how the paleness of a monk's face shows that he has to do without meat and without a wife. She herself had a female friend of whom she was very fond, and it was decided to take this friend away from her. She fought to retain her, but the friend had to depart and after a year pined away.

Hildegard lived a long and active life (1098-1179), and had many visions, which make her especially interesting. "When I was forty-two years and seven months old, the heavens burst open with fiery light," she recalls. It was such an overwhelming and dazzling flash that she did not know how to write about it. She was so frustrated by it that she fell ill, until she managed to pick up the thread and described the story of the universe in thirty-three visions; not as a city that is built, but as an organism born out of love. Sometimes she uses forcible images, such as the violation of a woman, who then bears a horrible monster—this refers to the Church. But the basic picture is that of the universe as a sort of vagina and, in the center, an egg from which everything emerges.

In the vision she had thirty years later, after she had become familiar with the Cathars, "love" is the symbolic figure from which everything is born. This contradicts the Cathars, who preached about a world made by Satan. In ten pictures, she showed how Satan was crushed from the beginning, how the cosmos—with humanity as its midpoint—was born from the womb of Love, how human beings cultivate the earth, how a divine fire goes through humanity and purifies it, how a city of God is built—the world in which "love" sits enthroned.

The remarkable thing about Hildegard's world picture is that "love" and being born are the important things. It is noteworthy, too, that evil plays no part in the formation of humanity for she said that when God created the world, He had already decided to make human beings. Not sin, but love alone, plays a role here. Sin comes into view only when humanity is full-grown and wants to build a city of God.

The Free Nuns or Beguines

In the course of the 11th century, women joined the preachers of poverty in increasing numbers. They accompanied them, took part in the preaching, and were respected and influential. They had no wish to be shut up in convents. The Church, and later St. Bernard, too, was fiercely opposed to this. According to the Church, the proper place for them was a nunnery. These women, who were itinerating with the men, clung to the argument used by St. Paul: "Have we not power to lead about a sister, a wife, as well as other apostles, and as the brethren of the Lord, and Cephas?" (I Corinthians 9:5). Those women who did comply with the demands of the Church but, because they were inspired by the new spirituality of St. Bernard, did not wish to enter Benedictine abbeys, built cloisters close to the abbeys of the Cistercians. Often there were "double cloisters." Men and women were segregated, but lived under a single leadership. However, this did not last long. It was quickly decided that Cistercians must accept no responsibility for women; so the nuns went their own way in their own abbeys. By the end of the 13th century, there were twice as many Cistercian nuns as monks.

Figure 84. Following in the footsteps of St. Bernard, Cistercian nuns and Beguines, such as Hadewych, experienced mystical union as oneness with the man Jesus. The love between man and woman in all its aspects (the ecstasy of love, devotion, longing, forlornness, companionship, and union), was for a long time the most important symbol in which the mystical life was expressed. (Miniature, ca. 1430. Badische Landesbibliothek, Karlsruhe, mg St. George 89, f. 9 v.)

Many women went further than this. They did not want to submit to a man in any respect, and did not relish being affiliated with a male religious order. They claimed the right to be alone with God in a little house adjoining a church, often as a recluse. These women settled in great numbers around hospitals, plaguehouses, and cloisters. "Beguine houses" developed out of their humble little dwellings; but many Beguines wished to be free from having a fixed place of residence. They linked up with the itinerant religious men. They dressed in nuns' habits, and were poor, asked alms, preached and sang in the churches, wrote poems, and "gave their testimonies." In fact they shared the way of life of the contemporary subculture, together with vagabonds, wandering students, and other impulsive artistic types. It was a hazardous existence. For instance, it quite often happened that these women, when they trod on the toes of the clergy, were sent to the stake. But during the 13th century, Rome began to give them more protection; especially after Jacob de Vitry (1170-1240), who had traversed the whole of Europe and had encountered a new sort of religiosity everywhere, became a cardinal. He made sure in 1216 that Beguines were legally protected and had a form of organization that was not governed by cloister rules. Partly due to his efforts, the Beguine movement was soon flourishing. It is estimated that, in 1250, there were 1200 Beguines in Liège, 1500 in Mechlin, and 5000 in Paris.

The Beguine movement was characterized from the beginning by an ecstatic experience of a love that is full of longing and grips the whole individual. Jacob de Vitry writes a report on it as someone who had witnessed a new and special phenomenon:

> You have seen certain women here whose hearts were so overflowing with affection and love for God that they were sick with longing and were virtually confined to their beds for years. Their sickness had no other cause than the Loved One, who melted their souls with longing . . . I knew a woman who regularly experienced up to twenty-five ecstasies a day. I myself observed seven of them.[54]

Similarly, Jacob de Vitry records many of the phenomena of this pining love, such as prolonged weeping that etched marks on the cheeks, fits of insensibility, spiritual inebriation so strong that one woman lost her voice for days, sensory gratification by an "extremely sweet taste" in the mouth upon reception of the host.

This form of mysticism fitted into the culture of Northern Europe but made little headway in Italy, where there were hardly any signs of love mysticism. In the Southern Netherlands and in Germany, the contact between men and women was much freer than further south. Of course, there was the well-known friendship of St. Francis and St. Clare; St. Dominic, too, had tender feelings toward women: but only in the North was a woman able to befriend a man and give him spiritual training. The Beguines, who had settled near hospitals, were soon joined by men who wanted to live as they did. Jacob de Vitry, born in Liège, was taken under the wing of one of these women when he was a student in Paris, and she followed him from Nijvel[55] to Oignies to live as a

---

[54] Translation mine. Tr.
[55] Or Nivelles.

Figure 85. Being in love and having holy mystical experiences and ecstasies are transitory. Mystics attach more importance to permanently altered consciousness. Different pictures have been used to illustrate this. It is remarkable that one of these, the mystical marriage, occurs at almost the same time in the South of India and in Western Europe. Catherine of Siena was one of the first to experience it. St. Teresa of Avila and St. John of the Cross are those who have elaborated it most deeply and extensively. (*The mystical marriage of Catharine of Siena*. Panel, painted by Barna of Siena, 14th century. Museum of Fine Arts, Boston.)

recluse near the priory he had entered. Maria "of Oignies," as she was known, kept a kindly eye on him from 1207 until her death in 1213. He was her confessor and she was his leader. Jacob wrote her "Life" and dedicated it to the bishop of Toulouse, who had been driven into exile by the Cathars; he wanted to let him see from a real-life example that what the Cathars advocated could be used within the Church.

Thomas de Cantimpré (1201-1270) was convinced by the example of Jacob de Vitry that he would greatly benefit from instruction by one of these women, and he accepted the leadership of sister Lutgard of Tongeren (1182-1246), a Cistercian, although eventually he joined the Dominicans. He wrote a *Life of the pious Lutgardis* and a supplement to the book by Jacob de Vitry on Maria of Oignies, as well as "Lives" of Christina the Miraculous, and of Margareta of Ieper.

Contacts between the Dominicans and female religious became very intense in Germany, and contributed to the fact that Eckhart, Tauler, and especially Suso, were able to formulate mysticism so specifically.

"MINNE" MYSTICISM

Most of the independent women of the 12th and 13th centuries whom we now lump together under the name Beguines—one of the many terms of abuse in those days—came from aristocratic circles or rich families. Generally speaking, they did not fulminate against wealth, but quietly turned their backs on it. Nor did they disdain sexuality, but they wanted to channel it toward the supreme Man. The form taken by their mysticism was largely influenced by the minnesingers, nobles who were both poets and songsters and cultivated a new ideal of chivalry: courtliness in the service of the lady love. It was a male cult of the unattainable female, who may be desired but not possessed. This cult

Figure 86. The most famous representation of an ecstasy that is both sexual and mystical is Bernini's vision of St. Teresa of Avila. In itself, what St. Teresa saw was banal—lovers often speak of an arrow piercing their hearts. (The church of Maria della Vittoria, Rome.)

Free Love

Sexuality is used as a symbol in mysticism. Apparently, it does not lead to concrete experience as in India, unless in the form of friendship. Many mystics have gone in for friendship with a partner, and this was not something completely separate from their mysticism. Explicit sexuality as a form of mysticism is seen only on the fringes of the Church and the community. Groups who practiced it were often called Adamites, because they sought to recover the sex life of Adam and Eve before sin entered the world at the Fall.

The art historian W. Fraengers deduces from *The Garden of Earthly Delights* by Hieronymus Bosch that the painter belonged to some such sect. Even if his conclusion is denied, the fact remains that in this "garden" we find depicted the very ideas of the Adamites. What these were we learn from the protocols of an interrogation that took place, in Northern France in 1411, of the Carmelite William of Hildernisse, the spiritual leader of a group in Brussels calling themselves "People of Insight." He had undertaken to initiate individuals into the most difficult "secret of love," experiencing sexuality without physical consummation as "the way on high" to the "bliss of paradise." This was a matter of "platonic love," sexuality aimed not at propagation but at reproducing the "original image" of humanity; at an experience of the union of man and woman as they were made "in the image of God" (Genesis 1: 27). This Brussels group was not an isolated phenomenon. Similar ideas are found, for example, in the "Brothers and Sisters of the Free Spirit." These wanted to promote the liberty of the children of God by distancing themselves from whatever can corrupt love—lust, possessiveness, being locked up in a matter-of-fact marriage. By avoiding carnal desire, jealousy, lust for power, and the impulses of life, they hoped to remove the cause of violence.

The Inquisition made no allowances for a mystical experience of sexuality. "To say anything good about sexuality is hypocritical," was their standpoint. And the general reaction was one of, "They treat us to a lot of pious talk in public, but who knows what they do in private?" The same thing had been said earlier in Syria, and of the Cathars in the 12th century; as it was to be said later on of the "Alumbrados" surrounding Francesca Hernandez in 16th century Toledo.

Nor is the situation any better now. Certainly, after the "sexual revolution" of the 60s, everything has come out into the open and the authorities have developed a high level of tolerance. However the possibility of experiencing a spiritual dimension in sexuality is doubted, and could do with thorough discussion. The traditional symbolism is not only threadbare, it has been dragged so completely into the sphere of pornography that it is virtually unusable.

Figure 87. The common opinion of the Cathars, who said they were striving after an uncommitted form of love, is shown by the sly fox at the top of the picture which conveys the message: "Their pure love is a hypocritical sham." (The Bodleian Library, Oxford, MS 270 b, f. 123 v.)

Figure 88. "Such games ruined the morals of the Romans," says St. Augustine to a council of wise men as he points out a group of Adamites dancing under the direction of an instructor, Scipio, who, himself, is pointing upward at the saint. This is how one miniaturist updated a description in Augustine's *The City of God.* (*De Civitate Dei*, translated by Paoul Pralles. Museum Meermanno-Westereenianum, The Hague, MS II, f. 36 v.)

Figure 89. Paradise in an edenic world as it was meant to be—an experience of union with nature and with other humans without coercion and free from stifling desire. (Hieronymus Bosch, *The Garden of Earthly Delights*, The Prado, Madrid.)

Figure 90. Controlled sexuality produces paradisal fruit. Detail of center panel. A sense of being cherished by nature. Bird and meditating man. Community of love without sexual or racial discrimination. (Hieronymus Bosch, *The Garden of Earthly Delights*, The Prado, Madrid. See further pp. 89-102 of *The Hidden Art*, by Fred Gettings, Studio Vista, Cassell, 1978. This explains the mystical sexual meaning in some details of Bosch's work. Tr. note.)

developed not only out of a need to distinguish oneself as superior to the barbarian nobility who stayed at home on their estates, but also out of the new form taken by marriage in the 12th century. Previously, marriage had been more polygamous than monogamous, and was dominated neither by the man nor by the woman. In the 12th century, however, it became a feudal arrangement: henceforth, man and wife had the same obligations, but the man was the master and supported the woman in return for her subservience and submission. Thus marriage was based on a contract of the same sort as that on which the whole of society was based—the contract between lord and serf. The purpose of marriage was reproduction; sexual pleasure came second, and love was a poor third or even unplaced. If it was love anyone wanted, they would go looking for it outside marriage.

A female response to the male cult of love was inevitable. Large numbers of well-to-do women, married, unmarried, and widowed, bade home and marriage farewell in order to devote themselves to the "Minne," or ideal lover. They did not go after married men, nor were they looking for the counterpart to the knight's "Lady," but they gave their hearts to the man Jesus, who is God. The special feature of this female mysticism was that they let it be seen that their bodies, too, were affected by their mystical experiences, and that such experiences can be expressed not only in cold words but also in visionary pictures—the picture of an exchange of hearts, for example. What is more, realistic sexual imagery was used to represent union with God. More tellingly than other descriptions, it conveys the intensity of joy felt when the whole person is involved.

HADEWYCH, MECHTILDE, AND OTHER "MINNARESSES"

What is known as female mysticism is found not only in the Beguines but also in the cloistered nuns; especially among the Cistercians—which is not to be wondered at in view of St. Bernard's erotic mysticism.

One of the high points of this mysticism is the work of Hadewych, a Beguine of noble birth, very well-read in mysticism and courtly literature, and apparently hailing from the region of Antwerp in the middle of the 13th century. She adopted a considerable part of the theme and style of contemporary Minne literature, yet she was also original, as were most female mystics. In courtly love there was no thought of union with the beloved; its essence was unfulfilled longing. "Minne" was different from sexuality. The latter had to do with the procreation of children within marriage. In female mysticism, however, interest was centered on meeting and being united with the Beloved; also on the desolation when the sense of union disappears. Hadewych often penned plaintive verse about the absence of the Beloved. Sometimes she gives way to despair in such words as these: "It is an abomination to me that I live!" This has to do with what every mystic undergoes, the contrast between ecstatic experience and the mundane. "And I returned in my grief with manifold and great sorrows," says Hadewych at the end of her fifth vision. And in her sixth letter, she writes:

> You should always bear in mind that life has its good days and its bad days. Jesus, too, experienced this as man. . . . "Minne" invariably involves something elevated and something painful.

Especially in the female mysticism of those days, there was also an element of personal "pride," with the notion that a person may love God on His level. Hadewych observes that people can misuse precious insights, and says among other things:

> Our rational view is that we must fear God, and that God is great and we are puny. But if we then fear the greatness of God because of our littleness, and do not venture to reach out a hand to the greatness of God because we conclude that it is impossible to be God's dear child . . . this is a lack of insight.

It is in the very soul of the individual that God and the individual can be on a level, she believes.

> The soul is a way along which God travels to His freedom from His deepest point. And God is the way along which the soul travels to her freedom; namely His Ground, which is attainable only with her deepest ground. And if God were not wholly hers, what she had would not satisfy her.[56]

---

[56] Translation mine for all previous quotes from Hadewych here. Tr.

Chivalry also entails the endurance of such negative feelings as loneliness, despair, and sorrow, while we keep courage, and cross each hindrance and barrier on the unfamiliar way. Love is a school, not a repetition of what others have already demonstrated. Here we can recognize the authenticity of Hadewych.

Of Hadewych's life we know very little; but rather more is known of Beatrix of Nazareth (1200-1268) a Cistercian nun of Tienen in Belgium. She was educated by the Beguines of Nivelles. She, too, experienced an exchange of hearts and concluded a marriage with the Bridegroom. Her fame rests on her *Seven Manners of Holy Love* in which she describes the process of mutual loving. There we read of the longing, of the human effort to purify the heart, and of how God comes unexpectedly without any intervention of human activity. Then she feels that she is completely absorbed and swallowed up in the abyss of love and that she herself has become altogether love.

Again in Beatrix, the first step on the way to mystical union is the personal pride mentioned above: the idea of personal greatness through which the individual, in the ground of the soul, can love God on the same level. In Germany, it was mainly women in and around the Cistercian abbey at Helfta who experienced minne mysticism in a special way. This abbey was founded in 1258 without actually being given recognition by the Cistercians.

The most impressive female mystic was the Beguine Mechtilde of Magdeburg (1210-1282), who came on the scene late in life and met two kindred spirits in Helfta—the 28-year-old Mechtilde of Hackeborn and her pupil, 14-year-old Gertrude of Helfta. All three wrote mystical works. Unlike Mechtilde of Magdeburg, the two younger women were educated in a convent school and knew Latin. Mechtilde spoke only her native language. The Dominican Heinrich of Halle prepared a treatise from her notes. This is the oldest known mystical work written in German. Its title, *The Flowing Light of the Godhead*, points to a picture of God that we find also in William of Saint-Thierry and in Hadewych, and is based on the Gospel according to St. John: "All things were made by him; . . . In him was life; and the life was the light of men" (John 1:3-4). This is a picture of creation as a birth, an outflowing of life from the source of all life. The living life, which is the source of all things, is Hadewych's "minne" and Mechtilde's "light." But even in Mechtilde and in the whole group from Helfta, minne and its communion and the heart are important symbols.

A distinct echo of these female mystics is found in Sister Bertken, a recluse who spent fifty-seven years in a cell at the parish church of Utrecht. She died at age 87 in 1514.

Female mysticism has often been rather uninhibited emotionally; but, in its best representatives, this is not something that destroys the understanding. On the contrary, these women were well aware of the male mysticism based on pseudo-Dionysius, but thought they could go further than that. Hadewych once expressed this very clearly in terms of the "eyesight of the soul." The soul has two eyes—reason and love. Reason maps out her way and reaches out via what is known to the God whose being is beyond all knowledge. Love realizes her limitations and perceives no easy way.

> . . . but her powerlessness takes her further than Reason. Reason proceeds to what God is via the things that are not God. Love does not concern itself with what God is not, but finds joy in succumbing to what God is. Reason is more easily satisfied than Love, but Love has greater satisfaction in salvation. And yet these two are very useful to one another; for Reason teaches Love and Love illuminates Reason. Therefore when Reason is enthused by Love and Love allows herself to be ruled by Reason, then they are ready for something very great. But what that something is, can never be discovered except by personal experience.[57]

Hadewych called the idealized, courtly love known as minne a primary passion, a secret impulse (of hidden origin) to know Him who is unknowable except in the enjoyment of the Beloved. Mechtilde of Magdeburg called it "a storm in my heart."

FEMALE AND MALE MYSTICS

Minne mysticism tended to flounder in the hyperemotional experience of being the bride of Jesus. Especially when the sisters tried

---

[57] Translation mine. Tr.

to relive the motherhood of Mary as St. Bernard had done in relation to Jesus. They went through the bearing of, nursing of, and caring for Jesus in visions; and they turned all this into specific devotions.

Franciscan leaders, such as David of Augsburg, warned against a hotbed of emotions. Dominicans were scandalized by the extravagance of female piety "in its search for hugs and kisses" and the "overrating of each little so-called grace." According to them a serious danger was that these women might identify their own spirit (or the spirit of some other visionary nun) in an uncritical way with the Spirit of God.

These free women sought to maintain their pride in a male-dominated church while staying in the church; but it was a hard task. Male theologians were quick to interpret their self-respect as conceit. Thus Albertus Magnus, in 1270, construed the attitude of the women of Ries in the bishopric of Augsburg as a heretical mentality, because they refused to submit to the theologians on the grounds that these men had no idea what a mystical experience was. What is more, they would not be tied by cloister rules. Rules always enslave the spirit. The difficulties encountered by these Beguines may be seen in the fact that Mechtilde of Magdeburg, after trying to put her experiences into words, was warned by the theologians that she was being pantheistic and therefore heretical. She conformed to their doctrine but, at the same time, clung to her own experiences. "You are right and I am right," she said. How she had managed to reconcile the two sides, she was unable to explain. She sought guidance from Dominicans, but, to resolve her uncertainty, she joined the Cistercian nuns when ill and nearly blind.

Women wanted to strive for union with God and to become as near perfect as possible in this life. Old exhortations meant a lot to them; for example, "Let Jesus be born again in you,"—or texts from the Bible and from tradition that speak about being "a child of God," "born of God," and "like God." They had experienced these things and had no need to fit their experiences into some generally accepted doctrinal framework. But this is what they were expected to do.

The main heresy with which Albertus Magnus charged the women of Ries is that they said they were able to be like God in their own strength. Theologically, "in their own strength" meant "by nature" and thus "without the need of grace," or, to put it another way, without the Church. They felt that the dogmatic separation of "nature" and "grace" was a thought-structure designed to shore up ecclesiastical power: it was not something they had experienced. Obviously, these women had difficulty in handling thought-structures of this sort when they wanted to express their personal experiences in their own words.

The gulf between dogma and experience also played a role in the persecution by the Inquisition of the "brothers and sisters of the free spirit," the collective name for a group of Beguines and Beghards who saw minne mysticism as the attainment of a paradisal church in their own inmost beings. Serious errors were made during this persecution. In 1311, all these Beguines or Beghards were named and condemned en bloc. In 1317, at a church council in Vienna, Pope John XXII published that decision, but had to retract it rather hastily, because there seemed to be only a small obscure group whose members explicitly claimed that they lived through God apart from the Church and therefore could not sin, and that they were free to do what they felt like doing, for love is of God and those who love do not sin. As generalizations, these statements are untrue. As formulations of an individual experience, they may well be true. What is more, we find in these heretical women the same formulation of the same experience as in the Upanishads: "Whatever sins the one knowing this may seem to commit, he is clean, pure, not aging, immortal." Also in Tantra, consciousness is supposed to change the morality of the sexual act: "By the same deeds for which some people burn in hell for millions of years, the yogi attains eternal bliss."

Before the condemnation in Vienna, the Beguine Margreet Porete had been burned at the stake in Paris in 1310. She came from Valenciennes, and had written a book that caused quite a stir—*The Mirror of Simple Souls*. Parisian theologians found two heresies contained in two of its propositions. These involved what Porete called the annihilated soul, by which she understood someone who is completely absorbed in God. In this event, the practice of virtue is no longer necessary, the person is automatically virtuous. And Margreet Porete can no longer be bothered with consolations; the need for consolations would only be inhibiting. She wanted to tell about the "liberty of the children of God" as she had experienced it. She quoted St. Augustine's saying: "Love, and do what you like," but cautioned that he meant a special kind of love. Her burning is a tragic example of the alienation between the theology relied on by the Church and the mysticism based on experience.

On the same square in Paris, the Beguine Jeanne Dabenton was burned in 1372, tied to the corpse of a Beghard who had died in the prison. These were macabre panic reactions of a Church in decline. Anyway, of all the Dutch Beguines, Porete had the most influence on late medieval mysticism. Her book was distributed anonymously and was sometimes even attributed to Ruysbroeck.

In a book called *Women Writers of the Middle Ages*, Peter Dronke summarizes the period commencing with Hildegard and ending with Porete as follows:

> Whereas Hildegard used her visions to show her individual chart of the Christian cosmos, the women of the 14th century show the chart of the individual soul, however much this soul is itself filled with the presence of everything that is Christian.[58]

Hildegard was very well-grounded in the learning of her times, and wrote in Latin. Porete looked into her soul and wrote of her experiences on her own behalf, in her mother tongue. Unlike the men, these free women could appreciate the unusual and did not try to assimilate it to what was generally accepted.

THE JOURNEY INWARD

The ecclesiastical city of God was finally built in the 14th century, and immediately started falling apart. The papal power was at its height when Boniface VIII published a bull making it an article of Catholic doctrine that the pope held supreme sway over the whole world and over all the rulers of the earth. This happened in 1303. Six years later, his successor moved to Avignon and became the hireling of French kings. When, after seventy more years, the pope returned to Rome, the papacy itself was divided. There were two legally chosen popes, and later even three. This Great Schism lasted until 1417.

---

[58] Peter Dronke, *Women Writers of the Middle Ages: A Critical Study of Texts from Perpetua (d. 203) to Marguerite Porete* (Cambridge, 1984), p. 203.

The peace of society was shattered, too. Relationships everywhere were more aggressive; burghers fought burghers, towns and villages were wantonly razed to the ground, and discrimination against women, Jews, and mystics grew fiercer. And all this took place at a time when natural disasters and plagues were decimating the population of Europe.

At the end of the century, Christine of Pizan wrote a letter to the God of love concerning her vexation over the spiteful and humiliating way in which men were writing and speaking about women, whereas at one time the woman had been greatly honored and respected. She went on to write a trenchant volume summoning all women from all times and all classes to join her in building a new society. Its expressive title was *The Book of the City of Dames*, and it signaled the transition from the Middle Ages to modern times. The era in which men and women were all the same, when it came to burning them as heretics, gave way to a male culture where the woman was a natural suspect and could be burned as a witch. Witch-mania is not a modern, but a medieval European phenomenon. In 1484, the papal *Malleus Maleficarum* or *The Witches' Hammer* was published. Until the 18th century, it was the standard guide for witch-finders, Protestant as well as Catholic.

The security offered by life in a city of God was also shaken in the field of learning. The bond between the divine and the earthly worlds was severed by two Franciscans, the Scots or Irish Duns Scotus and the English William of Occam,[59] for whom the key formula was no longer, "I believe in order to understand," but, "I believe because it is something I cannot understand." It was a question of belief in another reality than the one open to our senses and subject to our mental analysis. This set the scene for the split between faith and science. The only solace offered by Occam was that God had willed the world and the Church to be as they were, and that human beings must order their lives in the hope of receiving His grace.

---

[59] The author calls Duns Scotus "English." Bertrand Russell in *A History of Western Philosophy* (Allen & Unwin, 1946) says: "He was born in Scotland or Ulster" (op. cit. p. 489). Bertrand Russell says William of Occam was born in Ockham, but he uses "of Occam" (p. 491). I have assumed that Russell, as a British philosopher, can be trusted to provide correct information regarding another British philosopher. Tr. Note.

In these times of schism, mystics looked for unity. Prompted by the wreck of Rome, which had been reduced by the plague to a village of 20,000 inhabitants, the mystically gifted, visionary widow, St. Bridget of Sweden (1303-1373), fulminated against the corrupt Church. More vehemently still, and with greater authority, Catherine of Siena (1347-1380) did the same. She was convinced that her will coincided with that of God. She wrote to monarchs and to the pope: "You must do God's will and mine." A tall order, and even less realistic than the search for unity between theologians and mystics. A new mysticism was born out of all this, but it was not able to rejuvenate theology. On the contrary, the theologians were in power and compared the new mystical language with their fossil formulas. What did not fit must disappear. The mystics had to do a careful balancing act, and once more looked for a way inward. Pomerius, speaking of the writings of Bloemardin, a Beguine of Brussels, said that no one could find a particle of heresy in them if he receives help or a special gift from God that teaches the whole truth. However, Ruysbroeck thought that he could find heresy in them. And Ruysbroeck, himself, was later accused of heresy by the Parisian theologian [and mystic] Gerson. The dividing line between heresy and orthodoxy had become so fine that the non-specialist was unable to discern it. No wonder the mystics eventually retired, book in hand, to a quiet corner.

IN THE SILENT DESERT—ECKHART

When the high summer of the Middle Ages was over, mysticism had a revival in connection with a feeling of alienation, as in Hellenistic times. It had an affinity with the latter, being a path inward that is a path upward. And yet it was original, and it is generally seen as a high point in Western mysticism.

The foundation was laid by Meister Eckhart (ca. 1269-1327). He was a Dominican who received the title of Master as an award for his theological studies in Cologne and Paris. He had a leading position in his order, taught in Paris, Strasbourg, and Cologne, and was an authoritative man with wide interests who exercised a great deal of influence. What had a big effect on his teaching was his contacts with women, especially Dominican nuns, who were eager for religious guidance. At the start of the 14th century there were in Germany seventy-four cloisters, each housing on average eighty to one hundred Dominican nuns. For the benefit of these nuns, Eckhart preached in their native language; and we may thank them that his sermons were written down.

Eckhart was a mystic. He felt free to look for a new mystical language based on his own experience, on his mother tongue, and also on theology, and thus to clarify female mysticism and to replenish theological language. He harks back to Hellenistic mysticism and refers to Dionysius, Origen, Gregory of Nyssa, and St. Augustine. There is no trace of dualism in him, no attribution of evil to creation. He appreciated the world in which we live. On the question of the behavior of people who prefer to withdraw into the church or into themselves, he says that this is not the best thing to do.

> But if a man does wed, God is really in him, and with him everywhere, on the streets and among people, just as much as in church, or a desert place, or a cell.[60]

Eckhart, like any other mystic, wishes to rise above the everyday world. Like the Hellenists, he sets out from a sense of alienation and from disenchantment with existence. But it would be a mistake to call everything evil. "Complain only that you are still complaining," he says. Life definitely has meaning even if we do not know what that is; but it does need to be anchored in the living life, in the spark of the soul that hangs in God. Each one of us possesses this spark: it cannot be extinguished, not even in Hell. And through it the individual can come in contact with God. It is created in the image of God, and is in God as a latent image. So the mystic way for Eckhart is a way back to the original pattern of ourselves in God.

He describes mystical experience as a nonvisual and nonverbal union with God, and explains this in terms of the old neoplatonic concept that the spirit is in God and longs to return to God. He also says that God's being is one until He becomes conscious of Himself and expresses Himself in a Word.

Speaking about the place where God is one, Eckhart refers to "the still desert in which no difference was ever seen." Other words for it are: "Immovable Rest," "Wordless Godhead," "Naked

---

[60] Raymond Bernard Blakney, *Meister Eckhart* (New York: Harper Torchbooks, 1941), p. 7.

Godhead," "Nameless Nothing." When this Godhead brings forth, Eckhart speaks of God. The "still desert" then becomes a fruitful field from which everything is produced—the image, Word/Son, and the Spirit. Humanity, too, is born of this desert; not as an image, but *in the image of* the inner divine birth. And in each human being is a "little tip of the soul" where all is indistinguishably one, a still desert out of which life springs anew.

For Eckhart, the mystical process is two-way. It goes out from the Godhead, the still desert within us—a movement that draws us inward. Afterward there has to be a response on our part that begins with self-knowledge: He says that we are always carrying all truth inside us. Where creation ends, God begins. God desires nothing more from us than that we withdraw from ourselves and let God be God in us. When we think of God's birth, and open ourselves up to this, all the powers of the soul come to life; and, in a single moment, we receive more wisdom than anyone could teach us.

This turning inward goes further and further, for it wishes to know from whence our existence comes; it wishes to penetrate to the simple ground (the still desert in which no difference has ever been seen, neither Father, Son, nor Holy Ghost), to the innermost where no one is at home.

Via our understanding, we can come to know the Creator God in ourselves through creation; but, beyond this knowledge, we descend into a space where nothing can be understood, where there are no more paths, into the ground of the soul that is one with the ground of the Godhead. Thus, the mystical process is a gradual retirement into the self, into the "I" that goes out above the ego which wants to have, to know, to comprehend. The "ground of the soul" is also "the spark of the soul," which is roused by the spirit into a tempest of love. The way inward is not only intellectual, it is also ascetic, and the will is purified in it by love. One must detach oneself from all covetousness and cultivate "poverty of spirit" and "purity of heart," and must empty oneself of all pictures one has formed of oneself, of the hereafter, and of Heaven and Hell, and even of God as an object of desire.

> . . . as long as ye possess the will to do the will of God and have the least desire for eternity and God, ye are not really poor.[61]

---

[61] Franz Pfeiffer, *Meister Eckhart,* translated by C. de B. Evans (London: John M. Watkins, 1924), p. 218.

Eckhart called this theory his detachment, or taking leave of everything, even of God. He sees "loving God as nobody" as the reverse of "loving God as the One who is all."

For him, poverty and chastity, or the ascetic side of love, mean, among other things, accepting circumstances just as they are with no ulterior motive. And the point Eckhart wanted to make was that this is how we ought to love God because life lives out of its own ground and wells up out of itself. Those who seek nothing, neither honor, nor profit, nor inner surrender, nor sanctity, nor reward, nor the kingdom of heaven really honor God.

The turning inward is important and we realize that while we are of high nobility in the depths of the "I," we are "nothing" insofar as the ego returns to nothing. The nothingness of an individual apart from God also applies to sin. Evil is not something next to God; it is nothing in itself, but just an absence of good. It is nothing; or is something only insofar as God takes part. In which event the following applies:

> You may, however, fully trust God not to have put the sin upon you, except to bring out the best that is in you.[62]

Guilt feelings about the past hardly make sense:

> God is a God of the present; as he finds a man, so he takes him and accepts him, not for what he has been but for what he is now.[63]

Again, in this doctrine, sin can have a positive value:

> All the evil and outrage done to God in sin, he will gladly suffer and suffer for many years to come, if only he may bring man to a better knowledge of His love, and make man's affection and thankfulness warmer, his struggle more passionate—as so often it is, after one has sinned.[64]

---

[62] Raymond Bernard Blakney, *Meister Eckhart*, (New York: Harper Torchbooks, 1941), p. 19.

[63] Op. cit., p. 19.

[64] Op. cit., p. 19. Tr. note: As we shall see, many of Eckhart's teachings were held to be heretical. This is hardly surprising. Jesus said, "Seek ye first the kingdom of God and his righteousness" (Matthew 6: 33). Eckhart bids us "wave good-bye to all that." Paul said, "Shall we continue in sin, that grace may abound? God forbid!" (Romans 6:1-2).

The significance of Eckhart lies in the fact that he was the first to formulate the following:

◆ How we must achieve self-development through self-knowledge: the knowledge that we are nothing in ourselves and yet, at the same time are of high rank because we come from God;

◆ How mysticism in its highest form leads to action;

◆ How the ultimate standard of our behavior lies in ourselves: the "ground" out of which God desires to be born in us; our conscience;

◆ How we should be ourselves with God, and "leave God in exchange for God," abandoning Him as a possession or object of desire;

◆ How detachment from externals (asceticism), goes well with an openness to everyone and everything in daily life;

◆ How mysticism is a twofold process: God will come in us to the extent that we concentrate everything in us on the "ground."

Figure 91. Jan van Leeuwen in his kitchen, miniature. (Koninklijke Bibliotheek, Brussels, Albert I, MS II 138, f. l. r.)

Clearly this form of mysticism is suitable for the laity. It is a call to the majority, a call to the individual conscience. It is a summons to high spiritual nobility in humble everyday life. Eckhart's followers, in particular, took this message to the people.

INWARD AND OUTWARD—RUYSBROECK

At the end of his life, Eckhart met with hostility. In the troubled sphere of rivalry between clergy and religious, Franciscans and Dominicans, the archbishop of Cologne took proceedings against him. He was condemned, but appealed to the pope in Avignon. The inquisitor of the Cathars, Jacques Fournier, was his judge. After Eckhart's death, apparently in Avignon, the archbishop of Cologne obtained from the pope a list of twenty-eight articles extracted from Eckhart's writings which contained errors or at least were too vaguely formulated. The motive of the papal condemnation was: "that these articles may no longer sully the hearts

Figure 92. Ruysbroeck writing his books in the forest of Soignes near Brussels. A colleague is making fair copies of them. His inspiration is still visible in the form of a dove flying out of the tree. This is the only speaking likeness known of Ruysbroeck. (The Royal Library, Brussels, ms 19, 295-297, f. 2 v.)

of the simple to whom they have been preached." They had been preached to nuns, but perhaps the persons intended were the "Sisters of the Free Spirit," who were also being examined by the Inquisition at this time and were often condemned. Because of this judgment, the name Eckhart fell into oblivion. However his writings continued to circulate and his doctrine was elaborated by Tauler and Suso in language that was rather more prudently phrased, and less speculative.

Tauler informs us that there is little he can say about his own mystical experiences, except that everything said about it is as different from what it is as the point of a needle is from the sky above us. He lays heavy emphasis on the works of love. Eckhart had already given an unorthodox twist to the story of busy Martha and her quieter sister Mary, the one who sat and listened to Jesus' word: according to him, Mary had not attained the highest form of mysticism in which love finds expression in deeds. Tauler makes much of such deeds. He also thinks that the worth of love will not appear until it has passed through barrenness of spirit. He describes a path to total "poverty of spirit," moving away from self-preoccupied asceticism toward forgetfulness of self and concentration on God. Like Eckhart, Tauler proposes a radical method of self-improvement by confining the attention to the uppermost tip of the soul while, on the other hand, turning from all egocentric anxieties. And, as Eckhart also did, he says that if we withdraw completely from ourselves, God will fully enter, neither more nor less, and as we withdraw from our self-preoccupation, He will enter in the same measure.

Heinrich Suso was a more sensitive individual. He wrote poetry and painted miniatures. We have a woman, Elsbeth Stagel, to thank for the fact that so much of his life and teaching has been preserved. His life was characterized by attacks from "wolfish" individuals. When he defended Eckhart, he was dismissed from his university lectureship. He liked women and was slandered for it. This depressed him. His doctrine is based on that of Eckhart; but he modified it, made it plain, and above all practiced it with tender devotion.

Tauler and Suso belonged to the Friends of God and exercised a great influence in this circle. The Friends of God were male and (especially) female religious, plus lay people from all stations of life. They spread over Switzerland and Southern Germany, and downstream along the Rhine. With very little organization, they formed a circle in which a wide variety of documents circulated: in addition to the works of Eckhart, Tauler, and Suso, they passed round among themselves chronicles and registers of deaths from nunneries, diaries and biographies. The best known are the diaries of Christine Ebner (d. 1356) and Adelheit Langman (d. 1375), and the correspondence of Hendrik von Nördlingen with Margaretha Ebner (d. 1351). Popular, too, was the *Book of the Nine Rocks* by Rulman Merswin (d. 1382), a rich Strasbourg banker who had insightful mystical experiences. To the Friends of God in Strasbourg, Ruysbroeck sent his major work, *The Adornment of the Spiritual Marriage*. Eckhart's ideas, as communicated in this circle, were collected at the beginning of the 15th century in the book *Theologia Germanica*, which Luther translated in 1516. Also one of Switzerland's most interesting mystics, the hermit Nicolas of Flue, came seeking guidance from the Friends of God in Strasbourg.

The Friends of God did not fight the Church, and they did not want to build a new Church. All they wanted was to be God's friends and to stretch out their hands to one another. Merswin describes how the individual Christians must break through the network of the corrupt Church via nine steps, and how Jews and Mohammedans are closer to God than many Christians. Tauler bears witness to the incurable corruption in the Church. His hopes for the survival of Christianity are pinned on the Friends of God. The female Friends of God sought to point out a way to others by setting them a concrete example of how life should be lived with God.

The question of the hour was: what is the right road to mysticism? The simple, radical way of Eckhart had become a minefield after the condemnation of his doctrine and of the writings of the Brothers and Sisters of the Free Spirit. Therefore, the leaders among the Friends were particularly anxious to show how the dangers could be avoided. Heinrich Suso, for example, named four temptations. These are: spiritual atrophy through letting the innermost life lie fallow; looking blankly at mystical phenomena; showing off the knowledge received by illumination, even though some effort is made to hide it; regarding meditation as an end in itself—a sort of drowsing away and sinking into oneself in an inner, empty, blind rest without love or longings. The last point, especially, required elucidation, because what Eckhart had said about resignation and mystical sinking into oneself could be taken to mean the very thing of which Suso complained. Suso thought that novices expect too much of it and then stay stuck in it. For him, the devotional way, with Jesus and Mary, was important, too. He said that the way of self-denial involves becoming detached from created things, being molded by Christ, and refashioned in the Godhead.

The Southern Netherlands have always been a breeding ground for mysticism. From the beginning of the 11th century through the 14th century, the bishopric of Liège, and women, came to the fore; later the scene shifted to Brabant, and men became more prominent. The latter period culminated in the work of Ruysbroeck, a man who spent a long and rather quiet life in and around Brussels. Little can be seen in his writings of the turbulence and cruelty of his times. What strikes us most in him is the rippling, broadly spun, sappy writing, owing to which one quickly and automatically glides over fairly horrible passages, especially those in which he describes the love relationship between God and the mystic as each devouring the other.

He says that Christ's love is both miserly and generous; that His hunger is extremely great; He gobbles us up, for He is a greedy guest and has a gaping hunger. Or, he says that if we could clearly perceive the passionate desire that animates Christ for our salvation, we should not be able to restrain ourselves. Or another passage on the mystical impulse mentions that the soul that loves is especially voracious and gluttonous: her (the Soul's) mouth stands wide open, she wants to have everything that is shown her. She is a created thing, and it is not possible for her wholly to swallow God, or to contain Him. And therefore she must yearn and hanker, and experience hunger and thirst forever.

Twelve of Ruysbroeck's works are extant; one of them consisting mainly of pieces by Eckhart. The latter was translated almost immediately, by Gerard Groot among others, and in its entirety in 1552. And so this work, together with those of Suso and Tauler became widely known very quickly.

Ruysbroeck does not describe any individual experiences, but is a born teacher: he lays down guidelines for dealing with experiences. He embroiders Eckhart's picture—the invisible God who is one, and the flowing life in the Son and Spirit of the God who brings forth. He fits this into what Eckhart calls the highest form of mysticism, going outward and inward, actively and reflectively, engaged without the unity of the Godhead being disturbed. He uses images of the seas, and of the seasons, to describe this ebb and flow in God and in the mystic. He also speaks of the "common man and woman," the open individual who shares all with all, just as God is "common" or sharing.

He describes the mature mystic in this way: he has a "common" life, for vision and work are both alike to him; as we open our physical eyes, look out of them, and shut them again—and it happens so quickly that we are unaware of it—so we die in God, live in relation to God, and remain continually one with God. In Ruysbroeck, the way to this height is the way of the "Spiritual Marriage." The book bearing this title begins with the Bible text from the parable of the wise and foolish virgins: "Behold, the bridegroom cometh, go ye out to meet him" (Matthew 25:6). The bridegroom comes, the bride goes to meet him. Each goes part way to encounter the other, as described in the Song of Solomon in the Hebrew Scriptures and fully realized in Christ. In those who are mystically endowed, this historic event repeats itself in a very individual fashion.

In Ruysbroeck, medieval mysticism reaches its culmination and its end. He explains the way along which a person can reach rest in everyday life, and which method is safe. In doing so, he draws copiously from a long tradition, to safeguard himself against the Inquisition. He is contemplative, speculative, and, at the same time, a spokesman for minne mysticism.

MODERN DEVOTION

In 1378, Ruysbroeck received a visit from a remarkable man. This person came from Paris, where he had been buying new books, and he was on his way back to his birthplace, Deventer, where apart from one or two rooms, he had handed over his house to pious women—in penitence—after recovering from a deadly disease. Gerard Groot had read Ruysbroeck's work. The peace of the "common man" was the goal for which he earnestly longed, too.

The two of them were in agreement that human beings cannot compel God and that, therefore, mystical experiences cannot be promoted methodically. They were also in agreement that one can certainly prepare oneself by doing and thinking everything possible that would enable one to concentrate on "the light that shines from within," as Groot called it. However, Groot did not concur with Ruysbroeck on the type of preparation needed.

Both of them saw the need for something to cling to in a period when all certainty offered by structures had been swept away. Ruysbroeck had, in line with Eckhart, chosen the ground of

Figure 93. Toward the end of the Middle Ages, mysticism was rather maudlin. There was an emotional attempt to enter into the feelings of Jesus and Mary. The "gift of tears" was part of the picture and was highly regarded. Margery Kempe earned herself a great reputation for this. Here two nuns are weeping. The text comes from the first line of a song, "Och nu mach ic wel trueren" (Ah, now I truly grieve). (Pen-and-ink drawing. Leiden University Library. MS Ltk 2058 f. 39 v.)

Figure 94. In women, minne mysticism often ended in being spiritually occupied with the baby Jesus. Here "Meditatio" (contemplation) and "Oratio" (prayer) are tucking the Child in bed. (Woodcut from *Van die gheestelijker Kintsheyt Jesu* [The Spiritual Childhood of Jesus], Antwerp, 1488.)

Figure 95. The gift of tears was also esteemed in Mary. (Dirc Bouts, "Mother of Sorrows," 15th century, The Louvre, Paris.)

Figure 96. Sharing the life of Jesus also meant a willingness to share His sufferings by bearing with Him the sufferings that befall us, or even by enduring self-inflicted sufferings, like this monk who is scourging himself under the gaze and blessing of Christ. (Miniature made by Venturino Mercati in Milan, ca. 1470. Photo: George Weidenfeld and Nicholson, London.)

existence as his handhold, and so he followed the way of self-knowledge, of the knowledge that everything rests on nothing and therefore offers no external security if it is not built on the ground of the soul. But Gerard Groot elected to have a more comprehensible handhold, that of good deeds, self-denial, and, above all, methodical meditation. For him, the ultimate handhold was not "Love" as the ground of existence, but the "Will of God," as Occam had taught. This will, which is bound by nothing, is not something we can come to know through "love" or "goodness," but only through what He has willed, through exercising a more sober realism. The way is something we have to seek in the world and in the Church such as they are. And this way is principally that of the creation of order.

Groot was a serious-minded man, converted by the fear of death, and firmly resolved to break all opposition to God's will, both in himself and in the Church. The Church had run off the rails, and it was essential to bring it back into line with God's order! Gerard Groot died of the plague in 1384 at age 44. The movement he started quickly spread over the whole of the Northern Netherlands and over Northern Germany and into Scandinavia. It was called the New Devotion—an explicit name, chosen for the benefit of the laity. All through the Middle Ages, devotion was the most important result of mystical experiences as far as the laity were concerned. The devotions to the Sacred Heart, to the wounds of Jesus, to His holy steps, to His Mother, to the sorrows of Mary, and so forth, were not made by the Church but were "seen" by mystics and taken up by the people. These devotions were now internal, from a sympathy arising from within, and were not stimulated from outside by such things as pilgrimages. It was more convenient to do the Stations of the Cross internally with little pictures in front of one. The devotions were modern insofar as people had had enough of the speculations, which, at the same time, were sniffed at by theologians, and also insofar as the way was more suitable for the laity. There was no need to fear the Inquisition. The path could be trodden everyday while one was living on the same level as the majority of the human race. The exercises by which the individual learned to disavow the greedy world were within everyone's capabilities. Of course, the Modern Devotion entailed forgoing what most people desire—wealth, fame, pleasure, power. It was also a northern devotion, not excessively emotional, but sober as possible; what was done was the main thing, and all the rest was subsidiary.

The inner way of the Rhineland and Brabant mystics, in which every hold was given up in order to attain to the one security, the spark in the soul was seen as difficult and dangerous. As a single point of security, the love impulse ("Love, and do what you like") was not trustworthy. When is love that is directed inward self-love, and when is it love for the spark in the soul? Instead, these pious people sought the mystical way in the inner world of feeling and tried, in a variety of writings, to gather from one another what concrete practices had been discovered. They engaged in ejaculatory prayer, repeating the Psalms over and over again, examining the conscience every day, being constantly aware of Jesus, gathering pious thoughts, meditating by means of various techniques.

The followers of Gerard Groot, who went to live as brothers and sisters of the common life, did not surrender their lay status. They did not wish to have special clothing and dwellings, or to follow rules or take vows. But they were certainly devoted to the common-life ideal and were open, too, to the recent invention of book printing. They gave tuition in schools and attached importance to the use of their national language, to pictures and to every accessible publication. The movement was pietistic, like so many that would arise after it, especially in Protestant churches. It was inward-looking, devout, and caught up in a revelation of Jesus. In its modern representatives, emphasis is laid on the figure of Jesus, who is Christ and God; who suffered every hour of His life, and who did so for our sins. All the inner attention is directed toward this Christ—the triune God scarcely comes in sight. And ecclesiastical literature plays no role here.

The Imitation of Christ written by Thomas à Kempis at the Agnietenberg monastery in Zwolle (ca. 1424-1427) is the most perfect work of this Modern Devotion; and the work most reprinted, translated, and widely disseminated, after the Bible. It is free from any kind of speculation, theology, and churchiness; and is comforting, and very suitable for being occupied with one's own spiritual condition. In the opinion of Thomas à Kempis, reading a book is more fruitful than conversing with someone. "With a little book in a little nook" reads his epitaph. Huizinga characterizes later developments like this:

Figure 97. The New Devotion was very practical. People collected methods of prayer and meditation, and developed new methods of their own that were focused on something concrete, such as the secrets of salvation by Jesus, the seven sorrows of Mary, the limbs of Jesus, His five wounds, etc. Pictures were used as helps, and so were pieces of lace, rosaries, medals, etc. A splendid example of a meditation board of the period is this one by Hieronymus Bosch. It hung in the living room of Philip II in the Escorial. It is a sort of mantra: in a circle, the seven deadly sins surround a radiant center containing the risen Christ in the heart of it and the text, "Cave, cave, Dominus videt," a warning that God sees us. Depicted at the four corners are the last things—death, judgment, heaven, and hell. (The Prado, Madrid.)

Figure 98. The meditation diagram of Nicolaus van Flue (d. 1487) was very popular and is still used today. It is concerned not with the Last Judgment, but with the Good News. Here, too, are circles, and Christ occupies the center. Many woodcuts have been made from the original print, which appeared in a book for pilgrims published in Augsburg ca. 1480.

Figure 99. Entering in sympathy into the sufferings of Jesus was something that was promoted on a wide scale by the mass production and distribution of prints such as this one on a letter of indulgence in Nuremberg, from the second half of the 15th century.

Figure 100. In the 13th century, entering into the sufferings of Jesus budded into the cult of the Sacred Heart, which was to captivate millions of Catholics over the next few centuries. The big impetus came from the visionary, St. Margaret Mary Alacoque. This representation was drawn by herself in 1685 in Turin.

> The snug, spiritual intercourse in the quiet intimacy of simple little men and women, whose wide heaven spread its vault over a minuscule world that was bypassed by the stir and tumult of the times.[65]

Everywhere in the 15th century in Northern Europe we find a new spirituality oriented toward the laity. In France, the chancellor of the University of Paris, Jean Gerson, attacked Ruysbroeck and drew a distinction between speculative and practical mysticism which he maintained for life. But he defended Gerard Groot. The New Devotion and the Friends of God concurred on many points. After the *Imitation of Christ* came *The Life of Christ*, written by Ludolph of Saxony in 1377, which was also very influential. Suso, too, was much loved in pious circles. Gerard Groot had an affinity with him, and translated his *Little Book of Eternal Wisdom*, a sort of service book for lay people. Suso's one hundred points of meditation were included in many breviaries. At this period meditation was no longer a matter of being still and emptying the mind in order to find the self, but, on the contrary, consisted of mental activity with a picture or a reading in front of one. The meditation diagram painted by Nicolas von der Flue was widely distributed in the form of woodcuts. Picture diagrams of this kind were made everywhere, by among others Hieronymus Bosch. Their purpose was to keep the end of life before one's eyes— death, judgment, heaven and hell—and to serve as a reminder of how Jesus Christ made a way to heaven for us through death. The center of these meditation diagrams was usually Christ in His heavenly glory, as an image of union with God.

IN THE CLOUD OF UNKNOWING—ENGLAND

In the 14th century, England, too, had its own mysticism. This was a mysticism of the recluse in which women played a leading role, either as an anchoress or because men like Richard Rolle and Walter Hilton wrote their works for certain women who were important to them. In this mysticism it was emphasized that God is not to be reached through knowledge, but through love. Also

---

[65] J. Huizinga, *Herfstij der Middeleeuwen* [The Fall Time of the Middle Ages] (Groningen, 1984).

the largely lay character of those involved is very evident. These women were not nuns, but free agents who had chosen the life of a recluse. They had no convent rules, and the handbooks they followed could hardly be termed priestly, having been cleansed of all theological speculation and being very practical. Not that anything was said about the need to build the city of God: salvation was sought in a tiny corner of the Church with God alone.

The best known handbook in use with the female recluses is the *Ancren Riwle* written in Old English and emphasizing exercises designed to arouse emotional ardor. An older rule for female recluses comes from the hand of Aeldred of Rievaulx (1110-1167), the first mystical writer to recognize the importance of personal friendships. And the hard side of human and divine love seems to have been poignantly experienced by Aldred. He gives the following account of it:

> You called me, Lord, You called, You shouted, You startled me, You forced my deaf ears to hear You, You struck me down, You defeated me, You conquered my hard heart, You sweetened and allayed and dispelled my bitterness.[66]

In the best known mystical writings of two women, there is also a marked preoccupation with violence. Margery Kempe (ca. 1373-1440), the mother of fourteen children, is a typical example of a woman who was so upset by the violence of her times, that the slightest contact with violence—an injured animal, a smacked child, a crucifix—made her weep hysterically and fly into a rage. Whenever she saw or heard anything of that sort she thought she saw how our Lord was scourged or wounded. She endeavored to control herself, especially by bringing to mind the ultimate goodness of all things in God.

> For You are so good that You cannot be any better. Therefore it is a wonder that a person should be separated from You forever.[67]

---

[66] Translation mine. Tr.

[67] Translation mine. Tr.

Kempe looked for guidance from another woman, Julian of
Norwich (1342-1422). The latter lived as a recluse in Norwich, a
thriving English city that traded with Holland and the Rhineland.
It is not by chance that the many recluses in this city had much in
common with the Beguines. For instance, like the Beguine
Mechtilde of Magdeburg, Julian also wrestled with the problem of
how to write something about her own experiences without being
untrue to herself or coming into conflict with the Church. Julian
made the assumption that her own experiences and the teachings
of the Church were both true, but she was not able to bridge the
gap between them and spoke of the two kinds of secret things.[68]

More strongly than Margery, Julian had acquired a balanced
and original view of God through her mystical experiences and
visions. She says, "I believed soothfastly that Hell and Purgatory
is for the same end that Holy Church teacheth . . . But for all my
desire, I could see of this right nought."[69] To see evil as an expression of God's "wrath" is a mistake, she believed. The only proper
description of God is "Love." "It behoved that there should be
sin; but all shall be well, and all shall be well, and all manner of
thing shall be well."[70] The dark night of sin will end in light, even
though, at present, we do not understand how: "And at the end of
woe, suddenly our eyes shall be opened. . . . Thus I saw that our
faith is our light in our night: which light is God, our endless
Day."[71]

> And He is very Father and very Mother of Nature: and
> all natures that He hath made to flow out of Him to work
> His will shall be restored and brought again into Him
> by the salvation of man through the working of Grace.[72]

In male mysticism, we certainly encounter speculation, but their
basic theme is that whereas understanding and contemplation do
not approach the essence of God, love does. Richard Rolle (d.
1349) gives us a very personal description of this experience of
love:

---

[68] See *Revelations of Divine Love recorded by Julian, Anchoress at Norwich, anno
Domini 1373*, Chap. XXXIV. Edited by Grace Warrack. (London: Methuen,
1901), p. 69.

[69] Op. cit., Chap. XXXIII, pp. 67-68.

[70] Op. cit., Chap. XXXVII, p. 56.

[71] Op. cit., Chap. LXXXIII, p. 200.

[72] Op. cit., Chap. LXII, p. 156.

My soul pants after You. My being thirsts for You. Yet You will not show yourself to me. You ignore me. You bolt the door and shun me. You pass me by. You laugh even at my innocent sufferings. Surely You snatch your lovers away from all things. You raise them above all desires for worldly things. You enable them to love You. And they do love You.[73]

Rolle even goes so far as to see all love to their fellow humans as something from which mystics are drawn away for the sake of God. In the most important work of English mysticism, entitled *The Cloud of Unknowing* (ca. 1360), this being drawn away from everything that is not the love of God is the main theme. But there it is elaborated under the strong influence of pseudo-Dionysius: all thoughts, ideas, and images must be buried beneath the cloud of forgetting so that our naked love (naked because it is stripped of all thinking) can ascend on high to God, who is hidden in the cloud of unknowing. The author exhorts us to "break down all witting and feeling of all manner of creatures; but most busily of thyself," and adds:

For . . . thou shalt find when thou hast forgotten all other creatures and all their works—yea, and thereto all thine own works—that there shall live yet after, betwixt thee and thy God, a naked witting and a feeling of thine own being: the which witting and feeling behoveth always be destroyed, ere the time be that thou feel soothfastly the perfection of this work.[74]

A very special grace is required for something like this, and an exceptional "ableness" to respond to it. "And this ableness is nought else but a strong and a deep ghostly sorrow." It can induce us to go in for rigorous asceticism, but that is not advisable. "But in this sorrow needeth thee to have discretion . . . sit full still, as it were in a sleeping device, all forsobbed and forsunken in sorrow." ["Forsobbed" means "soaked," and "forsunken" means "immersed".] The author adds, "For he may make sorrow earnestly, that wotteth and feeleth not only what he is, but that

---

[73] Rolle: *The Fire of Love* (London: Penguin, 1972), p. 45. Translation mine. Tr.
[74] *The Cloud of Unknowing*, Chap. 43. Edited by Evelyn Underhill. (London: Watkins, 1922), p. 209.

he is." ["Wotteth" means "knows".] This comes of a realization that the individual's own existence rests on nothing. If this sorrow is "truly conceived" it will create a desire for the true ground of existence. A dangerous period is that during which this desire remains unfulfilled. The author then "goeth nigh mad for sorrow. Insomuch, that he weepeth and waileth, striveth, curseth, and banneth; and shortly to say, him thinketh that he beareth so heavy a burthen of himself that he careth never what betides him, so that God were pleased."[75]

In Walter Hilton, too (d. 1396), who had read Rolle and *The Cloud of Unknowing*, the interest centers on a love beyond thought, which blots out the self: "I am nothing. I have nothing. Nothing do I desire except one." However, he is more genial in his description of the mystical process, which he sees as a ladder. In fact, he thinks that mystical experience is part of the normal growth of a good Christian; though for some it may occur on a lower rung than that of "perfect contemplation," in which the self is lost in the cloud of unknowing.

THE EUROPEAN PHASE

As the New Devotion of the Middle Ages came to a close in Northern Europe, a new culture arose in the South. This ushered in the period when Europe grew into a world power, and started with the development of a new way of thinking. No longer did people look with the "eye of faith" that sees all things as symbols and icons of the divine. They did not see with the time-honored bird's-eye of the Chinese, but with the eye of the individual who has both feet planted firmly on the ground.

This way of looking, this perspective, was scientifically described in Florence in 1415. One of the first masterpieces showing that the artist possessed a sound grasp of perspective is a mural by Masaccio in the Carmelite church in Florence (1426-1428). He painted the Gospel Story as an ordinary human event, such as a contemporary spectator might have seen it. The holy is earthly, and the vertical reference to heaven has disappeared.

---

[75] Op. cit., Chap. 44, pp. 210-213.

In this approach to looking, the human being is central, and the same applies to the culture that arose out of it. Interest was now focused, not on the city of God, but on the world of humanity. People did not look in the Bible to improve their understanding, but set about using their eyes, plus optical instruments to extend their range of vision. And it was no longer the clergy, but the laity, who were the cultural leaders. The new, horizontal outlook also meant that reality was investigated differently. Reliance was placed on the five senses, and on a scientific method consisting of observation followed by analysis. The method was rational, and free from ecclesiastical dogmas.

Each age has its own way of trying to solve the riddle of creation. In the Renaissance, a fresh look was taken at history and

Figure 101. In the many miniatures that were made for Suso's mystical work, *Horologium Sapientiae* [The Clock of Wisdom], we can see how opinions changed after 1450, with even the "pious" showing an appreciation of technology. The machine was considered an image of virtuous life; a prime example was the clock, which measured time without regard to human feelings. It counted the hours in the dark, and day and night, summer and winter, with great regularity. An upright individual was expected to live by it. Measure and moderation were the highest virtues. White has thoroughly documented this development. One of the earliest of these illustrations shows "Wisdom" pointing to the mechanism of which Suso says in his Introduction that it "rouses the sluggard from uncaring slumber and urges him to be vigilant in the performance of good deeds." (Koninklijke Bibliotheek, Brussels. MS IV, III, f. 13 v., ca. 1450.)

Figures 102 and 103. The difference between the religious attitude of the New Devotion and that of the Renaissance becomes strikingly obvious when these two pictures are set side by side. On one hand, there is a man who is actually suffering, and on the other, there is a man who has endured as a hero—a flawless athletic man of evident virility, who boldly displays his wounds. (Top: A. Bouts, *Man of Sorrows*, Musée des Beaux Arts, Lyons. Photo: Bernard Lontin. Bottom: M. van Heemskerk. *Man of Sorrows*, 1532. Museum voor Schone Kunsten, Ghent. Photo: ACL, Brussels.)

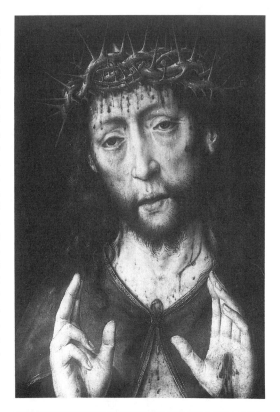

scholars delved into the forgotten cultures of the ancients in the hope of rediscovering some high civilization. The further back they went, the greater their chance of finding the source of wisdom—or so they believed.

The new culture can also be described as emancipative. People threw off their dependence, especially their dependence on the Church. The Church has sighed over this secularization, but more and more areas of life have been taken out of her hands during the course of the modern cultural period. She, herself, withdrew into an ivory tower of anathemas, and majored on individual salvation in the world to come.

The Renaissance was humanistic, and it was human dignity that was upheld. The human being was a microcosm—the universe in a nutshell. Not dependent on the stars, mankind could learn to control and influence the universe by the exercise of its innate powers. It did not expect a new world produced by divine intervention, but would create this world itself. And God was completely humanized. In paintings of Jesus after His crucifixion, He is shown displaying the wounds on His handsome half-naked body, and the loin-cloth suggests rather than disguises His virility (see figures 102 and 103). He is also a beautiful baby.

This humanistic culture originated in Florence and had become so strong by 1450 that it spread all over Europe. And when, after fifty years, Spain took over as the center of this culture, it started to cover the globe. Here, too, a new outlook set events in motion. Columbus did not turn eastward to the overland and coastal route to India, but westward to where there was nothing but water. He did not fall off the rim of Earth, neither did he reach India from the other direction, but he made the discovery of an unknown continent. With this discovery, there began a European phase of world history, which is now drawing to a close because the rational investigation, discovery, and control of nature is encountering limits. Now we find people searching for new religious sources elsewhere in the world and in history.

THE REBIRTH OF HERMETIC MYSTICISM

One of the most remarkable men to usher in this new era was Nicolas of Cusa (1401-1464), a brilliant scholar, diplomat and mystic. The son of a boatman in Cusa, he was educated in the Hanseatic city of Deventer by the Brothers of the Common Life.

Figure 104. The idea that everything flows forth from the One God is closer to the experience of the mystics than that God created something outside Himself out of nothing. The latter suggests a hiatus. Now theologians drew a clear distinction between the Creator and His creation; in their view it was a delusion to imagine that anyone could become a god. To be "born of God" was clearly a grace bestowed exclusively through the Church. The alternative doctrine, as proposed by Scotus, came under suspicion and was in fact condemned. Here is the doctrine of Scotus Erigena in picture form: the properties of the invisible God, with Goodness in the middle, create (in and out of Chaotic Material made subject to Time and Space) the four elements—Fire, Air, Water, and Earth—together with all they contain. Nature itself is *non creans* and creates no more. Christ closes the circle. (Honorius van Autun, *Clavis physicae*, 12th century. Bibliothèque Nationale, Paris, MS lat. 6734, f. 3 v.)

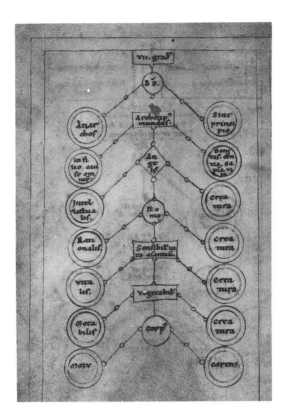

Figure 105. The same world picture in another form. Here we have a stylized stream that flows downward from the seven properties and *Bonitas* [Goodness], and ends in *corpus* [the body]. This representation can also be read as a "scale of being." The lowest form is the body, the highest form is the divine Goodness. Each individual can climb this ladder to God. (Honorius of Autun. *Clavis physicae*, 12th century. Bibliothèque Nationale, Paris, MS lat. 6734, f. 3 v.)

Imbued with the New Devotion, he continued his studies at the Universities of Heidelberg, Padua, and Cologne, and became a bishop, a cardinal, and finally a member of the Roman Curia. He had a clear plan for the reformation of the Church, traveled widely in the Netherlands and Germany to make a beginning there, and worked to set up a council intended to lead to the reconciliation of East and West. He drew the first map of Germany, and occupied himself with the reformation of the calendar and with infinitesimal calculus.[76]

Usually he is thought of as a late medieval figure, and he did adopt much of the current medieval theology. However, he was modern insofar as he did not let this theology hinder the search for a new picture of the world that would match his experiences. It was not Copernicus, but Nicolas of Cusa a century earlier, who was the first to propose that Earth orbited around the Sun. Nicolas was even further in advance of this time than this because he suggested that the universe is not limited to one solar system, but contains an infinite number of them.

He also sought for a new mysticism along forbidden paths by exploring Scotus, Eckhart, and Ramón Lull. The Irishman, John Scotus Erigena (ninth century), was condemned in 1210 when the followers of Amalric appealed to his writings as authoritative. Forty-five years later the pope ordered the destruction of all copies of Scotus' works in France because the Cathars were employing them. Ramón Lull latched onto Scotus' vision of creation, and Eckhart followed Scotus in picturing creation as a birth out of God. Both enjoyed the favor of Boniface VIII initially, but were condemned later. Nicolas ascribed all these condemnations to "weak eyes" and "lack of insight," and he was not deterred from dabbling in the heterodoxy or from allowing it to help in the formation of a new doctrine. He tracked down the three men's writings for his library at Kues, where they may still be seen.

Scotus Erigena had translated pseudo-Dionysius, and Nicolas of Cusa said of this fifth-century Syrian book, which had its source in Hellenistic mysticism, that it was not suitable for weak eyes. But he himself read it and was inspired by it.

---

[76] "It was an instinct that guided Nicolaus Cusanus, the great Biship of Brixen (circa 1450), from the idea of the unendingness of God in nature to the elements of the infinitesimal calculus." From *The World of Mathematics*, Vol. 4, by James R. Newman (New York: Simon & Schuster, 1956), p. 230.

In Florence at this time, people were eager to rediscover forgotten lore, especially anything to do with classical antiquity; and here, too, they stumbled on Hellenistic mysticism—and in a fairly undiluted form. It was purveyed in a manuscript brought from Macedonia by a monk in 1460. The writer purported to be someone called Hermes Trismegistus. People had a vague notion that he was one of the wise ancients. The ruler of Florence, Cosimo Medici, commissioned Marsilio Ficino to start on a translation of the manuscript which was finished two years later. Nine years later, in 1471, the first edition was published as *Corpus Hermeticum*. Right from the start, this Alexandrian production inspired great respect because it was assumed to predate the Bible.

The Platonic and Christian ideas contained in it were interpreted as a sort of prescience. Since it was seen to have certain things in common with ecclesiastical tradition, this piece of Alexandrian Gnosticism was able to form part of the new intellectual climate without arousing opposition. As a result, the teachings of Scotus, represented by Ramón Lull, began to carry more weight. All this fitted in splendidly with the high hopes that were being held about the so-called "new man." The old Gnosis supported the individual who took union with God in his or her own hands, and became a kind of demigod containing the whole cosmos and able to understand and rule it. The ability to do the latter was sought in mathematics, natural science, medicine, astronomy, and combined with things no longer regarded as scientific—numerology, geometrical contemplation, astrology, and white magic. I refer to the latter as occult sciences, but in those days these subjects were not "occult" (secret, concealed), but were included in the arts and sciences in imitation of Pythagoras, who had also blended the knowledge gained in ecstasies with the knowledge obtained by observation and had then used numbers to portray this amalgam. Pythagoras was another figure who was revered as an authority by hermetic Europe, the history of which has been well researched—from its beginning under Scotus and Lull to its end under Giordano Bruno—by Frances Yates. The following section is based on her studies.

A New Language—The Geometric

Characteristic of the Scotus tradition was a picture that had already been formed from mystical experience in Hellenistic times:

Figure 106. There is obvious approval of technical equipment in this vision of a remote and inaccessible Deity: God as the framer of the great cosmic machine. (William Blake, "The Ancient of Days," painted etching, 1824. Photo: The Whitworth Art Gallery, University of Manchester, England.)

that the one Godhead, resting in Himself, is clearly differentiated from the first unfolding of this Godhead in the Word. According to Scotus, the Word contains the Names of God, which are also "first causes," the flowing out of the divine into creation, in time, space, and matter, multifariously and tangibly. This is a picture of the ambiguous nature of mystical experience.

On the one hand, the Unity is experienced as unnameable and unknowable and, on the other hand, there is a multiplicity of physical objects that constantly change in time and space—the environment of daily life. It is a simple picture of the reconciliation of two poles: the manifold is shown as an "emerging from and returning into" the One, which is "breathing it in and out"—something like Jacob's ladder. Out of the manifold, the aspirant climbs the "mystical ladder" rung by rung to the One who is exalted above time and space. Scotus described this way as follows:

Creating and not created: the Godhead;

Created and creating: the Names.

Created and not creating: the created universe in generation, time and space;

Not creating and not created: God as the end of all.[77]

Unlike Eckhart, who worked this out theologically as a birth from the Godhead, Ramón Lull went back to Scotus' teachings in order to devise a language that was not theological. Climbing the mystical ladder signified, for Lull, union with creation at all levels, mainly through love. He used the language of love. In his *Book of the Lover and the Beloved* (written ca. 1285), his Beloved is so great "that You can abundantly and totally be the person who yields to You." In nature, too, he finds a mystical love song:

The birds sang of the dawn, and the lover who is the dawn awoke. And the birds ended their song, and the lover died in the dawn of his Beloved.[78]

To express mystical union, Lull employed images taken from what was for him living "dead" matter: "Their love mingles like water and wine, and they are bound together as intimately as heat and light." Lull was not by chance a follower of St. Francis; but, unlike the other lovers of God, he used an abstract learned language in order to define the object of his love more precisely, and depicted the mystical ladder in a geometrical form. His complicated patterns were based on Scotus' picture of creation and on the suggestion that the circle should be central in theological thinking. Thus the "names" of God are interconnected in a circle: "Justice" is "Goodness," "Goodness" is "Truth," "Truth" is "Justice," and so on. With the help not only of circles, but also of triangles, squares, lines, and letter codes, he constructed a comprehensive system.

---

[77] Frances A. Yates, *Lull & Bruno*, Vol. 1 (London & Boston: Routledge & Kegan Paul, 1982), p. 82.
[78] Translation mine. Tr.

Figure 107. An example of how Ramón Lull chose to translate his mystical experiences into a scientific symbolic language. (Woodcut in Lull's "*Ars brevis*," in *Opera Omnia*, Mainz, 1721-1742.)

Ramón Lull, who was born on the island of Majorca in 1232, spent his youth at courts that were in contact with the Cathars, and had a mystical vision on Mt. Randa in the same Spain and in the same year (1272) as that in which the Jewish Kabbalistic book The Zohar saw the light of day. Now Lull agrees not only with the Cathars in the values he attaches to Scotus, but also with The Zohar in regard to letters, geometrical forms, and images such as trees and stairways. Just as, in The Zohar, the named Sephiroth unfold out of the nameless *Ain Soph*, so, in Lull's doctrine, the nine-name circle (which can be labeled with the letters BCDEFHIK) arises out of the nameless divine state. Lull envisages an interplay between this circle and another circle labeled with the letters ABCD, the code of the four elements (water, air, fire, and earth) which were raised by the Spirit out of chaos. Numerous lines can be drawn from one circle to the other, and also between the parts into which a given circle is divided, in order to determine the creative influences on things, and thus their characteristics. According to Lull, this geometrical language is sufficient to represent and elucidate creation in its variety, structures, and connections. He sees it as the basis of all sciences and calls it an art. The insight gained by means of his letter code is applicable, he says, both to the mystic way and to practical sciences such as medicine, which he himself practiced.

Lull was convinced that he had discovered a universal science, and that it could also be understood and approved by Jews and Moslems. He presented this to Pope Boniface VIII, taught his *ars* (art) in Montpellier, Paris, and Naples, and traveled in the Islamic world in order to gain acceptance for his method.

His efforts there were in vain. Apparently he was stoned to death in Tunisia. The Spanish inquisitor, Eymericus, condemned him posthumously in 1357, but Lull was rehabilitated and had a significant influence on what is now called "occult" mysticism.

Figure 108. The following miniatures were painted in Florence at the very time when the Hermes Trismegistus corpus was discovered and translated. In the alchemical work ascribed to Ramón Lull he is depicted as a bearded monk displaying his reborn soul on a piece of cloth. In another picture he is plowing a field, while standing on the plow playing a pipe in Hermes Trismegistus himself. Again, Lull is shown cooking two "Tartars." The black fumes hanging over the oven are full of monsters. This represents the alchemical purification. Incidentally, the real Ramón Lull never engaged in activities of this kind. (*Opera Chemica*, 1470-1475. Bibl. Nazionale Centrale, Florence. MS BR 52, resp. f. 211, 21.)

Figure 109. Alchemy was seen as a serious matter. Here "Nature" in the form of a winged naked woman crowned with the seven metals, is telling the alchemist what to do: he must not restrict himself to the mechanical work represented by the oven with its retorts, but must immerse himself in her work. Out of the burning *prima materia*, a tree with two intertwined trunks is growing. Nature says to the alchemist in the text of the manuscript: "And you will never see anything if you do not enter my forge. . . . if you do not first go seeking the seed of all metals, animals, and plants, which I have in my power and sit in the earth." (Miniature by the court painter of Margaret of Austria, Jehan Perréal, 1516. Musée Marmottan, Paris. Photo: Routhier, Paris.)

Part of the purpose of Lull's *ars* was to calculate influences from the cosmos; and, in order to give it a general validity, he introduced Arabic astrology into his system, calling it "new astronomy." Its novelty resided in the fact that he had replaced the heavenly bodies by the "names" in the circle BCDEFHIK, and thus had incorporated in its entirety a system derived from Alexandria and refined by the Arabs. This was unlike his treatment of alchemy—also of Alexandrian origin and refined by the Arabs—which had spread into Europe from Moorish Toledo in the 12th century. Lull rejected this alchemy, but the stress he laid on the four elements, and on calculating their influence, seemed so alchemical that treatises on the subject were soon being widely issued under his name and eventually had a big influence.[79] Lull did not see any connection between goldmaking alchemy and mysticism. In Europe, this connection was first made in Franciscan circles, by the Fraticelli, the author of *Book of the Holy Trinity*, who was associated with them, and by John of Rupescissa. These groups were opposed to the covetous making of gold, and advocated an alchemy that was a search for "the mystical gold." However, their movement was condemned and petered out. A century later in Florence, alchemy was linked to hermeticism, and speculative alchemy was increasingly able to express itself through that, while operative alchemy gradually developed into chemistry. The alchemist Paracelsus (1493-1541) was the first to make a study of chemical substances and their reactions, and to apply them in medicine. This was the beginning of chemistry. Operative alchemy was an unsuitable means of manipulating matter.[80] But speculative alchemy survived.

---

[79] See, for example, *The Hermetic Mercuries of Raymund Lully* (The Alchemical Press, 1984). Reprint of old recipes. Tr. note.

[80] The practical alchemists believed in the possibility of the transmutation of elements such as lead or mercury into other elements such as silver or gold. Chemists came to believe that the elements could be combined, but not transmuted. However, they are now able to transmute one element into another in the extreme conditions of atomic piles. Even so, it is not thought possible to carry out such transmutations at the lower temperatures and pressures available to the old alchemists. In the last century, A. von Herzeele published reports on repeatable experiments with germination seeds, which suggest that "alchemical" processes occur in plants at low temperatures and pressures. See Rudolf Hauschka's *Substanzlehre* (Germany: Vittorio Klostermann, 1946). Tr. note.

A New Human Being—The Microcosm

Typical of the Scotus tradition is the emphasis placed on human dignity. The human being is put at the center of creation: in space, he or she is the cosmos in miniature (so to speak); in time, the hinge on which creation turns back to God after opening out away from him. This is because "human" was created in the image of God and, in particular, because the Word who created all things became human.

Little allowance was made for the distance between God and humanity expressed in orthodox terms by St. Anselm: that humans have sinned and can be saved only through the death of the Son of God; which is why God became human. One consequence is that humans have no cause for pride. Being born of God happens by "grace." Creation does not flow out from God, but has been made by Him out of nothing. Life that is born of God is obtainable only through the ecclesiastical sacraments. Without the Church, men and women are lost.

Eckhart speaks of human beings as "nothing" in themselves, but he does emphasize the value of the individual because he or she has been created (or, in other words, born of God). In Ramón Lull, astrology is merely a helpful influence. Matter is not an evil principle, but quite the opposite; and human beings are inherently good. Nicolas of Cusa, too, stressed the worthiness of human beings purely on the grounds of their existence. He also indicates their limitations.

The human being is the midpoint of creation insofar as he or she is a microcosm. According to Nicolas of Cusa, this does not imply that our dwelling place, Earth, is central, too. Earth orbits round another focal point, the Sun; and our solar system is one of the many systems in an unending universe. Men and women are centers only to the extent that they are specially rooted in the center of all: "We find the middle of the world not on earth, but in God." And God is central in each part of the universe, down to the tiniest atom.

We can come to know everything, even God Himself; but even so there are limits, according to Nicolas. The understanding is faced with contradictions it cannot grasp. All it can do is assume that these contradictions are reconciled in God. How this happens is beyond comprehension. God is the unfathomable ground, remoteness, silence. The highest wisdom, according to Nicolas, is the eventual realization that God is unknowable. Nicolas called his most important treatise, written in 1440, *De docta ignorantia*

[Learned Ignorance]. To the wise person each piece of knowledge is an awareness of what he or she does not know.

Fitting in well with the Renaissance culture, which had already taken fixed form, a new mysticism arose in Florence out of all these sources. It treated humanity as the perfected creation of God. Its founders were Marsilio Ficino, the translator of Hermes Trismegistus, and his pupil Pico della Mirandola. The clearest formulation of this new mysticism was made by Pico in an introduction to nine hundred theses he wished to defend in Rome in 1486. He was condemned, fled to France, returned to Florence at the instance of Savonarola, became a Dominican, and died a year later. However, his "Introduction" survived and was published under the title, *Human Dignity*. The dignity to which it refers is the idea that human beings contain the cosmos in themselves and, at the same time, can become all there is:

> If he indulges sensual passions, he runs wild like an animal. . . . If he cultivates his mind, he becomes an angel and a son of God. . . . And, finally, if dissatisfied with the lot of a created being, he withdraws to the midpoint of all being, then he becomes one with God Himself, one spirit, and lifted up into the lonely height in which the Father is enthroned above all, he himself will set up his throne above all.[81]

He looked on knowledge as having only limited value as far as mysticism is concerned. Love is more important. "We can love God more easily than we can understand Him or speak about Him," says Pico. Just as the microcosm is an ensouled body, so is the macrocosm animated by the world soul [*Anima Mundi*]. This soul, too, tends to return to the One from whom everything originated. The cosmic urge takes the form of a love impulse in mankind. "Love is the eternal knot and bond of the cosmos," says Ficino. By love he means all the forms taken by this passion: voluptuousness, and physical, cerebral and mystical love, and even such things as dying to win the love of God.

---

[81] It is hardly surprising that the Church sniffed brimstone in this. There is a marked similarity to the words in Isaiah 14:12-14: "How art thou fallen from heaven, O Lucifer, son of the morning! . . . Thou hast said in thine heart, I will exalt my throne above the stars of God . . . . I will be like the most High." Tr. note.

Figure 110. In the 15th and 16th centuries, alchemy was more than a controversial attempt to make gold. It offered an opportunity to express, in non-ecclesiastical language, experiences of the deeper dimensions of the cosmos. The work with matter was also a work with the alchemist's soul. A comprehensive picture of the insight sought, the "stone of the wise," is to be found in this emblem from *Atalanta Fugiens* of 1617, a work that closed the alchemical period. The outermost circle stands for the universe, which is composed of three things: spirit, soul, and body (the triangle), and of four elements: water, fire, air, and earth (the square). The square frames an inner circle representing the microcosm—man and woman.

By practicing this art, the alchemist can experience his or her own soul being dissolved, purified, and crytallized, and seeks the divine World Soul in the "stone of the wise" in each part of, and in the whole of, the cosmos. The intention is to rise through the material world to the One who is present in every part, and to attain to a new unity by the reconciliation of opposites. Usually this is shown by the symbolism of an androgyne, or sometimes by the risen Christ. The "stone of the wise" must be found by working. The principle is to separate and combine.

Figure 111. Two of many illustrations from the same book: Death (holding a raven) stands on a black sun between the influences of the sun and the moon in the sky. A picture of purifying fire and the melancholy that goes with it. "But the spirit renews, like before, the life," says the text. In the next illustration, the contraries are reunited: sun and moon, man and woman, are floating in the air above water that is filling the earth. (Woodcuts from: "*De Alchimia Opuscula*, Vol. II, in *Rosarum Philosophorum*, Frankfurt 1550.)

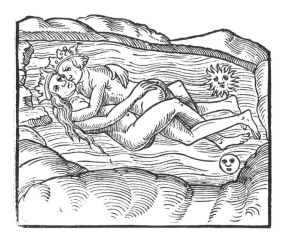

Figure 112. Modern art sometimes has an alchemical import—separation and combination. One example is a canvas by Paul Klee (d. 1940), painted when he knew he was going to die. He thought about his dying: about how everything in him would fall apart, and about what would remain after the process. For this painting he produced a new arrangement of signs—traces of his life—like the traces used to reconstruct vanished civilizations. (Paul Klee, "After the Fire," 1938. Hanover, Strengel Museum.)

Figure 113. A more complicated image of the "stone of the wise." The orb of the universe, inscribed with numbers and geometrical figures, is surmounted by the poisonous dragon of chaos, which has been conquered by the Rebis. The latter, in the form of an androgyne, is holding the square and compasses, and is connected to the seven planets. The whole is enclosed in the cosmic egg out of which everything hatches. (From the *Azoth* of Basil Valentine, Frankfurt, 1613.)

Figure 114. The alchemical idea of the individual who falls apart into a man and a woman and needs to be reunited has often been reworked in modern art. A well-known example is the "hommage à Apollinaire" painted by Marc Chagall in 1911. Many studies have survived which show how he wrestled with the idea of the androgyne. (The Municipal Abbe Museum, Eindhoven.)

For him, this love is the basis of alchemy. His aphorism is: "Dissolve and coagulate" [*Solve et coagula*]. Not only is this the fundamental dictum of those who want to refine matter (the later chemists), it is also the basic requirement for those who intend to climb the mystical ladder: they have to undo themselves and lose their identities in order to achieve a new unity. Ficino interprets alchemy as a burning fire that completes its work in three stages: the "black work" of detachment, the "white work" of ascetic purification, and the "red work" of ecstasy in which body and spirit become one.

The alchemical opus is possible on each level of being. Its basic idea is that things are differentiated from one another and in conflict. Yet, at the same time, all things are the same: fundamentally they are one. This gives the possibility of alchemical transmutation—the changing of one substance into another. For humans this means that even the soul can be dissolved, purified and recrystallized; and that the individual can become one with all minerals, plants, animals, and heavenly beings (heaven contains various of these). Climbing the mystical ladder also implies becoming immersed in nature, and realizing that all things are interconnected, and that a spiritual power is contained in "dead" matter. Salt and precious stones can be curative. The Anima Mundi curbs the evil in everything.

Out of the geometrical language of Ramón Lull, the synthesis of the Kabbalah and Hermeticism, the alchemical "work," and the number mysticism derived from Pythagoras, arose a symbolic language that is "occult" to outsiders. It incorporates puzzling complex methods for unlocking—in a manner that is different from the theological—the secrets of God, creation, and humanity. The aim was to discover connections, climb the mystical ladder, and (above all) find the universal truth that would resolve all religious conflicts. The latter was not only the express purpose of Lull; Pico della Mirandola had a similar objective and therefore incorporated the Jewish Kabbalah in his system. He was extremely tolerant, like the majority of those who studied "occult philosophy." Especially in the France of the 16th century, these scholars attempted to use magical poetry and music to restore the harmony of the inner man or woman.

Frances Yates has given the name "Renaissance magus" to savants who belonged to this tendency. Most of these mages were not practicing magic in the strict sense of the word but, like the ancient "magi," were concerned with a special form of knowledge. Frances Yates draws a distinction between Renaissance scholars on the one hand and 17th century scientists on the other. The magus tried to investigate the cosmos by allowing it to become one with his own spirit. He wanted to assimilate the world and to penetrate it with his soul and his understanding, to know things from within. Paracelsus said of himself and nature: "I have been born of her, and I follow her. She knows me and I know her." Alchemy and, above all, medicine, were for him a collaboration with nature. At the opposite extreme stands the present-day scientist, who does as much as possible to avoid any intimate connection with the outside world, who wants to learn at a distance, to perform an impartial analysis, and to obtain knowledge of the sort that will give power over nature. The latter attitude began to show itself in the late Middle Ages, as already mentioned; and, in the 17th century, it won the battle for supremacy over the magical approach.

THE EUROPEAN MAGES

The heyday of the mages came to an end with two great figures: John Dee, the Protestant mathematician at the court of Queen Elizabeth I of England, and the ex-Dominican from Naples, Giordano Bruno. Both traveled through Europe in an attempt to lay the groundwork of religious toleration. Dee returned in 1589, fell into disfavor with the queen's successor, and died in extreme poverty in 1608. Bruno went to Venice in 1591 at the invitation of the patrician Mocenigo, was extradited to Rome, imprisoned, and burned by order of the pope. A statue has been built where his stake stood in the Campo dei Fiori in Rome. He was rehabilitated as a martyr of modern science, although, strictly speaking, he was nothing of the kind.

Giordano Bruno had a modern vision of the cosmos. In his works, we encounter the system of Copernicus, the infinite universe of Nicolas of Cusa, the idea of many inhabited worlds, the concept of monads later elaborated by Leibniz (which is that the smallest unit into which the world can be divided is, at the same time, the world as a whole).[82] Nevertheless, Bruno did not

---

[82] ". . . every monad is a mirror that is . . . representative of the universe from its own point of view." Leibniz, *Principles* (New York: Everyman's Library, Dutton, 1934), p. 22. Tr. note.

possess the basic outlook of the modern scientist. His own brand of science was the opposite of objective research. He was a mystic who had profound experiences. Above all, he was an Italian who saw a lack of "mystical fire" in English Protestants. The picture he formed of the cosmos was, for him, only a symbol of a mystical experience he tried to express in poetry and imagery. He formulated his attitude as follows:

> Why, I say, do so few understand and apprehend the internal power? . . . He who in himself sees all things, is all things.[83]

What Bruno saw as a starting point for the unification of Europe was, in fact, the terminal point of what had been begun in Florence and had spread mainly in Germany. There the Benedictine abbot Trithemius (1462-1535) and especially Agrippa of Nettesheim (1486-1535) had conceived the idea that a human being can contain everything in his or her spirit when aided by magic in a very precisely defined sense of the word. Agrippa describes this as follows:

> A pure intellect that cooperates with the might of the gods; without which we shall never have the good fortune to look into secrets and to wield marvelous powers.[84]

For him, magic meant fathoming the "secrets" of the three worlds—the earthly, the starry, and the world of spirits and angels. These secret powers he termed "occult philosophy," which is also the title of his chief work, the most thorough summary we have of Western magic. He himself professed that this occultism was a form of Christian piety. John Dee and Giordano Bruno thought the same; and they were not condemned for it. Dee was falsely accused of diabolical "black" magic. He practiced "white" magic, which he connected with mathematics. Bruno was charged with heresy over his interpretation of Copernicus' views. According to him, the fact that the earth turns was a sign of life, a divine life,

---

[83] Henry Cornelius Agrippa of Nettesheim, *Three Books of Occult Philosophy* (London: Gregory Moule, 1651).
[84] Frances A. Yates, *Giordano Bruno and the Hermetic Tradition* (London: Routledge & Kegan Paul, 1964), p. 337.

like the Eucharist. The real reason why he was burned was a political one, according to Frances Yates.

Rome made up its mind to send a signal that the Europe of those days wanted to see: conciliation would no longer be tolerated. The Protestant Reformation of the Church was not accepted by Rome, but was repulsed by a counter-reformation. Attitudes had hardened on both sides. Bridge-building, a middle way, mediators, and compromises were no longer acceptable to either Catholics or Protestants. In the same way, science and faith had separated from one another and were soon poles apart. Both sides welcomed this. When Galileo demonstrated with his telescope that Copernicus was right, Rome decided (in 1632) to send another signal. Galileo was given an ultimatum: agree with Catholic dogma where it conflicts with science, or face the consequences. One of the brides to other religions, Hermeticism, was undermined by a demonstration in 1614 that Hermes Trismegistus was later than the Bible. This destroyed its authority for Christians, and they could not now rest any case on it.

In such an inhospitable climate "occult philosophy" went into hiding and became occult in the further sense of being "under cover." In 1604 and 1615, Rosicrucian manifestos appeared, implying the existence of an arcane society of that name; and, in 1616, *The Chymical Wedding of Christian Rosencreutz* was published. It is thought that the society did not exist outside the covers of these books, which were the creation of Johann Valentin Andreae and his circle, but the idea of its existence made a big impact. To this very day, Rosicrucian societies of various kinds abound, Freemasonry being one of them.

The Rosicrucian Outlook

The appearance in print of Rosicrucian documents was possible during the brief reign of the liberal "Winter King," Frederick V of the Palatinate and his English queen, Elizabeth. After the assassination of Henri III of France, Frederick was the last hope of those mages who saw themselves as reformers and peacemakers.

According to their manifesto, the Rosicrucians had in view a "Universal and General Reformation of the Whole Wide World." On the death of Frederick, an Englishman who had lived in Germany tried to lend solid support to this aim. His name was Robert Fludd (1574-1637). Fludd endeavored to gather the results of Renaissance mysticism into one great "museum" (in book

Figure 115. Robert Fludd conveyed alchemical (Hermetic) knowledge in pictures. One of these shows the human being as a microcosm in which good and evil are con-joined, as are day and night, body and soul, cre-ation and Creator. All the movements and relation-ships of the microcosm mirror those of the macro-cosm. (From *Utriusque Cosmi Maioris Scilicet et Minoris Metaphysica*, 1617.)

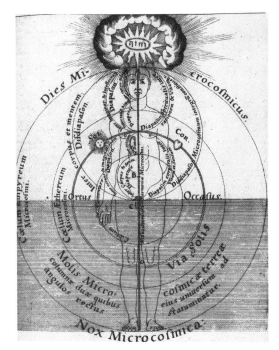

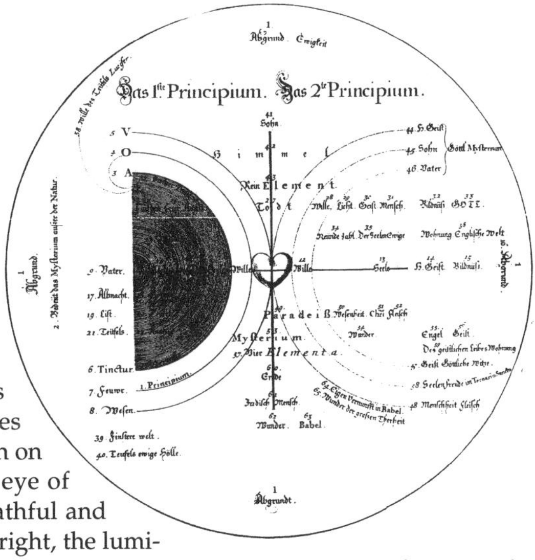

Figure 116. A contempo-rary of Fludd, Jacob Boehme, took God as his starting point and tried to show diagramatically how good and evil are not the same in Him, although they go together. He called the diagram reproduced here The Wonderful Eye of Eternity, explaining that, "The one eye (the outermost circle) is the eye of God. When this eye is divided and its halves are placed back to back, then on the left you have the dark eye of God the Father, who is wrathful and who condemns; and on the right, the lumi-nous eye of the Spirit who warms and enlightens. At the points of contact, the heart of the Son binds both parts of the eye." This fairly elaborate drawing is in keeping with the sayings of Joachim of Fiore: "God reveals Himself very dif-ferently in history," and of Nicolas of Cusa: "Good and evil go back to God and coincide in Him." Sentences like these are characteristic of Boehme: "Wherein then I found to be in all things, evil and good, love and anger, in the inanimate creatures, viz., in wood, stones, earth and the elements, as also in men and beasts." *Aurora*, 19: 6. (London: Watkins reprint, 1960).

form). What he wrote is abstruse, but he had a talent for simplifying his ideas in diagrams. He made numerous drawings, of which copper engravings were done by the German Johann de Bry and his Swiss son-in-law, Matthieu Merian. His works were printed and published in Oppenheim and Frankfurt. The undertaking was impressive, but was also something of an empty gesture. Fludd twice started on an ambitious series of books but was unable to complete either series. What he thought could be embraced in a single system was too unwieldy in practice. He came at the end of an era in which it had been believed that one individual could know all there is too know, and in which people had a well-defined picture of humanity and the universe and of the relationship between the two. Fludd was committed to this old picture, which put Earth at the center of the universe, and saw humanity as a single whole, linked to the cosmos—the latter being an organism, not a machine. In his day all this was decidedly old-fashioned. The intellect was given priority at the expense of intuition and the emotions. And people were aware of the split: they felt detached within the cosmic mechanism.

Science now prized cold objectivity, and was forever producing insights that, though novel, were not definitive. Knowledge of physical structure became so specialized in its various branches that no one could grasp all the details. And yet, in our own era, Fludd is still exerting a fascination and we often come across reproductions of his pictures. This continued interest reveals a longing for a new integration of knowledge, for a new insight into the interconnectedness of things.

ALL-EMBRACING WISDOM

From the beginning of the 17th century through today, Renaissance mysticism has promoted itself as Sophia, or wisdom. First there was pansophy or all-embracing wisdom, then theosophy or wisdom concerning God, and finally anthroposophy or wisdom concerning humanity.

At the head of this development stands a shoemaker, Jacob Boehme (1575-1624). He has much in common with Fludd, not only on account of his hermetic ideas, but because he liked to elucidate difficult and complicated concepts by means of drawings. However, he differs from Fludd in that he is no longer obsessed by the idea that it is possible for one to know everything.

He is concerned not with knowledge, but with wisdom, and with insight into the mysterious background of all things. He called it a *magnum pansophicum*. His insight was into the "spiritual world that is hidden in the visible world as the soul is hidden in the body," and he says, "We see then that the hidden God is very close to all, and is through all, yet completely hidden from sight." Boehme received an insight into this secret in an overwhelming experience which it took him a long time to put into words, as he himself explains:

> I saw and comprehended the Being of all Beings, the Byss and the Abyss; and the generation of the Holy Trinity. I saw the original and primal existence of this world and of all creatures. Within myself I perceived creation entire, in its order and movement; I saw, first, the divine world, of the angels and of paradise, second, the darkened world, the fiery realm, and third, this world around us, visible and tangible, as an issue and expression of the two inner, eternal, hidden worlds. Moreover, I comprehended the whole being and reason of Good and Evil.[85]

When he opened his mouth and talked about his experience, the clergyman of his home town, Goerlitz, threw a shoe at his head. Boehme picked up the shoe and replaced it on the pastor's foot. Then the town council forbade him to write, so he kept quiet for six years. Only a year before his death did anything from his hand appear in print. He was still going his own way without by or leave of the church and had not become any more popular. It was not until after his death that his influence began to spread. Serene thought and the desire to rise above religious conflicts express themselves, in Fludd and Boehme, in a specific religious formula—the identity of opposites in God. Here they are both in agreement with Nicolas of Cusa.

Boehme envisages creation as parturition, as God bringing forth the world in the pangs of childbirth. And the painful division

---

[85] From *Men Who Have Walked with God: Being the Story of Mysticism through the Ages Told in the Biographies of Representative Seers and Saints wth Excerpts from their Writings and Sayings*, ed. Sheldon Cheney (New York: Knopf, 1945), p. 249.

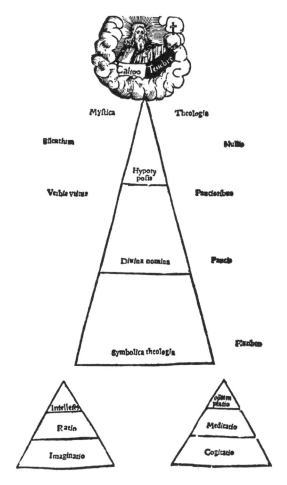

Figure 117. The mystical ladder of Nicolas of Cusa. The human being ascends to God by the use of imagination, reason, and understanding on the one hand, and thought, meditation, and contemplation on the other. The ascent is through theological symbols, divine names, the power of words, and silence. The Godhead in the clouds is obviously both light (Caligo) and darkness (Tenebre) at the same time: and is the Creator (shown holding the orb of the world) in whom all opposites are reconciled. (From the edition of Pseudo-Dionysius by Jean Eck, 1519. Taken from an edition of Nicolas of Cusa.)

between God and His progeny continues. What is a unified plenum in God fractures in His creation. Light and darkness, good and evil, love and wrath, are opposites, but are all reconciled in God. Whoever is blind to the fact that God is also "wrath," fails to understand the ground of our being, says Boehme. The tension between the opposites is fruitful, however, because of their origin.

Georg Hegel (1770-1831) was later to build his philosophical system on this idea. For him, creation is a process that unites contraries. Some new thing is continually being born out of painful tension. His philosophy seems much like the Chinese vision of the harmony of Yin and Yang. But what has a more stable structure in Chinese thought—the world is in harmony between opposites—is in Boehme, and especially in Hegel, a restless primary force producing sharp confrontations that have to resolve themselves in something new, and can find rest only in the place out of which the primary force itself arose: "the lions' den to which all footsteps go and from which none return," the absolute Being in which all are one.

Hegel's influence on culture up to and including Marx should not be underestimated. The power of Boehme's mysticism lies in the desire to see reality as it is, even its dark side, and having done so to look beyond it to the one ground out of which everything comes.

The practical aspect of pansophy was cultivated by John Amos Comenius (1592-1670). He was the last bishop of the Bohemian Brethren, and, due to persecution, moved from place to place, taking refuge in Amsterdam in 1656. He is buried in Naarden. His Czech name was Jan Amos Komensky.

He wanted to compile an encyclopedia of pansophy and to use the latter as a template for worldwide structures such as an international court of justice, a world college, and a system of tuition available to all, based on self-effort and general education. He attached great importance to learning from pictures.

Boehme himself had spoken of *theosofia*, and the term theosophist was later applied to a group of Protestants who adopted Boehme's views on wisdom but laid less emphasis on the "all" and more on the ground of the all as the source of wisdom. For them, reality was translucent and a symbol of the divine; it is even hard to distinguish between the material world and the world of spirits. Among these "Christian Theosophists" we must count F. C. Oetinger, F. von Baaden, J. G. Hamann, and, of course, Emanuel Swedenborg (1688-1772).

At the end of the 19th century, Theosophy received a fresh impetus from two women: the Russian H. P. Blavatsky and her successor, Annie Besant, an Englishwoman who became an atheist and then a Theosophist. Characteristic of this modern version of Theosophy is the incorporation of Eastern elements:

◆ Zoroaster's idea that from time to time a world teacher will be sent in order to give a new religious impetus.

◆ Buddhist Consciousness in which the unity of all things is experienced.

◆ Reincarnation as a transmigration of souls.

Blavatsky founded the Theosophical Society in New York in 1875. The Society intended:

◆ To form a nucleus of the Universal Brotherhood of Humanity, without distinction of race, creed, sex, caste or color.

◆ To encourage the study of comparative religion, philosophy and science.

◆ To investigate the unexplained laws of nature and the powers latent in man.[86]

The Theosophical Society has had an influence on the formation of the Theosophical Movement in the USA (1895), The Rosicrucian Fellowship (1909), Co-Masonry, and Anthroposophy. The latter was a movement founded by Rudolf Steiner (1861-1925) after his break with the Theosophical Society in 1913 when Annie Besant promoted Krishnamurti as the World Teacher. Steiner added a Christian ingredient to Theosophy and made mankind central: "man," fallen through sin, has to do with Lucifer and Ahriman, pride and matter (in 1906 he had studied Zoroaster),and the opposition of demonic forces. We have been trapped in matter, but,

---

[86] Irving S. Cooper, *Theosophy Simplified* (New York: Gordon Press, n. d.) p. 1. A revised edition is published by the Theosophical Publishing House, Wheaton, IL, 1989.

through Christ, new powers have entered the world by which the link with our Origin is recoverable and the "true humanity" can arise. The aim of reincarnation, he said, is not to release us from Earth but to rejoin us to Earth. Only on Earth is it possible to find the Christ forces.

The great merit of Steiner is that he encouraged a return to the source of all that exists in order to restore the unity of life, humanity, and the world, to this fragmented modern society of ours. His ideas were very attractive to painters such as Kandinsky, Mondrian, and Joseph Beuys. His success was greatest in the field of education. He believed that a school should educate people for life; that knowledge comes after feeling; that far from being "crammed" with facts, children need to have their innate faculties developed. Education in art is necessary if the child is going to learn to understand. The body and soul will not develop if the mind is trained too early. Many "free schools" based on Steiner's teachings already exist.

CONTINUATION OF MEDIEVAL MYSTICISM

In a distinct departure from humanistic mysticism, which was concerned mainly with the connection between humanity and the cosmos, with the fundamental goodness of humanity, and with everything that unites people, there arose in the 16th century a social mysticism.[87] This was concerned with the unjust structures in human society, with human wickedness, and with the spiritual alienation of the individual and society. What had been resisted throughout the Middle Ages, but had kept coming back in new forms, finally broke through in this century. It began to be said openly that the established Church was a temporary arrangement, that the "spiritual" Church was waiting to be ushered in, and that the Spirit that would create this new Church is a vital spark in the depths of our being. People sought to follow the "leading" of the Spirit within them. The emphasis was no

---

[87] *Theologia Germanica*, Chap. 6, translated from German by Susanna Winkworth (London: MacMillan, 1874).

longer on having a blissful experience, but on getting things done, as expressed in the *Theologia Germanica*, which was translated by Luther and published in 1516:

> Where men are enlightened with the true light. . . . they renounce all desire and choice, and commit and commend themselves and all things to the Eternal Goodness; . . . . so that every enlightened man could say: "I would fain be to the Eternal Goodness, what his own hand is to a man."[88]

In 16th-century Switzerland, Germany, and Holland, reformers appeared who were inspired to take radical action by this mysticism. Historians have lumped them together as "the left wing of the Reformation," or "the radical undercurrent of the Reformation." The most striking figure in this explosive movement was Thomas Müntzer (1490-1525). In the beginning, he and Luther thought alike on the subject of reformation. Both had had the same mystical impulse, but had experienced it differently. Their mysticism centered on the birth of Christ in the believer: a birth that can be experienced as the coming of the Bridegroom, but also as a coming without joy—a bitter embrace. Bitterness is an aspect of the mystical process insofar as the believer is transformed in spite of the longings of the fleshly nature.

Now, whereas Luther saw the transforming process as the pattern of every Christian life (bitterness, redemption, praise), Müntzer saw it as a transition to the Kingdom of God out of the prison of unrighteousness. According to Müntzer, this mystical process starts with the fear of God, who will one day separate the good from the bad. The ground of the soul is purged by this fear until it is "without form and void," like Earth at the start of creation, when "the Spirit of God moved upon the face of the waters" (Genesis 1:2). The Spirit of God descends upon the empty ground of the soul and Christ is born there in pain and sorrow, in ecstasies, and in blood, sweat, and tears. After large numbers of the elect have been born out of the ground of their souls in this way, society at large can be cleansed to await the coming of the Spirit.

---

[88] On the involvement of mysticism in social questions see: "Mystieke weerbarheid," in *Speling*, No. 3, 1981; and the contribution of H. A. Oberman and R. Hensen in *Mystiek in de Westerse Kultuur* (Kampen, 1973). Note: These are Dutch publications.

After 1520, the paths of Luther and Müntzer finally diverged. Luther repudiated pseudo-Dionysius and the whole neoplatonic mystical tradition. What is more, he realized the need for the protection of the nobility if he were to defend the Reformation against Rome in the political arena. Müntzer, on the other hand, was deeply concerned for those who were being treated unfairly by the wealthy and the landed gentry—for artisans and peasants who were living on the breadline. In the Germany of those days, approximately half the population belonged to this needy lower class. Müntzer called Luther "that spiritless soft lump of flesh in Würzburg." In his opinion, the Reformers were "book people with God in their heads" who did not stand by God and his elect to the end, but backed off when the going got tough.

In 1525 the peasants combined and made twelve specific demands for the relief of their miseries. Luther supported them and declared that in these proposals God Himself was coming against injustice. However, when the peasants, having failed to get their wrongs redressed, formed gangs that plundered castles and abbeys and burned them to the ground, Luther called on the nobility to quell them.

> Those of you who can should thrust, strike, strangle. If you die in the attempt—congratulations. A more blessed death could not fall to your lot.[89]

When Luther made this appeal, Müntzer placed himself at the head of the peasants and championed their cause. He had seen what ordinary folk had to suffer. He had studied Joachim of Fiore and had made the acquaintance of the "fanatics" in Zwickau and Prague. Everywhere he went, he was expelled because of his partisanship. Eventually, he found refuge in Mühlhausen, where he started building a Christian, democratic community without class distinctions. To him, the Peasants' Revolt was a harbinger of the millennium. He was convinced that the "rabble" were the elect who would be the first to enter this Kingdom of God on Earth. He tried in vain to persuade the nobility that it was right in the eyes of God to use force for the good of the people. The nobility came against him with an army. He accepted the challenge, and, mustering the peasants, marched out to meet them. Shortly before

---

[89] Translation mine. Tr.

the decisive battle, he made a final appeal, saying that he was not seeking power except to defend the right. He was not worried about class, but about justice for all. "If that is what you want, too, we shall do you no harm. Everyone ought to abide by this justice." His message made no impression. Müntzer's forces were crushed, and he himself was taken prisoner, tortured, and executed.

Movements of this kind, culminating in the occupation of a city, often occurred in this time of religious and political ferment. In Florence it was Savonarola who tried to set up a new form of government and a new way of life, based on the belief that divine justice now demanded that the career of one individual must not result in the impoverishment of another. In 1498, he was craftily cornered by Pope Alexander VI, and then hanged and burned.

The Anabaptists of Zürich, who did not find the reformation of Zwingli radical enough, moved to Strasbourg in 1532, when Melchior Hoffman was arrested there. Hoffman had prophesied that half a year after his arrest the millennium would dawn in this city. When that did not happen, Jan Matthys, a baker from Haarlem in the Netherlands, took over the leadership and went to Münster, where he seized power in 1534, only to be killed the same year. He was succeeded by Jan Breukels, a Leyden tailor who instituted such a Reign of Terror in Münster that the city was besieged by forces seeking to put this state of affairs to an end. Elsewhere, Dutch and Frisian Anabaptists made vain attempts to build the "new Jerusalem." A group under Jan van Geelen tried to occupy Amsterdam, but held it for no more than a single night. Meanwhile, in 1535, Münster was taken. The "king of Sion" and his followers were humiliated and tortured, and their bodies were left hanging in cages from the churchtowers. Of all the attempts to turn a city into a "City of God" only that made by Calvin (1541) in Geneva led to a permanent result.

MYSTICISM IN POLITICS

In the West, mystics have often tried to help the weak, usually by the path of non-violence taken by St. Francis. But a considerable number of them heard inner "voices" that compelled them to offer vigorous opposition to ecclesiastical and national politics. Hildegard, for example, and St. Catharine of Siena who—when they said, "I will," meant "God wills," or the other way round.

And sometimes the inner voice advocated violence. Thus St. Catherine wanted the pope to wage war against the Turks so that the Christian nobility would have something better to do than to fight among themselves. We have all heard of Joan of Arc's voices, and how she led a victorious army, but was eventually sacrificed to the religious-political powers. Luther, himself, excused his harsh call for bloodshed by placing the responsibility on an inner voice that said, "During the uprising, I caused peasants to be slain. But I ascribe this to the Lord God. He commanded me to say what I did."

In any case, in the Old Testament, God is quite often severe. But why should some mystics gain approval when Savonarola and Müntzer did not? Joan of Arc has been canonized, and Savonarola would have been declared a saint, too, if he had not resisted the corrupt pope. Müntzer has been revalued recently. He went through the mystical transformation process in an original way and remained true to it, even taking up the sword to defend it on behalf of the downtrodden. However, it is gruesome

Figure 118 During the conference of 1481, the priest went with a companion to ask the advice of the hermit Nikolaus von der Flüe. Everyone heeded his advice and the spirit of dissension was routed. This event is recorded in the illustrated chronicle of Diebold Schilling. If Nikolaus had not given his wise advice, Switzerland might be a very different place today. (From the facsimile edition of 1981.)

to see the enormous wave of aggression these people unleashed. And it is more gruesome to read about the terror of the tailor Jan Breukels of Leyden, who also claimed to hear an inner voice.

Their insurrection had a social character, but was also a political revolutionary version of contemporary mysticism, which had been popularized by the *Theologia Germanica*, for example. They said that humans can contact God in the "ground of the soul," and that God's purposes for the world can be revealed by this "spiritual spark." Anybody can be led by the knowledge imparted by this spark or fire. It is open to all, independent of human learning or ecclesiastical institutions. It is a knowledge "in which young girls and simple souls can excel," said Gerson. Those who live according to the spiritual spark are above the law, for the spirit liberates and bloweth where it listeth.

This particular brand of mysticism seems to be a two-edged sword. A great deal of political talent and strong-mindedness are required by anyone who would hold together a group of illiterate, unsuccessful nobodies and give them a voice and a sense of their own value. Especially if this voice is not heard by anyone but the leader, the danger of mass mania cannot be ruled out. And the sense of personal value can grow into a sectarian feeling that only "we" are good, and "they" are reprobates who have to be stopped. The frustration of being treated like scum can then lead to the force known as "blind terror." In modern times, the history of Jan Breukels has repeated itself in Jonestown. Nevertheless, politics and mysticism can work together harmoniously, as seen in such figures as Gandhi and Hammarskjöld. They, too, stood in the midst of a world in turmoil.

The mysticism that inspired the radical reformers has had nonviolent political consequences in the long term, especially the recognition of the right of individuals to obey their consciences, and the setting up of democratic forms of government. What is more, it became possible for the first time to be a Nonconformist. Sebastian Franck (1499-1542) is an example. A Catholic priest who became a Protestant and later earned a living as a soap-boiler, printer, and writer, Franck wandered from place to place, and eventually disassociated himself from Luther.

Franck had an affinity with the Anabaptists, but they were rather too sectarian and fundamentalist to please him. He, himself, was a liberal, committed to communion with all (even non-Christian) believers. He thought that the only true Church was a spiritual one and that the only authoritative word was an "inner word," taking as his premise that the Spirit who inspired the Bible is the same Spirit who is given by Christ to dwell in each person. Franck also looked at history and mankind in relation to God, and found little that was holy or noble. He saw a pigsty, a drunken dance, and a puppet show of people who are full of conceit in spite of the fact that God holds the strings. God Himself is so high that He is beyond description. What Franck did here was to clear the way for historical criticism. Franck possessed literary talent and exercised an influence on artists, especially on some painters known as the "godless painters" who belonged to a group in Nuremberg that included pupils of Dürer.

Another Protestant who felt drawn to the Anabaptists, and particularly to Melchior Hoffman, but (like Franck) recognized only the spiritual church as genuine, was Caspar von Schwenkenfeld (1489-1561). His followers later emigrated to America and are still in existence. In these Protestants, a Christian of a new type emerged: a non-churchgoer or, if belonging to a church, merely a nominal member, and yet a Christian; very unorthodox in matters of faith and yet a believer.

An example of the later development of this radical Protestantism is found in the shoemaker George Fox (1624-1691). In 1646, after an intense mystical experience, Fox rejected all external religion. He was convinced that each individual can find the truth within through the "inner light," a part of God the Holy Spirit. Jesus, he said, must be experienced without the help of guides, books, or scriptures. The Christian life is an everyday affair, and can be lived apart from rites and paid priests. He traveled widely in order to bring people into this inner church. He was a striking figure, with a broad-brimmed hat which he took off for nobody. His preaching was regularly done in the open air and, regardless of the rank of the person to whom he was speaking, he used the simple and unflattering "thee" and "thou."

His many followers behaved fanatically in a very serene and matter-of-fact way—often in opposition to the establishment. At any given time, twelve thousand might be sitting in jail. Their meetings began with a period of silent meditation, after which social and political problems were discussed. The discussions were a sharing of ideas without any attempt to persuade. Fox, himself, traveled to Ireland, the West Indies, North America and the Netherlands. After 1669, his international fellowship styled

Figure 119. A Quaker meeting. (Oil painting, ca. 1800, painted in England. Boston Museum of Fine Arts, bequest of Maxim Karolik.)

itself the Society of Friends; but the Friends were nicknamed Quakers, because they used to tremble with emotion when talking of their experiences. They clearly demonstrated how mysticism and politics could go together: they were trembling testifiers to their mystical experience, but sober advocates of other insights into practical living.

A friend of Fox's, William Penn, became governor of an American state which was named for him, Pennsylvania. He gave this state a democratic constitution with equal rights for Indians and Quakers. Because the state opened its borders to all comers, the Quakers were overrun by other groups. When these eventually made up the majority, the Quakers fitted in with them. Penn laid down the rights of man and, before other people began to interest themselves in such matters, the Quakers were working for the emancipation of the black slaves, the humanization of prisons and factories, and women's rights. They were opposed to dictatorship, war, and military service. If anyone thought it was right

Figure 120. In the background is represented William Penn's treaty with the Indians in 1682. In the foreground animals and humans are associating peacefully—a picture of the ideal of peace and unity for which Penn, as a Quaker, lived. The unity is one of opposites, such as the lion and the lamb—the Messianic vision of Isaiah 2: 4, and 11: 1-10. (Edward Hicks, "The Peaceable Kingdom" (1840-1845). Brooklyn Museum, New York. Dick S. Ramsay Fund.)

to take up arms, he had better search his conscience. As Fox had said, "Friends, be not hasty, for whoever believes in the inner light has no need of hastiness." Conscience is not only rooted in the "light" but is also tied in with culture. The Quaker tries to separate these two aspects before deciding what his or her political stance should be.

MYSTICISM OF
ACTION—IGNATIUS LOYOLA

At a time when people in Northern Europe were setting about the reformation of Christendom in such a pluralistic and therefore also chaotic way, the balance of power in the South was held by Spain which, after 1500, ruled an empire. Authority was strongly centralized there and was exercised by the king. The Moors had already been driven out of Spain, and the Jews had been expelled, too. In 1481, the Inquisition was established in Seville (Sevilla), and if an anonymous complaint was lodged against a converted Jew, the latter was interrogated under torture to see if he or she had retained any Jewish practices. After ten thousand unfortunates had been sent to the stake, the persecutors were still not satisfied that Jewish influence had been burned out of their culture, so all Jews were driven out of Spain (in 1492) and Portugal (in 1496). Anything that looked like a reformation as it was taking place in the North was ruthlessly suppressed, and those who wanted to spiritualize the Church and talked of inner enlightenment were condemned by the Inquisition as *Alumbrados* (Illuminati). All mysticism was suspect. And yet mysticism of an exceptionally high order flourished in this hostile environment. St. Ignatius Loyola, St. Teresa of Avila, and St. John of the Cross represent the cream of this mysticism.

Ignacio Lopez, a Basque born in Loyola in 1491, was a contemporary and, in a certain sense, an antipode of Martin Luther. He came from an aristocratic family and was brought up to believe in militarism and in the conquest of women. Seriously wounded in battle, he fell into a black depression, not only on account of disillusionment and mortification, but also because he had lost the sense of certainty and meaning in his life. He was almost suicidal. And then, in Manresa, in a cave on the bank of the Cardoner River, he had a saving enlightenment. Afterward, he saw visions of the world as a battlefield where a fight was in progress for the Kingdom of Christ.

Unlike his contemporary Müntzer, however, he did not regard this as a final battle. And he did not see the elect as coming from the dregs of society, but as an elite body. Like Müntzer, he took his own conscience as his starting point; unlike Müntzer, however, he did not look outside himself for the separation of good and evil impulses (in a judgment of God poured out here and now on mankind), but looked inside himself, and asked: By what standard can I discriminate between the good and evil spirits in my innermost being? In wrestling with this problem he produced his *Spiritual Exercises*, a methodical form of meditation by which an individual can attain a clearer understanding of himself or herself, and a technique for making wise choices based on personal experience. The whole being, including the imagination, is involved.

Like Luther, Ignatius possessed a vivid imagination, and saw the world as a stage on which Christ and Satan were in combat. His was a masculine way of looking at things, which has since had a guiding influence on culture, and has been largely responsible for the tendency to cast women in the role of witches, on the grounds that they always know more than is good for them about Satan's goings-on. In the following centuries the *Spiritual Exercises* have been used not only to form an elite corps, the Jesuits, but also to help Christians to make clear choices in retreats. But this is hardly mysticism.

Ignatius himself was an avowed mystic who wrote about his experiences; although, in fact, they encouraged him to be more of a doer than an author. His first step out of the crisis in his life was to find (when on his own and "apart from the Bible and the Church"), a fixed point in his emotional turmoil, and to separate the positive, liberating forces from the negative, alienating ones. He saw that the freedom of the individual is rooted in the superior Freedom that emanates from the Ground of all and passes all understanding. Whatever deprives us of freedom, no matter how pious it may seem, belongs to the "evil spirits." On his return from a pilgrimage to the Holy Land, he asked himself what he should do and reached a radical decision: he would bring about the unity of all mankind (which had come to him so clearly) in a Society of Jesus (the Jesuits) and under the banner of Jesus.

He felt that the pope should be a central figure to oversee the world situation. Therefore he placed the Society under direct papal control, and it was not answerable to the local church. Also the freedom to explore personal experience had to relate to the overall context of the Society. The mystical vein of this particular kind of obedience has rarely been understood, not even by the popes. Ignatius, himself, came into conflict with the Inquisition in Alcala, Salamanca, Paris, Venice, and Rome. He was locked up in Spanish ecclesiastical prisons for weeks at a time, and was forbidden to preach. Paul IV had his room searched by the police, and refused to give him his blessing when he lay dying. Ignatius died without the last sacraments, in 1556.[90]

A great figure in this development of mystical experience is the Jesuit-trained bishop of Geneva, St. Francis de Sales. St. Ignatius had wanted to avoid any vestige of monasticism; his Society was to adopt an active lifestyle without monkish buildings, robes, hours, and so on. St. Francis de Sales went a step further and let the laity remain laity in their usual daily environment without any other "society" than existing friends. He said that it is necessary—and at the same time a joy—to help one another on the way to God. People must extend a hand to each other in order that they may go on seeking the Lord in the midst of a world that is often estranged from Him. He devised a method of meditation which he offered as a simpler version of the "Spiritual Exercises." One of its striking features is learning the Christ-role through meditation. He said that through daily meditation "your deeds will be conformed to the pattern of His." In sharp contrast to his contemporaries, St. Francis de Sales was very open and positive. He was an experienced leader who, with great practicality and psychological insight, led individuals to the state of maturity that was within their scope.

THE PSYCHOLOGICAL WAY—
THE SPANISH CARMELITES

The first woman after Margaret Porete to offer a map of her soul to a wider public was St. Teresa of Avila. And she did so in an extremely hostile environment—a misogynist, anti-Semitic, anti-mystical, male-dominated culture jealously guarded by theologians. Philip II of Spain once said that twenty clerics of the

---

[90] "He died of fever, unexpectedly, without being able to receive the last sacraments." *New Century Cyclopedia of Names* (New York: Appleton-Century-Crofts, 1954). Tr. Note.

Figure 121. Teresa of Avila. This contemporary portrait has long been in the possession of the Ahumada family. (Photo: NCI, Boxmeer.)

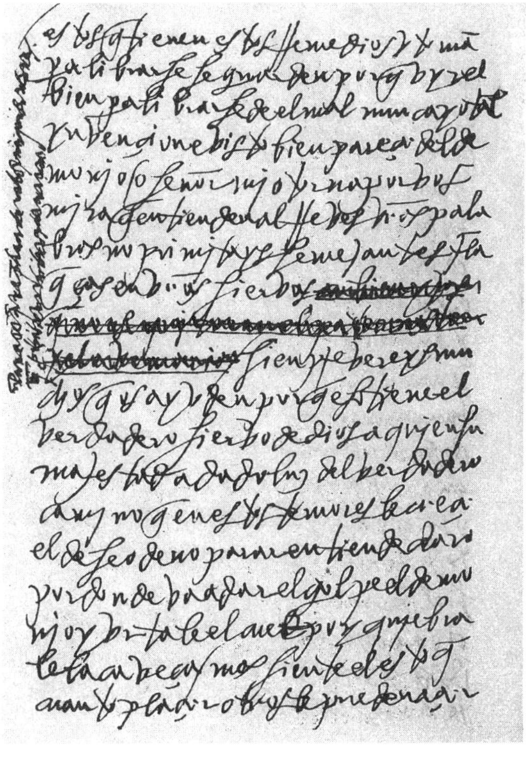

Figure 122. Teresa's handwriting, with "corrections" by her confessor who underlined: "Daughters, for they shall not deprive you of the Our Father and the Hail Mary," and added in a marginal note: "It seems that she is rapping the knuckles of the inquisitors because they are prohibiting books on prayer." People involved with the Inquisition (on which side we do not know) have tried hard to scribble this out. (Page from *The Way of Perfection*, MS Escorial, Madrid, f. 72 v.)

Inquisition could do more to keep the peace of his kingdom than a whole army. Coming from a family of "renegade Jews"—her father had been condemned by the Inquisition on this charge—St. Teresa was a woman who wrote about herself (in the language of the people, too) and publicized a new inner life. Such a woman already had several strikes against her, and she was frustrated by it: ". . . for the rest, it is enough that I am a woman. . . ."[91] Men of the church taught that women should spin and weave, and tell their rosary beads, and not bother their heads about anything else. St. Teresa did not agree: "What a blessing it is when God spares a woman from the tyranny of a husband, which very often ruins her body, and quite often her soul as well." However, she felt similarly hampered in her cloister. Her brothers had sailed for America in search of adventure, the whole Christian world was ablaze, and she was left doing nothing! She was hemmed in on all sides, and her discontent fostered severe neurosis and psychosomatic illnesses.

St. Teresa had never learned to read Latin, and when, in 1559, the grand inquisitor proscribed all spiritual works (even the Bible) printed in the national language, nothing remained to her but her imagination. She was soon seeing spectacular visions. But here, too, her father confessors started interfering. They told her to shake her fist at phantoms. And go crazy, thought Teresa. Her crisis lasted eighteen years. Afterward she called the process, "this struggle and hybrid desire to have God and keep the world too." For her, the world that was in opposition to God was the world of her emotional relationships and contacts, the products of her extrovert nature. "God be praised that he has delivered me from myself!" she exclaimed. She regained herself in the deepest center of her soul, from which vantage point she looked in a fresh way at people and things and was able to keep on the go without losing herself.

> Where was I when I sought you? You were present with me, but I was estranged from myself. You were in my innermost being but I was outside, and was looking for you outside.[92]

---

[91] *The Life of St. Teresa of Jesus (of the Order of Our Lady of Carmel)*, translated by David Lewis (London: Thomas Baker, 1916), p. 76.
[92] St. Augustine. Translation mine. Tr.

This characterization of a neurosis-causing life-crisis comes from St. Augustine. St. Teresa recognized herself in it. Afterward she was self-assured and more than a match for the Inquisition. She turned things round: instead of following a male reformer, she reformed a male order. She took the initiative with the inquisitors, nullified their objections and, as often as not, made them her friends. She continued to write in her native language. Having been warned that the Inquisition was out to trap her, she had this to say.

> . . . I told them I was not afraid of that, for my soul must be in a very bad state if there was anything the matter with it of such a nature as to make me fear the Inquisition; I would go myself and give myself up if I thought there was something amiss. . . .[93]

Though frustrated over having to wait impotently while feeling called to do something great, she rescued herself by looking at her options to make changes in the world. So in 1562, with four other women, she occupied a house in Avila in the early morning hours and started a reformation there on a small scale: these women tried to put into practice, as sincerely as possible, the original ideals of the order of recluses founded on Mt. Carmel (in Israel). Six years later she persuaded the newly consecrated Carmelite, John of the Cross, to do the same.

St. Teresa was especially gifted. She was astute yet benign, impulsive yet matter-of-fact, ecstatic yet coolly observant. As an author, she belongs to the top rank in Spanish literature. She writes spontaneously, without erasure and without revision. Her style is very direct, with humor and with great attention to the ordinary, to detail, to human types, and to the practical side of things. Not dogmatic, she writes from experience and with the reader in mind, and produces new imaginative representations of the mystical process while constantly looking for what she calls "new words."

She finds new words for a new kind of praying—silent prayer. Prayer can be articulate. St. Teresa is not against that, but ques-

---

[93] *The Life of St. Teresa of Jesus (of the Order of Our Lady of Carmel)*, tr. David Lewis (London: Thomas Baker, 1916), p. 313.

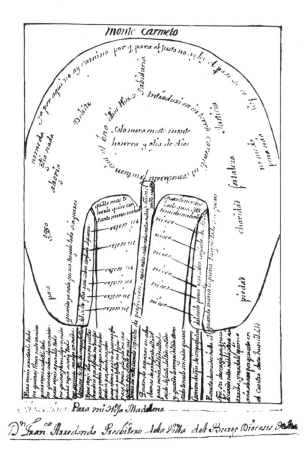

Figure 123. In 1578/1579, St. John of the Cross made a sketch of the ascent of Mt. Carmel for the nuns of Béas to keep in their breviary. The view from above downward is typical. The large circle is the base of the mountain, and the small circle—formed of letters—is the top of the mountain, a plateau. Several ways leading up from the bottom are marked—two broad paths and, sandwiched between them, a narrow one. Only the latter leads right to the top. In fact the vision of St. John of the Cross in his poems is also an extension from above downward—of the creation from God, and not of God from the creation. There are no further ways on the plateau itself. Looked at from this vantage-point, it is obvious what the shortest way is. (Made for *My Daughter Madalena*, Bibl. Nat., Madrid, MS 6926.)

tions the value of purely formal prayer and defends the importance of internal prayer against the cavils of the inquisitors—upholding it as a process that deeply moves the being and transforms the life, as a way of life and a source of active possibilities everywhere. ". . . Remember that the Lord walks among the pots and pans and that He will help you in inward tasks . . .,"[94] says St. Teresa to her Christian sisters. It is the point of rest in a life that can be full of doing.

> This love is always active and looking for what it can do. It cannot remain shut up in itself. Just as water, so it would seem, cannot stay locked in the earth, but seeks an outlet.[95]

In order to explain how one can penetrate to this rest-giving center, she employs a new picture for what is traditionally termed the "ground," "top," or "spark" of the soul. She calls it the innermost abode of the castle of the soul. The way is not climbing a mystical ladder, because the cosmos does not figure so largely for her as it does for some. She sees the earlier image of the cosmos as a picture of the human psyche with a central divine light and surrounding circular layers of the soul. Outside comes the darkness. Thus the human being must enter from the darkness and pass through all the layers (abodes in the castle) until he or she reaches the innermost abode where the most secret things are transacted between God and the soul. In this center, the person discovers what rises above him or her and what, at the same time, is the ground of his or her existence. St. Teresa describes this "way of perfection" in the form of an autobiography and from what she saw round about her. What is more, she portrays very accurately the accidental phenomena of mysticism and gives her opinion of them.

With St. Teresa, the modern psychological approach to the phenomenon of mysticism begins. It is a way through the psyche to the core of the personality, in which (almost as a matter of course) she sees psyche and body, earthly passion and spiritual love, as a unity.

---

[94] Joseph James, *The Way of Mysticism* (London: Jonathan Cape, 1950), p. 189. Quoted from *The Book of Foundations*, Chapter V.
[95] St. Teresa. Translation mine. Tr.

We are not angels: we have bodies. It would be foolish to want to make angels of ourselves as long as we are on earth and as earth-bound as I am.[96]

Now we come to a key figure. He was not St. Teresa's bosom friend, like Jeronimo Gracían, but was "the father of her soul." He was the Carmelite—St. John of the Cross—who was even less satisfied than she was with contemporary cloister life. He thought he would do better to become a Carthusian but, during a meeting with Teresa in 1568, changed his mind and joined her in an attempt to reform the Carmelite order. She was 52; he had just turned 25. She was extrovert and he was introvert. She wrote of her life in exuberant detail; he condensed his experiences into nine hundred verses of poetry. He did not have Teresa's self-assurance and adaptability. His enemies imprisoned him as a "rebel" in a monastery in Toledo, and, after the death of Teresa, he was stripped nearly naked by the brothers of his own order. Not quite 50 years old, and all but dead, he begged for a friar's habit saying, "I have nothing in which to be buried." He was removed from all his offices and, if he had lived a few more days, would have been expelled from the order he himself had started. His writings were subjected to prolonged probing by the Inquisition, and not until 1618 (four years before Teresa was canonized) were they cleared for publication. His own canonization had to wait for another century. But now his poems are part of the heritage of world literature, and he has been elevated to the status of a "doctor of the church."

His poems are a spontaneous initial reaction to what he experienced spiritually in the prison cell in Toledo. Afterward he elaborated, writing commentaries on them when asked to do so; and he wrote a new poem for the widow Ana de Peñalosa in Granada. Within the space of a fortnight, he prepared a commentary on it at her request. His entire output occupied eight years.

St. John of the Cross must not be thought of as a mystic who also wrote verse, like St. Teresa of Avila and Thérèse of Lisieux with her pious doggerel. He was a poet who clothed his mystical experiences in poetic form. In his interpretations one can feel him

---

[96] St. Teresa. Translation mine. Tr.

wrestling with the current idiom, which could not cover the subtle range of expression he required.

The imagery of St. John of the Cross is remarkably extrovert, and is not concerned with withdrawing into the castle of his soul, but with trudging through the desert and the dark night to the top of a mountain. He draws on age-old Hebrew pictures from the Bible—the joys and trials of love in the Song of Solomon, the Exodus, the pillar of cloud that led the children of Israel through the wilderness, and Mt. Carmel. He used a stylized sketch of Mt. Carmel to sum up everything he had explained to the Carmelite nuns in Béas, making thirteen copies of it for them to keep in their breviaries. The top of the mountain is outlined by the words, "I brought you into the land of Carmel that you may eat of its fruit, and of its good things." This is a text from the Bible (Jeremiah 2:7)[97] and is symbolic of an abundance of fruitfulness and enjoyment, and it served as a source of inspiration to the original Carmelites.

In this sketch by St. John of the Cross, we are presented with a bird's-eye view of the mountain and of the paths to the top. The view from above is also a striking feature of a drawing he made of the crucifixion, and is typical of his writings. His vision had to be interpreted so that people could understand it. In his poems he said it all; his prose explanations were more fragmentary. He wrote various commentaries simultaneously, some in poetry and some in prose. For him, the top of Mt. Carmel represents mysticism in its mature state. "The soul is divinized and participates in the divine nature." She "breathes in God just as God breathes in her." The pure essences of the human and the Divine come in contact. Their junction is permanent. The human becomes different and looks different:

---

[97] St. John of the Cross quotes the Latin Bible, which uses the Hebrew word "Carmel" as a place name. The modern *Catholic Jerusalem Bible* (London: Darton, Longman & Todd, 1966) uses "Carmel" as an adjective meaning "fertile" and reads: "I brought you to a fertile country to enjoy its produce and good things." So anyone turning to Jeremiah 2:7 will see no reference to Carmel in the Jerusalem Bible nor, for that matter, in the King James version except as a marginal note. Interestingly enough, Benedictus Arias Montanus, a contemporary of St. John of the Cross, who prepared an interlinear edition of the Bible for the King of Spain (Plantini, 1572, 1574), has "Charmel" in his text and *agri feracis* ("of a fertile land") in his margin. Tr. note.

Figure 124. This little drawing by St. John of the Cross has also been preserved. It's a crucified Jesus, also seen from above.

Figure 125. The vision of St. John of the Cross has become commonplace today. We look down on the clouds via satellites. In the past, however, it required great effort to imagine such a sight. Artists employed a technique called "foreshortening" to help them. Andrea del Castagno has used all his mastery of perspective here to display a vision of the crucifixion as a horizontal reality suspended above our own. (A. del Castagno, "The Trinity with St. Jerome," Church of SS. Anunziata, Florence.)

He can now say: "Of me are the heavens and of me is
the earth." Then the soul feels that all the world is one
ocean of love in which she is submerged, and she can
see no shores or margins beyond which love ceases to
exist.[98]

Pathways are not found on the summit itself, because whoever
reaches it will spontaneously walk in God's ways. There is no
more law, since the person is led by the Spirit of God. At the summit we possess consciousness of a new type. Not that we are
unceasingly conscious of God: "Usually He rests in the being of
the soul, sleeping." But we do have a different awareness of things
and of ourselves, and we see them from another point of view
and with a change in motivation. This summit is also seen by St.
John of the Cross as the end-point of a courtship—the spiritual
marriage. Falling love, as it were, and becoming a new person,
the aspirant—not unscathed—is the "wounded lover." Love's
arrow hits its mark, and the stricken soul runs after the Beloved
beyond nature and created things, which, though they are the
footprints of God, are also the signs of His absence. She searches
anxiously for the Beloved Himself. But He is not to be grasped.
Again and again, she is challenged by Him until she is empty of
desire, and through her very emptiness has room for the
Bridegroom.

What St. John of the Cross calls mature mysticism has been
described by others, too; for example, by the Brothers and Sisters
of Free Love and by the Illuminati. However, the power of St.
John of the Cross lies in the fact that he does not glory in being
lifted to a mountain peak above the masses who are living on a
low level; nor does he promise that mature mysticism is directly
attainable by all. On looking down from the summit, he sees the
steepness of the path he has climbed. And so he considers the
possibility of an easier way which does not lead so quickly to the
top.

Even though St. John of the Cross employs imagery for the
ascent, this is not a mystical ladder rising through creation, but the
psyche's path of inner purification and ever deeper penetration
into the ground of existence of the "I." The radical way is that of

---

[98] St. John. Translation mine. tr.

Figure 126. The clumsy but highly original little drawing by St. John of the Cross inspired Dali in 1951 to create a painting in which he combined this view from above to below with a horizontal vista. In the same year Dali wrote a mystical manifesto. (Salvador Dali, "The Christ of St. John of the Cross," Glasgow Art Gallery and Museum.)

nada ("nothing"). Apart from the creative Ground, our ground of existence is always "nothing," but in the Ground the "I" is all. We should practice becoming conscious of this "nothing" (the reverse of the "all"), by withdrawing from the "I" insofar as it is dedicated to itself—from the "I" that selfishly desires to possess. When God is desired, the circle is closed—closed around the ego. Only one way is possible out of this egocentric narcissism: we have to learn by experience that our real "I" is not full of desire. This exodus is a double movement: we dissociate ourselves from our false "I" and we leave ourselves to go to our true "I."

St. John of the Cross is known especially for his description of this mystical process. He calls it a "dark night." In his student days, he had become acquainted with the writings by pseudo-Dionysius which described God as "darkness." He also knew the Bible picture of the dark cloud (e.g., in Exodus 14:20), and he used these images in an original way—the pitch-black night is God Himself, but also a psychic event. We see and experience nothing but darkness and almost lose hope. Piety and images of God become meaningless, life no longer has any point, and prayer becomes a burden. And yet, in the total blackness, we are led by a dark light from within. Because of this shadowy inner guide, we do not fall into the depths of despair, but persevere, and emerge on the other side.

The "night" is something we bring upon ourselves when we renounce all our desires and all we have—including religion, our ideas about God, the experiences that have brought us joy, and mysticism, too. It is as if we are compelled to fight with the old images in order to keep the void open in a land without way or light, "where one feels that one is without God." However, the night is also God, Himself, insofar as what is happening to us is not intentional on our part, and also insofar as we are led through it. But this God is very unlike the "God" of tradition.

SALON MYSTICISM

Around 1600, the antimystical attitude of the Spanish establishment had waned and it became possible to publish and disseminate the works of Spanish and North European mystics throughout Spain and Europe. Chiefly in France, they became the inspiration for a new mysticism. "A mystical invasion" is what Bremond called it in his famous, eleven-volume, standard work on

French mysticism, which he started publishing in 1915.[99] Bremond was the first to describe the history of mysticism in a new way, "as seen by a reporter."

This French mysticism was mainly elitist—a salon mysticism in circles surrounding a "Madame." It began in the circle led by Madame Acarie in the house of Madame de Bérulle. Madame Acarie introduced the mysticism of St. Teresa of Avila. She founded Carmelite convents and, after the death of her husband, she and her three daughters became Carmelite nuns. Many Parisians met one another at her salons. The most inspiring was the Carthusian prior, Dom Beaucousin. He introduced northern mysticism. Both the English Capuchin, Benedict Canfield, and Pierre de Bérulle brought new insights to this study.

Benedict Canfield (1520-1611) wanted to shorten the many paths and spiritual exercises and "to reduce them all to a single point, namely the will of God." He saw growth to maturity in mysticism as occupying three stages: doing God's will by outward commandment, obeying God's voice from within and, finally, following God's will passively and spontaneously, "the real will of the incorporeal life." His work was translated into every European language and went through fifty impressions.

However, with Pierre de Bérulle (1575-1629), this short way has already become devotional and moral, fit only for the celibate clergy and the like. It was not for the ordinary person. The central image in his spirituality was "becoming a slave of God," which admittedly was not an attractive prospect to the average man or woman. Later on, the burning question was, if God wills my damnation, must I accept it gladly? The answer was yes.

After a stormy start, this branch of mysticism slowly but surely degenerated into an inextricable tangle of authentic experience and pathological overexcitement, of misconception and fanaticism, and of ecclesiastical intrigues and worldly politics. The baroque atmosphere of the time, and the glory shed by the Sun King, Louis XIV, made the drama complete.

Joanna of the Angels with her nuns of Loudun has been a continual source of inspiration to filmmakers, librettists, and novelists. She was a woman who, treated as one possessed, was driven

---

[99] H. Bremond, *Histoire littéraire du sentiment religieux en France* [A Literary History of Religious Feeling in France], 11 vols. (1916-1933).

by exorcists to the stake or the madhouse, and then paraded as a saint and mystic. A great fuss has also been made of the mystically inclined Madame Guyon (1648-1717). Bishop Bossuet attacked her, and Archbishop Fénelon defended her. With great literary skill, Bossuet drove the gentle Fénelon into a corner; and, by using his influence with Madame de Maintenon, the wife of Louis XIV, finally managed to obtain a papal condemnation of the archbishop. Fénelon capitulated, and Madame Guyon languished in the Bastille in solitary confinement until Bossuet's death in 1704.

A witches' cauldron bubbled around the convent in Port-Royal, too, where certain intellectuals living in small nearby houses shared a strong spirituality with the nuns. Pascal became involved in the life of the community, and so did Cornelius Jansen (Jansenius), bishop of Ieperen, and his opponents, the Jesuits. The nuns were used as pawns in the game. After they had been condemned of Jansenism, they were interned elsewhere by order of the king and, in 1709, their convent was torn down.

In this charged atmosphere, a certain Pierre Nicole tried to discover how a person could become a mystic. He had an aunt in Port-Royal and came to make a thorough investigation of the subject. His findings led him to take an intense dislike to mysticism, and he was convinced, from what he saw of it, that it had done a great deal of harm and he did his best to discourage it. In his view, the quest for mystical union amounts to tempting God, and the conviction of being one with God in a "pure love" is often false. Who knows the deepest motives of his or her heart? He considered the "dark night" of St. John of the Cross to be a superfluous and meaningless picture: only the sinner exists in God's darkness. He was equally dismissive of any "mystical contact of one's being with God." Even the being of the Devil is sustained by God. Nicole did not approach mysticism from personal experience but from theology and morals.[100] He is seen by Bremond as the instigator of "antimysticism," the spiritual climate that has prevailed in Europe ever since. In fact the whole climate sur-

---

[100] Nicole's rationalism appears in the fact that he helped Antoine Arnauld to write the *Logique de Port-Royal* [The Port-Royal Logic], first published in 1662 and still being printed in France two centuries later (e. g., by L. Hachette et Cie, Paris, 1869). In fact, *Logique de Port-Royal* was valued so highly that it was translated into German and English, and J. N. Keynes felt a need to refer to it seven times in his *Formal Logic* (Macmillan & Co., London, 1906). Tr. note.

Figure 127. Jean de Saint-Samson. (Engraving by R. Collin, Brussels. NCI, Boxmeer.)

Figure 128. Maria Petyt. (Contemporary engraving by Martin Bouche, Antwerp. NCI, Boxmeer.)

rounding mysticism was vitiated. Spanish mysticism had become merely ethical, and it was mistaken to think that an elitist mysticism was suitable for ordinary people or that they would have any real understanding of it.

In Italy the taste for mysticism soured because Jesuits, in their zeal for a popular, baroque devotion, attacked Molinos (1640-1696) as if he were really awful. This Spaniard was much in demand as a spiritual guide in various convents. He advocated an abstract mysticism with a complete cessation of the life of the will as its ideal, so that we "sink down and lose ourselves in the immeasurable sea of God's infinity." What is more, he thought that once there, being wholly at one with the will of God, we would no longer be able to sin. His teaching, drawn up in cut-and-dried propositions, was condemned as quietism. Some time before this condemnation, Madame Guyon came in contact with the teaching of Molinos. She recognized her own experiences in it and she elaborated the teachings in both poetry and prose. Her mysticism was the very counterbalance needed by the baroque, triumphal, intensely active, and devotional, counter-reformation. However, she was crushed by her own Catholic Church. Later her influence could be seen in certain Protestants who were very unhappy with an antimystical Protestantism in an antimystical culture—the Pietists, for example, and people like Labadie, Tersteegen, and Poiret.

Nevertheless, out of all the turmoil, there arose in France a mysticism that—by keeping a low profile—managed to survive. It was a mysticism of action, attainable by lay people in their daily lives, and was formulated and exemplified by St. Francis de Sales and Vincent de Paul. Each of these men wanted to preserve the freedom of women who felt called to a religious life. They did not feel that these women should be subject to convent and clerical rules. Only Vincent succeeded in this, and then only because he refused to ask for papal recognition.

Besides this form of mysticism, there is also Carmel mysticism. Not as cultivated by Carmelites, but as humbly experienced by two handicapped people—the blind brother in Rouen, Jean de Saint-Samson, and Maria Petyt, a Flemish woman who, having been rejected by the convents because of reading difficulties, shut herself up as a sort of Beguine in a small house next to the Carmelite church in Mechlin.

Jean de Saint-Samson (1571-1636) dictated his thoughts. Therefore his writings are rather disorganized; at the same time, they are firsthand testimony of his experience itself. Maria Petyt wrote down her experiences in letters that she sent regularly to her spiritual guide, the Carmelite Michael a Santo Augustino. Her experiences, which covered a long period of time, come to us "hot off the press" so to speak. From both sets of writings, we gather that the mystical way is not a vertical ascent or descent, or something that happens in three successive stages. That is too abstract. In reality, the way is a sort of spiral going up and down, slowly rising, and breaking through the circle that threatens to close round the "I." In Jean de Saint-Samson there is a clear statement of a double movement of death, dissolution, and self-annihilation on the one hand, and of a passionate, almost ecstatic feeling of love on the other hand. Death and love share an endless spiral movement with no finality. He used contemporary terms for love and death: pure love, real contact, rest in God, meeting of spirits, and the relinquishment of everything—even of God.

> When one deprives her of something, she immediately takes her flight to something else for support and enjoyment. When one deprives her of spiritual things, she avails herself of God . . . therefore during this period it will be good for those who experience anything painful not to resist it or to disregard it, except in the depth of simple longing.[101]

Maria Petyt (1623-1677), too, knew all the contemporary terms. What is especially striking in her is that she exhausted these terms and that, in the end, she wondered if there was language available to describe her new experiences. "But I am painting all this on such a grand scale. Perhaps I do not understand myself," she says. She wanted to make progress on the road to perfection, was able to stir up warm feelings and rich images, and had an excellent knowledge of the language of mysticism and could relate to it. At the same time, she knew that everything must relapse into silence and that, in the end, every effort—and every self-chosen way—must be given up. When she thought she had attained to "pure attachment to the Will and to the unpictured Being of God," she noticed later that this was not the case. Hidden under her

---

[101] Jean de Saint-Samson. Translation mine. Tr.

stereotyped mystical language, we often find something more authentic-sounding when we read between the lines. For example, this description of a deep crisis:

> It was as if a wall were between God and my soul. . . . At times I felt so pushed to the opposite extreme, so oppressed, and so full of suffering and vexation of spirit, that the world seemed to be too narrow for me: as if my soul were being ground between two millstones, or as if I were pierced with swords and hanging between heaven and earth without any support from above or below; that is to say, either from God or from man.[102]

She goes on to describe her suicidal thoughts.

In the atmosphere of antimysticism prevailing after the 17th century, an appropriate language was needed. This arose very unobtrusively out of the lonely state in which mystics found themselves—an example being Thérèse of Lisieux. From under the thick veil of bland respectability something like this peeps out:

> When, by dwelling on the comforting thought of eternal life, I try to set at rest a heart wearied by the surrounding darkness, my torment is twice as great. It is just as if the darkness takes the language of unbelievers on its lips and says to me jeeringly: you dream of light, of a homeland with the sweetest aromas, of the eternal possession of the Creator of these splendors, and you imagine you can escape from the mist in which you are pining. Make the most of it! Rejoice over death, which will not give you what you expect, but a night that is much deeper still, the night of nothing.[103]

The mysticism of action, which no longer mentions the experience itself, and can therefore flourish at the present time, will lose its mystical impulse if it does not endure the "wounds of love" and the "dark night of the soul" alongside its love in action. In the final analysis, it is only what happens to us (even, if necessary, a loss of our own idea of God), that can curb our "ego trips."

---

[102] Maria Petyt. Translation mine. Tr.
[103] Thérèse of Lisieux. Translation mine. Tr.

PART III

THE MYSTICAL WAY

THE NEW CHALLENGE

Our age is an age of religious decline. The once enduring vitality of religious people has been lost. Society has become superstitious, or credulous, or indifferent to religion. The flower of society is agnostic or skeptical, and political leaders are hypocrites. Young people are in open conflict with the establishment and with the authority of the past. People are experimenting with Oriental cults and meditation techniques. Most people are affected by the current decadence.

Here we have the current situation in the West in a nutshell; and yet it is a description of the Hellenistic world and comes from the *Annals of Tacitus*, written at the end of the first century of our era. There is nothing new under the sun! A culture spreads over the world, reaches the limits of its growth, and then returns like a boomerang from the colonized territories carrying foreign ideologies it is trying to assimilate.

Our technological culture is at the end of its growth. The indications are clearly visible—atomic weapons, environmental pollution, the depletion of natural resources, a sort of collective neurosis involving a sense of alienation, and an economic system in which the rich keep getting richer and the poor poorer. Society needs to change, with the help of the people who oppose its disintegration. If we do not share the world with one another, there will be no world to share.

As long ago as 1932, the Vice-Chancellor of the University of Nijmegen (in Holland), Titus Brandsma, maintained that mysticism is necessary for the solution of the world crisis—a mysticism that is seen as normal and attainable by all, leading to a "new and fruitful communism because it brings society to its senses." Pleas of the same sort are now being made more frequently, as in the book, *The Turning Point* by F. Capra (who says that today's world crisis is a crisis of consciousness),[1] and in the words of the restoration theologian Karl Rahner who, at the end of his life, summarized his experience of church renewal when he said that one has to be a mystical Christian or none at all.

We have already gone such a long way down that road that mysticism is now regarded as perfectly normal. Mysticism has

---

[1] F. Capra, *The Turning Point* (New York: Bantam, 1987).

come back into fashion. But whether or not this is cause for rejoicing is a moot point. Do we not find that mysticism is often a luxury indulged in by the affluent because they still have a small aching hole of dissatisfaction inside them? Is it not a macabre dance done by people looking for "kicks" performed on a volcano ready to erupt? Is not mysticism an evil when it forms part of an ego trip? When it is divorced from everyday reality with all its harshness and absurdities? Maybe not.

A modern mysticism is growing that challenges—and is challenged by—Western culture. And when I talk of Western culture I mean the scientific, rational, and technical culture, the secularized and atheistic world of today, the democratic consumer-society, the "ego-culture," the "hard sector," the confrontation of East and West. In my opinion, it is in this setting that a new mysticism can develop, if it will rise to the challenge.

THE TECHNICAL CULTURE

The alternative viewpoint which, as we have already seen, was adopted in the Renaissance, has finally made it possible for us to look out from Earth and allow the immensity of the universe to permeate our consciousness. We see the various strata, the slow deposits, that have brought Earth to its present condition. And, in these layers, we find the fossils that are studied in terms of evolution. Biologists cast doubt on a divine origin or special creation of the human being, and astronomers do not find heaven or hell out in space with its countless stars, solar systems, and galaxies. On Earth a human is a tiny dot, and in the universe the Sun is also a speck. That being so, it begins to sound like megalomania to say that we are at the center of the cosmos, and more realistic to say that we are miniscule particles in the vast reaches of time and space, with emptiness all around us. No intelligent life-forms have beamed back messages to the Earth-dwellers trying to contact them.

The person who popularized this style of thinking was Descartes (1596-1650). When he was 23, he had a visionary enlightenment which determined the rest of his life. In a flash, he saw the basis of true science from which a comprehensive knowledge could grow. He regarded himself as a born mystic in the line of the magi, but with one great difference: he did not intend to get to know the world by assimilating it in himself, by letting his own spirit and the universe become one; not at all. The knowledge he sought was to be obtained by severing every intimate connection between the inner world and the outer world, and by employing cold rational penetration into the world outside the mind without recourse to any preconceptions or beliefs. In an attempt to achieve absolute certainty, Descartes cast doubt on everything and then set out from this position of doubt like someone feeling his way in the darkness.

In the midst of all his doubt one thing was clear to him—the fact that he doubted. His conclusion was: "I think, therefore I am."[2] With him, "reason" (thinking, understanding) became the yardstick of human culture, which was then termed rationalistic. In this culture there is a deep divide between understanding and "all the rest" (including the body). "All the rest" is thought of as a machine. He saw no difference between machines manufactured by artisans and the various bodies assembled by nature herself. This machinery was imagined to have no soul, life, goal, or feeling, but to be made up of parts that gear into one another according to natural laws. To learn the laws governing nature's mechanism is the task of humanity.[3] And the aim is to discover how to control the world surrounding the mind, so we can "render ourselves the masters and possessors of nature."[4]

---

[2] *The Philosophical Works of Descartes*, Vol. 1., translated by Elisabeth S. Haldane and G. R. T. Ross (London and New York: Cambridge University Press, 1968), p. 101.

[3] *The Philosophical Works of Descartes*, Vol. 1, pp. 115-117.

[4] *The Philosophical Works of Descartes*, Vol. 1, p. 119. Tr. note: Bertrand Russell remarks that the philosophy of Descartes "brought to completion, or very nearly to completion, the dualism of mind and matter which began with Plato. . . ," *A History of Western Philosophy* (London: George Allen & Unwin, 1946), p. 590. Therefore, it is interesting to read the comments of a modern Greek philosopher on the subject: "The soul's first and primary congnition is consciousness in coincidence with perception—consciousness on the one hand of its own existence, and perception on the other hand of the existence of other beings, the aggregate of which is called the world. It is impossible for the soul to perceive without consciousness, or to be conscious of its own existence without perception . . . . Descartes, beginning unmethodically and irrationally with doubt, and in opposition to consciousness assuming his own existence as the only indisputable truth and the true first principle of philosophy, disregards the first principle of philosophical method, which is the acknowledgment of knowledge and ignorance, and the distinction between the known and the unknown." Apostolos Makrakis, *A New Philosophy and the Philosophical Sciences*, Vol. I., translated by Denver Cummings (New York: G. P. Putnum's Sons, 1940), pp. 192, 216.

"Knowledge is power." This motto is the key to the technological age in which knowledge, translated into technique, has
enabled human beings to rule and exploit nature. The motto
comes from the Englishman, Sir Francis Bacon (1561-1626).[5] He
likens this technical attitude to that of a man who seeks emotional
satisfaction by subjecting a woman against her will. It is the man-
date of the scientist to extract nature's secrets by means of torture. According to Bacon, nature has to be flushed out of her
hiding place, to be subjugated and enslaved. Nature may be
exploited remorselessly. And so he severs all emotional ties
between the human spirit and the cosmos. Only what is measurable (form, quantity, movement) is significant. Everything else
(color, sound, taste, etc.) is "subjective." What cannot be seen and
measured, cannot be controlled by reason. With a similar thought
in mind, no doubt, the witch-finders tortured their suspects, hop-
ing that the confessions wrung from them would provide information enabling the kingdom of Satan to be measured and
subdued. What is more, God began to be regarded as a "great
watchmaker." He made the mechanism of the universe, but left it
to keep running without further divine intervention. Therefore
He is not reached via the cosmos, but through the spirit in the
spirit, itself.

It was Blaise Pascal, in particular, who indicated a new concept for mysticism here: God is not knowable through nature.
God is knowable and approachable only through the non-mea-
surable, the human, and the spiritual. Faith, mysticism, and devotion must therefore be directed to this human aspect, to heart and
soul, to the enclosed garden of the soul. Thus the territories of
mysticism and science were fenced off. Science stepped aside from
church, faith, and piety, had its own methods and objectives, and
pursued its own goals to gain an exact and comprehensive knowledge of things. Mysticism was a spiritual, supernatural affair.

Rationalism and this technical approach have had an over-
riding and spectacularly successful influence on Western culture.
Alchemy developed in a non-mystical way and became chemistry: the principle of "dissolve and coagulate" was applied
without any direct link between the "work" and the "worker" as

---

[5] In *Meditationes Sacrae, De Haeresibus,* Bacon's actual words are: "Nam et ipsa
scientia potestas est" ["For knowledge itself is power."]. Tr. note.

had been the rule in alchemy.[6] Western culture became largely analytical, and focused on external reality. It spent its force in continual fragmentation, in the study of details, and in specialization; and its end product is a machine that has rung in a new era—the era of the computer. This machine operates on questions that have to be answered by "Yes" or "No." It can act as a substitute for the human brain, and possibly store the enormous amount of information the human race has accumulated—something that is no longer possible for a single individual to do.

As long ago as 1717, Julien Offray de la Mettrie defended the idea that there is little difference between mind and body—both belong to the human machine. Mystics, however, do not take such a mechanistic view, and are interested in knowing why—given its unitary origin—the world cannot be a better place.

People have always felt a need to find connections on a deeper level than the material, to gain an insight that lays bare the coherence of everything. At present, this need is being amply satisfied: often on a level of superstition or credulity in which whatever sounds different is liable to be thought of as better, and things that are no more than possibilities are accepted as facts. This aspect of the post-industrial culture has been christened the Age of Aquarius or the New Age—a new age dawning of harmony between humans and nature, without stress and without noise. The mystical core of this movement is that everyone share in cosmic love. On the sleeve of an LP of new age music (*The Light of Tao*, by Aeoliah) it is said that the music comes out of a deeply felt love of nature and the heavenly octaves of light, color, and sound as they blossom in the innocent, radiant life of the natural realm.

Modern new age music sounds spatial, the shapes and colors of this culture are "psychedelic," the politics are "green." We champion the rights of animals and crusade to protect and

---

[6] In other words, the practical laboratory operations of alchemy were carried over into chemistry, but its theoretical basis was not. For example, dissolving and coagulating are simultaneous in alchemy: "This corrosive being a volatile acid saline spirit, by dissolving the earth is thereby destroyed and with the dissolved earth become corporeal, vitriolic, or aluminous according to the nature of such an earth. The earth is dissolved and the spirit is coagulated." (From an alchemical manuscript on "The Generation of Metals," from a private collection.) Tr. note.

liberate them. The new age requires that the air, earth, and water must be made clean and kept clean. Aggressive people must learn peace, through music, meditation, dance, physical movement and breath control. And so, a spiritual journey is possible through unfolding spaces of divine love and glory. Many individuals have taken on board ideas and feelings of this sort. In her book, *The Aquarian Conspiracy*, Marilyn Ferguson pictures these scattered living individuals as a group. Through the book and also by organizing international gatherings, she hoped to take mystical fringe activity and make it the hub of the world culture of the future. A medley of yoga, Eastern meditation, Western mysticism, alternative medicine, macrobiotic diet, concern for the balance of nature, pacifism, astrology, magic, witchcraft, mythical thinking, shamanism, mysticism, and so on, was equated with some kind of global conspiracy:

> A leaderless but powerful network is working to bring about radical change in the United States. Its members have broken with certain key elements of Western thought, and they may even have broken continuity with history. This network is the Aquarian Conspiracy . . . It is a new mind—the ascendance of a startling worldview that gathers into its framework breakthrough science and insights from earliest recorded thought.[7]

Whether this new age will materialize remains to be seen. What we do know is that a fresh attitude is growing, which is discernible even in scientific circles. Indeed it was already present in the 18th century in the natural philosopher Swedenborg. He had mastered all the contemporary sciences and wanted to understand the whole world, even in the realm of the spirit.[8] He conversed with hundreds of spirits and tried to formulate his findings scientifically. Was this the search of a scientist for God? In retrospect, we

---

[7] Marilyn Ferguson, *The Aquarian Conspiracy: Personal and Social Transformation in Our Times* (Los Angeles: J. P. Tarcher, 1980), p. 23.

[8] ". . . hence the desire for wisdom becomes the special mark and characteristic of man. Unless, however, he is eager to attain a knowledge which lies beyond or above the senses, he is not truly rational, nor is there a due connection between the senses and the soul." E. Swedenborg, *The Principia*, I: 1, translated by Rendell & Tansley (London: The Swedenborg Society, 1912). Tr. note.

may prefer to see him as a forerunner of Freud, who was really investigating his own psyche and reducing the empty, infinite universe to human dimensions—which apparently is something the psyche needs to do.

More recently, it was a Swiss hotelier, Erich von Däniken, who made an imaginative study of the population of the universe, and produced as much scientific evidence as he could to support him.

> And so I step out of time. I stand outside and see everything simultaneously: the past, the present, the future. I hold conversations.[9]

He placed himself outside time with the knowledge of the archeologist. However, he saw something very different from what is seen by the scientist: his findings suggest that there are other intelligences and gods in the universe. Von Däniken has been read all over the world—which certainly says a good deal about the need of modern men and women for something different in life, for the fantastic and for such possibilities as encounters with space people.

A more convincing, and perhaps less ephemeral, answer to this need is given by scientists who have tried to dig back to some beginning that will show how all things are interconnected. By studying paleontology, Soloviov (1853-1900) and especially Teilhard de Chardin[10] (1881-1955) came to a mystical vision. In imagination, they stepped outside the universe to see it evolve. They saw dense matter fanning out. They saw the human spirit as something that came from within. At first, so it seemed to them, this spirit was locked up in matter; then it developed into individual consciousness; and now it looks set to be gathered into a collective unconscious and destined to become the soul of the universe. God, they said, was incarnated in this dawning consciousness. Matter, spirit, and the universe formed a divine milieu. There men and women could find Him. By seeing, feeling, experiencing, and thinking in

---

[9] Erich von Däniken, *Chariots of the Gods?*, translated by Michael Heron (New York: G. P. Putnam's Sons, 1969).

[10] *The Desire to be Human.* A global reconnaissance of human perspectives in the age of transformation, written in homage of Pierre Teilhard de Chardin (Wassenaar, 1983).

tune with the vital stream of matter, life, and energy, their experience of God would grow. By such means they would contact the Primeval Source of universal life (Soloviov).

> I actually feel Him, this God, through all the surfaces and depths of the world and of matter.

In the final analysis, the vision of Teilhard de Chardin was that of a believer. Admittedly he accepted evolution, but he pictured Christ as central to it. Humanity was Christ's "Mystical Body."

> The essence of Christianity is neither more nor less than the belief in the unification of the world in God through the incarnation. All the rest is merely clarification.

Teilhard thought that each one of us can experience this, even without naming it as "Christ." Christ is always,

> the invisible force that, underneath the discord and chaos of the world, guides the bright threads of the universal life and arranges the fragmented pieces of the universe into well-formed shapes.[11]

We can reach this force and immerse ourselves in it by our love. However, it is a vision of union that does not always make much impact.

Science has now reached a point where it is seeking unification of our splintered knowledge. Physicists, in particular, are looking for the beginning in various areas—for the fundamental forces that bind the atomic nuclei, the gases of the planets, and the universe itself. They are seeking the primary energy. By concerning themselves with such questions as the origin of life, consciousness, and the cosmos, scientists seem to be adopting a mystical attitude. Einstein once said that the most beautiful and deepest feeling that we can experience is that of mysticism. It is the strength of all true science. Whoever is a stranger to this feeling, whoever can no longer stand in awe and amazement, is as good as dead.

---

[11] The three previous quotes by Teilhard are from Siehe B. Borchert's, "Mystieke ervaring van de levensbron der lichamelijkheid: Teilhard de Charden en Solovjew" in *Speling* 26 (1974) 3, 88 f. Translation mine.

In recent years, more and more studies seem to have been giving the answer to this question. Vivid pictures have been drawn of black holes, the big bang, the cosmic soup. The ordinary viewer can explore on TV the beginning of the universe and the interior of the atom, and can learn about elementary particles which are both particles and non-particles (waves). Scientists are delving into Eastern mysticism in order to explain the results of their research.

Mystical texts fit the new discoveries surprisingly well. Consider "it both is and is not," and "all is one particle, and in each particle is all." Deep down, everything is one energy, on the surface are many shapes, says modern science. The same dynamic view of the universe is taken by oriental mystics.

The mystical culture that is now coming to the fore springs from the notion of an organic relationship between all that is. The "I" consists of the same primeval energy as the "all." Matter that seems so concrete, is built of elementary particles which are also flowing waves, relationships, and energies. Spirit and matter are two different forms of a single energy. The nuclear physicist, Jean E. Charon, suggested using the idea of the "black hole" to explain how consciousness is produced—not from the outside but—from the elementary, immortal electron. "My thinking is the thinking of my electrons." David Bohm sees the eternal basis of the universe as holographic, the whole, as it were, being "implicate" in each tiny part. The Danish physicist Niels Bohr was the first to make a connection between science and Oriental mysticism. And the Austrian, Fritjof Capra, has popularized this connection in best-sellers he has written in San Francisco since 1976. Like Teilhard de Chardin, his writing was prompted by a visionary experience:

> I "saw" cascades of energy coming down from outer space, in which particles were created and destroyed in rhythmic pulses; I "saw" the atoms of the elements and those of my body participating in this cosmic dance of energy; I felt its rhythm and I "heard" its sound, and at that moment I *knew* that this was the Dance of Shiva, the Lord of Dancers worshipped by the Hindus.[12]

---

[12] Fritjof Capra, *The Tao of Physics* (New York: Bantam, 1977), p. xv; and (London: Wildwood House, 1975), p. 9.

And he is not the only one to have had such an experience involving our scientific knowledge of nature. The German physicist Carl F. von Weizsacker says:

> We describe the material world, stars and atoms. We examine them, but at the same moment there comes over us a deep realization of the old truth, understood long ago by Buddha, that what we are telling is our own story. We ourselves, our bodies are composed of atoms. Our lives form part of nature that we are analyzing. We cannot separate them; we cannot talk about nature as if we do not belong to it.[13]

Capra, in particular, was called a traitor by his colleagues, and Teilhard de Chardin was not thought worth a mention. Both personified a break with current scientific theory, and were throwbacks to a researcher of another type—the mage. We certainly need to ask whether science can retain its keen edge if science is based on subjective experience. An accepted scientific hypothesis always goes through the stages of experimental support, modification, disproof, and replacement.

The case is different when scientific research (as now) is inwardly experienced and then popularized. At the moment it looks as if the mechanical picture of the world is being replaced by the picture of the world as an organism because the latter is more in keeping with the latest results. Also more in keeping with them is the cultivation of a mystical attitude that will avoid the dangers of a rationalistic and technological approach.[14] A good survey of the new tendency has been given by IKON. The text of this transmission appeared in "Natuurwetenschap en mystiek" ["Science and Mysticism"], in *VU-Magazine*, March 1986.

THE ATHEISTIC CULTURE

In the mid-60's, people were startled by the provocative announcement, "God is dead," as if He had recently expired. It made good copy for the media everywhere. The front cover of the world's

---

[13] "Naturwetenschap en mystiek," in *VU*-magazine, March 1986. Translation mine. Tr.

[14] Fritjof Capra, *The Tao of Physics* (New York: Bantam, 1977; and London: Wildwood House, 1975). Also see *The Turning Point* (New York: Bantam, 1987).

greatest magazine, *Time*, carried the obituary on a funereal black background (April 8, 1966). The source of the announcement was a little book from the pen of an Anglican bishop, Dr. Robinson. Four years later, the same magazine asked, on another cover, whether God was not very much alive again (December 26, 1969). In reaction against a rationalist culture, the neglect of religion, and the secularization of the church, religious feelings had exploded like fireworks. Maybe the old picture of God and ecclesiastical dogmas were rather threadbare, but this did not mean that pious sentiment was out of date. On the contrary, everything that humanity had ever clothed in religious forms was now on display in the Western market and was in great demand.

Although mainstream churches were being emptied, spiritual leaders were attracting followers and new groups (orthodox and otherwise) were growing fast. Was this a sign of declension? Were the faithful sinking in a morass of superstition, emotional instability, and irrational experience? Or was it perhaps an indication that religion is an impulsive affair? If the latter, then, like everything else impulsive, it needs to be turned into useful channels—but not suppressed. Atheistic religion, of course, is a challenge. I am speaking of an atheism that is "religious" in the sense that it does not arise out of skepticism and indifference but out of a loss of confidence in old images and an inability to find new ones. This lack of contact with God can prove to be a good breeding ground for a fresh form of mysticism.

The idea that God is dead suddenly hatched in the nest of learned minds where it had been incubating for a long time. German academics had said that religion and dogma were products of their age and rest on religious feelings (Schleiermacher, 1768-1834); or that one's image of God is a projection of one's own hopes and fears (Feuerbach, 1808-1872); or that the Son of God is a myth (Strauss, 1808-1874); or that Jesus of Nazareth must be discovered behind the myth (Schweitzer, 1875-1965); or that heaven and the promised paradise have to be sought on Earth and religion is an opium of the people that hinders them from seeking paradise on Earth (Marx, 1818-1883); or that God is dead and human beings must just learn to live with it and become different human beings (Nietzsche, 1844-1900).

The emptiness felt by the members of certain exclusive circles, after this "death of God," was accepted as a challenge to be human in a completely new situation. In other words, we need to learn to live adequately in the absence of any higher authority. People need to acquire fresh values, since the old ones appear to have gone stale. Humanism thrived in this void, which was also experienced as a sort of painful search for the meaning of life. Buddhism was found to be very attractive, too, because it rejected religious projections and talked of a way of liberation from suffering without a divine savior or a hereafter. Typical of this secularized religion is the tale of a monk who relieved himself against an image of Buddha. On being reproved, he replied: "Can you show me a place where I can answer the call of nature without defiling the Buddhist deity?" However, Buddhism also demonstrates that religion will not be killed off just by calling God dead. Asia is covered in images of various Buddhas, and they are larger than any images of Christian saints in the West. Actually, it is widely thought that the appearance of atheism within Christendom is no anomaly. Christianity has roots in Judaism, which strictly prohibits making images of God. The living God has no designation or shape. And the cosmos itself is not divine. A tree is a tree—nothing more. It is not an object charged with holy powers, which must be knelt to, prayed to, and placated.

Religious atheism, having dethroned God and the gods, is a test for the mystical experience that tries to come to terms with it. Mysticism has been left to endure emptiness, to carry out a search—in that emptiness—for the great Mystery. The "transcendent dimension" need not be described as God per se, nor experienced as anything sacred. God and divine worship are not taken for granted at this period in history. Failure to mention God does not seem odd. Therefore mystics who decide to keep quiet about God and religion no longer attract attention. On the other hand, there are still people who make no bones about being religious.

From the very earliest times, most religions and forms of devotion have been introduced by mystics. Mysticism often plays a key role in a religion and exposes the way in which high-handed authority is being projected on God. Even now we see monastic orders, which put at risk their very existence by doing so, developing an active mysticism in their "mission fields," while targeting the misery caused by the power of church and state. Carlos Mesters, a Dutch Carmelite in Brazil, explained this mystical attitude in a parable: what is happening in divided South America is, for him, like the innumerable pieces of the torn painting of a face. Many people are busy repairing the painting and he decided to lend a hand.

I want to see the Face that interests me so much. . . . So far I have not succeeded, but something tells me that one day I shall. And that—I assure you—will be the happiest day of my life. For in that Face is the key of life, the meaning of our existence and of our struggle for a better world. I want to see the Face that gazes at me so intently and attracts me in the fragments of life.[15]

THE CONSUMER SOCIETY

Shortly before he died, Aldous Huxley (1894-1963) vented his spleen about the behavior of mystics, and wanted to know why they do not tell the ordinary person living in the everyday world how to have mystical experiences, and why the words they use are so vague. He characterized as follows the situation in which mysticism has to make good nowadays: we are living in a democratic consumer-oriented society in which nothing is reserved any more for an elite group, each one must be able to satisfy his or her needs and for all these needs there is a market. Even mystical experiences are "needs." All his life, Huxley had been looking for a "quicker" way to satisfy these needs, and thought he would find it in mind-bending drugs. In the end, it seemed that these induce not only heavenly but also hellish experiences, and can form a destructive addiction. He discovered that the democratization of mysticism is by no means free from peril.

Nevertheless, this democratization will continue in response to a universal need, and no authority can stop it, as the Church would once have been able to do. Not only are mystics and mystical currents being studied, and mystical texts from every conceivable culture being published, they are also being popularized in the press and on TV. In addition, we frequently find lectures, training sessions, group therapies, and fellowships being formed around a mystical idea or around some guru.

What kind of mysticism can be democratized? Not the brief mystical experience itself—which is something personal that just happens. But everything else can be democratized—the mystical attitude, the mystical life, the mystical culture or devotion, the search and its expression in word and deed, the fruits of mysticism. Not everyone has a talent for putting experiences into words,

---

[15] Carlos Mesters, "Brief aus Brasilien," in *Speling* 3, 1981. Translation mine. Tr.

but they can recognize the experiences of others, and realize that life can be lived in a certain manner on the basis of the core of an experience, even if one is scarcely able to recall the experience itself. In order for this recognition to occur, however, mysticism has to express itself in contemporary imagery, language, and indications of the way, without introducing any unnecessarily involved and peculiar constructions or technical words, or using obfuscation.

Expressions of mysticism always relate to the spirit of the times. In cultures in which powerful emotions are valued, mysticism will be magnified; and in cultures in which they are distrusted, it will be neglected or eliminated. It has not been popular in the West during recent centuries. The well-educated thought it was a nonsensical, hazy superstition retained by unstable people who lagged behind the times. In the Catholic world, mysticism was certainly acceptable; but only for monks and nuns. And within the cloisters themselves, the mystic was thought of as someone special who was possibly on the way to sainthood. The normal path for normal "religious" Christians was asceticism, and they did not feel drawn toward mysticism. But nowadays, although people are not interested in the odor of sanctity, they crave for the spiritual ascent and expect it to be brought about by a "mystical attitude," "mystical life," or "mystical culture." They hope to be motivated by a source of inspiration deep inside them. To a large extent, they rely on openness to the unusual in the everyday world and on savoring their experiences, and they try to cultivate an intuitive, alogical[16] insight into the affairs of life.

---

[16] I have used "alogical" as if it differed from "illogical" in much the same way as "amoral" differs from "immoral." The insight being described here is not contrary to logic, it just runs on lines that have nothing to do with logic. Unfortunately, the examples of the (rather rare) use of "alogical" given in the *Oxford English Dictionary Supplement* show that in the past the word has not been employed with such precision, but has been more or less equated with "irrational" or "illogical." Nevertheless, I think it would be good to set a precedent and use it in the restricted sense of being unconcerned with logic, because such a usage is needed. In fact, this note has been written to make that point clear. In Jung, the word "irrational" is employed similarly "not as denoting something contrary to reason, but something beyond reason, something, therefore, not grounded in reason." C. G. Jung, *Dictionary of Analytical Psychology*, (London: Arkana-Penguin, 1987), p. 125. However, it is virtually impossible to alter the generally accepted meaning of a common word like "irrational," whereas with a rare word like "alogical" it may be done. Tr. note.

The framework of modern mysticism can be secular or, in the words of St. Teresa of Avila, an environment of "pots and pans." As St. Francis de Sales taught and Dag Hammarskjöld realized, it has to be suitable for everyone. This ordinary mysticism now seems possible in a number of ways. For many, the word mysticism may conjure up visions of holiness, the Orient, or exceptional visions and experiences, but today's mystics include executives and scientists, philosophers and poets, novelists and playwrights, artists and composers. Their story has yet to be written. A mystical attitude also seems to be often present in peaceworkers, environmentalists, and champions of the oppressed. And then there are those who, although they do not claim to have had a mystical experience themselves, enjoy reading books about mysticism. The ready sale of such books reveals how many people are trying to understand their own fleeting moments of inspiration, or to satisfy their curiosity about modern esotericism. The words "mystical impulse" can apply to almost anything—the need to get out of the rat race, a yearning for ecstasy, interest in unusual phenomena, a longing to lose oneself in something greater or to "cross thresholds." They may also apply to the rejection of our technical, rationalist culture which threatens to swamp the individual, and pays more attention to the mind than to the body and the emotions.

Some people embrace mysticism in order to become pure and perfect, and holy and happy, not to mention healthy, or in order to discover their origins. History teaches that mysticism often takes root in a culture that has reached a critical juncture where the people are alienated from themselves. At this very moment, we are living in a world full of alienation: a technological desert has been produced in which creativity is prostituted to consumerism, fertile land has been leveled and concreted, and air and water are poisoned by refuse and acid rain. We are also living in a spiritual desert in the midst of material prosperity. Existence is meaningless, empty, boring, because instant enjoyment is the order of the day. And when the instant is over, there is nothing left to enjoy. Denial of the God and heaven of our forebears leaves the future blank. Such a desert is the haunt of existential fears and neuroses. And, in this desert, not everything calling itself mysticism is worthy of the name. There are many forms of mysticism that cover the bare soil with artificial flowers. Instead of opening our eyes to reality and giving us the means to cross the wasteland successfully, these aberrant forms cause euphoria, create illusions, and conjure up *fata morgana*. They satisfy too quickly, and the search is abandoned because the real need has been pushed into the background. An Eastern adage is instructive here: "When you have found the Buddha, slay him."

The mystic way can bring happy and intense experiences, and can conduct us to an oasis in the desert, but the way is long and, after awhile, becomes very monotonous and dreary. Mysticism is often like being in love. When the fires of passion have died down and the lovers have taken a good look at one another, a period of patience is required, a painful phase that has to be endured while each learns that the other is. . .different. We can lose our self-love in the desert. Not wanted, yet it can have everything to do with love. The Gestalt psychologist, Fritz Perls calls this a homicide. *Nothing* is what is experienced:

> If we accept this nothing and enter into this nothing, then the desert begins to blossom. The void comes alive, it is filled. The sterile void becomes a fruitful void.[17]

Thus mysticism brings us into contact with love itself.

THE EGO-CULTURE

In a book titled *Culture of Narcissism* Christopher Lasch described how Western—and in particular American—culture is dominated by the narcissistic personality, preoccupied with its own lot in life and incapable of lasting relationships.[18] Since this was written, we speak of the "ego age."

The individual is central in the Western World, together with his or her rights, conscience, freedom,[19] improvement and experiences. At first sight, this aspect of our culture might seem helpful to mysticism, for mysticism itself is an individual matter. The

---

[17] Fritz Perls, *Gestalt Therapie. Verbatim*, compiled and edited by John O. Stevens (The Hague, 1973).
[18] Christopher Lasch, *Culture of Narcissism: American Life in an Age of Diminishing Expectations* (New York: Norton, 1991).

experiences of a mystic are personal. He or she cannot rely on a leader, a doctrine, or on any external authority. Nevertheless, an "ego age" poses challenges to mysticism, for how can mysticism escape from narcissism and ego trips in a process that is ultimately bogged down in the ego?

"Retirement into oneself" is not exclusive to people who practice Eastern philosophy. The West also has a rich tradition in this respect. However, unlike what has happened in the East, the way into the "self" has also been trodden by scientists, who have carried out research into the soul (or psyche). Dreams, symbols, myths, and psychological illnesses have been recognized as a language of the unconscious. Freud thought that the sexual drive was the deepest part of the psyche; his disciple, Jung, thought that the religious drive was the deepest.

Because psychoanalysis, designed as a therapy, often gave inadequate results, Fritz Perls looked for an efficient method. He saw not only dreams and myths, but also behavior as the language of the psyche. From group discussions and analysis of this behavior, it became clear how the conscious "I" had turned the unconscious "I" into an underdog. What "I" expect of myself, the role "I" will play in society, what "I" refuse to recognize as part of myself, all this represses the "true I"—which then has no chance to make good.

This psychotherapeutic attitude has subsequently been adopted in many forms by groups with leaders. Often the intention is not so much the cure of psychological illnesses as the development of the true "I" in the mystical sphere (taking mystical in the sense of "expansion of consciousness"). The ego-conscious expands when it is penetrated by what has previously been hidden.

---

[19] A big trade-off between liberty and government is going on all the time, even in so-called "free" countries. Those who believe they are free should ask themselves whether they are free to preach any religion or politics on the streets without anyone's permission, to be a teacher, or educator, or practice alternative medicine without a certificate or license, to reject military service, to run any type of business (professional or nonprofessional) without a license, to buy, sell, and publish whatever, whenever, and wherever they like, to work in any trade without union membership, to jump on and off moving public transport, to drive anywhere at any speed consistent with safety, to build anything anywhere without planning permission, carry firearms, or even to feel free if they are the wrong color. There are fashions in freedom, even in the West, and "free" are those who follow the fashion. Tr. note.

Has the mystic way ended up as a psychological way? We know now that much of our behavior is motivated by the unconscious, that is to say, without our awareness of its motivation. This new knowledge unmasks our "I" and renders considerable mystical literature superfluous. Many of the earlier guides have become obsolete. But that's not the whole story. Mystics speak plainly about another reality in the deepest point of the soul: a "ground" that is more important than any projection, in which no image, idea, or emotion plays a part—no picture of what we are—and no picture of what God is. Just as in nature mysticism primeval energy is not the divine reality that the mystic experiences, so in psychology, the "true I" is not the same as the deepest ground of existence. In the Western tradition, this aspect is more clearly worked out than in the Eastern, probably because it is more necessary to do so in the West, where the emphasis placed on the individual increases the danger of ego trips.

Of course, the deciding factor is not which theory a person uses to interpret an experience, but whether or not the experience itself, and the mystic way, becomes entangled in the ego. Great mystics like Buddha and Jesus talked about abandonment of the egocentric, grasping "I," renunciation of desire, and becoming poor in spirit. Other Oriental ways regularly emphasize that mysticism must always remain something to search for if we are to escape being trapped by the"I." We must never stop at any supposedly safe haven along the path. St. John of the Cross gave some marvelous advice that is still suitable for this egotistic age we live in. Even for him, the shortest way is renunciation of the ego and its desires, but he specifies just how this is to be carried out—not only through mental effort, but through a love that spurs us on, and draws us out of ourselves and nearer to our desire. He also indicates the danger of what we might call "consumerism" in things of the spirit—the deliberate attempt to have experiences, visions and blissful feelings, or the keeping of vigils in the hope of becoming a saint and a mystic. It is not possible to rise above self if we do not let go of ourselves when we set out on our mystic quest.

For many of us, letting go will not take place without a "dark night of the soul," which is something that is not in our power to prevent. It is an emptiness that often takes the form of a deep depression. The feelings are numb and there is no light anywhere. According to St. John of the Cross, whoever will hold out—so that the depression does not lead to suicide, but to the loss of the greedy self—will arrive at a "new comprehension of God in God." The "I" then experiences its deepest ground; not from the vantage point of the "I" itself, but from the other side of this ground—which is God.

The darkest night is not even the pain of the absence of the Beloved (the reverse of desire). The darkest night is the night in which no more desire is perceived, even though, in retrospect, a deeply hidden will-to-live seems to have everything to do with love. It is hard not to interpret this "dark night" as being entirely negative, as something in which God is not to be found and we cannot exist, as a technical desert from which we must flee to so-called mystical regions—in accordance, one might say, with the practice, so popular in our modern ego-culture, of divorcing "incompatible" partners and looking for new ones.

COMBINING MYSTICAL PATHS

Like Alexandria in the Hellenistic world, California and Northern Europe in today's world are melting pots of many tendencies. And it looks as if, once again, something new might grow out of a clash of creeds. Many, like Teilhard de Chardin or the adherents of certain modern religious movements, await the dawn of a "universal religion."

The Mazdaznan movement, based on Zoroaster, sees itself as the religion behind all religions. The Sufi movement, inspired by the Sufi mystics of Islam, but founded by the Indian mystic Kahn (1882-1927), professes to perceive fraternity as the universal element in all religions. so does Bahai, founded by two Iranian mystics in the 19th century and now fiercely persecuted in Iran itself by Moslem fundamentalists. Ramakrishna (1836-1886), too, a Brahmin from Bengal, was encouraged by an insight into the unity of creation to attempt a synthesis of the many forms of worship. His pupil, Vivekananda (1863-1902), made an original synthesis between the technical West and Vedantic mysticism, which he unveiled at the World Parliament of Religions held in Chicago in 1893. The German, Schopenhauer (1788-1860), was the first Western philosopher who was open to the East. This openness eventually spread among the elite, especially in Germany, the Netherlands, and England. In America, California became a hotbed of exotic ideas, not only because Americans now had their

Figure 129. A special unity with nature has been earnestly sought in China from early times. The path taken is characterized by such keywords as I Ching (The Book of Changes), yin-yang, and Tao (The Way). An agelong observation of the relationships that rule in the starry world and in human society, and form the basis of all changes. The wisdom [of the I Ching] can still be consulted by asking a question and throwing [yarrow stalks or] coins. Heads or tails are counted after each throw to obtain long or broken lines, and six throws give two trigrams = one hexagram. The total of possible hexagrams is 64.

The purpose of using the Book of Changes is to have one's thinking pointed in the right direction, and the underlying premise is that each thing is a pole with a corresponding anti-pole—yin-yang. The art of living is not to choose the pole and avoid the antipole, or vice versa, but to bring them into harmony with one another. Lao Tsze formulated the art of living as following the Tao, the great cosmic Way.

YIN	YANG	YIN	YANG
Female	Male	Cooperating	Competing
Contracting	Expanding	Intuiting	Rationalizing
Conserving	Demanding	Synthesizing	Analyzing
Reacting	Acting	Uniting	Fragmenting

[Yin-yang is an abstract idea. Its symbol is two droplike shapes. The form of the one determines that of the other. The one is the opposite of the other: they are white and black. They embrace one another, however, and constitute an undivided unity, the circle.]

Figure 130. "The Fishing Hermit" by Ma Yuan (13th century) illustrates a typically Taoist attitude to life—the way of non-action. (Copy of the original in the National Palace Museum, Taipei, Republic of China.)

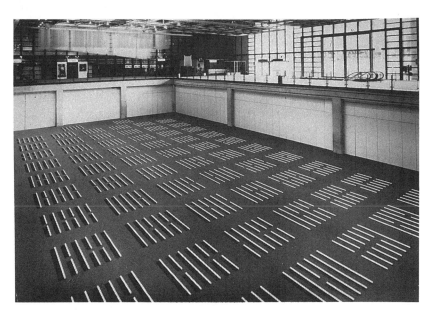

Figure 131. The 64 I Ching hexagrams are laid out as modern sculpture in the foyer of the Georges Pompidou Art Center, Paris. By Walter de Maria in 1982. (Photo: B. Hatala.)

interest aroused regarding Eastern mysticism, but also because Oriental gurus had sensed it would be worthwhile to come to America with their mysticism specially packaged for a new audience. And now, the encounter with the East is no longer a matter for the elite, but has become part of a heterogeneous subculture, in which all kinds of mysticism, magic, old traditions, and new trends, are cross-pollinating one another.[20] Perhaps, in this melting pot, the ancient schism of East and West will finally disappear. Some important choices still have to be made. For example, the West needs to adopt a different attitude to nature, while the East must find a solution for the problem of the pariahs on the basis of the "equal rights for all" recognized in the West. We have a choice between, on the one hand, a heroic mysticism with little understanding of the failures, the sick and the weak, and, on the other hand, a mysticism of the repressed. Should we opt for a heroic mysticism in which the cosmos is central, and human beings are worth neither more nor less than anything else, the mystic way being a method of getting good order in our innermost being? Or should we opt for a mysticism in which the weaker individual can pass through a negative experience to reach God as a helper and lover; in which all are "of noble birth" (Eckhart), and we are aware of the importance of justice for the individual as we strive toward the One?

Eastern, and especially Chinese, mysticism majors on harmony, stillness, conformity with the Tao (the Way), resignation, and "absorption." Following in the steps of Zoroaster, Western mysticism is more aggressive, because humans are seen as fighting alongside God against evil and injustice The East holds to a profound nature mysticism in which the individual feels absorbed into the great whole. The West is mistrustful of this kind of nature mysticism because it can easily deify the cosmos; whereas, it is not the cosmos, but man, that is "made in God's image," according to Western tradition.

Whether this distinction is really quite so sharp is a moot point. Centuries ago, St. Francis of Assisi was talking about created things as his brothers and sisters, and the Buddha came to his

---

[20] For a discussion of how modern management and Eastern and Western mysticism can be combined, see: Stikker, *Tao, Teilhard en Weseters denken* [Tao, Teilhard and Western Thought] (Amsterdam, 1986).

doctrine through compassion with suffering. In Krishna and Bhakti yoga, Eastern mysticism becomes human and warm; and, in neo-Platonism, reality is a shadow of the true Reality. But now, the baneful side of the technical frame of mind is very evident in the smugness of those who behave as if they were the center of the universe, and are devoid of proper reverence.[21] On the other hand, self-indulgent affluence at the expense of others is just as impossible for those who seek nothing but harmony, nothing but respect for nature, nothing but restfulness, nothing but inner order, nothing but conformity with the great cosmic Way, as it is for those who struggle to remove poverty and injustice.

THE MANY WAYS OF MYSTICISM

History teaches that human beings are concerned with the improvement of their material circumstances and the satisfaction of their needs, and also with their spirits and highest aspirations. They are always trying to rise above the everyday world. They crave for paradise, for a moment of eternity beyond their restless, unsatisfying lives, for a refuge in the soul where they know that they are loved and accepted by the "All."

In this section I want to discuss the deepening process that takes place as new life emerges from the kernel of living experience with all the characteristics of growth—just as from a tiny fertilized ovum a human being develops over a period of years according to a certain "code" which specifies arms, legs, brain, etc., though never in exactly the same way twice. The growth of the body is limited; at a certain moment it stops; the individual's appearance begins to change and to reflect the wear and tear of life, until at last the frayed body rather suddenly collapses.

---

[21] *The Zohar*, for example, stresses the importance of reverence in the following passage: "Job displayed preeminently the sense of religious awe and fear; for in the sphere of supramundane relationships, whether in the region of holiness or of unholiness ("the other side"), man cannot draw down the spirit from above and unite himself with it without a sense of fear and awe, the concentration of heart and mind, and self-effacement." *The Zohar, Vol.* III, 69a, translated by Maurice Simon and Dr. Paul P. Levertoff. New York: Soncino Press, 1934.

THE TURNING-POINT

Mystical experience evokes something from "up above," higher than everyday life. Vague as this realization is, it is often clothed in concrete imagery. Formerly, it meant that the individual desired to feel one with a God who occupies a world of His own, far above the cosmos He has made. From the standpoint of Earth, His heaven is located beyond the stars. And men and women can ascend, step by step, through creation, away from mundane things toward God. This picture of a mystical ladder has often been used to represent the mystical path, though details differ. The shamans were early exponents of it.

The "God is dead" school can no longer relate to any mystical ladder. They have blocked off the ascent to heaven, and are forced to turn inward. And, indeed, they themselves represent a turning point. Mysticism depends on various attitudes and turning points that are relative but not unimportant. Consciously or unconsciously, people rely on concepts. The following illustrations bring home, in a vivid way, the significance of the above-mentioned turning point.

Figure 132. In the ancient world picture, the Earth was the center of the cosmic movement. The universe was not empty. Stars were grouped in well-defined constellations and coursed through space, enclosed by the belt of the zodiac. (Bibliothèque, Paris, MS fr. 9140, f. 169.)

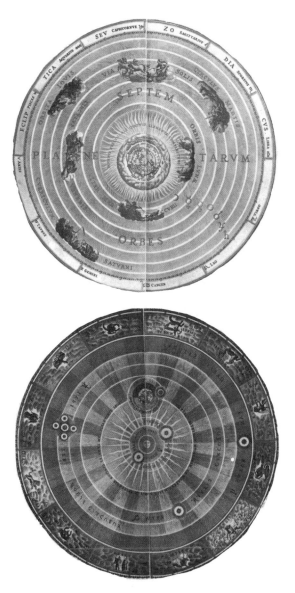

Figure 133. The Ptolemaic view of the universe (inherited from second century Alexandria) was eventually undermined by Copernicus (d. 1543), who made the Sun central instead of the Earth. More than a century later, Hans Keller placed the two astronomical models on a par with one another in his *Atlas van het Universum* [Atlas of the Universe] published by J. Janszoon in Amsterdam in 1661. In both maps of the heavens, engraved by J. van Loon, it is interesting to note that the boundary of the universe is the same—the zodiac.

Figure 134. The mystic vision—the cosmos as wholly born out of Wisdom, the "wisdom that embraces all things"—is being celebrated in song by the poet. The line of vision of a medieval person ran through the cosmos to God. It could hardly do anything else—the cosmos was a great symbol and every detail in it had a symbolic value. Everyday life was governed by this point of view. (Miniature accompanying a poem by Petrus de Ebulo, 1194. Burger-Bibliothek, Bern, MS 120, f. 140a)

Figure 135. The mystical vision of Hildegard of Bingen—love originates in the Godhead. Everything is born from this love. In the universe, which is embraced by the love that brings it to birth, humanity and Earth are the central point.

Figure 136. This woodcut without its neo-Gothic frame is sometimes used as a sort of icon by some people who are part of the New Age movement. Its maker was Nicolas Flammarion (1842-1925), an astronomer who made thousands of observations of the night sky and believed that there must be life on some other planet. He was a good popularizer, and an illustrator, too. Because he could not find a suitable contemporary picture showing the Copernican discovery, he himself drew one and dated it as early as possible. In fact, he was reflecting the revolution in astronomy of his own time, because his starry heavens are no longer bounded by the zodiac. Beyond our solar system lies a whole new, endless space waiting to be discovered. The heavens, which used to be just above the clouds, and then relatively near outside the zodiac, can no longer be localized. Tr. note: The picture was published with its neo-Gothic frame in *The Rainbow Book*, Fine Arts Museum, San Francisco in association with Shambhala, 1975.

Figure 137. Just a few centuries ago people thought the Earth stood still. Human beings lived on its top half. Whether the Earth was round or flat hardly mattered if it was not turning. But, when it seemed likely that it *was* turning, people felt spatially disorient. Nevertheless a "sane individual" could experience freedom in this space—balancing on water and earth and reaching for the stars. (Woodcut from *Von gluckseliger Gesundheit*, Augsburg, 1532.)

Figure 138. In the comfort of our own homes, we can now see how Earth appears from outer space. We have even had a view of Earth rising and setting from the Moon. (Photo: ABC-Press Service, Amsterdam.)

Figure 139. The ordered universe of centuries ago seems like a minute speck in the universe as we now know it. Our Earth is a small member of the solar system, which is part of one of perhaps 500 million galaxies And everything seems to be in an expanding vortex. Though Earth feels quite static, it is a tiny dot in this expanding universe. (The spiral galaxy in Canes Venatici. Photo: Govert Schilling, Utrecht.)

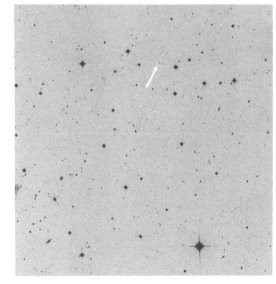

Figure 140. The most distant known object in the universe—Quasar 0046-293—estimated to be 12 billion light years away. When viewing this object, we are also looking far back in time toward the origin of everything at the "Big Bang." (Photo: Govert Schilling, Utrecht.)

Figure 141. Research is also penetrating deep into the fundamental energy of which everything else seems to be made. The first photo taken at the nuclear research center, CERN, in Geneva in 1973, of the evidence for a new sort of elementary particle. (Photo: CERN, Geneva.)

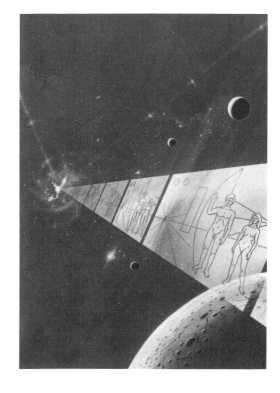

Figure 142. The universe is everpresent but empty. People no longer feel at home in it. They turn to science fiction and stories of space-gods in order to overcome their fears. Pioneer 10, which exited our solar system after photographing Jupiter, carried a message in code for the benefit of any intelligent space beings. Eight years afterward, the magazine "Bild der Wissenschaft" featured the cover illustration reproduced here and inquired: "Why don't the extraterrestrials contact us?"

The Mystical Ladder Ends Nowhere

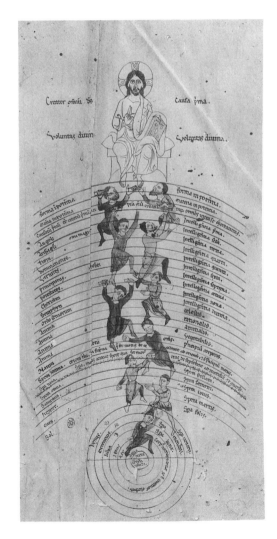

Figure 143. The traditional *scala mystica* (mystical ladder): the Earth is round, stands still, and is inhabited only on the upper half. Human beings endeavor to ascend from it to their place of origin—traversing the spheres of the elements, of the stars, of the *anima* (soul), of *intelligentia* (intellect), of the choirs of angels, of causes, of prime matter, and of prime form—until they reach the Creator and Lord of all, the *causa prima* (first cause). (12th century drawing, Bibliothèque Nationale, Paris, MS latin 3236 A, f. 90.)

Figure 144. A more spiritualized representation of the ascent to the divine light through the heavenly spheres. (Hieronymus Bosch, "Paradise." The Doge's Palace, Venice.)

Figure 145. The mystical ladder (*scala*) of Ramón Lull. Pictured as a stairway having the following steps—stones, fire, plants, animals, humans, the starry sky, angels, and God. The teacher holds in his hand another *scala* with steps going round in a circle. This is a "ladder of thought," showing how God can be reached with the mind. (Woodcut from Ramón Lull, "Liber de ascensu et descensu intellectus," p. 41, Valencia, 1512.)

Figure 146. Fludd simplifies the traditional mystical ladder, and places the main emphasis on human powers of observation. The rungs are: the senses, imagination, calculation, intellect, intelligence, and word. (Engraved by J. de Bry, 1619, from a draft by Fludd.)

Figure 147. Anselm Kiefer has frequently employed the motif of the mystical ladder. His starting-point is Jacob's ladder on which the angels ascended and descended—a favorite picture from the Hebrew Bible. In him, the ladder rises out of a dark and barren landscape with a venemous desert snake in it, and ends in a turbulent cloud. (A. Kiefer, untitled, 1984. Antony d'Offay Gallery, London.)

Figure 148. In modern times, mystical ladders do not seem as natural as they used to do. Start climbing one and there does not seem anywhere for it to end. Escher drew a striking illustration of this—not a ladder but a hall of stairs, in which little "spiral staircase animals" are crawling up and down. What is a ceiling for one animal is a floor or a wall for another animal. ("The Staircase," lithograph, 1951. Photo: Cordon Art, Baarn.)

WHAT IS THE INNER "I"?

What ideas are involved when we contemplate the way to the innermost sanctum of the "I"? Is this "I" the point from which we try to arrange and control the world around us? That the human being is a microcosm and also "the measure of all things" are fundamental concepts of Western culture. The harmful side of these concepts is the belief they foster that we are the masters of nature and at liberty to exploit it. We need to behave as the partners, not the rulers, of nature. In the last century, many people tried to find their own image in nature; it was a romantic longing—now deepened into environmentalism, or the realization that we are responsible for this "mother" and "sister" of ours.

Figure 149. In the Middle Ages, educated people felt linked with the cosmos. This picture, created in 1165, shows the "microcosm." The Sun, Moon, and planets issue from its eyes, mouth, nose, and ears, and are all encircled by the halo of the heavenly spheres. It breathes out Saturnus, and this becomes the atmosphere with clouds and birds. Its abdomen is the sea into which rivers flow, and so on. (Bayerische Staatsbibliothek, Munich, Clm. 13002.)

Figure 150. The romantic longings of the last century. (Caspar David Friedrich, "The Wanderer." Hamburger Kunsthalle.)

Figure 151. "Environmental awareness." (Cover of *Omni*, August 1979, designed by Peter Goodfellow.)

Figure 152. In the Renaissance, the emphasis was no longer placed on the cosmos, of which the human being is a tiny replica, but on the human being as the "measure of all things." (16th century woodcut.)

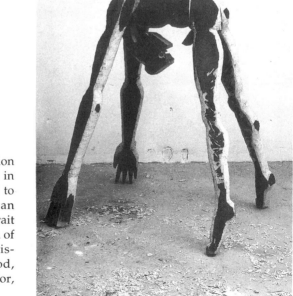

Figure 153. The attention paid to the individual in our own times has led to an ego-culture. Jos van Oosterhout's self portrait is a graphic illustration of this introverted narcissism. (Painted wood, 1982-83. Museum Fodor, Amsterdam.)

Figure 154. After the Renaissance, the individual moved to center stage. A strik-ing painting by Parmigianino, whose real name was Francesco Mazzalo (1503-1540), is a self-portrait seen in a convex mirror. The hand that painted the portrait is so placed that it becomes the center around which the space is curved. The artist's face is pushed into the background, but is central even so. The picture was offered to the Pope in 1523. (Parmigianino, "Self portrait." Kunsthistorisch Museum, Vienna.)

Rising Above Myself Into My Inmost Silence

It is possible to experience the self by searching for the true "I" that is hidden under subconscious or unconscious layers of the psyche. Modern people who explore the mystic path find the inward search most rewarding. The difficulty is this—how can we really surmount the ego? In the traditions of both East and West, mention is made of rising into a transcendent reality, the ground of the soul, described as a void, a stillness, a desert, etc. This place or state can be reached through meditation, but usually something needs to happen that "awakens" us.

Figure 155. To quote Meister Eckhart: "In the midst of the deepest stillness, God speaks to us His Word. And indeed, He does so in the purest and noblest place the soul has to offer, in her essence. There perfect quiet prevails: neither creature nor image ever gain access to it . . . . Certainly, our activities spring from the ground of the soul, but the ground itself is deepest silence. Here there is room and quietness only for God's word. No one and nothing but God alone is able to affect the ground of the soul." "The silence" of those who retire into themselves. (Painting by Odilon Redon, 1911. Museum of Modern Art, New York [Lillie P. Bliss Collection].)

Figure 156. A superb, sympathetic portrait of a person who has retired into himself and meditates broodingly in peaceful and beautiful natural surroundings. ("St. John Meditating in the Desert." Gemäldegalerie, Staatl. Museen Preussicher Kulturbesitz, Berlin.)

Figure 157. A Zen monk in the garden of Daisen in Kyoto, Japan. Nature is completely replaced by meticulously raked white sand. The purpose of this method of meditation is to do away with all the contents of consciousness in the hope that enlightenment will drop into the void during a timeless moment. (Photo: ABC-Press Service, Amsterdam.)

Figure 158.
Eastern inward-
ness in a West-
ern form.

Rousing From Sleep

A certain form of meditation of Chinese origin has been practiced in Japan, and uses harsh methods, even physical violence, in order to awaken the conscious mind suddenly. In the West, these methods are sometimes used by practitioners of Zen, by psychotherapists, and also by artists.

Figure 159. A sanguinary ritual "stage" in 1979, by the artist Herman Nitsch of Vienna. (Photo: Kurt Will)

Figure 160. The horror of the death of Jesus has been hidden, sweetened, and embellished in Christian liturgy and devotion. Artists have tried to tear off this veil. The Spaniard, Antonio Saura, sets to work on the popular pretty picture of the crucifixion and mutilates it. ("Sweat-cloths," six repainted picture postcards. Neue Galerie, Aken, 1986.)

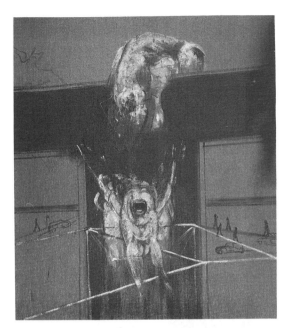

Figure 161. Francis Bacon, "Fragment of a crucifixion," 1950, Van Abbemuseum, Eindhoven.

Figure 162. An awakened or shocked consciousness can totally change the life with profound consequences, and not always for the better. Lynette Phillips of Australia, who inherited millions, joined the Indian Ananda Marga sect and set herself on fire in front of the Palace of the League of Nations in 1978. Before pouring gasoline over herself, she said: "I have a fiery wish to fight against the luxury and egotism of this world." (Photo: ANP)

Figure 163. "The Scream" has become a sort of icon, a picture of what we are experiencing in our era. (Edvard Munch, "The Scream," lithograph, 1895.)

Figure 164. The picture of a low-point in a human life. In the flames the monk cries: "Take pity on me, especially you my friends, for God has touched me." (Painted page in a *Liber pro infirmorum* [Book for the Sick] once used in the Carthusian monastery in Waard near Utrecht. 15th century. University library, Amsterdam, MS XII, A 16, f. 66 v.)

TESTED BY SUFFERING

Figure 165. The suffering endured by an individual often plays a big, and sometimes decisive, role in mysticism. Suso was tormented by his religious fraternity, and by demons, and felt like a rag being shaken by a dog. He considered that he was participating in the sufferings endured by God Himself. All this was recorded by his friend Elisabeth Stagel, who is seen in this painting offering him a moist sponge on a stalk of hyssop to comfort him, as had been done to Jesus. (Stiftsbibliothek, Einsiedeln, MS no. 710, f. 57.)

Figure 166. People with a melancholy temperament, who take life seriously, are (as a type) rather prone to mysticism. According to Ficino and the "mages" who came after him—those who knew how to live with their temperament were melancholics of the first kind. *Melencolia I*, ruled by Saturn and born to be a genius, a poet, or a mystic. A mystic of this type was depicted by Dürer in this famous engraving, made in 1514, showing Melancholy as a winged woman, crowned with a garland, and in an introspective mood. The mystic ladder reaches to heaven. The hound, symbolizing keen perception, slumbers—a prerequisite for the inner vision of the melancholic. The hour glass stands for Time - Saturn. A comet shoots past, there is a rainbow, and the place is filled with hermetic symbols such as a sphere representing the androgyne. (Photo: Koninklijke Bibliotheek, Brussels.)

Figure 167. In a psalter ca. 825 we find this representation of the anima, the soul (not the anima of Jungian psychology). She is seated on a mountain, wrapped in melancholy, and listening to a cither player. It is an illustration of the verse in Psalms that says: "Why art thou cast down, O my soul? And why art thou disquieted within me?" (Psalms 43: 5). This is a good illustration of the "dark night of the soul," as St. John of the Cross calls that sense of darkness and loss of light that can be an important end-phase before a permanent mystical experience. (The psaltery of Stuttgart, originally from *Saint-Germain des Prés.* Württembergische Landesbibliothek. Photo: Marburg.)

(Figure 166 continued): Tr. note: "A bunch of keys hangs topsy-turvily from the woman's left, and her satchel lies on the ground, with loosened strings. The significance is given by Dürer himself in a sketch made for the plate, on which he has written slüssel-gewalt, pevtell-reichtum betewt (key means power, satchel wealth). The woman seems to care neither for power nor wealth, allowing their symbols to lie or hang about." (*Albrecht Dürer* by Ivan Fenyo, tr. Ann Biener Tauber, Corvina, Budapest, 1956, p. 51.) The name '"Melencolia I" may be explained by this quotation from Robert Burton's famous *The Anatomy of Melancholy* (1621 and many later eds.): '"Love melancholy (saith he) is twofold; the first is that . . . affection of those which put God for their object, and are altogether about prayer, fasting, &c., the other about women."' (Part. 3. Sec. 4. Memb. 1. Subs. 1. Burton himself was quoting Hercules de Saxonia.)

Figure 168. "The Dark Night," a woodcut made for the magazine *Carmel* in 1964 by Marianne van der Heijden. (Photo: Lambert van Gelder.)

TESTED BY RESEARCH

One can be confused by experiences, feelings, ideals, and paths, so it is good to expose them to the test of reason. Descriptions of mysticism that use words like "supernatural" and "secret" discourage a more rational approach to the mystical experience. The secrets in mysticism relate to *what* is experienced, not to *how* it is experienced.

Figure 169. If experiences are rooted in the brain, it is natural to want to investigate the connection. As far back as the 14th century, people were trying to locate consciousness. In this drawing, the faculties located in the brain areas are fantasy, appreciation and estimation, memory and understanding, and the head is surrounded by a list of mental disorders. One of these is melancholia. (Drawing from a 14th century medical manuscript. Bibliothèque Nationale, Paris, MS lat. 11229. f. 37 v.)

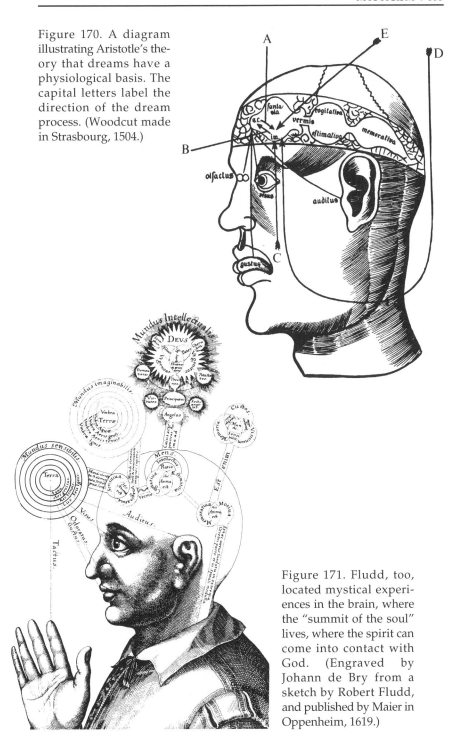

Figure 170. A diagram illustrating Aristotle's theory that dreams have a physiological basis. The capital letters label the direction of the dream process. (Woodcut made in Strasbourg, 1504.)

Figure 171. Fludd, too, located mystical experiences in the brain, where the "summit of the soul" lives, where the spirit can come into contact with God. (Engraved by Johann de Bry from a sketch by Robert Fludd, and published by Maier in Oppenheim, 1619.)

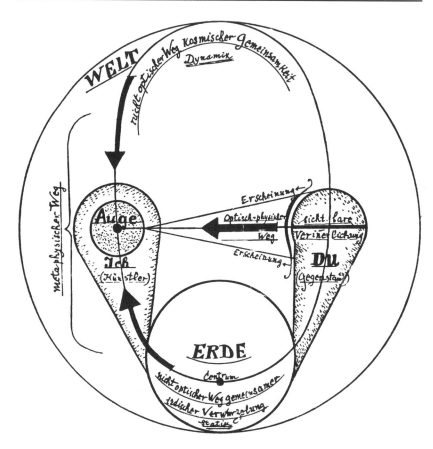

Figure 172. A drawing by Paul Klee where he tries to bring order into the many kinds of perception. The "eye" of the "I," the artist, receives along an "optico-physical pathway" the image of the "you," a visible object. However, a "non-optical pathway" is involved, too, because of our common rootedness in the earth (static) and our oneness with the cosmos (dynamic). All these in combination set up a "metaphysical pathway."

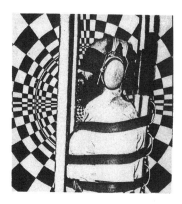

Figure 173. The earlier explanation of experiences as brain-work strikes us as very naive. In the last few decades, laboratory tests have been run to discover how individuals react when isolated from all external stimuli. (Photo: Don Snijder taken in the Maimonides Hospital, New York.)

Figure 174. Does medita-
tion itself (here that of
the yogi Swami Rama),
provide data on the func-
tioning of the brain? (Bio-
feedback test by Elmer
Green of the Menniger
Foundation. Photo: ABC-
Press Service, Amsterdam.)

Figure 175. Using one's
understanding remains
important, even in a mys-
ticism that relies on experience to give a sense of a
reality full of secrets. "The
sleep of reason bears monsters" is the title of this
aquatint by Francisco de
Goya made in 1799. And
he ought to know.
(Philadelphia Museum of
Art, Smith Kline Beckman
Corporation Fund. Photo:
Joan Broderick.)

The mystical process has a beginning point as well. This is often a longing for love, passion, and solace, a desire to live in higher spheres, and so on. The there comes a time when the desire wanes, grows stale by custom, or is even forgotten. It is okay to remain in this valley for a while, though one should want to eventually move on. St. John of the Cross is rather critical of spiritual teachers who, when any of their disciples enter a period of stagnation, try to get them praying again in the old way, instead of encouraging them to endure the emptiness in the hope of something new. Molinos, Madame Guyon, and the Quietists made the opposite mistake. In their theoretical expositions, they neglected the practicalities of the process. The attitude of pure selfless love—that has to be developed along way—is something they treated as a prerequisite.

The mystical process has an initial phase, a growing phase, and an end phase. Various accounts have been given of these phases—the seven-runged ladder to the sky (shamanism and the cult of Mithras), the eightfold path to Nirvana (Buddhism), the threefold way of the West.[22]

These schematic descriptions have all been made in retrospect. The goal is manifold. It can be the regaining of the lost paradise (shamanism), absorption into the All (Hinduism), learning the dark wisdom of God (pseudo-Dionysius), union with the Beloved (the West), the achievement of adult freedom (Maslow). The nature of the goal determines the way in which the path to it is conceived. Schematization can be helpful at the beginning, but not a few mystical approaches have come to grief because their schematizations have taken on a life of their own. The aspirant who starts with a clear-cut goal and keeps to it come what may, runs the risk of eventual delusion. The goal is imposed from outside on a living process that needs to grow from inside. Life is not a logical straight line, but a journey with ups and downs, intense longings alternating with deep depressions, and splendid insights that later seem to lose their meaning. The various

---

[22] For more information about the threefold way, see "The Meaning of Initiation" in *Shakespeare's Mystery Play: A Study of the Tempest* by Colin Still and Cecil Palmer (London: 1921), pp. 83-119. Still calls the three stages passional, rational and intuitional, respectively: or purification, self-conflict, and "closing of the eyes" to await a revelation. Tr. note.

outlines merely indicate certain mystical landmarks in the capricious journey of life: mention is always made of purification, of the renunciation of desire, of something that has to be endured; and of a clear light and a blissful feeling of love, but also of darkness and of an emotional state as arid as a desert.

Mysticism is characterized by a personal experience and a change in life, but not every mystic goes the same way. Preference and character enter into the selection or rejection of a given path and in the affinity felt for a particular mystic or mysticism.

In 16th-century Germany, the melancholic individual was thought to be the most suitable candidate for mysticism. But, in the Spain of this period, the melancholic individual was the least suitable one. It was thought that women had a greater aptitude for mysticism than men. Today, mysticism is usually associated with the "soft sector" and with a dedication to "green" issues. However, this is very one-sided, for when we consider a general historical view of the subject, two mystical types stand out—the contemplative type that rests in God, and the restless type that strives with God. Modern mystical people seek a life where everything is paradisiacal, harmonious, and One. Keywords for mystics of this type are: meditation, absorption in the one Ground, cosmic consciousness, mastery of mind and body, healing, well-being and bliss. Evil is rarefied into not-being, shadow, illusion, maya. Roughly speaking, the contemplative type follows a more Eastern path, although not entirely so, because this kind of thinking is also found in the West. Nevertheless, what has come to the fore in the West is a restless search, and the burning question is how contemplation or meditation can be combined with action. The hard reality of evil has also increasingly made itself felt.

Many Western mystics have proved that the inner way can still allow an active life. St. Bernard traveled all over Europe, and St. Teresa all over Spain. They were contemplatives, yet both took a hand in politics, were good organizers, and could be extremely business-like. They found peace in the center of their lives. In women, the center they seek is often an "inner voice." St. Catherine of Siena said that the inner voice she heard was the voice of God, and that deeds show obedience to God, for when one is passive— no matter what happens—the soul stays free; there is only attention, stillness, and immobility in times of suffering or joy. She said that passive activity of this sort is the highest activity of all, and is fully described in the Bhagavad-Gita and by Lao Tse. So committed was she to this view that she toiled away at the most menial tasks, and eventually died of exhaustion.

Eckhart clearly states his opinion that an active mystic should be valued more highly than a non-active mystic. He speaks of the point of rest in the activity as "being caught up in God" and being united with Him in the "spark of the soul." Ruysbroeck calls the true mystic a "ghemeyne" person, that is to say, someone who is at everyone's beck and call. The reason why the mature mystic can keep busy, untroubled by worldly affairs, is explained in the following terms by St. John of the Cross:

> he will come to consider the things of God not to be God's, and those things which are not God's to be the things of God.[23]

His modern, active, fellow religious, Titus Brandsma, saw the separation of mysticism and action as an evil of our times. He says:

> God is perceptible in our being, we can see Him and live in His presence. And His presence will not fail to influence our behavior. And it will also reveal itself in what we do. . . .The deed itself is not sufficient. It must be consciously derived from the indwelling of God, as commanded or advised by Him in the inner being.[24]

Mysticism in the Western tradition has matured by making itself useful; at the same time it is "original" in the sense of being rooted in the deepest ground of the individual's being, involving not only the conscience but also the source of creativity, which fuels political and social endeavor as well as science and art.

Among those who champion this mysticism we find both depressives (Simone Weil) and optimists, such as Titus Brandsma, who approached the problem of atheism with respect but could not understand it; who knew what suffering was but could not

---

[23] St. John of the Cross, *The Living Flame of Love*, translated by David Lewis (London: Thomas Baker, 1919), p. 110.
[24] Titus Brandsma, *Mystiek leven*. Translation mine. Tr.

represent the night of St. John of the Cross as pitch black; who persisted in seeing the conflict in the light of potential harmony, and evil as good that has not yet come into its own.

Jacob Boehme's idea of evil was different again. According to him, it is not permissible to call God "good." God is love, but, at the same time, He is also "wrath." This is easier to understand if we remember that goodness would be weak-kneed piety if we could not be angry at injustice.

There have been mystics, such as Nicolas of Cusa, who have surmised that good and evil coincide in God, and also that good is in some way connected with evil, and evil with good. Everything has its reverse side, and it is no use copying the Cathars and trying to separate the good from everything in order to create a paradise free from evil. This quest for purity and innocence is as appealing, but also as primitive, as a picture of the Garden of Eden from the brush of a Sunday painter.

There Are Many Paths

Many paths of life have been explored during the course of history; many avenues and methodologies are available for those who look for the mystical path. Not all these paths are promising, attractive, or practical. We cannot assume that the teachings of great classical mystics will interest modern people. In the classical work of pseudo-Dionysius, the interminable narrative of the choirs of angels and their upward progression is not easy for modern readers to grasp, unless they already celebrate Byzantine liturgies and revel in their pomp and splendor. As to understanding oriental mysticism, tyros must delve into a bowlful of exotic beliefs before scooping out anything of use. The same applies to Western mystics who lean heavily on dogmatic theology. People want to know why they should have to take the trouble to comprehend them.

To some extent, therefore, one can agree with Huxley's complaint that mysticism is too difficult a way today. But when mysticism becomes fashionable and readily available, it can be pernicious, as was the case with Huxley's "short cut" with drugs, which avoided anything difficult. Shamans used this path, but only after being tested and waiting until they were thought ready to receive powerful experiences they could use for the benefit of the tribe. Nowadays, we see the reverse in operation—first the ecstasy, then the testing, and then maybe the people who try the drug path end up being a burden to society.

The choice of paths is open in some respects but not in others. Some paths rely on the unity of spirit and body: the science of breath in the East and the Jesus prayer in the West, the dance of the whirling Dervishes, and the asanas of Yoga. However there is also the way of release of the spirit from the body, as in Mani and the Cathars. There is a way that emphasizes the "light," understanding, expansion of consciousness, and concentration. There is also the path of the emotions, which emphasizes passion, pangs of love, purification and holiness. In both East and West, there is the path of pleasure (Tantra), and the path involving the refusal of pleasure; just as, also in both East and West, there is a way of non-action, creating a hollow or void. "The more I wanted it, the less I found it; the more I looked for it, the less I was able to discover it, "said St. John of the Cross. And Lao-Tsu said, "We make a vessel

Figure 176. "God." Timber with doll's eyes, by Wim de Haan, 1962. The fact that action, word, and imagination are not the only ways to gain enlightenment by mystical experience, that artistic designing, as such, is another way, was convincingly demonstrated by Wim de Haan (1913 - 1967). In him it became clear that the "moderns" have made art so free that it can be a form of "mystic life." (Photo: Louise van der Veen.)

from a lump of clay; it is the empty space within the vessel that makes it useful.[25] However, there is a way of action, too, of "good deeds," of "self-denial," of the deed that is rooted in the spark of the soul. There is the way of meditation which, in the West, is directed toward active devotion and, in the East, toward stillness and inner emptying,[26] helped by one-pointed concentration on a mantra or mandala. The path can be sought outside society, in a hermitage or cloister, or even in the midst of the culture itself. And one can be dependent on a book, on a fellowship using a book or liturgy, on a "master" or guru, and on courses, sects, communes, or colonies.

The path is also heavily influenced by environment, culture, and the spirit of the age, and by personal disposition and taste, as well as by personal belief. Not everyone needs emptiness. There are southen or "Roman" types who embody their experiences in their activities. St. Francis of Assisi is an example. Then there are the devotional types, who (so to speak) build a cosy nest for themselves. What St. Francis expressly refused, Suso welcomed—the safety of a cloister cell surrounded by a monastery. Outside the monastery wall Suso felt like a wild animal with hunters on its track.

There are leaders like Krishnamurti and his female friend Virnala Thakar, who teach that there is *no* way. Thakar says:

> Perhaps there is no place where we should expect to arrive. . . .Perhaps life itself is the goal and has an inherent direction. Life is dynamic, and those who live are eternally journeying.[27]

Naturally, all these options don't make it easy to choose a particular path. Matters are simplified if we ask ourselves why we are

---

[25] Lao-Tsu, *Tao Teh Ching*, translated by John C. H. Wu (New York: St. John's University Press, 161), § 11, p. 15.

[26] "What difficulty is there in inverting yin and yang? You should exercise spiritual observation in quietude. When the mind of Tao is not obscured, the human mind vanishes; right away you ascend directly to the peak experience." *The Inner Teachings of Taoism*, by Chang Po-tuan, commentary by Liu I-Ming, and translated by Thomas Cleary (Boston: Shambhala, 1986), p. 111. Tr. note.

[27] Virnala Thakar, *On an Eternal Voyage* (Hilverson, 1966).

looking for this in the first place. Perhaps we have little interest in the mystical experience or in living in the light of such an experience, but want to enjoy some of its benefits. If we are searching for health or peace in a hectic world, the question is simple: which way is the most efficient? We may then look at the pros and cons of transcendental meditation, yoga, Za-Zen, a monastic retreat, or something of that sort.

If people are seeking intense ecstasy, there are other methods: the techniques of fasting and isolation, rooms with a special atmosphere, a disco, a Roman carnival, a pilgrimage, or a big demonstration. However, it must always be borne in mind that the tiger of addiction often prowls round the edges of the ecstatic experience.

Hundreds of books are available to teach us all we need to know about every possible mystic way, old or new. Thousands more have been written on the subjects of sexuality, marriage, and every imaginable aspect of love; yet one cannot make love while studying a book, even though it may offer good advice. Each case has its own direction, limitations, and possibilities. The secret of success is to discover and follow your particular path. The mystical process has an internal compass, which can be consulted once the way itself is clearly seen, and can help you find your bearings in the maze of life.

I end this book with two poems. They follow the internal compass intuitively, in the dark, and without deliberation. Four centuries separate them.

Songs of the Soul

Into the darkness of the night
With heart ache kindled into love,
Oh blessed chance!
I stole me forth unseen,
My house being wrapped in sleep.

Into the darkness, and yet safe
By secret stair and in disguise,
Oh gladsome hap!
In darkness, and in secret I crept forth,
My house being wrapt in sleep.

Into the happy night
In secret, seen of none,
Nor saw I ought,
Without, or other light or guide,
Save that which in my heart did burn.

This fire it was that guided me
More certainly than midday sun,
Where he did wait,
He that I knew imprinted on my heart,
In place, where none appeared.

Oh Night, that led me, guiding night,
Oh Night far sweeter than the Dawn;
Oh Night, that did so then unite
The Loved with his Beloved,
Transforming Lover in Beloved.

On my blossoming breast,
Alone for him entire was kept,
He fell asleep,
Whilst I caressed,
And fanned him with the cedar fan.

The breeze from forth the battlements,
As then it tossed his hair about,
With his fair hand
He touched me lightly on the neck,
and reft me of my senses in a swoon.

I lay quite still, all mem'ry lost,
I leaned my face upon my Loved One's breast;
I knew no more, in sweet abandonment
I cast away my care,
And left it all forgot amidst the lilies fair.[28]

---

[28] San Juan de la Cruz, *The Dark Night of the Soul*, translated by Gabriela
Cunninghame Graham (London: Watkins, 1922), p. 29.

THE TRAVELING COMPANION

Having departed one unearthly hour
Averse to all, without a traveling plan,
Not taking thought,
And wandering in happy freedom
As the puppets' strings danced round me,
I was festively aware that in my pocket
Lay the compass that under Arkel
I as a child one morning
found on the grass.

It was my pride, and is so still,
And I christened in Boreas.
It has never failed me.
Even if south I go or zigzag,
Irreversibly, inexorably,
The magnet needle points to north.
In the end we travel together again;
Two who belong,
Two who are well-matched.

—Ida Gerhardt, ca. 1980[29]

---

[29] Ida Gerhardt, *NKL-Handelsblad*, cultural supplement, "Poesie," December 27, 1991.

APPENDIX I

MAPPING
MYSTICAL INFLUENCES

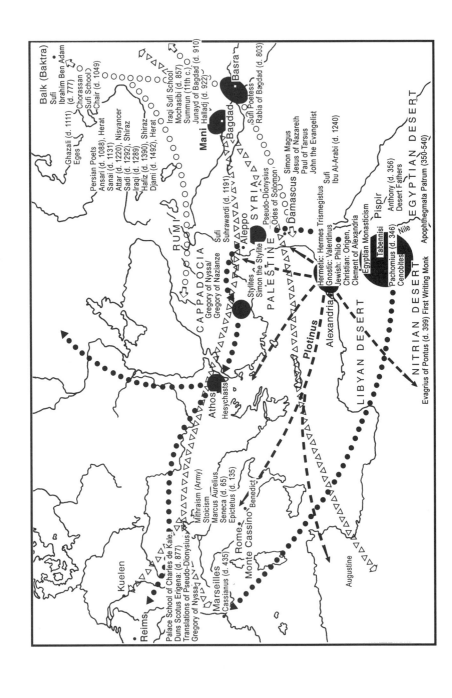

MYSTICISM IN THE FAR EAST

Shamanism. Spread over Central Asia and via the North Pole to America (Indians).

● *Zoroastrianism.* The doctrine of Zoroaster contained in the liturgical Gathas, entered Persia in the eighth century B.C. via Raga. Cyrus made it a state religion.

Jewish Mysticism. It originated with the historical experiences of the Hebrews, who were led by Moses from the region of the Nile to the land of Canaan, which became the land of Israel. There was a significant meeting of Jews and Zoroastrians during the exile in Babylon. The record of this history is contained in the Holy Scriptures (called the Torah, Bible, or Old Testament).[1]

▮ *Hindu Mysticism.* Aryans invaded the regions of the Ganges and the Indus, and eventually reached Sri Lanka (Ceylon). They surpassed the original cultures but were also influenced by them. Their writings reflected this course in history. In the South of India the prevailing mysticism was personal, devotional, and nourished by love. Tantra plays a big part in it.

△ ▲ *Buddhist Mysticism.* Arose out of compassion and as a reaction to the bloodless indifference of Aryan mysticism. Originated in the Ganges region from the inspiration of Buddha. Spread in a strict form to the south, and in a devotional form to the north (Mahayana), especially by translations of the Lotus Sutra. Brought to China in the eighth century by teachers from the South of India, and through the translation of seventy-five manuscripts in 664. The Chinese form is Cha-en (Zen), developed in two schools—the Gradual and the Sudden Way. Zen was brought to Japan in two waves: by Chinese in the ninth century, and by the Japanese themselves in the 13th century. In the West, Rinsai is the best known of the many forms of Zen.

Taoism is typically Chinese. It originated in China and is confined to China.

---

[1] Strictly speaking the Torah is the Pentateuch or Five Books of Moses. The Hebrew Bible also contains the Neviim (Prophets), and the Ketuvim (Holy Writings) including the Magillot (Five Rolls). Passages from these, known as Haftorahs, are read in the synagogue along with the readings from the Torah. "Old Testament" is the Christian term, and implies the "New Testament." Tr. note.

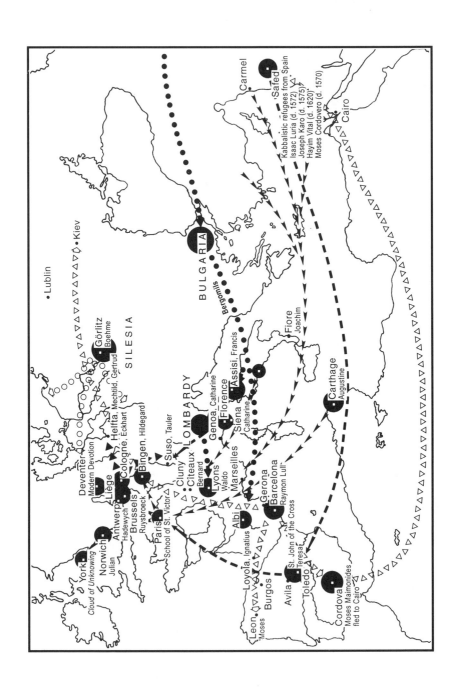

York

Norwich
Julian

Cloud of Unknowing

Deventer
Modern Devotion

Helfta. Mechtild, Gertrud

Görlitz
Boehme

SILESIA

Lublin

Kiev

Antwerp
Hadewych

Liège

Brussels
Ruysbroeck

Cologne. Eckhart

Bingen, Hildegard

Suso, Tauler

Paris

School of St. Victor

Cluny

Citeaux

Bernard

LOMBARDY

Lyons
Waldo

Genoa. Catharine

Florence

Siena
Catharine

Marseilles

Albi

Gerona

Barcelona
Raymon Lull

Leon.
'Moses

Loyola, Ignatius

Burgos

Avila
St. John of the Cross
Teresa

Toledo

Cordova
Moses Maimonides
fled to Cairo

Assisi. Francis

Fiore
Joachim

Carthage
Augustine

BULGARIA

Bergomils

Carmel

Safed

Kabbalistic refugees from Spain
Isaac Luria (d. 1572)
Joseph Karo (d. 1575)
Hayim Vital (d. 1620)
Moses Cordovero (d. 1570)

Cairo

MYSTICISM IN THE MIDDLE EAST

■ *Hellenistic Mysticism.* Characterized by a religious pluriformity: mystery cults (Mithraic, Christian), Stoicism, Gnosticism, Hermeticism. Alexandria was the center, important for its writings (Hermes Trismegistus) and philosophers (Philo, Origen, and Plotinus—neo-Platonism). Gnosticism also flourished in Palestine and Syria.

● *Monasticism.* Arose on the outskirts of the Nile culture and spread to the deserts of Libya, Palestine, and Syria. Hermits preserved their cultural links by going to live on a pillar near a city (Antioch), and monks did the same by adopting a rule that made it a duty to serve the city dwellers (Cappadocia). To this day, Mt. Athos is a center of Eastern monasticism. The ideal here is to find rest by rising above the passions (hesychasm).

△ *Manicheism.* Arose out of the dualistic doctrine of Mani and spread as far as Turkestan, Africa (Augustine), and via Turkey and Bulgaria (Bogomils) through Provence (Cathars).

○ *Islamic Mysticism (Sufism).* Cradle—the area between the Euphrates and Tigris. Sufi schools later arose in Egypt, Iran and Afghanistan. This love mysticism was opposed in Syria and Iraq, even with executions. Many love poems were written in Persia until the 15th century. After Ghazali had reconciled orthodox and mystical Muslims, Sufi orders were founded all over the Islamic world.

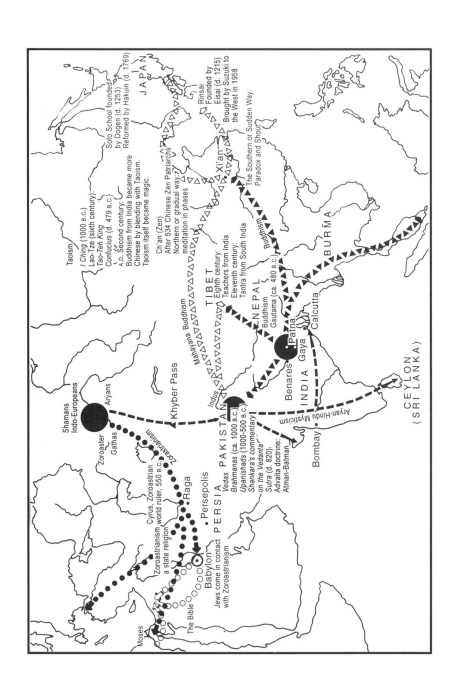

Taoism

I Ching (1000 B.C.):
Lao-Tze (sixth century):
Tao-Teh King
Confucius (d. 479 B.C.)

A.D. Second century:
Buddhism from India became more
Chinese by blending with Taoism.
Taoism itself became magic.

Ch'an (Zen)
After 534 Chinese Zen Patriarchs
Northern or gradual way:?
meditation in phases

Mahayana Buddhism

Eighth century:
Teachers from India
Eleventh century:
Tantra from South India

Khyber Pass

Indus

JAPAN

Soto School founded
by Dogen (d. 1253)
Reformed by Hakuin (d. 1769)

Rinsai
Founded by
Eisai (d. 1215)
Brought by Suzuki to
the West in 1958

Xi'an

The Southern or Sudden Way:
Paradox and Shout

TIBET

NEPAL
Buddhism
Gautama (ca. 480 B.C.)

Buddhism

BURMA

Patna
Benares Gaya Calcutta
INDIA

CEYLON
(SRI LANKA)

Shamans
Indo-Europeans

Aryans

Zoroaster
Gathas

Zoroastrianism

Cyrus, Zoroastrian
world ruler, 550 B.C.

Raga

Persepolis

PERSIA PAKISTAN

Vedas (ca. 1000 B.C.)
Brahmanas (ca. 1000 B.C.)
Upanishads (1000-500 B.C.)
Shankara's commentary
on the *Vedanta*
Sutra (d. 820)
Advaita doctrine:
Atman-Batman

Bombay

Aryan-Hindu Mysticism

Zoroastrianism
a state religion

Babylon

Jews come in contact
with Zoroastrianism

The Bible

Moses

MYSTICISM IN EUROPE

▲ *Love Mysticism.* Sources—mysticism from the Middle East, made available by translations of Scotus (pseudo-Dionysius); Augustine was studied in Paris; Cistercian abbeys. Inspirational figures—Bernard, Hildegard of Bingen. The cradles of female mysticism were—Brabant and Liège and, later on, central England and nunneries in southern and central Germany.

● *Poverty Movements.* Arising from dissatisfaction with the prosperity and outward show of the Church. Strong in the thriving regions of southern Europe—Provence, the Rhône area, Lombardy. Influenced by the Bogomils, who reacted against Byzantine power and splendor. Attacked as heresy. Grew within the Church into full-blown mysticism, especially through St. Francis of Assisi.

▲ *Rhineland Mysticism.* Arose within the Dominican order, and had its center in Cologne; the inspirational figure was Eckhart. Influenced by women and vice versa (Helfta near Halle). Spread up the Rhine to Switzerland among the Friends of God.

△▽ *Jewish Mysticism.* Three major areas: 1) In Provence; the Kabbalah was developed here and in Spain (Gerona). A key test was the Zohar. The Kabbalah was taken by Spanish Jews to Palestine, where Safed became the new center. 2) In the Rhineland around Worms, about the same time. 3) In the region between Lublin, Minsk, and Kiev, as Hassidism.

■ *Humanistic Mysticism.* Cradle—Renaissance Florence. From there it developed into a form of Hermeticism in South Germany. In the North it became a more intimate devotion.

■ *Spanish Carmelite Mysticism.* Carmelite cloisters from the Spain that had discovered the "New World." Inspiration—the ideal lived out by a group of hermits on Mt. Carmel beside Elijah's Well. Brought to Europe in the 13th century. Spanish Carmelite mysticism provided the stimulus for a fresh flowering of mysticism in France.

○ *Protestant Mysticism.* The most important figure was Jacob Boehme in Silesia. He influenced many spiritual movements and stands at the beginning of the "-sophies."

APPENDIX II

TIMELINES

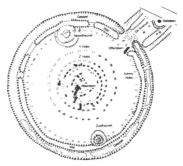

Stonehenge

8000 B.C. ———————————————————— 1200 B.C.

Notion of the All-high-est to whom one can travel

Horse and chariot from Sinai.

Notion of cosmic con-nections

Stonehenge
Creation myths

Everywhere a search was in progress for a basic principle in the divine world. Akhenaten (1372-1354).

Notion of harmony

Shaman

Notion of God-with-us, who delivers from injustice
Experience of injustice

Moses: Historical deliverance becomes a memorial to God entering the life of His people.

Zoroaster: History is a battle on the side of God against Evil. This history has an end—Judgment.

Aryans

Sense of heroism

I Ching: the search for a balance between:

Yin	Yang
Female	Male
Darkness	Light
Negative	Positive

Mazda (Zoroastrian deity)

1100 B.C. ━━━━━━━━━━━━━━━━━━━━━━━━━━ **600** B.C.

The Bible
Ezekiel. Vision of the throne of God (Merkabah).

The Gathas
Cyrus (538): world ruler. Zoroastrianism a state religion.

The Vedas
Notion of God-in-me

Upanishads. The ground of the cosmos is the ground of the "I."

"Deutero-Isaiah" (597-538)? Jews in Babylon. Dialogue with Zoroastrian priests.

Sense of the misery of everyday life.

Confucius (551-470) Application of the Tao to daily living.

Akhenaten

Pythagoras

Lao Tze

575 B.C. ——————————————————————— 350 B.C.

Notion of mankind and its history

Buddha (563-483)
Way of liberation: the "I" is an illusion.
Extinction of every desire.

Lao Tze: Cosmic process = Tao;
The Way = conforming to the Tao;
The Tao is inexpressible.

The Books of Moses.
The story of deliverance applied to humanity. Expectation of the Messiah.

Mysticism combined with research

The structural basis of the universe is number.

Plato (427-347): The One Good is the source of all. What we see are shadows of the One true reality.

Yoga Sutras: basic text of Raja Yoga. Yoga: a means of gaining control of one's inner being by transforming it into a cosmos.

Buddha

Moses

Alexander the Great

331 B.C. ————————————————————— **200** B.C.

331: Alexandria founded by Alexander the Great; the city became a center of Hellenistic culture.

Hermes Trismegistus

Hermeticism: the universe is a macrocosm; the human being is a microcosm.

The Bhagavad Gita

Uprooted people call for an answer to their plight.

New roots sought in a fatherland above in the hereafter.

Constantinople

Jesus

Paul

100 B.C. ──────────────────────────── **0**

Fresh concepts:
Creation = the descent of light into darkness. Matter is evil. The body is matter. The spirit is a divine spark. The spirit is good. The mystic way consists of the release of the divine spark.

Gnosticism
Deliverance through Gnosis (knowledge of the self sought in the here and now).

Mysteries: Deliverance through ecstasy. Sober inebriety. Dionysian drunkenness. Ladder of increasing spiritualization.

Atheistic Taoism becomes religio-magical.

Simon Magus

Philo of Alexandria

Jesus of Nazareth: taught that the ground of reality is the "Father."

Paul of Tarsus: taught that Jesus is the Christ (the Messiah) and that the return to source is to die and rise with Christ.

Mithras: experience of new life through death.

WHY? YIN YIN WANTS to ADD "BELOVED FATHER" to COLIN'S CHINESE NAME MAY 2021

Simon Magus

Philo

A.D. **50** ━━━━━━━━━━━━━━━━━━━━━━━━━━━━ A.D. **200**

General insight: the ineffable Godhead is expressed in the Logos (the Word). The Word creates. The divine aspect distinguished from the creative aspect.

John the Evangelist proclaims Jesus as the Word.

Unity of all in humanity as the mystical body of Christ.

Merkabah: (Chariot) Mysticism: The difficult and dangerous journey to the unapproachable Lord.

There is One source of all being. Humans are independent individuals but are united with the ground of all being, to which they will return.

Stoa. Zeno. Epictetus (50-130). Marcus Aurelius (121-180). Greek philosophers.

Clement of Alexandria (150-215).

Origen (185-253).

The Book of Creation (Sepher Yetzirah). We can be involved in God's creative act by studying the numerics of reality. Numbers and letters are the primary ground of creation.

Marcus Aurelius

Constantine

A.D. **200**

Plotinus (204-270)

Mani (216-276): Matter is evil, spirit is good.

313: Edict of Milan.

330: Constantinople founded.

Christianity emancipated and becomes a state religion.

The mystic way is sought in the wilderness

Monasticism
Anchorites living alone.

Cenobites living in communities.

Stylites living on top of pillars.

Plotinus

Hermit's dwellings

Augustine

Anthony

A.D. **300** ———————————————————————————— A.D. **600**

Anthony (251-356)

Paul of Thebes (228-341)

Paschomius (287-347) 320. First cloister in Tabennisi.

Basil of Cappadocia (330-379). Monastery participating in civic life.

Evagrius of Pontus (346-399): first writing monk.

Simeon (389-459). Simeon Jr. (521-592). Alypius (seventh century).

Cassianus (360-430): A bridge between the Middle East and Europe.

Concept: God is unknowable. The beholding of God in the ground of the soul must be free of every passion. The way is to deny, and to rise above, all knowledge.

Gregory of Nazianze (329-390): "Thou art No One."

Augustine (354-430)

Pseudo-Dionysius

Mohammed (570-632)

Benedict (480-547)

Simeon the Stylite

Gregory of Nazianze

Visnu
contemplating
Creation.

A.D. 800

Rabia (d. 801): Woman from Basra: formulated the ideal of disinterested love without hope of paradise or fear of hell.

As a reaction against secularization, austere ascetic groups come into existence.

Sankara (780-820). The doctrine of Advaita (non-duality).

Andal (ninth century): poetess.

860: Pseudo-Dionysius translated by Scotus Erigena (810-877).

Founding of religious houses: 963: Athos.

Love Mysticism

Asceticism becomes mysticism through love. Iraqi school. Munasibi (d. 857).
Ascesis: paving the way to union with God.
Iranian school: Abu Yazid (d. 874).
Doctrine of self-annihilation (fana).
Egyptian school: Dhu-an-nun (d. 857).
The learned versus "internal knowledge" (*marifah*).

Eighth to 13th centuries: mystical poets in South India: love directed toward Krishna.

Founding of religious houses: 963: Athos.

Central Iraqi school: The lover who gives his life:

Nuri and Sumnun (10th century): "Inebriation with God": Hallaj (d. 922): Key figure: Junyad of Baghdad (d. 910).

Bhagavata Purana (ninth century):
Poetic description of Krishna, a *bone fide* type of the divine: his love is human, his essence is spiritual.

Constantinople

Rome

Bruno

A.D. 900

The way is *hesychia* = "tranquillity" gained by *apatheia* = "freedom from passion."

Al Hallaj executed because he gave the name "Love" to Allah. After this, it became necessary to write books in defense of the orthodox character of Sufism.

900-1100: New methods sought for kindling the spirit: enigmatic questions or answers, paradoxes, sudden shouts and blows. The idea is to wrench the mind away from its conditioning.

Simeon the New Theologian (949-1022).

Reflections on Sufi tradition:
Sahl-at-Tustari (d. 896);
Hakim-at-Tirmidhi
(d. 898);
Qushari (d. 1047).
Ghazali (d. 1074), made Sufi mysticism accessible to the great mass of Moslems.

The void, Nirvana, all distinction or thought stripped away.

1054: Schism between Eastern and Western Christendom

Rome becomes the new center

Benedict

Milarepa

A.D. 1000

11th century; Seeking new ways.

1083: Vallombrosa
1084: Carthusians
1098: Cistercians

Development of a distinctive Tibetan mysticism

Marpa (1012-1096)
Milarepa (1052-1135)
After them ten schools.

Tantra introduced into Tibet: Dampa Sangargyas and Labkyi Sgtonma are votaries, married person and nun.

Growing awareness that God is love. God became man. God has to be loved in a human way.

Love mysticism. John of Fécamp (1078)

Poverty Movements. Desire to copy the life of Jesus—as poor itinerant preachers.

Longing for a poor, unsullied church, in which God is seen.

Bernard (1090-1153)
Hildegard (1098-1179)
William of St.-Thierry (d. 1148)

Poverty movements in prosperous areas:
Waldenses
Poor men of Lyons
Humiliaten
Arnold of Brescia (1100-1155)

Cathars: 1145: emerge in Cologne. Council of Toulouse.
1208-1229: Crusade against the Cathars around Albi.
1244: Last fortress in Montségur laid waste.

Interpretation of Vedanta:
Ramanudya (d. 1137)
Madha (d. 1278)

Mahadeviyakka
(12th century): poetess of Central India; felt she was wedded to Siva.

Hildegard

Francis

A.D. **1100**

Women wanted to love Christ with heart and soul, but without constraints: "Love and do what you will."

Apocalyptic longings for the Kingdom of God on earth.

Joachim of Fiore (1130-1202).

13th century Japan: A turbulent time with popular preachers of mysticism going from village to village, with apocalyptic visionaries, and with many sects.

Ippen (d. 1289) sang, danced, and saw the Buddha in all things.

In the footsteps of St. Bernard: Cistercian nuns

Beatrice of Tienen (1205-1268).

Kabbalah.
The unknowable God.
Part of God turned toward human beings: God's "attributes" [or "emanations"] (Sephiroth).

Self-reliant recluses and Beguines

Maria of Oignies (1177-1213)

Hadewych

Francis of Assisi (1181-1226) Clare (1194-1253)

The mystic wants to intervene and share God's responsibility.

From the 12th century, Sufi orders were being formed around the doctrines of various teachers.

Suhrawardi (d. 1191): tried to assimilate Zoroastrianism and Hermeticism to Sufism. He was executed.

Joachim of Fiore

Eckhart

A.D. 1250

Under the influence of Dominicans:
Helwich of Magdeburg (d. 1252)
Mechtild of Magdeburg (1207-1282)
Mechtild of Hackeborn (1241-1299)
Gertrude of Helfta (1256-1301)

1170: Kabbalah arises in Provence, develops in Gerona 1230: spreads throughout Spain.

In the 13th century Sufism spread through the whole Islamic world.

Sufi love poetry:
Beginning: Ansari (1006-1088)
High point: **Rumi** (1207-1273)
Final exponent: Jami (1414-1492)

Bonaventura (1217-1274)
Ramón Lull (1232-1315)

Ca. 1270: Composition of the Zohar (the basic text of the Kabbalah). Interaction between higher and lower forces within a circuit that includes humanity and is capable of being influenced by human beings.

Eckhart (1260-1327)
Brethren of the Free Spirit;
1310: Margaret Porete burned;
1311: Council of Vienna: condemnation;
1372: Jeanne Dabenton burned.

Maimonides (1135-1204)
Continual absorption in God in everyday life.
Desire for the way of disinterestedness.

Catherine of Siena

Bernard

Tauler

A.D. **1300**

1348-1350: the Black Death.

The plague

Suso

The "Friends of God" and their Circle:
Suso (1295-1366)
Tauler (1300-1361)
R. Merswin (1307-1361)
Margaret Ebner
(1291-1351)
Christina Ebner
(1277-1356)
Elisabeth Stagel (d. 1360)
Adelheid Langman
(d. 1375)
Henry of Nördlingen
(d. 1351)

Intimate Mysticism in England Centered on Recluses and Devout Women
The Ancren Riwle
(ca. 1135-1154)
Richard Rolle
(1300-1349)
Walter Hilton
(1330-1337)
Julian of Norwich
(1342-1422)

Margery Kempe
(1373-1440)
The Cloud of Unknowing (14th century)

Ruysbroeck (1293-1381)
Jan van Leeuwen
(1314-1378)

Bridget of Sweden
(1301-1373)
Catherine of Siena
(1347-1380)

Ruysbroeck

Nicolas of Cusa

A.D. **1400**

Modern Devotion:
Sense of personal responsibility toward God;
Life from the ground of the soul;
The discovery is made that mysticism is also for lay people.

Gerard Groot
(1340-1384)

Henry de Herp
(1431-1477)

Catherine of Bologna
(1413-1463)

Catherine of Genoa
(1447-1510)

Nicolas of Flue
(1417-1487)

Nicolas of Cusa
(1401-1464)
"The center of the world is found not on earth but in God."

15th-16th century, Vaisnavas in Bengal. Description and analysis of the love process with Krishna.

Krishna playing his flute.

Paracelsus

Pico della Mirandola

The Gospel Pearl
(ca. 1500)
Sister Bertke (1426-1514)

New picture of humanity.

Human beings are central in the cosmos. They are the hinge on which the creation, that came from God, turns back to Him. Man is created in the image of God.

Rediscovery of Hermetics.
1471: the *Corpus Hermeticum* issued in translation by Ficino.
Pico della Mirandola (1463-1494)
Humanity contains the cosmos, and can become all things. The Kabbalah fits into this vision. Love reaches further than reason.

Ficino (1433-1499)
"Love is the eternal knot and tie of the cosmos."

Mystical poets:
Ramanda (d. 1440)

Theologia Germanica:
1516 translated by Luther

Alchemy.
"Dissolve and coagulate, is the secret of operating with matter, but also of the mystical process."

Agrippa (1486-1535)
Paracelsus (1493-1541)

Chaitanya (1485-1533)
Esctasies with weeping, shouting, dancing. Krishna as mantra. Helping the destitute. Love rises above all laws.

Reaction to a reformation that had reverted to set forms.

The typical researcher is a "mage," who investigates the cosmos by letting it become one with his own spirit.

Safed: center for a Kabbalistic group belonging to those Jews who had been expelled from Spain.

Alchemical symbol

Quakers

A.D. 1500 ——————————————————————— **A.D. 1545**

Formation of a new fellowship of the Spirit

Radical choices made from the ground of the soul.
Radical experience of the birth of Christ in the ground of the soul. The painful crisis purifies this ground.

Part of the divine light has been lost. The mystic collects the splinters of light and brings them back to God.
The task of mysticism— to restore the scattered creation.

Sebastian Franck (1499-1542)
The only true church is the spiritual church, the only binding word is the inner word.

Müntzer (1490-1525)

Anabaptists:
1532: Strasbourg, around Hoffman

1534-1535: Münster

J. Matthijs of Harlem

J. Breukelz of Leiden

Isaac Luria (d. 1534)

Chaim Vital (1542-1620)

Josef Karo (1488-1575)

1545-1563: Council of Trent

Start of the Counter-Reformation.

Boehme

Maria Petyt

St. John of the Cross

A.D. **1550** ——————————————————————— A.D. **1575**

Psychological outlook on the mystical process

Ignatius (1491-1556)
Mysticism that induces action and decision-making.
The problem of attaining clarity with oneself.

Madame Acarie
(1566-1618)

Teresa of Avila
(1515-1582)

Detailed description of the mystical process and of the path inward.

St. John of the Cross
(1542-1591)
Poetic narrative of mystical experiences.
Accurate analysis of crises, especially the "dark night of the soul."

John Dee (1527-1608)

Giordano Bruno
(1548-1600)
"He who sees all things in himself, is all things."

Benedict Canfield
(1562-1610)
Pierre de Berulle
(1575-1629)

Jean de Saint-Samson
(1571-1636)

Maria Petyt (1623-1677)

Beginning of the "-sophies"
Knowledge is not just a matter of information; wisdom is involved too: insight into the ground of all things.

Jacob Boehme
(1575-1624)
All antitheses are reconciled in God.
The new is born from the tension between opposites.

Teresa of Avila

Francis de Sales

Francis de Sales
(1567-1622)
Mysticism in ordinary everyday life with no other companions than one's usual friends.

Vincent de Paul
(1628-1660)
Maria Guyart (d. 1672)
Blaise Pascal (1633-1662)

Mysticism is of the heart and soul—not of the mind.

Comenius (1592-1670)

In practice, pansophy entails multinational structures.

Spinoza (1632-1677)
Jewish mysticism combined with rational thought in a single vision.

A psychological question: what is pure love?

Molinos (1628-1696)
Guyon (1648-1717)
Fénelon (1651-1715)

Emphasis on Things of the Spirit—Inner experience versus the external church.

Hassidism
The task of the mystic—to become aware of God's presence in everything.

Antimysticism
Labadie (1610-1674)
Tersteegen (1697-1769)

George Fox (1624-1691)
Truth is to be found in the inner voice.

Oetinger (1702-1782)
F. von Baaden
(1765-1841)
Emmanuel Swedenborg
(1688-1772)

Nothing is trivial; an experience of God is open to all; a rabbi with continual access to God is necessary for communion.

Masonic apron given to George Washington.

Madam Blavatsky

A.D. **1750** ———————————————————————— A.D. **1900**

Need for the accidental phenomena of mysticism

Need for mystery

Occultism and secret societies;

The Philosophical Approach
Schopenhauer (1788-1860)
First philosopher to be receptive toward Eastern mysticism.

Israel ben Eliezer (d. 1760)

Levitation—Joseph of Copertino (1603-1663)
Stigmata—Catherine dei Ricci (1552-1590)
Visions—M. M. Alacoque (1647-1680)
Possession—Maria of the Angels

1616—Rosicrucians
Freemasons
Theosophical and Anthroposophical Societies

Theosophy
Blavatsky (1831-1891)
1875: Theosophical Society founded

Annie Besant (1847-1933)
Rudolf Steiner (1861-1925)
1913: Anthroposophical Society founded

Ramakrishna (1836-1886)
Vivekananda (1864-1902)

Synthesis of Western technical culture and Vedanta mysticism introduced in Chicago in 1893.

Steiner

Secret symbols

GLOSSARY

For explanation of the sources abbreviated in the following text, refer to page 405.

ADAMITES
Recurring group within Christianity: in the second century in Syria; in the Middle Ages as the Brethren of the Free Spirit; and, later still, as the Anabaptists. The Adamite ideal was a mature way of life free of selfish desire.

ALCHEMY
Arose simultaneously in Egypt and China in the second century B.C. The alchemical work was conceived as a way of manipulating nature in which forms are transmutted into one another. Forms had to be dissolved and then reassembled in a new unity. Alchemy was also envisaged as an attitude to life: that of death and rebirth. From the 14th century onward, a non-ecclesiastical pictorial language for a certain mystical process became prevalent, being used in a host of illuminated alchemical MSS.
WP 1, 487, 488.
Bibliography: *Prelude to Chemistry*. John Read. G. Bell & Sons Ltd., 1936 (reprinted by AMS Press). *The Alchemist in Life, Literature and Art*. John Read. Thomas Nelson & Sons Ltd., 1947 (reprinted by AMS Press). *The Great Art*. Antoine-Joseph Pernety. Samuel Weiser, 1976. *Alchemy, the Ancient Science*. Neil Powell. Aldus Books, 1976. *Chinese Alchemy*. J. C. Cooper. The Aquarian Press, 1984. *Psychology and Alchemy*. C. G. Jung. Tr. R. F. C. Hull. Princeton, NJ: Princeton University Press, Bollingen Series; and London: Routledge. *Alchemical Studies*. C. G. Jung. Tr. R. F. C. Hull. Princeton, NJ: Princeton University Press, Bollingen Series; and London: Routledge.

ALVARS (seventh-tenth century)
Group of South-Indian mystics who traveled from temple to temple, ecstatically singing hymns in honor of Vishnu. Twelve such groups are known.
NEB 20, 592.

AMALRICANS
Followers of Amalric, who were persuaded that the kingdom of the Spirit, in which they themselves were already living, would break through within a few years and make the Church redundant.
WP 2, 48.

ANABAPTISTS
Followers of Zwingli who did not find him radical enough and so formed their own congregation in 1523. Under persecution they were scattered from Strasbourg along the Rhine as far as The Netherlands. Often they were artisans who had a vision of a city of God.

ANTHROPOSOPHY
System of belief devised by Rudolf Steiner [and further developed by him] after his break with the Theosophical Society in 1913. The Center of the Movement is the Goetheanum, which he built [and rebuilt] in Dornach near Basel. One key thought is the unfolding of the human being out of what he or she really is. Anthroposophical research has been particularly rewarding.
WP 2, 289, 290.

APATHEIA
To the Stoics this meant impassivity in the face of influences from outside and of urges from inside. It was adopted as an ideal by the first Christian mystics and monks, but was rejected in Western Europe.
TW, 173-175.

ASTROLOGY
Originally a belief that the stars are divine beings, and that the soul occupying the body has passed through the starry sky during its descent from its heavenly origin. The star gods were thought to mold it on its way.
WP 2, 575, 576.

BAHAI
A movement that arose after the death of Baha Ullah (appellation of Mirza Hussein ali Nuri, 1817-1892). Advocates the unity of all human beings. Central sanctuary on Mt. Carmel. Persecuted by Khomeini, but very active in the West.
POP, 63.

BEGUINES
Women who wanted to dedicate themselves to the service of God independently of the male orders and without being bound by a cloister "rule." Men under their guidance were called Beghards.
The movement started with groups of woman around hospitals in the area between Nijvel and Liège. After papal approval (1230), the movement spread over France and Germany. Its contribution to history is an original, intensely felt love-mysticism.
WP 3, 523, 524.

BHAGWAN MOVEMENT
Named for Bhagwan Shri Rajneesh (Ohso), a guru who integrated Hindu traditions and Western psychotherapy. A group of Western chelas was formed in Poona, but broke up after moving to the USA.
POP, 202.

BHAKTI SCHOOLS
Form of Hindu mysticism in which loving devotion is central. Arose in South India.
WP 4, 257. NEB 20, 593-595.

BOGOMILS
Balkan religious sect between the tenth and 15th centuries. Derived its teachings from Mani via the Paulicians (in Turkey). Reacting against the pomp of

church and state, it rejected everything visible as bad. The Cathars had their roots in it.
WP 4, 473.
Bibliography: *Bogomils: A Study in Balkan Neo-Manichaeism*. Dmitri Obolensky (Reprint of 1948 ed. AMS Press).

BRETHREN OF THE FREE SPIRIT
Collective designation of groups that, from the 14th century (and especially in Northern France, Germany, and The Netherlands), majored on the realization that the Spirit gives liberty and whoever lives in the Spirit does not sin.
WP 5, 208. DS V, 1242-1267.

BROTHERHOOD OF THE COMMON LIFE
Religious group that inspired the New Devotion. They played a significant part in spreading spiritual reading-matter via the press and for education.
WP 5, 208.

CAMBRIDGE PLATONISTS (17TH CENTURY)
Group of academics belonging to the University of Cambridge who wanted to integrate faith and mysticism with rational thought on the basis of neoplatonism and nature mysticism.
RGG I, 1601, 1602.

CATHARS
A sect derived from the Bogomils and inspired by Manicheeism. They arose in the Rhineland and Northern Italy, but their main center was in Provence. Opposed from the start. The sect held out longest in the region around Albi; hence they were called "Albigenses." Hildegard, Dominic, and Francis were inspired by them to create an alternative picture: love as the basis of creation, truth as the highest standard of purity, poverty for those who follow in the footsteps of Jesus.
RGG III, 1192-1193.
Bibliography: A. C. Shannon, *The Medieval Inquisition* (Washington, 1983).

CHASSIDEI ASHKENAZ
Jewish movement in the region around Mainz and Worms in the 13th century. Affected by the local pogroms, which led the Jews to believe they would be totally destroyed. Its leading light was Eliazer of Worms.

EXPERIENTIAL RELIGION
In Protestantism, the movement that lays a strong emphasis on personal experience and faith. Came to the fore in Germany during the second half of the 18th century.
WP 4, 234, 235. RGG II, 457-461.

FEMALE MYSTICISM
Women have made a special contribution to the development of mystical consciousness, especially in times when "love" has come to the fore, both in the revealed religions and in those of the Far East. It is striking that this first happened in the Islamic world (Badia of Baghdad) and almost simultaneously in Western Europe and the South of India in the 12th and 13th centuries.

Bibliography: E. A. Petroff (ed.), *Medieval Women's Visionary Literature* (Oxford, 1986).

FRATICELLI (14th century)
Small groups of Franciscans scattered over the whole of Italy and spreading into Greece, Persia, Catalonia, and Bohemia. They regarded themselves as the true "spiritual" church.
WP 9, 178.

FRIENDS OF GOD
Mystical movement among the religious and the lay people in the 14th century; especially widespread in the Rhineland and in Southwest Germany. Little organization. They were held together by the Dominicans. They exchanged ideas via diaries and tracts.
WP 10, 69. EM, 43, 44 and 302.
Bibliography: *Jean Tauler: Aux 'Amis de Dieu'*. Sermons, 2 vols. (Paris, 1979-1980). B. Gorceix, *Amis de Dieu en Allemagne au siècle de Maître Eckhart* (Paris, 1984).

GNOSTICISM
A mystical attitude to life based on the idea that knowledge (gnosis) of oneself and the world is a way of salvation. In a more strict sense, it means a religious movement arising out of the merging of Greek culture with that of the Middle East. The history of this movement was recovered through the finding of an ancient library in Nag Hammadi (1945).
Bibliography: *Nag Hammadi Library*. James M. Robinson. Harper-Row, 1978. *Gnostic Scriptures: A New Translation with Annotations*. Bentley Layton. Doubleday, 1987.

GRAIL
Holy chalice. The object of a difficult quest, of which there are many versions. Its origins are unknown. The Grail quest can be seen as mysticism of the nobility.
WP 10, 151, 152.
Bibliography: *Y Seint Greal: The Holy Grail*. Ed. and tr. by R. Williams (1876). Jones (Wales) Publishers, facsimile, 1987. *The High History of the Holy Grail*, tr. Sebastian Evans, E. P. Dutton, New York, 1910 and reprinted (this is a fuller version of the Second Part of Y Seint Greal). *The Ancient Secret: In Search of the Holy Grail*. Flavia Anderson. Victor Gollancz Ltd., 1953. *King Arthur in Legend and History*, Richard Barber. The Boydell Press, Ipswich, 1973 (with attractive color reproductions of Arthurian paintings and illuminated MSS).

HASSIDISM
Jewish movement that arose at the beginning of the 18th century in Eastern Europe among an impoverished rural population that had fallen into despair after the collapse of the ecstatic Messianic hope of Sabbatanism. In contradistinction to Rabbinic teaching, there was an awareness of God's presence in all the things of life. People felt called to release God from matter by gathering the divine spark that had been dispersed everywhere. The founder was Israel ben Eliezer.
WP 6, 135, 136.
Bibliography: *Hasidism*. Ed. by Aryeh Rubinstein. ADL.

HESYCHASM

Fourteenth-century movement among the monks of Athos, who strove for the "rest of contemplation" and the vision of the Divine Light by such means as breath control and the "Jesus prayer."

WP II, 159. DS VII, 381-399.

Bibliography: I. Hausherr, *Solitude et vie contemplative d'après l'hésychasme* (Abbaye de Bellefontaine, 1980); *The Power of the Name: the Jesus Prayer in Orthodox Spirituality*. Bishop Kallistos of Diokleia. SLG Press, Oxford, 1982.

HUMILIATI

Poverty movement in 13th-century Lombardy.

WP II, 391.

ILLUMINATI

Also: Alumbrados. Name given to people in Spain who applied themselves to mysticism in the 16th and 17th centuries. It was later also used for any who held unorthodox views. From 1527 onwards, the Spanish Inquisition swung into action against them, often completely unjustifiably. The term was also employed for the French Quietists, for the secret societies of the 18th century, for a group in the South of France, *Les Illuminés*, founded in 1623, and for a group of religious enthusiasts in Bavaria, established by Adam Weishaupt in 1776.

WP II, 479.

KABBALAH

Doctrine that flourished in Provence and Northern Spain. Continuation of Jewish Merkabah mysticism. Its main work is the Zohar. It was cultivated in the 16th century by Spanish Jews who had fled to Safed in the Holy Land. A late off-shoot was the Hassidism of 18th-century Eastern Europe.

WP 12, 419.

Bibliography: *On the Kabbalah and its Symbolism*. Gershom Scholem. Tr. Ralph Manheim. Shocken Books, NY, 1977; *Origins of the Kabbalah*. Gershom Scholem. Tr. Allan Arkush, ed. R. J. Werblowsky. Princeton University Press, 1987; *The Qabalah*. Papus. Samuel Weiser, 1977.

LABADISTS

Followers of Jean de Labadie (1610-1674), who was a Protestant Pietist. They started as a house fellowship in Amsterdam, and later became a mystical sect in Herfold and in Altona. After Labadie's death, his group removed to Wieuwerd in Friesland. It ceased to exist in 1732.

WP 13, 444.

LAMAISM

Name for Tibetan Buddhism. It is a Mahayana Buddhism with an exceptional number of Buddha figures and very many monasteries. It was imported from Northern India by Padmasambhava.

WP 13, 463.

LIBERATION THEOLOGY

A movement that started in Latin America based on awareness that the Church has to champion the oppressed and work for changes in social structures. Often mystically inspired.

MERKABAH MYSTICISM

Also: Halakha mysticism. Earliest form of Jewish mysticism experienced as a journey to God's throne.

POP, 235-243.

Bibliography: G. Scholem, *Jewish Gnosticism, Merkabah Mysticism and Talmudic Tradition* (New York, 1965).

With reference to Jewish mysticism in general: G. Scholem, *Judaica*. 3 vols. (1977-1981); S. Sharot, *Messianism, Mysticism and Magic: A Sociological Analysis of Jewish Religious Movements* (Chapel Hill, 1982); Sed, *La mystique cosmologique juive*, Etudes juives, XVI (1981); S. Shaked (ed). *Irano-Judaica: Studies Relating to Jewish Contacts with Persian Culture Throughout the Ages* (1982).

NEOPLATONISM

One of the most important philosophical movements. Lies at the heart of Medieval mysticism, although going back to Plotinus. Its leading idea is that everything arises out of the Infinite One, which descends into an increasingly varied number of forms and ends in the opposite extreme: Nothing. The mystical element in this mode of thought lies in the concept that one can look beyond the visible to its origin, yet can never reach the Ultimate One by the use of reason because it transcends all being.

WP 16, 288.

NEW AGE

Term that refers to the arrival of the astrological Aquarian Age. Used as a general term for a coming together of various forms of reaction to the rational technical culture.

Bibliography: *Aquarian Age Philosophy*. E. Doane. Am. Fed. Astrologers, 1969.

NEW DEVOTION

Religious revival started by Gerard Groot. The New Devotion strove for "inwardness." Making common cause with what was modern at that time (humanism, the Renaissance), it advocated a personally experienced, human attitude to life, open to others. The New Devotion was spread by two organizations: "The Brotherhood of the Common Life," and the "Congregation of Windesheim," and most of all through the book *The Imitation of Christ*.

WP 15, 440.

OCCULTISM

Blanket term for teachings and practices which, according to their advocates, only initiates can understand or experience. Much that now passes for mysticism is occultism. Usually the things involved are either phenomena that can be stripped of their mystery by parapsychology, or secret activities.

WP, 20, 273.

PANSOPHY

Sought to summarize all knowledge in a single system, in order to reform the world and prepare for the Realm of lasting peace. Its proponents were: Paracelsus, the Rosicrucians, Weigel, Boehme, Angelus Silesius, Comenius, and Oetinger. Comenius, in particular, has had great influence on peace movements.

LthK 8, 23-4.

PIETISM

Movement, mainly found in German-speaking countries, and placing more emphasis on internal experience than on the external church.

Bibliography: *Pietists. Selected Writings*. Ed. Peter C. Erb. Paulist Press, 1983.

POVERTY MOVEMENTS

These arose from the beginning of the Middle Ages in the prosperous regions of Europe. People wished to live like Jesus: traveling around without possessions and preaching the Gospel. Women, too, claimed the right to preach.

WP 2, 493-494.

QUAKERS

The name given to the followers of George Fox because they shook with emotion. Officially, they called themselves The Society of Friends.

WP 18, 498.

Bibliography: *Quaker Spirituality: Selected Writings*. Ed. Douglas V. Steere. Paulist Press, 1984.

QUIETISM

Indicates an essential aspect of the mystical process—receptiveness, silence, not-doing. In a narrower sense, the term refers to any movement that aimed to put these things into practice: Apatheia, Hesychastic teaching, the doctrine of the Brethren of the Free Spirit, of Molinos and of Madame Guyon.

RGG V, 736-738.

RECLUSES

Original form of religious life for the single woman who did not wish to live in a nunnery. They were "immured" with special rituals; usually next to a church.

WP 19, 85.

SABBATANISM

Jewish movement in the 17th and 18th centuries, started by Sabbatai Zevi. Strongly Messianic with intense ecstasies and visions of the approaching end of the age and of the throne of God. Each leader fancied that he was the Messiah.

SHAMANISM

The primitive religion of the steppe dwellers. The shaman is the pivotal figure in the tribe. He is the priest who, through ecstasy, can journey to heaven and hell and to the All-highest. Modern notions of shamanism all have to do with trance techniques and with some sort of paranormal healing.

WP 20, 411.

SPIRITUALS

Franciscans who fought to observe the testament of St. Francis in opposition to the system-builders. Later inspired by Joachim of Fiore's vision of a spiritual church. The fiercest resistance was offered by the Fraticelli. The term "spirituals" was also used for a group of Protestants who, resisting the ossification of the Church, emphasized personal experience, piety, living from within, listening to the inner voice. They became known as Pietists, Enthusiasts, Experientialists, Neo-reformers, Revivalists.

WP 21, 85.

SUFISM

Islamic mystical movement. A reaction against rigidity and the abstract. It has schools and orders. Often entails a strongly erotic experience. Westernized Sufism was founded by Inayat Khan.
WP 20, 561-562.
Bibliography: *Oriental Mysticism*. E. H. Palmer (1867) Octagon Press reprint, London, 1974.

TANTRA

A kind of mystery religion of Ancient India, which survived in later Hinduism and Buddhism, especially in South India. It employs many meditation techniques and images, also sexual mysticism.
WP 21, 449-500; POP 336-337.
Bibliography: *The Tantric Way*. Mookerjee & Khanna. Thames & Hudson, 1977.

THEOSOPHY

A system of belief that seeks to turn knowledge into wisdom (sophia) through mystical experience of the divine. Modern theosophy sees this wisdom as the core of all religions. This universal theosophy was reworked by Madame Blavatsky. In 1875 she founded the Theosophical Society. The Theosophical Association split from this in 1895.
WP 22, 33.24; POP 345-500.

TM MOVEMENT

Founded by Maharishi Mahesh Yogi of Madras in 1958. This guru has since traveled around the world and has persuaded the Western elite to join a widespread organization in which the integration of Eastern and Western meditation is studied and practiced. Its religious character is being pushed into the background. Its main aim now seems to be to find rest while remaining involved in the consumer society. TM is short for Transcendental Meditation.
WP 14, 478-479; 22, 189-190.

VAISHNAVISM

Religion centered on the god Vishnu and his incarnations, especially Rama and Krishna. One of the three main trends in Hinduism.
WM 22, 444.

WALDENSES

Initially a poverty movement started by Peter Valdes in Lyons. It survived denunciation and persecution in Lombardy. Since the 16th century, it has formed part of reformed Protestantism.
WP 7 19, 634-635.

GLOSSARY OF MYSTICS

This book came into being because of an issue of *Speling* (a Dutch magazine, Volume 33, published in 1981) that was devoted entirely to the subject of mysticism. I went on to explore mystics through the ages using the following references to gather data. The various sources have been abbreviated as shown in the following list so readers can quickly see the sources.*

EM J.G. Ferguson, *An Illustrated Encyclopaedia of Mysticism and the Mystery Religions*; Dutch edition prepared by Simon Vinkenoog (Baarn, 1979). This is the most highly regarded systematic encyclopedia of mysticism, with mystical texts. However, there is no bibliography and there are very many errors. Unreliable.

WP *Grote Winkler Prins Encyclopedie*, 25 vols (Amsterdam, 1984[8]). Reliable, with bibliography.

EB *Encyclopedia Britannica*, 29 vols (1985[15]).

NEB *New Encyclopedia Britannica*, 29 vols (1986). A complete revision of the old encyclopedia. The old format was: first the overview and then everything in detail. Whoever looks up mysticism in the new edition must consult the alphabetical listing in the first section. In the last parts, the main trends are dealt with including Buddhist, Islamic, Hindu, and Taoist mysticism. The articles are very full and thorough, but not so clearly expressed as those in the old encyclopedia. We followed the old encyclopedia when preparing the charts and the chronological table. Both encyclopedias are very reliable, and give bibliographies and suggestions at the end of the articles.

EdM Marie-Madeleine Davy, *Encyclopédie des Mystiques*, 4 volumes (Paris, 1972); pocket edition (Paris, 1977); A collection of articles on all historic forms of mysticism, with a short bibliography. The articles are uneven in value.

DS *Dictionnaire de la Spiritualité ascétique et mystique* [A Dictionary of Ascetic and Mystical Spirituality]. Very circumstantial with a comprehensive bibliography. However publication has been very slow: the first volumes (from 1937) are much dated; the final volumes are still not published.

EJ *Encyclopedia Judaica*, ed. C. Roth and G. Wigoder, 16 volumes (1971-1972). Detailed and reliable, with bibliography and considerable attention to mysticism within Judaism. See also: Philadelphia, Coronet Books, 1982.

---

* Publisher's Note. This book has been translated from Dutch and the many Dutch references to books published about mystics are unavailable in English. See bibliography for additional references.

Hi *Handwörterbuch des Islams* [Pocket Dictionary of Islam] (Leiden, 1976). Contains all the articles on religious themes and persons to do with Islam that were published in the *Encyclopedie des Islams*, brought up to date by A. Wensinck and J. Kramers, a translation to *The Encyclopaedia of Islam*. Brill reprinted this English encyclopedia unaltered, and began a new one. Six volumes are out now. We had no time to consult them.

RGG *Die Religionen in Geschichte und Gegenwart* [Religions Past and Present], revised by E. Werbeck (Tübingen, 1957-1965; 1987³). Gives a good survey under the word *Mysticism*. Reference is also made to other key-words relating to mysticism.

LthK *Lexicon für Theologie und Kirche* (Freiburg, 1957; 1967²). [A Theological and Ecclesiastical Lexicon].

ThW *Theologisch Woordenboek*, 3 volumes [A Theological Dictionary] (Roermond, 1952-58). Data on Dutch mystics not in the big encyclopedias.

OGE *Ons Geestelijk Erf* [Our Spiritual Inheritance]. A periodical carrying information about Dutch mystics and others noted for their piety. Every year a bibliography is published of mysticism in general, and the history of piety in particular, limited to Western Europe, with special reference to the Netherlands and Germany.

POP Cris Popenoe, *Books for Inner Development* (Washington, Yes Books, 1974). The most complete presentation of all the books that have appeared in English on mysticism and related topics. With descriptions of their contents and value, and with brief, pithy introductions to the themes under which the various books are arranged.

A. Toynbee *De cultuurgeschiedenis van China en Japan*, [The Cultural History of China and Japan] (Amsterdam, 1977). Not encyclopedic, but instructive on the layer of mysticism in the culture; the text is illustrated with pictures and maps.

ABRAHAM BEN DAVID OF POSQUIÈRES (ca. 1125-1198)
Jewish mystic in Provence. Not a Kabbalist himself, but his children became Kabbalists.
EJ 2, 136-140.

ABRAHAM BEN ISAAC (middle 13th century)
Important Kabbalist in Gerona. Student of Isaac the Blind.
EJ 2, 144.

ABRAHAM BEN ISAAC OF NARBONNE (1186-1237)
Born in Narbonne, Spiritual leader in Provence. Kabbalist.
EJ 2, 146.

ABRAHAM BEN MOSES BEN MAIMON (1186–1237)
Son of Maimonides. Influenced by Sufis, whom he saw as disciples of Elijah.
EJ 2, 150-152.

ABRAHAM BEN SAMUEL ABULAFIA (1240-after 1291)
From Zaragoza, wandered through Europe. Important representative of the prophetic-Kabbalistic tradition.
EJ 2, 185. WP I, 205.

ABULAFIA, see Abraham ben Samuel Abulafia; see also Todros.

ABU YAZID (ca. 801-874) Also known as: al-Bistami of Bayazid/Abu Yazit al-Bistami.
Persian Islamic mystic. Abandoned all rituals and devotions. Doctrine of self-annihilation (fana). EM 7, 8. Hi, 82-83.

ABU SA'ID IBU AL-CHAIR (967-1049)
Persian mystic. Gave an account of practical experiences. One of the great Sufis.
WP I, 178.

ACARIE, BARBE JEANNE (1566-1618)
Also Known as: Madame Acarie/Marie of the Incarnation. Widow, Carmelite. Introduced Carmelite mysticism into France.
WP 15, 55.

ADELHEID VAN SCHAARBEEK (d. 1250)
Brabant Cistercian. Mystical devotion to Christ. No writings.
WP I, 278.

AELRED OF RIEVAULX (1110-1167)
Also of Hexham. English Cistercian, famous for his work *On Spiritual Friendship*.
WP I, 317-318.
Publication: *Spiegel van de liefde* [Mirror of love], Monastieke cahiers 28 (Bonheiden, 1985).

AGREDA, MARIA DE JESUS (1602–1665).
Spanish Franciscan nun. Wrote *The Mystical City of God* and letters to Philip IV.
WP I, 425.

AGRIPPA OF NETTESHEIM, Heinrich Cornelius (1486-1535)
Magician and alchemist. Reduced everything to a system in his *Occult Philosophy*.
WP I, 430.

AKHNATEN (1372-1354 B.C.)
Egyptian Pharaoh. Early monotheist, but his religion failed to survive. Famous for his Hymn to the Sun.
Literature: R. Hari, *New Kingdom Amarna Period: The Great Hymn to Aten* (Leiden, 1985). D.B. Redford, *Akhenaten: The Heretic King* (Leiden, 1987).

AKIBA (ca. 50-135)
Also known as: Rabbi Akiba. Spiritual leader of the Jewish people after the fall of Jerusalem. Practiced Merkabah

mysticism. Regarded the Song of Solomon as the most sacred book.
EJ 2, 488-492.

ALACOQUE, MARGARETHA MARIA (1647-1690)
French mystic. Her visions led to widespread devotion to the Sacred Heart.
WP I, 455.

ALBERTUS MAGNUS (ca. 1200-1280)
German Dominican. Taught theology in Paris and Cologne. Pioneered a more naturalistic, humanistic way of thinking. Alchemical works have been ascribed to him.
WP I, 477-478.

ALVAREZ, BALTASAR (1533-1580)
Spanish Jesuit. Guide of Teresa of Avila. Described methods of prayer.
WP 2, 42.

ALYPIUS THE STYLITE (7th century)
Lived for 76 years on top of a pillar in Adrianopolis (Asia Minor). Two communities formed around the pillar.
WP 2, 45.

AMAURY (d. ca. 1206)
Also Known as Amalric. Teacher from Bena with a mystical vision of the Church. In Paris. Posthumously condemned.
WP 2, 48.

ANDREAE, JOHANN VALENTIN (1586-1654)
Claimed authorship of the "Chymical Wedding of Christian Rosencreutz" (1616), a basic text of the "Rosicrucians".
WP 2, 171.

ANGELA OF FOLIGNO (ca. 1249-1309)
Visionary mystic. Inspired by Franciscans. Widow.
WP 2, 183.

Literature: P. Lachance, *The Spiritual Journey of the Blessed Angels of Foligno*, according to the Memorial of Frater A., *Studia Antoniana, 29* (Rome, 1984).

ANGELUS CLARENUS (ca. 1250-1337)
Leader of Franciscan-inspired spirituals.
WP 2, 187.
Literature: Lydia van Auw, *Angelo Clareno et les spirituels italiens* [Angelus Clarenus and the Italian "spirituals"] (Rome, 1979).

ANGELUS SILESIUS (1624-1677)
Also known as: Johann Scheffler. Mystical poet of Silesia. Lutheran who converted to Catholicism.
WP 2, 187.
Anthologies: *Zwerver tussen hemel en aarde* [Traveler between heaven and earth], translated and introduced by J. Benoit (1971). *Cherubinischer Wandersmann* [Cherubic Traveler], compiled by Hans Urs von Balthasar (Einsiedeln, 1980). *Der Himmel ist in dir* [Heaven is in you], compiled and introduced by G. Wehr (Einsiedeln, 1982).

ANNA VAN SINT-BARTHO-LOMEUS (1549-1626)
Companion of Teresa of Avila. Founded a Carmel nunnery in Antwerp.
WP 2, 213

ANSARI, ABDALLAH (1006-1088)
Persian Sufi mystic and poet.
WP 2, 288.

ANTHONY, ABBOT (251-356)
Hermit in the Egyptian desert. Fought demons. Pioneer of Christian monasticism.
WP 2, 284 - 285.
Bibliography: N. Devilliers, *Antonius de Grote* [Anthony the Great], Monastieke cahiers 18 (Bonheiden, 1981).

ANTHONY OF PADUA (1195-1231)
Portuguese Franciscan. Preacher of poverty. Legendary popular saint and visionary wonder-worker.
WP 2, 285.

APPELMANS, GHERAERT (ca. 1250-1325)
Brabant mystic.
WP 2, 352

ARNAUD, ANTOINE (1612-1694)
Leader of Jansenism. Retired to Port-Royal.
WP 2, 495.

ARNAUD, JACQELINE-MARIE-ANGÉLIQUE DE SAINTE-MADELEINE (1591-1661)
Known as Mère-Angélique, abbess of Port-Royal.
WP 2, 495.

ARNAUD, JEANNE-CATHERINE-AGNES (1593-1671)
Known as Mère Agnes. Abbess of Port-Royal.
WP 2, 495.

ARNDT, JOHANN (1555-1621)
Lutheran. His influence on pietism was felt after his death.
WP 2, 496.
Bibliography: C. Braw, *Bücher im Staube. Die Theologie Johann Arndts in ihrem Verhältnis zur Mystik* [Books in the Dust: The Theology of Johann Arndt in Relation to Mysticism], Studies in Medieval and Reformation Thought 39 (1986).

ARNOLD OF BRESCIA (ca. 1100-1155)
Political mystic, who strove for a spiritual church. Gifted preacher
RGG I, 632-633.

ARNOLD, GOTTFRIED (1666-1714)
Pietistic clergyman. Describes church history as actually powered by mysticism.
RGG I, 633-634.

ASHIK PASHA (1271-1332)
Turkish mystical poet.
WP 2, 545.

ASVAGHOSA (1st century)
Also known as: Ashvaghosa. Brahman who became a Buddhist. Poet, musician, mystic. First formulator of Mahayana Buddhism.
NEB I, 658 and 27, 724. POP, 71.

ATTAR, FARID AD-DIN (1142-1220)
Persian mystical poet. Pantheistic Sufi.
NEB 22, 19-20/ POP, 219.

AUGUSTINE, AURELIUS (354-430)
One of the most influential Christian thinkers. North African. His mysticism was characterized by restless seeking.
WP 3, 99-103.
Works: *De Civitate Dei*, translated (with introduction) into Dutch by G. Wijdeveld as *De stad van God* (Ambo, 1984).
[Tasker's revision of Healey's English translation, with introduction and notes, has been published in two volumes by Everyman's Library, E.P. Dutton & Co., New York, 1945].
Regel voor de gemeenschap [Community rule], translated with commentary by T. J. van Bavel, (Averbode, 1982).

AUROBINDO GHOSE, SRI- (1872-1950)
Hindu mystic. Founded the ashram in Pondicherry that launched the Sri Aurobindo Society. His French wife founded Auroville.
WP 3, 109. POP, 191-193.

AZRIEL OF GERONA (beginning of the 13th century)
Most famous Kabbalist of Gerona. Influenced by Neoplatonism.
EJ 3, 1012-1014.

•

BAADER, FRANZ XAVER VON (1765-1841)
Universal genius in the line of Boehme.
In his time, the best judge of European
mysticism.
EdM, 335-336.

BAAL SHEM TOV, see Israel b. Eliezer.

BACHYA BEN JOSEPH IBN PAKUDA (1040-
1110)
Also: Bachya ibn Pakuda. Spanish Jew,
known for *The Duties of the Heart*, a
guide strongly influenced by Arab
mysticism.
EJ 4, 105-108.

BAKER, AUGUSTINUS (1575-1641)
English Benedictine living in northern
France. Strongly influenced by Dutch
mysticism.
NEB I, 811. EM 31.

BARSANUPHIUS (d. ca. 540)
Coptic hermit in Gaza. Wrote letters
on hesychastic prayer.
WP 3, 382.

BASIL THE GREAT (ca. 330-379)
Also: of Caesarea. Cappadocian.
Reorganized monasticism.
WP 3, 399-400.

BAUDELAIRE, PIERRE, CHARLES (1821-1867)
French poet. Sought artificial paradises
and "Flowers of Evil."
WP 3, 429-430.

BEATRIX OF NAZARETH (1200-1268)
Prioress of the Nazareth convent, Lier.
Her *Seven Manners* is the oldest known
piece of mystical prose in Middle
Dutch.
WP 3, 449.
Works: *Van seven manieren van heiligher
minnen* [Seven Manners of Holy Love],
ed. H. Vekeman, (Zutphen, 1970).

BENEDICT CANFIELD (1564-1610)
Also: William Fitch. English Protestant
who became a Capuchin and a member of the Parisian mystical salon.
WP 7 3, 530.
Works: *La Regle de perfection* [The Rule
of Perfection]. Critical edition by
L.Orcibal (Paris, 1982); see the reactions to this work: OGE 84, pp. 41-45,
247-273.

BENEDICT OF NURSIA (ca. 480-547)
Initiated a new form of monastic life in
Subiaco and Monte Cassino. His rule
is the basis of Western monasticism.
WP 4, 90-82.
Works: *Regel voor monniken* [Rule for
Monks] (Slangenburg, 1973).
Bibliography: M. Coune, *Sint Bendictus
regal dag aan dag*
[St Benedict's rule day by day]
(Bonheiden, 1985).

BERNARD OF CLAIRVAUX (1090–1153)
One of the most important mystics of
Western Europe. His mysticism of love
inspired thousands of women.
Works: *Werken van Sint-Bernardus, abt
van Clairvaux*, 6 volumes [The Works
of St. Bernard, abbot of Clairvaux]
(Tilburg, 1973-1974²).

BERNARDINUS OF LAREDO (1482-1540)
Physician of Seville. Became a
Franciscan and was influential to
Spanish mystician with his *Ascent of
Mount Sion*.
WP 4, 165.

BERNIÈRES-LOUVIGNY, JEAN de (1602-1659)
Mystic who lived in a hermitage in
Caen.
LThK 2, 256.

BERTKEN, SISTER (ca. 1427-1514)
Mystic, poetess. Had herself immured
in a cell at the parish church, Utrecht.
WP 4, 183.

BÉRULLE, PIERRE DE (1575-1629)
French cardinal. His mysticism is centered on surrendering the will to God.

WP 4, 186. ThH, 157 and 505-507.
Works: *Het leven van Jezus en andere geschriften* [The Life of Jesus and other writings] (Utrecht, 1954).

BETKE, JOACHIM (1606-1663)
Berlin clergyman, inspired by Boehme. True church is hidden.
RGG I, 1099.

BESANT, ANNIE (1847-1933)
Left Anglicanism for Atheism, and Atheism for Theosophy.
WP, 4, 188. POP, 346-347.
Works: *Thought-Forms*, with 38 color and black-and-white illustrations (1986⁵). [And other books, some in collaboration. *Tr.*]

BIRGITTA OF SWEDEN (1303-1373)
Court lady, widow, founder of the Bridgetin nuns (the Order of St. Bridget). Visionary.
WP 4, 310.
Bibliography: F. Holböck, *Gottes Nordlicht. Die heilige Birgitta von Schweden und ihre Offenbarungen* [God's Northern Light. St. Bridget of Sweden and her Revelations] (Aschaffenburg, 1983).

BLAKE, WILLIAM (1757-1827)
English artist, poet, mystic.
WP 4, 348. POP, 266-267.

BLAVATSKY, HELENA PETROVA (1831-1891)
Russian theosophist. Founded the Theosophical Society in 1875.
WP 4, 359. POP, 347-348.
Works: *The Secret Doctrine*. 3 volumes (London 1888); reprint by J.J.V. Couvreur (The Hague, n.d.) [Also *The Veil of Isis*. Tr.]

BLOMMEVEEN, PIETER (1466-1536)
Of Leyden. Made the Carthusian monastery in Cologne a center for printing mystical works.
WP 4, 403.

BLUMHARDT, JOHANN CHRISTOPH (1805-1910)
Luther's chaplain in Möttingen, where he encouraged a revival that was continued by his son Christoph.
RGG I, 1325-1327.

BODELSCHWINGH, FRIEDRICH VON (1831-1910)
German, worked under the proletariat of Paris and gave the social misfits self-confidence.
RGG I, 1335-1336

BODHIDHARMA (ca. 470-543)
Buddhist who came to China from India. First Zen patriarch.
WP 4, 426. NEB 2, 315; 15, 289.

BOEHME, JACOB (1575-1634)
Shoemaker of Görlitz. Original vision of the reconciliation of opposites in God. Great influence on modern mysticism and on modern artists.
WP 4, 479. NEB 2, 329; 16, 374; 26, 640.
Literature: *Aurora, Way to Christ, Mysterium Magnum*, etc.

BONAVENTURA (ca. 1217-1274)
Also: Giovanni Fidanza. Italian Franciscan. Doctor of the Church. His *Journey of the Mind to God* is a very important contribution to mysticism.
WP 4, 510, 511.
Works: *Opera Omnia, Ad Claras Aquas*, 1902.

BONHOEFFER, DIETRICH (1906-1945)
German Protestant theologian, killed by the Gestapo. Advocate of "Christian worldliness."
WP 4, 515.
Bibliography: H. R. Pelikan, *Die Frömmigkeit Dietrich Bonhoeffers, Dokumentation, Grundlinien, Entwicklung* (1982). Short biography in: *A Third Testament*, by Malcolm Muggeridge, Little, Brown & Company (Canada) Limited, 1976.

BOOTH, WILLIAM (1829-1912)
Founded the Salvation Army in 1865.
EDM 369, 370.

BOURIGNON DE LA PORTE, ANTOINETTE
(1610-1680)
Native of Lille. Saw herself as a new
Eve called to preach a spiritual
Christianity. Extensive writings.
Followers in Amsterdam and England.
Died in Franeker, Friesland.
WP 5, 80.

BRANDSMA, TITUS (1881-1942)
Carmelite, professor, publicist.
Formulated a contemporary "mysticism of action." Died in the concentration camp at Dachau.
WP 5, 136.
Publications: *Mystiek leven*, an anthology by Bruno Borchert (Nijmegen,
1985).

BRUNO, GIORDANO (1548-1600)
Italian, ex-Dominican. Worked for reli-
gious tolerance. Traveled all over
Europe. Original mystic vision.
Executed in Rome.
WP 5, 260.
Bibliography: *Giordano Bruno & the
Hermetic Tradition*, Frances Yates,
Random, 1969; U. of Chicago Press,
1979.

BRUNO THE CARTHUSIAN (1032-1101)
Of Cologne. Founder of the Carthusian
order.
WP 5, 260.

BUBER, MARTIN (1878-1965)
Jewish philosopher. Made Hassidism
accessible. Formulated mysticism as
an "I and thou" dialogue.
EJ 4, 1429-1433; WP 5, 289, 290.

BUDDHA (ca. 560-480 B.C.)
Also: Siddharta Gautama/Siddharta
Gotama. Name ("Enlightened")
bestowed on Siddharta Gautama, the
founder of Buddhism.
WP 4, 433. POP, 73.
Works: *Dhammapada*, twenty-five
poems ascribed to Buddha.

BUNYAN, JOHN (1628-1688)
Tinker, lay preacher. His description
of life as a pilgrimage has been trans-
lated into a hundred languages.
WP 5, 336.
Bibliography: *The Pilgrim's Progress,
Grace Abounding*, and *The Life and Death
of Mr. Badman*. Reprinted New York,
Everyman's Library, Dutton. He also
wrote *The Holy War*, etc.

CAITANYA, BISYVRAMBHARA (1485-1533)
Also: Chaitanya and Gauranga.
Love mysticism with ecstatic song and
dance, devoted to Krishna. Great influ-
ence on Bengali piety.
WP 5, 440.

CASSIAN, JOHN (360-435)
Formed the bridge between monasticism in the Middle East and in
Western Europe, by founding cloisters
and making summaries of talks with
the desert fathers.
WP 5, 570, 571.

CATHERINE OF BOLOGNA (1413-1463)
Nun of order of St. Clare. Described
her mystical experiences.
WP 6, 44.

CATHERINE OF GENOA (1447-1510)
Married. Integrated her psychosis and
the care of the sick in a mystical life,
and described this as purgatory: a
process of purification.
WP 6, 44.
Bibliography: *Catherine of Genoa:
Purgation and Purgatory, the Spiritual
Dialogue*. Ed. by Serge Hughes.
Mahwah, NJ: Paulist Pr. 1979.

CATHERINE DEI RICCI (1522-1590)
Visionary mystic. Stigmatist.
WP 6, 44.

CATHERINE OF SIENA (1347-1380)
Daughter of a wool-dyer. Bride mysticism. Very influential on ecclesiastical policy. Her letters form part of the classical Italian texts (289 in all).
WP 6, 44.
Bibliography: *Catherine of Siena: The Dialogue*. Ed. by Suzanne Noffke. Mahwah, NJ: Paulist Press. 1980.

CHAIM BEN JOSEPH VITAL (1542-1620)
Also: Hayim Vital. One of the greatest Kabbalists. In Safed (Palestine).
EJ 15, 171-176.

CHANTAL, JEANNE-FRANCOISE FRÉMIOT (1572-1671)
Mother of six children. Founded the order of the Visitation with her spiritual guide, Francis de Sales. Suffered from timidity, but confiding in God is the core of her mysticism.
WP 6, 122.

CHAPMAN, JOHN HENRY (1865-1933)
Abbot at Downside. Good guide: especially in regard to the "dark night" in the mystical process.
LthK 2, 1016.

CHI-TSANG (549-623)
Chinese. Denied the existence of being and not-being. All phenomena resolve themselves into the "Center" and the "Void." Founded the Chung-lun (Doctrine of the Center) School.
Toynbee, 123.

CLARE OF ASSISI (1194-1253)
Adopted the "rule" of her friend St. Francis, and started the Clarist order for women in San Damiano.
WP 6, 293.

CLEMENT OF ALEXANDRIA (ca. 150-215)
Ecclesiastical writer who was receptive to Hellenism. The core of his teaching is the gnosis as saving awareness.
WP 6, 308.

COMENIUS, JOHAN AMOS (1592-1670)
Real name: Komensky. Czech scholar, bishop of the Bohemian Brethren. Devised a pansophy and an educational system aimed at unifying people around the essentials.
WP 6, 384, 385.

CONFUCIUS (551-479 B.C.)
Applied Taoism to society, which ought to be built—not on force or privilege—but on ethical principles. The Tao is honored by virtuous community life.
WP 6, 446. POP, 98.
Bibliography: *The Analects of Confucius*, translated by W. E. Soothill, Oxford University Press, 1910 and reprints.

CORDOVERO, see: MOSES BEN JACOB.

COSMAS DE ETOLIER (d. 1779)
Greek monk. Formulated a spirituality suitable for the ordinary person who is mystically inclined.
EDM, 236, 237.

CRASHAW, RICHARD (1612-1649)
Mystical poet, inspired by the Song of Solomon and by St. Teresa of Avila.
EM 58.
Bibliography: Two poems of his on St. Teresa are to be found (with some others) in *The Oxford Book of Christian Verse*, Clarendon Press, Oxford, 1940, reprinted.

DA FREE JOHN (born 1939)
Also: Naitauba Avodhoota Da Love-Ananda Hridayam. Became a spiritual teacher after an intense search in Eastern and Western traditions, which led to a total God-realization in which each form of duality is surmounted.
Publications: *The Knee of Listening* (Amsterdam, 1987), *The Method of the Siddhas* (Clearlake, CA, 1973), *The Dawn Horse Testament* (San Rafael, CA, 1985).

DANTE, ALIGHIERI (1265-1321)
The great poet who, in his *Divine Comedy* gave dramatic form to the Christian view of time and eternity. Native of Florence.
WP 7, 123-125.
Bibliography: Edmond G. Gardner, *Dante and the Mystics: A Study of the Mystical Aspects of the Divina Commedia and its Relations with some of its Mediaeval Sources* (London, 1913). Emelia Russell Gurney, *Dante's Pilgrim's Progress, with notes by the Way* (Elliot Stock, London, 1897).
[Many versions of *La Divina Commedia* have been made. Cary's has long been popular, and a profusely illustrated copy of it is *The Vision*, G. Fattorusso, Florence, n.d. An extremely literal, and therefore very useful, translation is that of the poet Longfellow (see editions of his works). Some translations include the Italian: e.g., L. Binyon's, Macmillan, 1933-38-43.]

DAVID OF AUGSBURG (1200-1272)
Franciscan mystical author. The first to write in his mother tongue about the mystic way.
WP 7, 142, 143.

DAVID BEN SOLOMON IBN ZIMBA (1479-1573)
Spanish Jew who settled in Egypt. Kabbalist.
EJ 5, 1356-1358.

DEE, JOHN (1527-1608)
Noted English hermeticist and mage.
NEB 3, 954.

DENCK, HANS (ca. 1500-1527)
German Anabaptist, elevated spiritual mysticism above the visible Church.
WP 7, 207.

DHU AN-NUN (d. ca. 861)
Egyptian Sufi school. Introduced *ma 'rifah* (inner knowledge) as the antithesis of book-learning. Hymnlike prayers in praise of God.
Hi 98, 99. EM 63.

DIADOCHUS OF PHOTICE (mid-fifth century)
His *Hundred Chapters on Perfection* was the most widely disseminated mystical work in the early ages of the Greek Church.

DIETERLEN, CHRISTOPHE (1818-1874)
Industrialist in Rothau (Alsace). Inspired by Boehme.
EDM 368, 369.

DIETRICH VON FREIBERG (d. after 1310)
Dominican who influenced German mysticism by his teaching on the "ground of the soul."
RGG II, 194.

DIONYSIUS THE CARTHUSIAN (1402-1471)
Also: Denys van Leeuwen, Denys van Rijkel. Carthusian in Roermond. Came at the close of the Middle Ages and made a grand summary of theological and mystical works.
WP 7, 338, 339.

DJAMI, ABD AL-RAHMAN (1414-1492)
Also: Jami, Narrudin Abdur Rahman. Last great Persian mystic poet.
WP 7, 360.

DOGEN (1200-1253)
The greatest of the Japanese Zen masters in literary skill. Rejected the koan. Taught Za-Zen: sitting erect without thinking of anything. Founder of the Soto order.
NEB 4, 150 (cf. 12, 901; 15, 289). Toynbee 240. EM 315, 316.

DOMINIC (1170-1221)
Member of the Spanish Guzmán family. In response to the Cathars, planned a new sort of monastic order.
WP 7, 360.

DOV BAER OF MEZHIRECH (d. 1772)
Also: of Mezritch. One of the first and most important of the Hassidic leaders.
EJ 6, 180-184.

DUTOIT, JEAN-PHILIPPE (1721-1793)
Also: Mambrini. One of the Protestants who carried on the Quietist mysticism interdicted by Rome.
RGG II, 293, 294.

EBNER, CHRISTINA (1277-1356)
Visionary mystical writer. Dominican nun in Engeltal.
WP 6, 239.
Bibliography: OGE 87, No. 430.

EBNER, MARGARET (1292-1351)
Also: Margaretha von Maria-Mödlingen. German visionary mystic. Her visions were very much in keeping with their times.
WP 12, 613.
Bibliography: OGE 84, No. 271.

ECKHART (1260-1327)
Also: Meister Eckhart. German theologian and mystic. Dominican. Rightly named "the father of German speculative mysticism." Shortly after his death certain of his articles were condemned [by Pope John XXII] and he fell into oblivion. Now he has been rehabilitated as one of the "greats."
WP 8, 52.
Bibliography: Meister Eckhart: Sermons and Treatises, translated and edited by M. O'C. Walshe, Watkins, 1979.

ELEAZER BEN JUDA OF WORMS (ca. 1165-ca. 1230)
As the victim of a pogrom, he felt called to record the whole of Jewish mysticism for fear the Jews might be exterminated.
EJ 6, 592-594.

ELIJAH (ninth century B.C.)
Israeli prophet. Carmelite mysticism found its inspiration in him.

WP 8, 211.
Bibliography: the Bible (I & II Kings and occasional references elsewhere), Josephus, The Midrashim, etc.

ELISABETH OF SCHÖNAU (1129-1164)
Visionary mystical writer. Benedictine nun. Her brother compiled a book of her visions.
See for spirituality directed to Jesus as a "mother" and to the feminine side of God: OGE 84, No. 182; 85, No. 180; 86, Nos. 148-150.

EMMERICK, ANNA KATHARINA (1774-1824)
Nun in Dülmen (Westfalia). Her visions, meditations, and stigmata attracted a great deal of attention.
WP 8, 247.
Bibliography: M. T. Loutrel. Anne Catherine Emmerick par elle-même et par ses contemporains (Paris, 1980).

EPHRAEM OF SYRIA (ca. 306-373)
The greatest hymnodist of the Syrian Church. His fifteen songs on paradise were very popular.
WP 8, 290, 291.

EPICTETUS (ca. 50- ca. 130)
Emancipated slave. Philosopher who wrote for the ordinary person. One of the main exponents of Stoicism.
WP 8, 291.

EVAGRIUS PONTICUS (346-399)
The first hermit to do much writing. In the desert of Nitria, Libya.
WP 8, 404.

EZEKIEL (sixth century B.C.)
Jewish prophet, carried captive to Babylon in 597. His visions of the throne of God influenced Merkabah mysticism.
WP 8, 452.
Bibliography: The Bible (Ezekiel). The Promise of Ezekiel's City: Wisdom's Seven Pillars, Bezzant and Pridham, Norwich, 1952. Numerous commentaries.

EZRA BEN SOLOMON (d. ca. 1238)
Kabbalist in Gerona (Spain). Commentary on the Song of Solomon. EJ 6, 1123-1124.
Bibliography: *Le commentaire d'Ezra de Gérone sur le Cantique de Cantiques, Etudes et textes de mystique juive* (Paris, 1969).

FALCONI DE BUSTAMANTE, JUAN (1596-1638) Spanish mystical writer, for whom Christian perfection implied mysticism. DS V, 35-43.

FELGENHAUER, PAUL (1593-1677)
Physician, preacher of the new birth. Influenced by Boehme. Combined "enthusiast" mysticism, pietism, and enlightenment.
RGG II, 894, 895.

FÉNELON, FRANÇOIS DE SALIGNAC DE LA MOTHE (1651-1715)
Archbishop of Cambrai. Defended in vain Madame Guyon and her teaching on "pure love" (quietism).
WP 8, 505.

FICINO, MARSILIO (1433-1499)
Italian humanist. Translated Hermes Trismegistus, Plato and Plotinus. Also formulated his own mystical world view.
WP 8, 532, 533.

FOUCAULD, CHARLES EUGENE (1885-1916) French explorer and hermit in the Sahara. Source of inspiration for a dozen religious groups.
WP 9, 103, 104.

FOX, GEORGE (1624-1691)
Shoemaker. Preached about the "inner light." Organized the Society of Friends (Quakers) in England and elsewhere in the world.
WP 9, 109.
Bibliography: *The Journal of George Fox*, New York: Dutton.

FRANCIS OF ASSISI (1181-1266)
A unique figure: spontaneous, radical, poor by choice, brother of all living creatures. Paramount influence on the spirituality of the Middle Ages.
WP 9, 115-117.
Bibliography: *The Little Flowers & the Life of St. Francis* with the *Mirror of Perfection*, New York: E. P. Dutton Everyman's Library edition of 1910 and reprints.

FRANCIS DE SALES (1567-1622)
Also: François de Sales. French bishop. Made mysticism accessible to the ordinary person. Founded the order of the Visitation with his close friend J. de Chantal.
WP 9, 117.
Bibliography: A. Dodin, *François de Sales, Vincent de Paul: les deux amis* (Paris, 1984).

FRANCK, SEBASTIAN (1499-1542)
Protestant mystic for whom the inner word was the only certainty. Attracted a large following in Germany.
WP 9, 118.

GABIROL, see SOLOMON BEN JUDAH.

GAGLIARDI, ACHILLE (1537-1607)
Italian Jesuit. Formulated a Quietist mysticism with the mystic Berinzaga Rabia.
LthK 4, 485.

GALGANI, GEMMA (1878-1903)
Italian ecstatic. Stigmatized.
WP 9, 265.

GANDHI, MOHANDAS KARAMCHAND (1869-1948)
Indian leader. Strove for co-operation between Hindus and Moslems, for liberation of the pariahs, and for Indian independence through passive resistance. Had a background of Jainism.

Central in his thinking was the concept of *ahimsa;* that is to say, universal love to and between all that lives.

GERARD GROOT (1340-1384)
Preacher of repentance in Deventer. Inspired the New Devotion.
WP 9, 339, 340.

GERLACH, PETERS
Also: Gerlacus Petri. Most important mystic of the New Devotion.
WP 9, 459.

GERONDI, see JACOB BEN SHESHET.

GERSON, JEAN (de) (1363-1429)
From the Ardennes. Chancellor of the University of Paris. Preference for practical mysticism.
WP 9, 469.

GERTRUDE OF HELFTA (1256-1302)
Also: Gertrude the Great. Mystic belonging to the nunnery in Helfta. Her writings were very influential, especially on devotion to the Sacred Heart.
WP 9, 470.
Bibliography: P. Luislampe, "La grâce est signe de l'amité de Dieu: Gertrude d'Helfta, une figure d'espérance de l'amour libérateur" in: *Collectanea Cisterciensia.* 48, 1986, pp. 71-87.

GEZELLE, GUIDO (1830-1899)
Priest and teacher in Roeselare, Belgium. Mystical poet.
WP 9, 517-519.

GHAZZALI, ABU HAMID MOHAMMED AL- (1058-1111)
Persian scholar. Led a wandering life following a crisis. Brought orthodox and mystical Moslems closer together. Made mysticism accessible to the great mass of Moslems.
WP 9, 533, 534. Hi 140-144. NEB 22, 19. POP, 221, 222.

GIBRAN, KHALIL (1883-1931)
Lebanese poet and painter. The progress from skepticism to mysticism can be seen in his work.
WP 9, 543.

GICHTEL, JOHANN GEORG (1638-1710)
German Protestant mystic who emigrated to Amsterdam. Deeply influenced by Boehme.
WP 9, 543.

GREGORY THE GREAT (ca. 540-604)
Roman. Pope. He recalled a mystical experience. He expressed mysticism along the same lines as St. Augustine.
WP 10, 207-208.

GREGORY OF NAREK (ca. 944-1010)
Also: Grigor Narekatsi. Armenian mystic and poet. He can be considered one of the great Christian mystics.
DS VI, 927-932.

GREGORY OF NAZIANZE (329-390)
"Cappadocian father." Often withdrew into isolation. Mystical poet.
WP 10, 211, 212.

GREGORY OF NYSSA (ca. 335-394)
"Cappadocian father." Devised a model, known as the "via negativa," since used by mystics when speaking of God.
WP 10, 212.

GREGORY PALMAS (1296-1359)
Byzantine theologian and mystic. His hesychastic doctrine has been officially approved by the Greek Church. Monk on Athos.
WP 10, 211.

GREGORY OF SINAI (1225-1346)
Also: Sinaiticus. Hesychastic monk.
DS VI. 1011-1014.

GROU, JEAN (1731-1803)
French Jesuit. Described a "simple way of prayer": turning the attention, with-

out undue effort, to a vague idea of God.
EM 109. DS VI, 1059-1083.

GUERRICUS OF IGNY (d. 1157)
Cistercian confirmed by St. Bernard. Christian mystic who thought the soul was the spiritual mother of Christ.
DS VI, 1114-1120.

GURDJIEFF, GEORGE IVANOVICH (1877-1949)
Native of the Caucasus. Traveled in the Far East. Settled in France, visited New York. Influence in artistic and literary circles through his method of ridding the "I" of all conditioning.
EM 109, 110. NEB 5, 574. POP 154-158. Bibliography: G. I. Gurdjieff, *Meetings with Remarkable Men*, New York: Dutton, 1969, and Viking Penguin, 1991; and London: RKP, 1963; Pan Books, 1978. P. D. Ouspensky, *In Search of the Miraculous*, RKP, 1950.

GUYART, MARIE (1599-1672)
Also: Marie de l'Incarnation. French mystic, writer, missionary in Canada. Widow, Ursuline.
WP 15, 55.

GUYON, JEANNE-MARIE BOUVIER DE LA MOTHE (1648-1717)
Also: Madame Guyon. French mystic. Very influential through her teaching on "pure love." Condemned and imprisoned as a Quietist.
WP 10, 390.

HAAN, WIM DE (1913-1967)
Described an intense mystical experience in a Japanese prison camp; but was not able to give it form until he took up art.

HADEWYCH (13th century)
Flemish mystic. Love mysticism. Her poetry and prose in her mother tongue have great literary merit.
WP 10, 420, 421.

HAKIM AT-TIRMIDHI, al- (d. 898)
Reflected theosophically on Sufi mysticism.
Hi 753, 754. NEB 22, 19.

HAKUIN (1685-1768)
Japanese Zen master, poet, painter, sculptor, writer. Revived Rinzai-Zen. Detailed description of mystical experiences and their accidental phenomena, based on episodes in his own life.
NEB 5, 627. POP 86. EM 111.

HALLADJ, MANSUR AL- (858-922)
Also: al-Husain ibn Mansur al-Hallaj. One of the most important of the "God-intoxicated" Sufis. Executed as a pantheist in Baghdad. Later seen as a "martyr for love": his statement, "I am God," being short for "God loves Himself, I am the image of that."
WP 10, 449. Hi 159, 160. NEB 22, 19, 20.

HAMMARSKJÖLD, DAG HJALMAR AGNA CARL (1905-1961)
Swedish diplomat. Secretary-General of the United Nations. His mystical outlook is seen in his diary.
WP 10, 468.

HAMZAH, PANSURI (ca. 1600)
Malay mystic. Also significant through his creative use of the Malay language.
WP 10, 471.

HEINRICH OF NÖRDLINGEN (d. after 1379)
Priest. Central figure in the circle of the Friends of God in Basel.
RGG III, 203.

HERACLITUS (ca. 544-484 B.C.)
Greek philosopher. *Panta rhei* (everything flows): The one is made up of all things, and all things issue from the one, impelled by the Logos. "God is day and night, winter and summer, war and peace, satiety and hunger."
WP 11, 131. EM 115.
Bibliography: J. Burnet, *Early Greek*

Philosophy, Adam and Charles Black, 1892. Warren A. Shibles, *Models of Ancient Greek Philosophy*, Vision Press Ltd., n.d.

HERMES TRISMEGISTUS
Mythical figure to whom the complete knowledge of God, heaven, and earth was revealed. In Europe he was reputed to be the author of a compilation of Egyptian writings from between the third century B.C. and the third century A.D.
WP 11, 131. POP 25.
Bibliography: See above: CORPUS HERMETICUM.

HERP, HENDRIK (ca. 1400-1473)
Dutch mystical writer. His works, published in many languages, have gained the Flemish mystic world-wide recognition.
WP 11, 136, 137.

HESSE, HERMANN (1877-1962)
German-Swiss author. Main theme: the search for the true self. Much read in the hippy culture.
WP 11, 158.

HESYCHIUS OF SINAI (eighth-ninth century)
Also Hesychius of Batos. Monk in Batos. Described the way of silent attention (hesychia) as a form of mysticism.
EDM 202, 203.

HIERONYMUS A MATRE DEI (1545-1614)
Also: Jeronimo Gracián. Friend of Teresa of Avila. Carmelite. Mystical writer.
WP 11, 179.

HILDEGARD OF BINGEN (1098-1179)
German mystic. Very talented in science, music and literature. Famous for her visions. Abbess of the Benedictine cloister in Bingen.

WP 11, 182, 183.
Bibliography: Hildegard of Bingen, *Scivias*, and *Book of Divine Works*, Santa Fe: Bear & Company, 1987. Strehlow and Hertzka, *Hildegard of Bingen's Medicine*, Santa Fe: Bear & Company, 1988. R. Boenig, "Music and Mysticism in Hildegard von Bingen's *O ignis spiritus paracliti*" in *Studia mystica*, 9, 1986.

HILTON, WALTER (ca. 1330-1396)
English priest. Chiefly known for his mystical treatise, *The Scale of Perfection*.
RGG III, 327-328.
Bibliography: Walter Hilton, *The Scale of Perfection*, ed. by E. Underhill, London, 1923. Josef E. Milosh, *The Scale of Perfection & the English Mystical Tradition*, Bks Demand UMI.

HOBURG, Christian (1607-1675)
German clergyman. Chief representative of the mystically minded "spiritualists."
RGG III, 373, 374.

HONEN (1133-1212)
Also: Honen Shonin/Enko Daishi/Genku. Founder of the Yodo-Shu (Pure Land) sect. Taught the gradual way.
NEB 6, 34 (see also: 9, 807; 10, 744 and 15, 288).

HSUAN-TSANG (597-664)
Also: Yuan-tsang/Chen-I/San-tsang. Chinese. In 645 returned to Ch'ang-an from India with 75 authentic Buddhist writings. Founder of the Wei-shih (pure consciousness) School.
Toynbee, 123. NEB 6, 104 (see also: 15, 285).

HSUN-TSU (313-238 B.C.)
Also: Hsuntze/Hsun Ching/Hsun Kuang. A Confucian, but one who laid emphasis on egocentric desires and on the necessity of laws.
Toynbee, 116. POP 100.

HUGH OF SAINT-VICTOR (1096-1141)
Leader of the contemplative school in the abbey of Saint-Victor in Paris.
WP 11, 370, 371.

HUI-NUNG (638-713)
Also: Hwei-neng/Hui-neng. Approached Buddhism, not as someone who had been in India, but as a Chinese. In place of prolonged meditation, he taught sudden enlightenment; a method of "catching the self" by springing traps for it, so to speak.
NEB 6, 128; 15, 289. Toynbee 125.

HUXLEY, ALDOUS LEONARD (1894-1963)
English author. Experimented with drugs and likened his experiences to those of the mystics.
WP 11, 413.

IBN AL-ARABI (1165-1240)
Also: Ibn'Arabi, Mocheiye al-Din, Mohammed ibn Ali al-Andalusi ibn al-Arabi. Spanish-Arab Sufi mystic and scholar, inspired by a Persian woman in Mecca and introduced to mysticism by two Spanish women.
WP 11, 443. Hi 182, 183. NEB 22 19, 20. POP 217, 218.

IBN-AL-FARID (1181-1235)
Egyptian Sufi. Mystical poems in Arabic.
WP 11, 443. Hi 183, 184. NEB 22, 19, 20.

IBRAHIM BEN ADHAM (d. 777)
Nobleman of Balkh. Became a convert while out hunting and adopted the life of a wandering Sufi.
Hi 193, 194.

IGNATIUS OF LOYOLA (1491-1556)
Also: Inigo Lopez de Loyola. Basque founder of a religious order (the Jesuits). His *Spiritual Exercises* is the fruit of his mystical experiences.
WP 11, 471, 472.
Bibliography: *Spiritual Exercises of St.*

Ignatius. Tr. by Anthony Mottola. Doubleday. Other editions also exist.

IKKYU (1394-1481)
Japanese Zen master of noble birth. Mixed with all kinds of people in order to experience various circumstances. Rejected the Amadist expectation of paradise. For him, paradise was to be found in the ground of the individual soul.
EM, 127. NEB 22, 315.

IPPEN (1239-1289)
Best known of the Japanese itinerant monks. Sang, danced, told tales, saw Buddha in every expression of nature. Founded the Amadist Ji-shu sect.
Toynbee 230. NEB 15, 288.

ISAAC BEN ABRAHAM IBN LATIF (ca. 1210-1280)
Spanish Kabbalist in Toledo.
EJ 10, 1446.

ISAAC THE BLIND (ca. 1160-1235)
Central figure of the early Kabbalists.
EJ 9, 35, 36.

ISAAC BEN JACOB HA-COHEN (13th century)
Spanish Kabbalist.
EJ 9, 19, 20.

ISAAC OF NINEVEH (second half of the seventh century)
Syrian mystical writer.
WP 12, 107.

ISAAC BEN SALOMON LURIA (1534-1572)
The central figure of the Kabbalistic school in Safed.
WP 14, 368. EJ 11, 572-578.

ISRAEL BEN ELIEZER (ca. 1700-1760)
Also: Baal Shem Tov. First leader of the East European Hassidic Jews.
EJ 9, 1049-1058.
Bibliography: A. Herschel, *The Circle of the Baal Shem Tov* (Chicago, 1985).

JACOB ISAAC OF LUBLIN (1745-1815)
One of the founders of Hassidism in Poland.
EJ 9, 1227, 1228.

JACOB BEN JACOB HA-COHEN (mid-13th century)
Spanish Kabbalist.
EJ 9, 1219-1220.

JACOB NAZIR (12th century)
Kabbalist, living with a group of recluses in Provence.
EJ 9, 1232.

JACOB BEN SHESHET GERONDI (mid-13th century)
Kabbalist in Gerona.
EJ 7, 507, 508.

JACOPONE DA TODI (ca. 1228-1306)
Rich and well-connected. After the death of his wife, became a whimsical mystic and a great poet. His Lauds sowed the seed of Italian drama.
WP 12, 199.
Bibliography: *The Lauds*, tr. S. and E. Hughes (London, 1982).

JEAN DE SAINT-SAMSON (1571-1636)
Blind Carmelite of Brittany. Original mystic.
DS VIII, 703-710.
Bibliography: *Oeuvres mystiques*, ed. H. Blommestijn and M. Huot de Longschamp (Paris, 1984). *L'eguillon, les flammes, les flèches et le miroir de l'amour de Dieu, propres pour enamourer l'âme de Dieu en Dieu même*, publication of the Rennes MS by H. Blommestijn (Rome, 1987).

JEFFERIES, RICHARD JOHN (1848-1887)
English author. Atheistic nature mystic.
WP 7 10, 375, 376.

JESUS OF NAZARETH (d. ca. 33)
Palestinian Jew. Words recorded by others. Preached that He was one with His Father, the deepest ground of reality. Was put on trial and crucified. He is central to the whole of European mysticism as the risen God-man.
WP 12, 295-298.

JILI, ABDU 'L-KARIM IBN IBRAHIM AL- (1365-1424)
Also: Djili. Sufi mystic.
Hi 6.

JIVA GOSVAMIN (seventh century)
Philosopher of the Bengal Vaisnava school.
NEB 21, 198.

JOACHIM OF FIORE (ca. 1130-1202)
Native of Calabria. Cistercian abbot. Founded his own society of hermits in Fiore. Influential through his original view of history: the Spirit will break through.
WP 12, 302, 303.
Bibliography: H. de Lubac, *La posterité spirituelle de Joachim de Fiore*, 2 vols. (Paris Namur, 1979-1981). McGinn, *Apocalyptic Spirituality: Treatises and Letters of Lactantius, Adso of Montier, Joachim of Fiore, the Franciscan Spirituals, Savanarola* (London, 1979).

JOENIAD, ABU EL-OASIM AL- (d. 910)
Also: Junayd of Baghdad. Sufi mystic in Baghdad.
Hi 116.

JOHN OF THE ANGELS (1536-1609)
Spanish mystic. Franciscan. Strongly influenced by Ruysbroeck.
WP 12, 372.

JOHN VAN DEN BOSCH (1588-1635)
Also: Gerard Verscharen. Dutch Capuchin. Made Northern mysticism accessible to ordinary people.
ThW, 2585, 2586.

JOHN CLIMACUS (d. 649)
Monk in Sinai. Wrote *The Ladder* (climax) *of Divine Ascent*.

WP 12, 330.
Bibliography: *The Ladder of Divine Ascent*, tr. C. Luibheid and N. Russell (London, 1982).

JOHN OF THE CROSS (1542-1591)
Also: Juan de Ypres Juan de la Cruz. Spanish mystic. Carmelite. Poet of world stature. Unique in his description of "the dark night."
WP 12, 333.
Bibliography: J. Array, *Christian Mysticism in the Light of Jungian Psychology: St. John of the Cross and Dr. C. G. Jung* (Chiloquin, 1986).

JOHN THE EVANGELIST (first century)
What he wrote on the Logos and on Love are foundational texts in Western mysticism.
WP 12, 329.
Bibliography: The New Testament and (numerous) Commentaries.

JOHN OF FÉCAMP (ca. 990-1078)
Much read writer in the Middle Ages. However, his works were usually issued under someone else's name.
WP 12, 338.

JOHN GUALBERTUS (ca. 1000-1073)
Florentine monk who founded the order of recluses known as "Camaldolensians."
WP 12, 332.

JOHN SCOTUS ERIGENA (810-877)
Head of the palace school of Charlemagne. Important for his translations of pseudo-Dionysius and for his neoplatonic view of the world.
WP 12, 337.
Bibliography: *Selections from Medieval Philosophers*, N. Y., 1930.

JORDAENS, WILLEM (ca. 1321-1372)
Flemish mystical writer and translator into Latin of Ruysbroeck's works.
WP 12, 356.

JORISZ, DAVID (1501-1556)
Glass-painter. Visionary Anabaptist. Strove for a spiritual church, and claimed to be a "new Messiah."
WP 12, 360.

JOSEPH OF COPERTINO (1603-1663)
Known as the "flying saint."
WP 12, 370.

JUDA BEN SAMUEL HA-CHASID (ca. 1150-1217)
Most important teacher of the Ashkenazi Hassidim in Germany.
EJ 10, 349.

JULIAN OF NORWICH (ca. 1342-1442)
English mystic. Recluse. Original concept of evil, and of Jesus as the Christian's "mother."
WP 12, 380.
Bibliography: *Julian of Norwich: Revelations of Divine Love*, ed. Grace Warrack, Methuen & Co. Ltd, 1901 and later editions. N. P. Tanner, *The Church in Late Medieval Norwich 1370-1532* (Leiden, 1984).

JULIANA OF CORNILLON (1192-1258)
Native of Liège. Her visions gave the impulse to the "feast of the sacraments."
WP 12, 379.

KABIR (ca. 1440-1518)
India's mystical poet. Sang praises of divine love in the vernacular.
Hi 245. NEB 6, 671.

KARO, JOSEPH (1448-1575)
Also: Caro. Central figure in a group of Jewish mystics in Safed (in the Holy Land).
WP 12, 519.
Bibliography: R. Zwi Werblowsky, *Joseph Karo: Lawyer and Mystic* (Philadelphia, 1977).

KEMPE, MARGERY (ca. 1373-1440)
Mother of fourteen children. Very emotional English mystic.
NEB 6, 795. EM, 149.
Bibliography: Cl. W. Atkinson, *Mystic and Pilgrim: The Book and the World of Margery Kempe* (Ithaca & London, 1983).

KHAN, HAZRAT INAYAT (1882-1927)
Came to the West in 1910 and founded the modern Sufi order. The first of his Sufi messages was "The Mysticism of Sound."
POP 225, 226.

KOTSK, see: Menahem Mendel of Vitebsk.

KRISHNAMURTI, JIDDU (1895-1985)
Indian mystic. Broke away from the Theosophic Movement, which had hailed him as a World Teacher. Stood up for our right to be independent seekers.
WP 13, 360.
The following books are recommended: *Krishnamurti to Himself: His Last Journal; Freedom from the Known; Think on These Things; Krishnamurti's Notebook; Meditations; On Freedom; On Living and Dying; On Nature and the Environment;* and the following books edited by Mary Lutyens; *Krishnamurti: His Life & Death. Krishnamurti: The Open Door. Krishnamurti: The Years of Awakening. Krishnamurti: The Years of Fulfillment. Krishnamurti's Journal.* Krishnamurti was a prolific modern writer.

KUHLMANN, QUIRINUS (1651-1689)
German poet. Overwrought mystic who sometimes found it difficult to express his visions in words or to translate them into action. Burned to death in Moscow.
WP 13, 400.

KUKAI (774-835)
Also: Kobo Daishi. Introduced esoteric Buddhism into Japan. Founded the Singhon school. Had a great influence. "Father of Japanese culture."
NEB 7, 28; 15, 294.

LABADIE, JEAN DE (1610-1674)
Native of Bordeaux. Founded a mystical sect which lasted in Friesland until ca. 1732 (Labadists).
WP 13, 440.

LABKYI, SGRONMA (11th-12th century)
Tibetan follower of Dampa Sangsrgyas, the Brahman from South Asia. Lived in turns as a married woman and as a nun. Her teachings, which are still practiced, are concerned with governing the passions through compassion.
EB 3, 416.

LABRE, BENOIT JOSEPH (1748-1783)
Unkempt wanderer from one European place of pilgrimage to another. Experienced mystical ecstasies. Canonized.
WP 13, 443.
Bibliography: P. Doyère, *Benoit Labre, ermite pèlerin* (Paris, 1983). A. Dhôtel, *Saint Benoit Joseph Labre* (Paris, 1983).

LANGMANN, ADELHEID (d. 1375)
Dominican nun in Engelthal. Visions of Jesus when she was a child, and as an 18-year old.
LthK 6, 787.

LAO-TSE (ca. 500 B. C.)
Also: Lao-Tzu. Legendary figure in whom Taoism finds its origin. The Tao Teh King is ascribed to him.
WP 13, 545. POP 101, 102.
Bibliography: *The Simple Way of Lao Tsze: an Analysis of the Tao Teh Canon with Comments.* Shrine of Wisdom, London, 1924. *Tao Te Ching: Lau Tzu* (Classics Series) Penguin, 1964. *Taoist*

Tales: The First Mystical Writings of Mankind's Religious Consciousness. Ed. Raymond van Over. Mentor, 1973.

LAURENTIUS VAN DE VERRIJZENS (1614-1691)
Also: Nicolaas Herman Kok of the Paris Carmel. His simple suggestions, derived from St. John of the Cross and published in various languages, were popular with Catholics and Protestants alike.

LAW, WILLIAM (1686-1761)
English religious author, profoundly influenced by Boehme.
EM, 155, 156. NEB 7, 201.

LEEUWEN, JAN VAN (1314-1378)
Mystical writer. Cook in Ruysbroeck's monastery.
WP 14, 27.

LEVI ISAAC BEN MEIR VAN BERDITCHEV (ca. 1740-1810)
One of the most celebrated of the third generation of the Hassidim in Galicia.
EJ 11, 102-104.

LUDOLF VON SACHSEN (ca. 1295-1378)
His *Life of Jesus Christ* was one of the most widely read books in the late Middle Ages, with 420 editions in all European languages.
WP 14, 343.

LULL, RAMON (1232-1315)
Also: Raymond Lully. Catalan mystic. Original mystic who tried to bridge the gap between Christians and Moslems.
Bibliography: *Selected Works of Ramon Lull (1232-1316)*. Edited and translated by A. Bonner, 2 vols, Princeton U. Press, 1985.

LUTHER, MARTIN (1483-1546)
Reformer (of the Church). Originally an Augustinian monk, he made a deep study of various mystical tendencies, where his greatest affinity was for Tauler. He rejected the neoplatonic mysticism of pseudo-Dionysius. As he said, he was able to "speak from experience."
WP 14.
Bibliography: B. R. Hoffmann, *Luther and the Mystics* (1976).

MACARIUS THE GREAT (ca. 300-390)
Hermit in the Egyptian desert.
WP 14, 435.

MADHWA (1199-1278)
Hindu. Many parallels with the life of Jesus. Dualistic: said that God and the self are opposite poles, independent and dependent. He founded a Bhakti sect.
NEB 7, 654.

MAHADEVIYAKKA (12th century)
Hindu poetess in Kannada. Mystical love poetry. Considered herself married to Siva.
EB 8, 925 (comparable with Catharine of Siena).

MAHAVIRA (ca. 560 B.C.)
Also: Vardhamana. Founder of Jainism.
NEB 7, 696; 8, 246; 22, 274.

MALLARMÉ, STEPHANE (1842-1898)
French poet. Important for modern mysticism.
WP 14, 512, 513.
Bibliography: *Mallarmé et le Symbolisme*. H. Nicolas. Larousse, 1985.

MANI (216-277)
The "apostle of the Light" who combined elements of Christianity, Buddhism, and Zoroastrianism to form a new religion in which there was a clear choice between Light and Darkness. A mystic who made drawings of his own visions.
WP 14, 539.

MARCUS AURELIUS (121-180)
Roman Emperor. Stoic. His "Discourses with Himself" are better known as *The Meditations*.
Bibliography: *The Meditations of Marcus Aurelius*, tr. Jeremy Collier, intr. & notes by Alice Zimmern, Walter Scott, London, 1887. *Meditations*, tr. M. Staniforth, Penguin, 1964.

MARGARETA OF CORTONA (1247-1297)
Concubine, penitent, and mystic.
WP 15, 41.

MARIA OF EGYPT (d. 421)
Sinner from Alexandria. Penitent in the Jordan desert.
WP 15, 46.

MARIE DES OIGNES (1177-1213)
Mystically gifted. Withdrew from marriage and became the pivot of the first Beguines.
WP 15, 47.

MA-RUF AL KARKHI (d. 815)
Also: Abu Mahfuz B. Firuz Firuzan. Islamic recluse belonging to the school of Baghdad. Native of Karkh. Son of Christian parents. He had many pupils. Only his sayings have been handed down. People's saint.
Hi, 420, 421.

MATSUO BASHO (1644-1694)
Japan's greatest poet. Mainly famous for his Haiku. Lived the life of a wanderer.
WP 3, 402.

MAUMIGNY, RENÉ DE (1837-1917)
Jesuit. Drawing on his own experience described mysticism as a normal development.
ThW, 3182.

MAXIMUS CONFESSOR (580-662)
Brilliant initiator of Byzantine mysticism. More than 90 works.

WP 15, 148.
Bibliography: *Selected writings*, tr. G. Pelikan (London, 1985).

MECHTHILD OF HACKEBORN (1241-1299)
Also: Mechthild of Helfta. German mystic. Her mystical experiences were recorded by her pupil Gertrude of Helfta.
WP 15, 166.
Bibliography: *The Book of Gostlye Grace of Mechtild of Hackeborn*, edited by Th. A. Halligan (Toronto, 1979).

MECHTHILD OF MAGDEBURG (ca. 1210-1282, or 1294)
Beguine, and later Cistercian nun, in Helfta. Her notes formed the basis of the oldest mystical work in German.
WP 15, 166.
Bibliography: OGE 87, No. 477-481.

MENAHEM MENDEL OF KOTSK (1781-1859)
Original leader of the Hassidic movement in Poland.
EJ 10, 1222-1224.

MENAHEM MENDEL OF VITEBSK (1730-1788)
Hassidic leader in Lithuania, Minsk and Palestine.
EJ 11, 1310.

MENG-TSE (372-289 B.C.)
Also: Mencius. Confucian philosopher with a mystical outlook, who laid emphasis on virtue rather than law.
NEB 8, 2. POP 103.

MERSWIN, RULMAN (1307-1382)
Merchant in Strasbourg. His writings were very influential among the "Friends of God."
WP 19, 462.

MICHAEL A. S. AUGUSTINO (1622-1684)
Flemish Carmelite. Mystical writer. Spiritual friend of Maria Petyt.
LthK 7, 399.

MILAREPA, JETSUN (1052-1135)
Also: Mi-la-ra-pa. Tibetan mystic, poet, and singer. After renouncing black magic, he spent many years under the tutelage of Marpa (1012-1096). He himself attracted many pupils, and is still influential in Tibet.
WP 15, 369. NEB 15, 294. POP 82.
Bibliography: W. Y. Evans-Wentz (ed.), *Tibet's Great Yogi Milarepa* (Oxford, 1978).

MOEHASIBI, AL-HARITH BEN ASSAD AL-(781-857)
Also: Muhasibi. Poet of the Iraqi school: asceticism is purification of the soul in order to pave the way for union with God.
NEB 8, 400, 401. Hi 541, 542. EM, 183.

MOHAMMED (570-632)
Politically talented prophet of Mecca. Founder of Islam. His mystical experience took the form of a heavenly journey.
WP 15, 458-460. POP 228, 229.
Bibliography of mysticism in Islam: NEB 22, 18-25 (bibliography 43). POP, 215-234.

MOLINOS, MIGUEL DE (1628-1696)
Spanish mystic. Influential leader in Rome. His teaching on silent prayer and absorption in God was denounced as "Quietism" and he was given a life sentence.

MORDECHAI BEN JUDA DATO (1525-1600)
Italian Kabbalist.
EJ 5, 1313.

MOSES (13th century B.C.)
Led the Exodus of the Children of Israel out of Egypt. Had a personal encounter with the Living God.
WP 15, 568.
Bibliography: The Bible. W. Coats, "Moses, Heroic Man", *Journal for the Study of the Old Testament*, Supplement 57, 1988.

MOSES BEN JACOB CORDOVERO (1522-1570)
Kabbalist. Systematized the Zohar and other writings.
EJ 5, 967-970.

MOSES BEN SHEM TOV DE LEON (ca. 1240-1305)
Also: Moses de Leon. Kabbalistic leader. Writer of the greater part of the Zohar.
EJ 12, 425-427.

MOSES BEN SOLOMON BEN SIMEON OF BURGOS (1230-1300)
Also: Moses de Burgos. Leading Kabbalist in Castile.
EJ 12, 427.

MOSES MAIMONIDES (1135-1204)
Spanish Jew, philosopher, and physician. Wrote the standard work of Jewish mystical philosophy, his *Guide to the Perplexed*.
WP 14, 483. EJ 11, 754-781. POP, 240.

MÜLLER, HEINRICH (1631-1675)
Lutheran. Religious writer in the mystical-erotic tradition.
RGG IV, 1169.

MÜNZER, THOMAS (1490-1525)
Also: Müntzer. Leader of a radical religious popular movement. Defeated at Frankenhausen.
WP 16, 59.

MUSO SOSEKI (1275-1351)
Celebrated Japanese Zen master. Wielded political power. Also known as an artist.
NEB 22, 315; and 2, 335. WP 15, 455-457.

NACHMAN OF BRESLOV (1772-1811)
Hassidic teacher in Eastern Europe.
EJ 12, 782-787.

Bibliography: A. Green, *Tormented Master: a Life of Rabbi Nachman of Bratslav* (Alabama, 1979). *Rabbi Nachman's Stories*, tr. with notes by Aryeh Kaplan, The Breslov Research Institute, 1983.

NACHMANIDES (1194-1270)
Catalan poet and Kabbalist.
EJ 12, 774-782.

NAJMUDDIN KUBRA (d. ca. 1220)
Sufi master of Central Asia. Described the psychological phenomena of the mystic way.
NEB 22, 19.

NAMMALVAR (eighth-ninth century)
Hindu mystic and poet. Bride mysticism focused on Krishna.
NEB 1, 304 and 27, 728.

NANAK (1469-1539)
Mystic. First guru of the Sikhs.
NEB 8, 499.

NEUMANN, THERESE (1898-1962)
German woman of Konnersreuth. Widely known for her mystical phenomena.
WP 16, 309.
Bibliography: E. Boniface, *Thérèse Neumann, la crucifiée de Konnersreuth, devant l'histoire et la science: essai d'introduction à l'étude de la phenomenologie mystique* (Paris, 1980).

NICEPHORUS THE HERMIT (13th century)
As far as is known, the first to practice the "Jesus prayer."
EDM, 228, 229.

NICHEREN (13th century)
Ardent priest, apocalyptic visionary. Founded a lotus-sutra sect named for him. He preached a return to the most ancient Buddhist texts.
NEB 16, 680, 681. WP 16, 361.

NICLAES, HENDRIK (1502-1580)
Merchant, mystic. Founded the "Family of Love" in Amsterdam.
WP 16, 362.
Bibliography: A. Hamilton, *The Family of Love* (Cambridge, 1981).

NICOLAI, PHILIPP (1556-1608)
Lutheran hymn writer in the mystical-erotic tradition.
WP 16, 366.

NICOLAS OF CUSA (1401-1464)
Son of a boatman in Cusa. Diplomat, mystic, versatile and original thinker. Trained by the Brethren of the Common Life in Deventer.
WP 16, 364-365.
Bibliography: P. Moffitt Watts, *Nicolaus Cusanus: A Fifteenth Century Vision of Man, Studies in the History of Christian Thought, 30* (Leiden, 1982).

NICOLAS OF FLUE (1417-1487)
Father of ten children. Retired to a cloister in Flueli. Big political influence on the Swiss Confederacy.
WP 16, 365.

NOVALIS (1772-1801)
Pseudonym of Friedrich Leopold Freiherr von Hardenberg. Poet and writer. Romantic mystic.
WP 16, 505.

OETINGER, FRIEDRICH CHRISTOPH (1702-1782)
German theosophical clergyman thinking along the same lines as Boehme. He believed that God was corporeal, and has been followed in this by Swabian Pietism and by Anthroposophy.
WP 16, 576.

OLIER, JEAN-JACQUES (1608-1657)
French mystic. Blind. Founded the priestly congregation of Saint-Sulpice.
WP 17, 62.

OMAR KHAYYAM (ca. 1062-1123)
Persian Sufi poet. One of the world's
great writers.
WP 17, 77. NEB 8, 945; 22, 47, 44.
Bibliography: *The Sufistic Quatrains of
Omar Khayyam in Definitive Form*,
including the Translations of
Fitzgerald, Whinfield, Nicolas. With
prefaces by each translator and a gen-
eral introduction dealing with Omar's
place in Sufism. Robert Arnot, Willey
Book Co., N. Y., 1908. *The Quatrains of
Omar –i Khayyam*. Persian text taken
from two newly discovered oldest
manuscripts with an English prose
version by Friedrich Rosen, Luzac &
Co., London, 1928. *Omar Khayyam as a
Mystic*. Jamshedji E. Saklatwalla.
Folcroft, 1928.

ORIGEN (ca. 185-254)
One of the most original thinkers of his
age. Lived in Alexandria. His mysti-
cism shows most clearly in his Bible
commentaries, especially the one on
the Song of Solomon.
WP 17, 263-265.
Bibliography: *Origen: Selected Writings*,
ed. Rowan A. Greer, Paulist Pr., 1979.
*Origen, the Song of Songs: Commentary
& Homilies*, ed. W. J. Burghardt, et. al.,
Paulist Pr., 1957.

OSUNA, FRANCISCO DE (ca. 1492-1540)
Spanish Franciscan. His comprehen-
sive mystical work, *The Spiritual
Alphabet* was used by St. Teresa of
Avila in her prayer life.
RGG IV, 1745.
Bibliography: L. Calvert, "Images of
Darkness and Light in Osuna's
'Spiritual Alphabet Books,'" in: *Studia
Mystica 8*, 1985, No. 2, 38-44.

PACHOMIUS (ca. 287-347)
Monk in Upper Egypt. Founder of the
cenobitic communities.
WP 17, 360.

PARACELSUS, PHILIPPUS AUREOLUS (1493-
1541)
Also: Theophrastus Bombastus von
Hohenheim. Swiss doctor and
alchemist. For him, God-knowledge is
self-knowledge.
WP 17, 434.
Bibliography: *Magic into Science: the
Story of Paracelsus*. H. M. Pachter,
Henry Schuman, New York, 1951.
*The Occult Causes of Disease, being a
compendium of the teachings laid down in
his Volumen Paramirum by Bombastus
von Hohenheim, better known as
Paracelsus*. E. Wolfram, tr. Agnes Blake,
Rider & Co., London, n.d.

PARMENIDES (ca. 512-443 B.C.)
Shaman and philosopher. Gained his
insights during visionary "journeys to
the sky": all that exists is the One.
WP 17, 458. EM 210, 211.

PASCAL, BLAISE (1633-1662)
Mathematician and scientist. Also a
defender of the Christian faith: the
heart has its reasons which are
unknown to reason.
WP 17, 477, 478.
Bibliography: *A Third Testament*.
Malcolm Muggeridge. Little, Brown &
Co., Canada Ltd., 1976.

PAUL OF THE CROSS (1694-1775)
Also: Paolo Francesco Danei. Mystic,
and missionary to the impoverished
peasantry of Northern Italy.
WP 17, 50.

PAUL OF TARSUS (d. ca. A.D. 60)
Raised in an orthodox Jewish sect.
Converted by a heavenly vision of
Jesus. Spoke of his ecstasies, and for-
mulated a mystical vision of Christ,
His Body (the Church) and the New
Man.
WP 17, 502, 503.

PAZZI, MARIA MADDALENA DEI (1566-1607)
Italian mystic. Ecstatic visions. Carmelite in Florence.
WP 7, 15, 195.

PETYT, MARIA (1623-1677)
Also: Maria a Sancta Teresia. Recluse attached to the Carmelite Church in Mechlin (Malines). Recorded in her diary astonishingly detailed descriptions of her mystical life. From both a literary and a psychological point of view, hers are among the most interesting of 17th century writings.
WP 18, 99.

PHILO OF ALEXANDRIA (ca. 25 B.C.–A.D. 45)
Jewish Hellenist, philosopher and mystic.
WP 18, 111, 112.
Bibliography: *The Contemplative Life. The Giants and Selections.* (London, 1981).

PICO DELLA MIRANDOLA, GIOVANNI (1403-1494)
Native of Florence. Expressed a new mystical vision of mankind.
WP 18, 125.

PINTO, FREI HEITOR (1528-1584)
Portuguese mystical writer. Also of literary importance.
WP 18, 142.

PLATO (428-348 B.C.)
Greek philosopher. He has been extremely influential on Western thought.
WP 18, 190, 191.
Bibliographical note: Plato's works are always in print in various editions. He has inspired the many authors of books on Atlantis (Ignatius Donnelly, *Atlantis: The Antediluvian World*, New York, 1882; Lord Arundell, *The Secret of Plato's Atlantis*, London, 1885; and the rest).

PLOTINUS (ca. 204-270)
Egyptian. Gave a more mystical interpretation of Plato. Spiritual father of neoplatonism.
WP 18, 207.
Bibliography: *The System of Plotinus: A Synthesis of the Plotinian Philosophic Religious Mysticism.* The Shrine of Wisdom, London, 1924. *Plotinus.* G. R. Mead. Holmes, 1983. *Plotinus: Essay on the Beautiful.* Tr. Thomas Taylor. Holmes, 1984.

POIMANDRES
Visionary teacher of Hermes Trismegistus. Also title of a treatise included in the Corpus Hermeticum, in which fundamental issues are discussed in a question-and-answer session with Hermes.
Bibliography: *The Divine Pymander of Hermes Trismegistus: an Endeavour to Systematize and Elucidate the Corpus Hermeticum.* The Shrine of Wisdom, London, 1923. Segal, R. A., *The Poimandres as Myth: Scholarly Theory and Gnostic Meaning* (Leiden, 1986).

PONTE, LUDOVICUS DE (1554-1624)
Also: Luis de la Puente.
Spanish Jesuit. Spiritual writer whose main concern was to give mysticism a theological foundation.
ThW, 3911, 3912. RGG V, 460.

PORDAGE, JOHN (1607-1681)
Anglican mystic who had a great affinity for Boehme.
RGG V, 463.

PORETE, MARGARET (d. 1310)
Also: Marguerite de Hainaut. A Beguine of Valenciennes. Wrote *The Mirror of Simple Souls*, which was later issued anonymously or under another name and was widely read. On

account of this book, Porete herself was condemned and burned in Paris. Bibliography: *Mirror of Simple Souls.* Ed. by John Griffiths. Crossroad, New York, 1981. "Le procès d'inquisition contre Marguerite Porete et Guiard de Cressonessart (1309-1310)" in: *Revue d'histoire ecclésiastique*, 81, 1986, pp. 47-94.
OGE 84, pp. 388, 389; 87, No. 375.

PORPHYRY (234-306)
Greek philosopher. Made the thought of Plotinus more accessible and added his own interpretation of it.
WP 18, 305, 306.

PSEUDO-DIONYSIUS THE AREOPAGITE, (ca. 500)
Unknown early Christian writer who concealed his identity behind the name of Dionysius the Areopagite, a convert of the apostle Paul. Was very influential on Medieval mysticism.
WP 18, 444, 445. DS III, 286-429.
Bibliography: *The Mystical Theology and the Celestial Hierarchies of Dionysius the Areopagite*, with commentaries by the editors of the Shrine of Wisdom and poem by St. John of the Cross. The Shrine of Wisdom. Fintry Brook, 1949. A. Louth, *The Origin of the Christian Mystical Tradition: From Plato to Denys* (Oxford, 1981).

PULLEN, JAN PELGRIM (ca. 1520-1608)
Limburg mystic. Most of his mystical works remain unpublished.
WP 18, 469.

PYTHAGORAS (ca. 575-after 500 B.C.)
Shamanistic philosopher of Southern Italy, invoked by the Pythagoreans. He himself wrote nothing. He taught purity through insight into the universe; which, he said, is determined by numbers.
WP 18, 469.

Bibliography: *Pythagoras: A short account of his Life and Philosophy.* Leslie Ralph. With a foreword by H. R. H. Prince Peter of Greece. "Krikos," London, 1961.

QUSHAYRI, AL- (980-1074)
Also: al Kushairi, Abu l'Kassim abd. al. Karim. Wrote a book on Sufism to demonstrate its orthodoxy.
NEB 22, 53. Hi, 362.

RABIA AL-ADAWIYA (d. 803)
Also: Rabia of Basra. Poetess of Basra. First to formulate the Sufi ideal of a disinterested love without hope of paradise or dread of hell.
NEB 22, 19. Hi, 603, 604. EM, 229.

RADHAKRISHNAN, SARVEPALLI (1888-1975)
Indian thinker, basing himself on the Vedanta and influenced by Western philosophers.
WP 18, 535.

RAMAKRISHNA (1836-1886)
Indian mystic and guru. Studied all religions and concluded that the essence of their mysticism was the same. His chela, Vivekananda, founded the Ramakrishna movement.
WP 18, 566. NEB 9, 917; 20, 596 and 584.

RAMANANDA (1370-1440)
Hindu mystic and poet. Inspirer of Kabir. Replaced erotic veneration of Krishna by mystical veneration of Rama-Sita.
NEB 9, 918.

RAMANUJA (1050-1137)
The first Hindu mystic who saw consciousness of *atman*, not as an end in itself, but as a phase of the process. The identity of the ego and God meant: I do not exist independently. Mysticism is a love affair.
WP 18, 567, 568. NEB 9, 918, 919.

RICHARD OF SAINT-VICTOR (1123-1175)
Mystical theologian of the school of
Saint-Victor in Paris. Exercised a great
influence through his methodical
description of the mystical process.
Scots by birth.
WP 19, 226.

ROLLE, RICHARD (ca. 1300-1349)
Also: Richard Rolle of Hampole.
English mystic. For a long time the
most widely read mystical writer in
England.
NEB 10, 146.
Bibliography: *Richard Rolle & de Holy
Boke Gratia Dei: An Edition with
Commentary*. Mary Luke Arntz. Ed.
James Hogg. Longwood Pub. Group,
1981. *Richard Rolle's Expositio Super
Novem Lectiones Mortuorum*. Malcolm
Moyes. Ed. James Hogg. Longwood
Pub. Group, 1984.

ROSA OF LIMA (1586-1617)
Also: Isabella of Lima. Mystic of Lima,
Peru.
WP 18, 388.
Bibliography: *The Life of S. Rose of Lima*.
Ed. F. W. Faber, London, 1847.

RUMI, JALAL AD-DIN (1207-1273)
Greatest mystical poet of Persia. His
love affair with Shamsi Tabriz in
Konya (Turkey) was a source for him
of mystical love, which he expressed
in poetry, song, and Dervish dance.
WP 7, 360. Hi, 105-107. NEB 6, 475.
POP, 232.

RUPERT OF DEUTZ (1075-1130)
Benedictine from Liège, abbot in
Deutz.
WP 19, 469.

RUYSBROECK, JOHN (1293-1381)
Brabant mystic. Wrote in his native
language. Trinitarian mysticism. His
works quickly spread abroad. He is
one of the "greats."

WP 19, 493, 494.
Bibliography: *John Ruusbroec: The
Spiritual Espousals, the Sparkling Stone
& Other Works*. Tr. James A. Wiseman,
Paulist Press, 1985.

SABBATAI ZEVI (1626-1676)
Kabbalist of Turkey. False Messiah
with many adherents in the Jewish
diaspora.
WP 20, 410.

SADI, MOSLIH AL'DIN ABU MOHAMMED
ABDALLAH (ca. 1200-1292)
Persian poet in Shiraz. Linguistic
virtuoso. Mystical tendency.
WP 19, 535.

SAHL AT-TUSTRARI (818-896)
Reflected theosophically on Sufi mys-
ticism.
Hi, 633, 634.

SAINT-EXUPÉRY, ANTOINE DE (1900-1944)
French writer, aviator, mystic.
WP 19, 545.

SAINT-MARTIN, LOUIS CLAUDE DE (1743-
1803)
French theosophist and admirer of
Boehme.
RGG V, 1316-1317.
Bibliography: *The Unknown Philosopher,
Louis Claude de Saint-Martin*. A. E.
Waite, Rudolf Steiner Publications,
1970.

SALOMON BEN JUDA IBN GABIROL (1020-
1057)
Also: Gabirol. Jewish poet. Native of
Spain. His poems have much in com-
mon with those of the Sufis.
EJ 7, 235-246.

SALOMON BEN MOSES HA-LEVI ALKABEZ
(1505-1576)
Also: Shelomoh Halevi Alkabez. Poet
and mystic. Kabbalist. His hymn:

"Come, my beloved, with chorusing praise, welcome the Sabbath Bride, Queen of the days," is still sung at the beginning of the Sabbath.
EJ 2, 635.
Bibliography: This hymn (tr. by Solomon Solis-Cohen) appears in editions of *A Book of Jewish Thoughts, collected and arranged by the Chief Rabbi.* Eyre & Spottiswoode Ltd., 1917.

SANAI (ca. 1050-1131)
Also: Sanayi. Persian poet and mystic.
NEB 22, 20 and 10, 402.

SCHLEIERMACHER, FRIEDRICH ERNST DANIEL (1768-1834)
German Protestant theologian. Reflected on the mystical core of religion.
WP 20, 187.
Bibliography: E. Benz, *The Mystical Sources of German Romantic Philosophy.* Tr. Blair Reynolds, et. al., Pickwick, 1983.

SCHWENKFELD, KASPAR VON (1489-1561)
German Evangelical theologian. Sought to base church life on a form of mystical spirituality.
WP 20, 251.

SHANKARA (788-820)
India's greatest philosopher. During his short life, vivified the Upanishads. Taught Advaita (non-duality): the one reality is Brahman, the rest is Maya. Repose is the experience of the identity of Atman and Brahman.
NEB 10, 418, 419. WP 20, 56.

SHEN-HSIN (606-706)
Chinese Zen Buddhist, leader of the Northern School, which taught the gradual path.
Toynbee, 125.

SHIBLI, BEN DJAHDAR AL- (861-945)
Official who, after his conversion, expressed his enthusiasm in a rather bizarre way in the mystical circles of Baghdad. He was locked up in a madhouse. His opinions have been handed down.
Hi, 692, 693.

SHINRAN (1173-1262)
Reformed the Jodoshu sect to Jodoshinshu (Real Pure Land). Taught the sudden way. He inclined to Quietism, but founded an active sect.
Toynbee, 240.

SIMEON THE STYLITE (ca. 389-459)
Withdrew to the top of a pillar outside Antioch, making it higher and higher until it had risen twenty meters.
WP 20, 379.

SOLOVYEV, VLADIMIR SERGEIEVITCH (1853-1900)
Russian philosopher and poet. Mystically inspired.
WP 20, 530.
Bibliography: Sutton, J., *The Religious Philosophy of Vladimir Solovjov: Towards a Reassessment.* Library of Philosophy and Religion (1988).

SPENER, PHILIPP JAKOB (1635-1705)
Leader of the Lutheran Pietists in Germany.
WP 21, 63.

SPINOZA, BARUCH DE (1637-1677)
Also: Benedict Spinoza. Sephardic Jewish philosopher born in the Netherlands. Attempted to combine Jewish mystical tradition with physical science.
WP 21, 80-82.
Bibliography: *Spinoza: Selections.* Ed. John Wild, Charles Scribner's Sons, New York, 1930.

STAGEL, ELISABETH (d. ca. 1360)
Also: Stagelin. Dominican nun in Zürich. Friend of Suso. Suso's work

has been preserved through her notes and correspondence.
LthK 9, 1006.

STEINER, RUDOLF (1861-1925)
Developed Anthroposophy and then broke with the Theosophical Society. Great influence on modern mysticism, education, and the arts. The *Complete Edition* of 1956 already comprises 200 parts.
WP 21, 194. POP, 330-334.
Bibliography: *Sun at Midnight: The Rudolf Steiner Movement and the Western Esoteric Tradition*. Geoffrey Ahern, Aquarian Press, 1984. *Teaching and Initiations of the Old Rosicrucians: Three Lectures Delivered by Dr. Steiner in Dornach, January, 1924*. Distributed privately but probably in the *Complete Edition*.

SUHRAWARDI-AL-MAQTOEL (ca. 1155-1191)
Persian Sufi. Leader of the "enlightenment" school. Preached a mystical doctrine in which Zoroastrianism and Hermeticism went together. Executed in Aleppo.
NEB 22, 22.

SURIN, JEAN JOSEPH (1600-1665)
French mystic. Jesuit. Unable to assimilate his experiences.
LthK 9, 1194.
Bibliography: S. Breton, *Deux mystiques de l'excès: J.-J. Surin et Maître Eckhart* (Paris, 1983).

SUSO, HENRY (ca. 1295-1366)
Also: Seuse. Dominican. Impressionable mystic. Pupil of Eckhart. Worked in Switzerland and the Upper Rhine area. Friend of Elisabeth Stagel.
WP 21, 362.

SWEDENBORG, EMANUEL (1668-1772)
Swedish scientist. Attempted a scien-

tific description of the spirit world he saw in visions. In 1788 his followers founded the church of "The New Jerusalem."
WP 21, 370.
Bibliography: *Compendium of Swedenborg's Writings*. S. M. Warren, Swedenborg Society, 1885. *Swedenborg: Life and Teaching*. G. Trobridge, Swedenborg Society, 1945. *The Universal Human and Soul-body Interaction*, ed. G. F. Dole (London, 1984).

SYMEON THE NEW THEOLOGIAN (ca. 949-1022)
Byzantine mystic.
RGG VI, 554.
Bibliography: B. Fraigneau-Julien, *Les sens spirituels et la vision de Dieu selon Syméon le Nouveau Théologien* (Paris, 1985).

TAGORE, RABINDRANATH (1861-1941)
Also: Thakur. Bengali poet, philosopher, and mystic. Attempted to combine Eastern and Western thought. Nobel prize for literature.
WP 21, 422.

TAULER, JOHN (1300-1361)
Dominican, mystic, pupil of Eckhart. Central figure in the circle of the "Friends of God."
WP 21, 466.
Bibliography: *Johannes Tauler: Sermons*. Tr. Maria Shrady, Paulist Press. *Johann Tauler: Predigten*. Insel-Verlag, Leipzig, 1923. G. Eschnach, *Jean Tauler: la naissance de Dieu en toi* (Paris, 1986).

TEILHARD DE CHARDIN, PIERRE (1881-1955)
Jesuit. French geologist, paleontologist, and philosopher. Mystical vision of an evolving universe which is also an unfolding of consciousness and of the mystical body of Christ.
WP 21, 488.

TENNYSON, ALFRED (1809-1892)
English poet. Described his mystical experiences.
WP 21, 522, 523.
Bibliography: Tennyson's early poem, "The Hesperides." Not in the Works, but quoted in Flavia Anderson's *The Ancient Secret*, p. 83. Gollancz, 1953.

TERESA OF AVILA (1515-1582)
Also: Teresa de Cepeda y Ahumada. Spanish mystic. Carmelite. Very efficient reformer. Provided an exact description of the mystical way and its phenomena.
WP 22, 35.
Bibliography: *Collected Works of St. Teresa of Avila*, tr. Kieran Kavanaugh & Otilio Rodriguez. ICS, 1976-80-85.

TERSTEEGEN, GERHARD (1697-1769)
German mystical poet and pastor. Very much under the influence of Madame Guyon's Quietism.
WP 21, 540.

THAKAR, VIMALA
Friend of Krishnamurti. She was an Indian mystic.
POP, 253.

THÉRÈSE OF LISIEUX (1873-1897)
Also: Thérèse Martin. French mystic. Carmelite. Experienced and described the "short way." Original mystical passages were left out of the first editions of her writings.
WP 22, 35.

THOMAS AQUINAS (1225-1274)
Dominican. Systematized Medieval thought. Only at the end of his life did he have a mystical experience.
WP 22,53.
Bibliography: *Aquinas Reader*. Ed. Mary T. Clark, Doubleday. *Thomas von Aquino: Abhandlung uber den Stein der Weisen*. Tr. Gustav Meyrink. Leipzig, 1925. (C. G. Jung regards these two short treatises on alchemy, ascribed to Thomas Aquinas, as spurious, but Meyrink argues in favor of their authenticity.)

THOMAS À KEMPIS (1379-1471)
Writer of the world-famous book, *The Imitation of Christ*.
WP 33, 53.

THOMAS OF VERCELLI (d. 1246)
Also: Thomas Gallus. Turned the Andreas cloister in Vercelli into a study center for mysticism. Considerable influence on Franciscan mysticism, especially through his pupil, Anthony of Padua.
LthK 10, 149.

THOMPSON, FRANCIS (1859-1907)
British poet. Addicted to opium after unsuccessful studies. Passionate portrayal of his vision of the human being as relentlessly pursued by the love of God.
WP 22, 55.
Bibliography: *The Hound of Heaven & Other Poems*. Francis Thompson. Branden Pub. Co. *Francis Thompson: Poet & Mystic*. John Thompson. Folcroft, 1974.

TIKHORN OF ZADONSK (1624-1783)
Also: Tychon of Sadonsk. One of the greatest of Russian Christian mystics.
RGG VI, 1091-1092.

TODROS BEN JOSEPH HA-LEVI ABULAFIA (1220-1298)
Linked Gnostic Kabbalah in Castile with the school of Gerona.
EJ 2, 194-195.

TRAHERNE, THOMAS (ca. 1637-1674)
English poet and mystic.
WP 22, 186.
Bibliography: *Centuries of Meditations: Thomas Traherne*. Ed. Bertram Dobell. London, 1908, and reprints.

Tsjwang-Tse (369-286 b.c.)
Also: Chuang-tse, Chuang-tze, Chwang-tse, Chuang-chou, Tsjwang-tse. Amplified Taoism in a more mystical direction.
POP, 98. NEB 3, 297; 28, 396.

Tsou-yen (305-240 b.c.)
Combined the Yin-Yang doctrine with the equally ancient doctrine of the five elements.
Toynbee, 118.

Tung-Chung-Shu (ca. 176-104 b.c.)
By specifying everything as Yin, Yang or an element, everything is reduced to numbers.
Toynbee, 119, 120 and 142.

Unamuno y Jugo, Miguel de (1864-1936)
Spanish poet and novelist in the line of traditional Spanish mysticism.
WP 22, 379.

Underhill, Evelyn (1875-1941)
Mystical poet. She wrote pioneering works on mysticism.
NEB 12, 126.
Bibliography: *Mysticism*. Evelyn Underhill. Methuen, 1911 and many editions. (Her other works include: *The Life of the Spirit and the Life of To-day*; and *Concerning the Inner Life*).

Valentinus (second century a.d.)
Of Alexandria. One of the most important Gnostic teachers.
WP 22, 457.
Bibliography: *The Writings of Tertullian*, tr. Peter Holmes, T. & T. Clark, Edinburgh, 1870. (*Against the Valentinians*).

Vallabna (1473-1531)
Founder of a Bhakti sect that revered Krishna.
WP 22, 463.

Vaughan, Henry (1622-1695)
Welsh poet and mystic. [The mystical bent of his brother, Thomas Vaughan, led the latter to study alchemy, and Henry himself translated the *Hermetical Physick* of Nollius. Tr.]
WP 22, 499.
Bibliography: *The Works of Henry Vaughan*. Ed. Leonard Cyril Martin, Oxford, 1914.

Vincent de Paul (1628-1660)
Mysticism of action.
WP 23, 203.

Vivekananda (1863-1902)
Pupil of Ramakrishna. Introduced Hindu mysticism in the U.S.A. Proclaimed the World Parliament of Religions in Chicago, 1893, and saw a similarity in the mystical core of all religions.
WP 23, 244.

Weigel, Valentin (1533-1588)
German mystic. Developed a theory of knowledge on the basis of mysticism. Saw the Church as avowedly spiritual.
WP 24, 55.

Weil, Simone (1909-1943)
Jewish agnostic. Sought to clarify her experiences through Stoicism, Hinduism, Catholicism, and through solidarity with "the workers."
WP 24, 56. RGG, 1258-1259.

Wichmann von Arnstein (ca. 1230-1270)
Also: von Ruppin. Dominican of Magdeburg. Letters to nuns on the subject of mystical experiences.
WP 24, 234.

William of Saint-Thierry (1085-1148)
Also: Guillaume de Saint-Thierry. Mystic of Liège. Friend of St. Bernard. Has strongly influenced Dutch mysticism.
WP 24, 234.

Bibliography: *L'expérience spirituelle selon Guillaume de Saint-Thierry* (Paris, 1985).

YUNUS EMRE (13th century)
Sufi poet. Turkish mystical poetry and the Dervish order begin with him.
NEB 22, 22.

ZERBOLT OF ZUTPHEN, GERARD (1367-1398)
One of the Brothers of the Common Life. Was their most successful spiritual writer.
WP 24, 522.
Bibliography: G. Gerrits, *Inter Timorem et Spem, A Study of the Theological Thought of Zerbolt of Zutphen* (Leiden, 1986).

ZINZENDORF, NIKOLAUS LUDWIG VON (d. 1760)
Founder of an Evangelical Group known as the Moravian Brethren. Wrote some two thousand spiritual songs.
WP 24, 562.

ZOROASTER (between 1500 and 1200 B.C.)
Also: Zarathustra. Shaman priest. Poet. Founder of the Zoroastrian religion, which became the state religion in the Persian kingdom. Preached one God, the end of the ages, the judgment leading to heaven or hell, the thousand year reign.
WP 24, 459. NEB 29, 1078-1083.
Bibliography: *The Philosophical, Spiritual and Ethical Interpretation of the Gathas of Holy Zarathustra*. Framroz Rustomjee, Bombay, n. d. *Daily Prayers of the Zoroastrians*. Framroz Rustomjee. Colombo, 1967.

SPIRITUAL SOURCEBOOKS

For explanation of the sources abbreviated in the following text refer to page 405.

ANCRENE RIWLE (between 1135 and 1154)
Anonymous rule for recluses of Kilburn, England.
WP 2, 155.
Bibliography: A. Zettersten, *The English Text of the 'Ancrene Riwle,'* edited from Magdalene College, Cambridge MS. Pepys 2498 (Oxford, 1976). L. Georgianna, *The Solitary Self: Individuality in the 'Ancrene Wisse'* (Cambridge, MA and London, 1981).

APOPHTHEGMATA PATRUM (between 350 and 450)
Also: Sayings of the fathers/Desert fathers. Sayings of Coptic hermits and monks of Scetis (desert in Western delta of Egypt).
WP 2, 337.
Bibliography: *Apophthegmata Patrum.* E. A. Budge, Eastern Orthodox, 1975.

BHAGAVAD-GITA (ca. 200 B.C.)
The most read and appreciated text in Hindu mysticism. It forms part of a great epic, *the Mahabharata*, a collection begun ca. 1100 B.C.
WP 4, 257. POP, 195-197.
Bibliography: *The Bhagavad-Gita, with a Commentary Based on the Original Sources* by R. Zaehner (Oxford, 1979).

BHAGAVATA-PURANA (ninth-tenth century)
South India. Poetical description of the many aspects of Krishna as a divine figure. His love is human, although he himself is a spiritual being.
WP 4, 257. POP 204-205.

BOOK OF CREATION (Sefer Yetzirah)
Jewish mystical vision of the Creation: reality can be expressed numerically. Its basis is ten primordial numbers, or principles, which, together with the twenty-two letters of the Hebrew alphabet, were used by God in creating. The mystic can enter into this creative activity by counting and scanning them.
Bibliography: *Sepher Yetzirah: The Book of Formation.* W. Wynn Westcott (1887). Samuel Weiser, Inc., 1975. *The Book of Creation: Sepher Yetzirah.* Irving Friedman. Samuel Weiser, Inc., 1977. *Sefer Yetzirah: The Book of Creation.* Aryeh Kaplan. Samuel Weiser, Inc., 1990. *The Sepher Yetsira.* Carlos Suarés. Shambhala. 1976. *The Qabalah.* Papus. Thorsons Publishers Limited. 1977.

BOOK OF THE HOLY TRINITY (Buch der Heyligen Dreyfaldekeit)
Anonymous work produced at the time of the Council of Constance in 1419. Ascribed to the Franciscan, Ulmannus. Its theme is the use of alchemical gold in the service of the true faith as it fights against antichrist, who makes false gold.
Bibliography: J. van Lennep, *Alchemie* (1984). pp. 70-78.

BOOK OF THE PIOUS (Sefer ha-Chassidim)
Comprehensive work of German Hassidism.
WP 20, 273. POP, 239.

BRAHMANAS (ca. 1000 B.C.)
A collection of texts compiled by "Brahmins," in which the rituals are no longer performed in honor of a divinity but have become an end in themselves.
WP 5, 122, 123.

CLOUD OF UNKNOWING (14th century)
An anonymous English mystical treatise by someone familiar with pseudo-Dionysius.
WP 6, 320.
Bibliography: *Cloud of Unknowing*. Ed. James Walsh. Paulist Pr. 1981.
R. A. Lees, *The Negative Language of the Dionysian School of Mystical Theology: An approach to the Cloud of Unknowing*. Analecta Cartusiana, 107 (Salzburg).

CORPUS HERMETICUM (1471)
The two main treatises of Hermes Trismegistus were published in Florence under this title in 1471. This book became the basis of Western hermeticism.
WP 11, 131.
Bibliography: *Hermetica: The Ancient Greek & Latin Writings which Contain Religious or Philosophic Teachings Ascribed to Hermes Trismegistus*, 4 vols. Ed. and tr. by Walter Scott. Shambhala Publications. "The Sayings of Hermes," quoted in the *Ma' Al-Waraqi of Ibn Umail Ambix*, Vol. III, Nos. 3 & 4, London, 1949.

EVANGELICAL PEARL (early 16th century)
Written by a Beguine who died at the age of 77 in 1540. She also wrote *The Temple of our Soul*. Both works were published by Nicolaus von Essche (in 1534, 1542, and 1543 respectively).
WP 8, 408.
Bibliography: OGE 84, pp. 30-40.

I CHING (ca. 100 B.C.)
Also: The Book of Changes. The fundamental idea of this ancient Chinese work is that our well-being depends on keeping in balance with nature. Nature is composed of opposites—yin and yang. The *I Ching* takes the form of an oracle intended for consultation.
POP, 100, 101. EM, 133. Toynbee, 119, 120, 126-130.
Bibliography: *The I Ching*. Tr. James Legge. Dover, 1963. *I Ching*. Tr. Wilhelm & Baynes. RKP, 1983. *Creative Energy. Being an Introduction to the Study of the Yih King*. I. & L. E. Mears, John Murray, 1931.

MAHABHARATA. See: BHAGAVAD GITA.

ODES OF SOLOMON (early second century)
Forty-two Gnostic poems. Syrian.
WP 16, 534.

RAMAYANA (fourth century B.C.)
Great epic poem telling the story of Rama and Siva. By the sage, Valmiki.
WP 18, 568. POP, 204, 205.
Ramayana of Valmiki, 3 vols. Shri Valmiki. Tr. Hari P. Shastri. Methuen Inc., 1985.
Ramayana at a Glance. Satguru S. Keshavadas. Vishwa, 1978.

SONG OF SOLOMON
Hebrew song cycle in the Bible. Secular love is the symbol of love between God
and His bride (Israel, the Church, the mystic). Hence the book is of great impor-
tance to Western mysticism.
WP 11, 316.
Bibliography: *Le Cantique des Cantiques par Origène, Grégoire d'Elvire, Saint Bernard*.
Homélies traduites par R. Winling et par les Carmélites de Maille. Introduction
par R. Winling & A.-G. Hamman. Indications doctrinales par A.-G. Hamman.
(Paris, 1983). P. Dronke, *The Medieval Poet and his World*, pp. 209-236: "The Song
of Songs and medieval love-lyric."

TAO TE CHING (between 500 and 300 B.C.)
Also: *Tao Teh King*. Ascribed to Lao-tse, but in fact a collection of writings that
grew from the sixth century through ca. 300 B.C. Content: Tao is the way of
nature. It is the inexpressible Unity, which gives rise to duality (Yin-Yang).
WP 21, 470. See also under LAO-TSE.
Bibliography: *The Illustrated Tao Te Ching*. Element, 1993. *The Simple Way of Lao
Tsze: An Analysis of the Tao Teh Canon*. The Shrine of Wisdom, London, 1924. *The
Tao of Long Life*. Chee Soo. Gordon & Cremonesi, 1979.

TEMPLE OF OUR SOULS (ca. 1530). See EVANGELICAL PEARL.

THEOLOGIA GERMANICA
Anonymous mystical work, ascribed to Tauler, but in fact composed by an
unknown member of the Friends of God. It was highly valued by Luther, who
published it in 1516.
Bibliography: *Theologia Germanica*, tr. Susanna Winkworth. MacMillan &
Co., Ltd., 1874 and reprints. *Theologia Germanica of Martin Luther*. Ed. Bengt
Hoffman. Paulist Press, 1980.

TIBETAN BOOK OF THE DEAD
Handbook of advice for the soul after death. Used by Tibetan monks as a primer
of mystical phenomena.
WP 22, 72.
Bibliography: *Tibetan Book of the Dead*. Ed. W. Y. Evans-Wentz. Oxford University
Press, 1960.

UPANISHADS (between 1000 and 500 B.C.)
Collection of various speculations written in India between 1000 and 500 B.C.
WP 22, 393. POP, 208, 209.
Bibliography: *Upanishads: A Selection for the Modern Reader*. Tr. Eknath Easwaran.
Nilgiri Press, 1987. *The Upanisads*. Tr. by F. Max Muller. Dover, 1962.

VEDANTA SUTRAS
System of 555 sutras by Badaryana interpreting the Upanishads. They served as a basic text for later Hindu mystics such as Shankara, who commentated on them.
WP 22, 503. POP, 211.
Vedanta Sutras of Badarayana with the Commentary of Baladeva. Tr. by Srisa Chandra Vasu. Reprint of 1912 ed. AMS Press.

VEDAS (from ca. 1500 B.C.)
A compilation of writings in four parts. In order of age, starting with the earliest, these are: *Rigveda, Samaveda, Yajurveda,* and *Atharvaveda.*
WP 22, 503. POP, 210-212.
Bibliography: *Vedic Hymns.* F. Max Müller & H. Oldenberg. Gordon Press, 1974.

YOGA SUTRAS
A basic text consisting of pithy summaries of Yoga collected by Patanjali, who must have lived between the second and fifth centuries A. D.
WP 24, 390. POP, 201, 203, 355, 356.
Yoga Sutras of Patanjali. Tr. Charles Johnston. Brotherhood of Life, 1987.

ZOHAR (ca. 1280)
Basic text of the Kabbalah from the period when it was flourishing in Provence and Northern Spain. Written, in part at least, by Moses of Leon.
Bibliography: *The Zohar.* Tr. by Harry Sperling & Maurice Simon. 5 vols. The Soncino Press Ltd., 1984. *The Kabbalah Unveiled.* Tr. S. L. MacGregor Mathers. Samuel Weiser, 1983 (contains important supplementary parts of the Zohar omitted from the above). *The Kabbalah Decoded.* Tr. George Sassoon. Ed. Rodney Dale. Duckworth. 1978 (non-mystical, "manna-machine" interpretation, but offers some useful corrections and improvements of the Mathers translation). *The Holy Kabbalah.* A. E. Waite. University Books. 1976 (not a translation, but has much material on the Zohar). *The Kabbalah.* Christian D. Ginsburg. George Routledge & Sons Ltd., 1925 (contains a summary of, and notes on *The Zohar.* Is a reprint of a lecture originally published in The Proceedings of the Literary and Philosophical Society of Liverpool, 1864-1865, but without the latter's Index of Passages of the Sohar (sic) Quoted and Translated, or its Glossary of Hebrew words. Formerly the standard work in English on the Kabbalah).

BIBLIOGRAPHY

Aalders, C. *Spiritualiteit, geestelijk leven vroeger en nu* [Spirituality: Religious Life Then and Now]. The Hague, 1980.

Aarnink, L., et al. *Verkenningen in de mystiek* [Explorations in Mysticism]. On mystical experiences and how they may be cultivated. Delft, 1985.

Abelson, Dr. J. *Introduction to the Zohar.* New York: Socino Press, 1984.

Acht, C. van. *Mystieke poezie, poetische mystiek* [Mystical poetry, Poetical Mysticism]. Nijmegen, 1980.

Allis, Dr. O. T. *The Unity of Isaiah.* The Presbyterian and Reformed Publishing, 1950.

Arnauld, Antoine, and Pierre Nicole. *Logique de Port-Royal.* First published in 1662.

Aurelius, Marcus. *Meditations.* Translated by M. Staniforth. New York: Viking Penguin, 1964; New York: The Limited Editions Club, 1956.

Bacon, Sir Francis. *Meditationes Sacrae, De Haeresibus.*

Barthes, Roland. *Fragments d'un discours amoureux*, 1977. An English version titled *A Lover's Discourse: Fragments* was published by Hill & Wang, London, 1978.

Bernard of Cluny. *De Contemptu Mundi.* 12th Century.

Bernardi, S. *Abbatis Primi Clarae-Vallensis, Opera Omnia.* Editio Nova, Paris, 1854.

Blakney, Raymond Bernard. *Meister Eckhart.* New York: Harper Torchbooks, 1941.

Boyce, Mary. *A History of Zoroastrianism*, Volume 1: *The Early Period* (Leiden, 1975); and Volume 2: *Under the Achaemenians* (Leiden, 1982).

Brandsma, Titus. *Mystiek leven* (Mystical Life), an anthology gathered and introduced by Bruno Borchert. Published by Nijmegen, 1985.

Bremond, H. *Histoire littéraire du sentiment religieux en France*, 11 vols. (1916-1933).

Brewer's Dictionary of Phrase and Fable. Odhams Press Limited, n. d.; An edition edited by Ivor Evans is published by HarperCollins (New York, 1989).

Brown, J. C. *A History of Chemistry.* J. & A. Churchill, 1920.

Buber, Martin. *Ecstatic Confessions.* Edited by Paul Mendes-Flohr. San Francisco: HarperCollins, 1985.

———. *I and Thou.* New York: Macmillan, 1978.

Campbell, Joseph. *The Masks of God*, Vol. IV. New York: Viking Penguin, 1991.

Capra, Fritjof. *The Tao of Physics.* New York: Bantam, 1977; and London: Wildwood House, 1975.

———. *The Turning Point.* New York: Bantam, 1987.

Catholic Jerusalem Bible. London: Darton, Longman & Todd, 1966.

Chang Po-Tuan. *The Inner Teachings of Taoism.* Commentary by Liu I-Ming, and translation from Chinese by Thomas Cleary. Boston: Shambhala, 1986.

Cheney, Sheldon, ed. *Men Who Have Walked with God: Being the Story of Mysticism through the Ages Told in the Biographies of Representative Seers and Saints with Excerpts from their Writings and Sayings.* New York: Knopf, 1945.

The Cloud of Unknowing. An anonymous work, edited by James Walsh. (Classics of Western Spirituality Series). New York: Paulist Press, 1981.

The Confessions of Jacob Boehme. Compiled and edited by W. Scott Palmer. New York: Harper & Row, 1954. Cited in William Williams, *Unbounded Light*. York Beach, ME: Nicolas-Hays, 1992.

The Confessions of St. Augustine. Translated by F. J. Sheed. New York: Sheed & Ward, 1943.

Cooper, Irving S. *Theosophy Simplified*. New York: Gordon Press, n. d.; A revised edition is also published by the Theosophical Publishing House (Wheaton, IL, 1989).

Cruz, San Juan de la. *The Dark Night of the Soul*. Translated by Cabriela Cunninghame Graham. London: Watkins, 1922.

Culianu, Ion Petru. *Psychanodia I*. Leiden, 1983.

Däniken, Erich von. *Chariots of the Gods?*. Translated by Michael Heron. New York: G.P. Putnam's Sons, 1969.

Deblaere, A. *De Mystieke Schrijfster Maria Petyt 1623-1677*. Ghent, 1962.

A Dervish Textbook (1891); reprinted by Octagon Press, London, 1980.

The Desire to be Human. Wassenaar, 1983.

A Dictionary of the Bible, Vol. IV. Edited by James Hastings. London: T. & T. Clark, 1902.

Dionysius the Areopagite. *Mystical Theology* and *The Celestial Hierarchies*. London: Shrine of Wisdom, 1924.

The Divine Pymander and Other Writings of Hermes Trismegistus. Translated by John David Chambers. London: T. & T. Clark, 1882. Reprinted by Samuel Weiser, New York, 1972.

Dronke, Peter. *Women Writers of the Middle Ages: A Critical Study of Texts from Perpetua (d. 203) to Marguerite Porete*. Cambridge, 1984.

Dupre, Louis. *Licht uit licht: een inleiding in de christelijke mystiek*. Amsterdam, 1983; or *Light from Light: An Anthology of Christian Mysticism*. Mahwah, NJ: Paulist Press, 1988.

Eliade, Mircea. *Encyclopedia des mystiques* (Encyclopedia of Mystics) Vol. 1. Paris, 1977.

———. *Images & Symbols: Studies in Religious Symbolism*. New York: Sheed & Ward, 1961.

———. *Shamanism*. London, 1964.

Ferguson, Marilyn. *The Aquarian Conspiracy: Personal and Social Transformation in our Time*. Los Angeles: J. P. Tarcher, 1980.

Frickel, Josef. *Hellenistische Erlösung in christlicher Deutung, Die gnostische Naasenerschrift* [A Christian view of Hellenistic Salvation: The Gnostic Naasene Writings]. Leiden, 1984.

Gerhardt, Ida. *NKL-Handelsblad*, cultural supplement, "Poesie," December 27, 1991.

Gieraths, G. *Rijnlandse mystiek*. Haarlem, 1981.

Greeley, Andrew M. *Extase, een vorm van gewaarworden* [Ectasy: a Form of Awareness]. Haarlem, 1975.

Gutmann, Joseph. *Hebrew Manuscript Painting*. London: Chatto & Windus, 1979.

Gyselen, Mark. "Mijn patient was meer dan ziek" in Mark Gyselen, Paul Mommaers and J. J. C. Marlet, *Hoe Menselijk is Mystiek?* Baarn, 1979.

Hadewych, Brieven. *Oøspronklelijke Tekst en nieuw-Nederlandse Overzetting met in leidingen en aanteken ingen.* Bezorgd door F. van Bladel en B. Spaapen, Tielt, 1954.

Hammarskjöld, Dag. *Markings.* New York: Alfred A. Knopf, 1964.

Happold, F. C. *Mysticism: A Study and an Anthology.* London: Harmondsworth, 1975; and New York: Viking Penguin, 1963.

Hauschka, Rudolf. *Substanzlehre.* Germany: Vittorio Klostermann, 1946.

Henry Cornelius Agrippa of Nettesheim. *Three Books of Occult Philosopy.* London: Gregory Moule, 1651.

The Hermetic Mercuries of Raymund Lully. The Alchemical Press, 1984. Reprint of old recipes.

Holloway, Reverend Benjamin. *Originals Physical and Theological, Sacred and Profane,* Vol I. Oxford, 1751.

Huizinga, J. *Herfstij der Middleleeuwen* [The Fall Time of the Middle Ages]. Groningen, 1984.

Huxley, Aldous. *The Doors of Perception* and *Heaven & Hell.* New York: HarperCollins, 1963.

Ionesco, Eugene. *Journal en Miettes.* Saint-Armand, 1967.

Jager, Willigis. *De mystiedke weg: traditie an ervaring.* Nijmegen, 1984; or *The Way to Contemplation: Encountering God Today.* Mahwah, NJ: Paulist Press, 1987.

St. John of the Cross. *The Ascent of Mount Carmel.* Translated by David Lewis. London: Thomas Baker, 1922.

———. *The Living Flame of Love.* Translated by David Lewis. London: Thomas Baker, 1919.

———. *The Mystical Doctrine of St. John of the Cross.* An abridgement made by C. H., with an introduction by R. H. J. Stewart. London: Sheed & Ward, 1953.

James, Joseph. *The Way of Mysticism.* London: Jonathan Cape, 1950.

James, William. *The Letters of William James,* Vol. 2. Boston, 1920.

———. *Varieties of Religious Experience: A Study in Human Nature.* New York & London: Longmans Green, 1902. A recent edition was published by Viking Penguin (New York, 1982).

Jung, C. G. *Alchemical Studies.* Translated by R. F. C. Hull in *The Collected Works of C. G. Jung,* Bollingen Series XX, Vol. 13. Princeton, NJ: Princeton University Press, 1967.

———. *Dictionary of Analytical Psychology,* Arkana, 1987.

———. *Flying Saucers: A Modern Myth of Things Seen in the Skies.* New York & London, 1958. Translated by R. F. C. Hull in *The Collected Works of C. G. Jung,* Bollingen Series XX, Vol. 10. Princeton, NJ: Princeton University Press, 1970.

Jung, C. G. et al. *Man and His Symbols.* London: Aldus Books, 1964; and New York: Dell, 1964.

Kallistos, Bishop of Diokleia. *The Power of the Name, the Jesus Prayer in Orthodox Spirituality.* SLG Press, Oxford, 1977.

Kaplan, Aryeh. *Sepher Yetzirah.* York Beach, ME: Samuel Weiser, 1990.

Keynes, J. N. *Formal Logic* (Macmillan & Co., London, 1906).

Kitto. *Cyclopaedia of Biblical Literature.* 3rd ed., Adam & Charles Black, 1876.

Klimkeit, Hans-Joachim. *Manichaean Art and Calligraphy. Iconography of Religions,* XX. Leiden, 1982.

Lamoen, G.J. *Prana*, No. 37, pp. 100-104, 1984. An extensive bibliography of modern shamanism.

Lans, J., van der *Religieuze ervaring en meditatie* [Religious Experience and Meditation]. Deventer, 1980.

Lao Tsu, *Tao Teh Ching*. Translated by John C. H. Wu. New York: St. John's University Press, 1961.

Lasch, Christopher. *Culture of Narcissism: American Life in an Age of Diminishing Expectations*. New York: Norton, 1991.

Laski, Marghanita. *Ecstasy: A Study of Some Secular and Religious Experiences*. Westport, CT, 1968; *Ecstasy*. Bloomington, IN, 1961. Now available as *Ecstasy in Secular and Religious Experiences*. Los Angeles: J. P. Tarcher, 1990.

Legge, F. *Forerunners and Rivals of Christianity*, Vol. II. Columbia University Press, 1915. Reprinted by Peter Smith, New York, 1950.

Leibniz. *Principles*. New York: Everyman's Library, Dutton, 1934.

Lewis, I. M. *Religieuze extase*. Utrecht, 1972; or *Esctatic Religion*. London: Routledge, 1989.

The Little Flowers & The Life of St. Francis with the Mirror of Perfection. New York: E.P. Dutton & Co., 1910.

L. N. R. *The Book and Its Story*. London: Samuel Bagster & Sons, 1854.

Maccoby, Hyam. *De Joodse wereld* [The Jewish World]. Edited by Elie Kedourie. Antwerp, 1980.

Magdeburg, Mechtild. *Ecstatic Confessions*. Collected and introduced by Martin Buber. San Francisco: HarperCollins, 1985.

Makrakis, Apostolos. *A New Philosophy and the Philosophical Sciences*, Vol. I. Translated by Denver Cummings. New York: G. P. Putnam's Sons, 1940.

Martindale, C. C. and S. J. Burns. *The Message of Fatima*. Kent: Burns, Oates & Washbourne, 1950.

Maslow, Abraham. *Religions: Values and Peak Experiences*. New York: Viking Penguin, 1976.

———. *The Highest State of Consciousness*. Edited by John White. New York: Doubleday/Anchor, 1972.

McKeon, Prof. *Selections from Medieval Philosophers*. Charles Scribners Sons, 1930.

Merton, Thomas. *Wijsheid uit de woestiin*. Haarlem, 1979; or *The Wisdom of the Desert*. New York: New Directions, 1970. Sayings of the fourth-century desert fathers.

Mommaers, P. *Wat is mystiek?* [What is mysticism?]. Nijmegen, 1977.

Neale, J. Mason. *The Rhythm of Bernard de Marlai on the Celestial Country*, 7th ed., London, 1865.

New Century Cyclopedia of Names. New York: Appleton-Century-Crofts, 1954.

Newman, James R. *The World of Mathematics*, Vol. 4. New York: Simon & Schuster, 1956.

Nicolas, Antonio de. *The Bhagavad Gita*. York Beach, ME: Nicolas-Hays, 1990.

Oberman, H. A., and R. Hensen. *Mystiek in de Westerse kultuur*. Kampen, 1973.

Ouweneel, W. Het domein van de slang. *Christelijk handoek over occultisme en myticisme* [The Serpent's Domain: A Christian Handbook of Occultism and Mysticism]. Amsterdam, 1978.

Palmer, Cecil, and Colin Still. "The Meaning of Initiation" in *Shakespeare's Mystery Play: A Study of the Tempest*. London: 1921.

Perls, Fritz. *Gestalt Therapie. Verbatim*, compiled and edited by John O. Stevens. The Hague, 1973.

Perry, Whitall. *A Treasury of Traditional Wisdom*. Cambridge, England: Quinta Essentia, 1971.

Pfeiffer, Franz. *Meister Eckhart*. Translated by C. de B. Evans. London: John M. Watkins, 1924.

Phillips, J. B. *The New Testament of Modern English*. Geoffrey Bles, 1960.

The Philosophical Works of Descartes, Vol. 1. Translated by Elisabeth S. Haldane and G. R. T. Ross. London and New York: Cambridge University Press, 1968.

Revelations of Divine Love recorded by Julian, Anchoress at Norwich, anno Domini 1373. Edited by Grace Warrack. London: Methuen & Co., 1901.

Richard of Saint-Victor. *De Quatuor Gradibus Violentae Charitatis*. Migne, Patrologia Latina, Vol. 1. cxcvi, col. 1207.

Rümke, H. C. *Karakter en Aanleg in Verband met het Ongeloof*. Amsterdam, 1963.

Russell, Bertrand. *A History of Western Philosophy*. Allen & Unwin, Ltd., 1946.

Ruysbroeck, Jan Van. *Adornment of the Spiritual Marriage: the Book of Truth; & the Sparkling Stone*. Introduction by Guelyn Underhill. Kila, MT: Kessinger Publisher, 1992.

Scholem, Gershom. *On the Kabbalah and Its Symbolism*. New York: Schocken Books, 1969.

The Simple Way of Lao-tse. London: Shrine of Wisdom, 1924.

St. Clair, George. *Creation Records Discovered in Egypt*. David Nutt, 1898.

St. Teresa. *The Life of St. Teresa of Jesus*. Translated by David Lewis. London: Thomas Baker, 1924.

St. Thomas Aquinas. *Summa Theologica*.

Stikker. *Tao, Teilhard en Weseters denken*. Amsterdam, 1986.

Stuip, R., et al. *Visioenen* [Visions]. Utrecht, 1987.

Swedenborg, E. *The Arcana Coelestia* [Heavenly Secrets]. New York: the Swedenborg Society, n.d. *The Principia*, I: 1. Translated by Rendell & Tansley. London: The Swedenborg Society, 1912.

Thakar, Virnala. *On an Eternal Voyage*. Hilverson, 1966.

Theologia Germanica. Translated from German by Susanna Winkworth. London: MacMillan and Co., 1874.

The Thirteen Principal Upanishads. Translated from the Sanskrit by Robert Ernest Hume. London: Oxford University Press, 1921.

Tholens, C. *Teksten om bij stil te staan. Bifeengebracht uit Oost en West* [Words for Standing Still from East to West]. Delft, 1984.

Uleyn, Arnold. *Religiositeit en Fantasie*. Baarn, 1978.

Underhill, Evelyn. *Mysticism:A Study in the Nature and Development of Man's Spiritual Consciousness*. New York: E. P. Dutton, 1930.

Underhill, Evelyn, ed. *The Cloud of Unknowing*. London: John M. Watkins, 1922.

Verhulst, A. *Spiegel Historiael* (1988).

Vitry, Jacques de. *Vita Beatae Mariae Orgniacensis*. Paris, Analecta Sanctorym.

Waaijman, Kees. *De mystiek van ik en jij* [The Mysticism of I and Thou]. Utrecht, 1976.

Waite, A. E. *The Holy Kabbalah*. New York: University Books, 1960.

Walshe, M. O'C. *Meister Eckhart: Sermons and Treatises*. London: Watkins, 1979.

Ward, R. H. *A Drug-taker's Notes*. London: Victor Gollancz, 1957.

Way, B. *Wijsheid uit Engeland* [Wisdom from England]. Sayings of English mystics. Haarlem, 1979.

White, Lynn Jr. *Medieval Religion and Technology*. Berkeley: University of California, 1978).

Yates, Frances A. *Giordano Bruno and the Hermetic Tradition*. London: Routledge & Kegan Paul, 1964.

———. *Lull &Bruno*, Vol. 1. London & Boston: Routledge & Kegan Paul, 1982.

The Zohar, in 5 volumes. Translated by Maurice Simon and Dr. Paul P. Levertoff. New York: Soncino Press, 1934.

ILLUSTRATION CREDITS

ABC-Press Service, Amsterdam, 62, 76, 166, 332, 346, 357
Alte Pinakothek, München, 205
American Academy in Rome, Rome, 158
ANP-Foto, Amsterdam, 349
Anthony d'Offay Gallery, London, 338
Archief Bruno Borchert, Maastricht, 35, 38, 52, 73, 74, 103, 104, 113, 117, 118, 122,
    123, 131, 132, 162, 167, 179, 183, 191, 192, 194, 196, 211, 234, 235, 239, 254, 260,
    261, 262, 267, 270, 285, 298, 325, 331, 332, 337, 340, 342, 351, 353, 354, 355, 356
Archiv fur Kunst und Geschichte, Berlin, 175
Archivi Alinari, Florence, 292
Badische Landesbibliothek, Karlstruhe, 44, 208
C. Barton van Flymen, Zuiderwoude, 65
Biblioteca Apostolica Vaticana, Vatican, 148
Biblioteca Nacional, Madrid, 288
Biblioteca Nazionale Centrale, Florence, 256
Biblioteca Statale, Lucca, 26, 329
Bibliothèque Municipale, Troyes, 203
Bibliothèque Nationale, Paris, 102, 174, 248, 249, 335, 354
Bibliothèque Sainte-Genevieve, Paris, 173
Bild der Wissenschaft, Stuttgart, 347
Bildarchiv Foto Marburg, Marburg/Lahn, 154
Bildarchiv Preussischer Kulturbesitz, Berlin, 163, 345
Bodleian Library, Oxford, 99, 180, 213
The Brooklyn Museum, New York, 281
Burger Bibliothek, Bern, 330
C.E.R.N., Geneva, 277, 334
Centre Georges-Pompidou, Paris, 325
Cincinnati Art Museum, Cincinnati, 103
Cordon Art, Baarn, 339
Corpus Christi College, Cambridge, 48, 185
Faksimili Verlag, Luzern, 277
Werner Forman Archive, London, 98
Glasgow Museum & Art Gallery, Glasgow, 294
Greek Museum, Newcastle upon Tyne, 132
Hamberger Kunsthalle, Hamburg, 341
Robert Harding Picture, Ltd., London, 98, 166
The Israel Museum, Jerusalem, 106
King's College, Cambridge, 203
Koninklijke Bibliotheek Albert I, Brussels, 228, 229, 245, 352
Kunsthistorisches Museum, Vienna, 343
Metropolitan Museum of Art, New York, 77
Musée des Beaux-Art, Lyon, 246
Musée Marmottan, Paris, 256

INDEX

A

Abaris, 122
Abbey of Cluny, 183
Abel, 116
Abiri, 108
Absolute, 24
Abyss, 24
Acarie, Madame, 296
Acts of the Apostles, 136
Adamites, 212, 213
Aeldred of Rievaulx, 241
Agrippa of Nettesheim, 265
Ahra Manyu, 100
Ahriman, 100, 103, 120
Ahura Mazda, 100, 103, 105
Akhnaten, 98
Alacoque Margaretha Maria, 59
alchemy, 30, 139, 257, 263
alcohol, 49
Alexander the Great, 124, 125
al-Qushayri, 57
alumbrados, 42, 282
Amalric of Bena, 189, 190
Amalricians, 190
Amos, 114
Anabaptists, 276, 279
Andreae, Johann Valentin, 266
androgyne, 262
Anima Mundi, 259, 263
Anthroposophy, 272
apparitions, 47
Aristeas, 122
Arjuna, 87
Arnold of Brescia, 186
ars, 257
Artaxerxes II, 120
Aryans, 77
Ascent to Throne of God, 141
astrology
    Arabian, 30
    Babylon, 119
atakkavacara, 23
atheistic culture, 314, 316

Atman, 24, 80, 82, 95, 159
Aurelius, Marcus, 129

B

Baaden, F. von, 272
Baal worship, 111
Bacis, 122
Bacon, Sir Francis, 308
Bahai, 323
Barthes, Roland, 37, 39
Basil of Caesarea, 168
Beatrice of Nazareth, 51, 218
Beaucousin, Dom, 296
Beghards, 221
Beguines, 32, 207, 208, 209, 211, 216,
    221
beloved, 24
Benedict of Norcia, 170
Bernard of Clairvaux, 39
Bernardone, Pietro, 195
Bernini, 59
Bertken, Sister, 219
Bérulle, Madame de, 296
Bérulle, Pierre, 296
Besant, Annie, 272
Beuys, Joseph, 15, 273
Bhagavad Gita, 86, 87
Bible, 116
biblocation, 63
Bloemardin, 224
Boehme, Jacob, 15, 29, 267, 268, 271,
    361
Bogomil, 187, 188
Bohm, David, 313
Bohr, Niels, 313
Bonhoeffer, Dietrich, 33
Bosch, Hieronymus, 212, 240
Bossuet, Bishop, 297
Boyce, Mary, 96
Brahman, 80, 94, 95, 159
Brahmanas, 79
Brandsma, Titus, 45, 305, 360
Breukels, Jan, 276, 278

Bruno Borchert is the senior researcher on art and mysticism at the Titus Brandsma Instituut, and a board member for the magazines *Speling* (published by the Titus Brandsma Instituut, under the leadership of Dr. Otger Steggink, professor of mysticism at the University of Nijmegen), and *Kruispunt*. He has taught theology in Holland, and is a member of the Carmelite Order.